Understanding Henri Lefebvre

Theory and the Possible

Stuart Elden

continuum
LONDON • NEW YORK

Continuum
The Tower Building,   80 Maiden Lane
11 York Road   Suite 704, New York
London SE1 7NX   NY 10038, USA

Reprinted 2006

www.continuumbooks.com

British Library Cataloguing-in-Publication Data
A catalogue record for this book is available from the British Library.

ISBN: 0–8264–7002–5 (HB)   0–8264–7003–3 (PB)

Typeset by Refinecatch Ltd, Bungay, Suffolk
Printed and bound in Great Britain by
MPG Books Ltd, Bodmin, Cornwall

Contents

Acknowledgements

Elgin Diaz, Elizabeth Lebas, Adam Holden and Warren Montag read the entire manuscript of this book and it has benefited immeasurably from their careful and generous comments. Neil Brenner's report for the publishers was extremely helpful. Some early parts of the work here were improved by Mark Neocleous' useful suggestions, and I learnt much from working with Eleonore Kofman. Conversations with those already mentioned, and Sharon Cowan, Jeremy Crampton, Laurence Hemming, Morris Kaplan, James Olsen, Marisa Richardson, Maja Zehfuss and my colleagues at Durham helped me to sharpen up many of my ideas. Working with Imogen Forster and Gerald Moore on translations has improved my ability to render Lefebvre into appropriate English. As an editor, Tristan Palmer has been extremely supportive of this and other Lefebvre projects. I am grateful to them all.

I have given papers on Lefebvre at the University of Manchester, Brunel University, Friedrich-Alexander Universität Erlangen-Nürnberg, University College London, University of Durham, Open University and the Bath Royal Literary and Scientific Institution. I would like to thank these venues and their audiences for the opportunity to develop this work and improve its presentation. Tracking down Lefebvre's books and articles has taken me to a wide range of libraries. I am particularly grateful to the staff of the rare books and manuscripts library at Columbia University for access to Norbert Guterman's papers which include works and letters by Lefebvre.

Some of these ideas first appeared in print in other places: part of Chapter 2 as 'Through the eyes of the fantastic: Lefebvre, Rabelais and intellectual history', *Historical Materialism* 10(4), December 2002, pp. 89–111; and a version of parts of Chapters 2 and 5 as 'Between Marx and Heidegger: politics, philosophy and Lefebvre's *The Production of Space*', *Antipode: A Radical Journal of Geography* 36(1), January 2004. Some early ideas were outlined in 'Politics, philosophy, geography: Henri Lefebvre in recent Anglo-American scholarship', *Antipode: A Radical Journal of Geography* 33(5), November 2001, pp. 809–25, although little of that text finds its way in here. I am grateful to the editors of these two journals for giving me the opportunity to try out some arguments, and to their referees who provided helpful comments and criticisms. I would also like to thank Jesko Fezer for translating a lecture of mine into German, which appeared as ' »Es gibt eine Politik des Raumes, weil Raum Politisch ist.« Henri Lefebvre und die Produktion des Raums', *An Architektur* 1, July 2002, pp. 27–35. This was a valuable experience, especially given the argument here that much of Lefebvre's work is the translation of German ideas into a French context.

As ever I owe an incalculable personal debt to my mother, grandmother, Ian, Nicky, and Rachel; and to Susan, now my wife, for her love, patience and support.

Stuart Elden
Durham, July 2003

Introduction: Henri Lefebvre 1901–91

Lefebvre had an extraordinary life. It stretched from the very beginning of the century until a decade before its end. It is no surprise that his French biographer has accordingly called his work the adventure of the century.[1] Born eighteen years after Marx's death, and only six after Engels', Lefebvre was a youth of sixteen at the Russian Revolution, in his late thirties at the outbreak of World War Two, 60 at the time of the Cuban missile crisis, and still writing at the fall of the Berlin Wall. He obtained his *licence* in philosophy the year Althusser was born, and published his first articles two years before Foucault's birth, yet outlived both of them.

In 1950, introducing his work to a French audience in a survey volume of contemporary thought, he wrote the following biographical note:

> Born in 1901, of a family belonging to the middle class. A strongly religious (Catholic) education. Youth tormented, rebellious, anarchistic. Found balance around his thirtieth year in and through Marxism. Has not followed a regular career, either University or otherwise. Currently in charge of research in the *Centre National de la Recherche Scientifique*, sociology section. Sees philosophy as a critical conscience on real life. Places theatre above philosophy (as he conceives it, not as it is!) Has only accomplished a small part of the programme of life and work that he has planned. Doesn't hope to arrive at the end.[2]

The parallel American volume of this collection cuts this down to a purely academic 'Born in 1901, formerly professor of Philosophy in Toulouse. At present, in charge of studies at the *Centre National de la Recherche Scientifique*, sociological section, in Paris',[3] before listing some of his books. This is unfortunate, because the longer version seems revealing in terms of giving a glimpse of his formative years and the broad outlook he took. Lefebvre here explicitly states his Marxism, and how he sees philosophy 'as a critical conscience on real life'. This Marxism and this view of philosophy will be the guiding threads of this study, which seeks to situate Lefebvre within his intellectual context, to show how his many writings on disparate topics interrelate, and to demonstrate the importance of Lefebvre's writings for a range of contemporary concerns.

Although this is a book about Lefebvre the thinker, the biographical, especially in the context of his two autobiographies, will inform the substantive chapters of this book. However it is worth providing a brief outline of his life at the outset, both for background and to introduce and outline the themes to be discussed in this book as a whole. Whereas Nietzsche claimed that 'I am one thing, my writings are another matter',[4] Lefebvre argues that his work is his life.[5] I would not want to reduce Lefebvre's writings to Lefebvre the man, but in his case, perhaps more legitimately than with many other writers, the work and the life were closely interrelated.

Lefebvre was born just outside the Pyrenees in 1901 at Hegetmau. His mother was Béarnaise, with some Basque blood; his father had roots in Breton and Picardy. In his own terms, his father gave him a robust and stocky body; the mother a long face, almost Iberian. This led to his being described as having 'the head of Don Quixote on the body of Sancho Pancha'.[6] Although he left the Pyrenees in his early teens he was to retain strong attachments to it. Lefebvre was educated at the Louis-le-Grand Lycée in Paris, and originally intended to be an engineer, but following a bout of pleurisy he transferred to philosophy with Maurice Blondel at Aix-en-Provence, chosen, Hess claims, because of its climate.[7] From 1919 he was educated at the Sorbonne with Léon Brunschvicg, writing on Jansen and Pascal. He attained his degree in philosophy, and in the early 1920s he was a member of a small group of left-wing students including Georges Politzer, Norbert Guterman, Georges Friedmann and Pierre Morhange. They founded the journal entitled *Philosophies* from which they took their name and in which Lefebvre published many of his first articles. This journal was founded with the belief that a challenge to the dominant philosophy of Bergson was necessary.[8] Leading on from some of this work, he associated with the surrealists, particularly Tristan Tzara and André Breton, and he and Guterman were among the signatories to a piece in *La révolution surréaliste*.[9] He was later to break with them acrimoniously.[10]

With the dissolution of *Philosophies* and its successor *L'esprit* Lefebvre moved away from academic work and during this time did his military service, worked in a factory, and drove a cab in Paris. Of this he wrote in 1946

A huge volume could not contain the adventures and misadventures of this existentialist philosopher-taxi-driver. The Paris underworld unfolded before him in all its sleazy variety and he began to discover the secrets of its brothels, knocking-shops and gambling dens, dance halls (for white and coloured), fancy hotels and greasy spoons, shady dealers, high and low-class pederasts, bookmakers, armed robbers and police squads. I plumbed some of the smelly depths of 'existence' and what I dragged up would have sent the neo-existentialists of the Café Flore into transports of delight.[11]

Following a bad car accident he became a teacher, initially in Privas, and then in Montargis, just south of Paris. He commuted between the capital and his place of work.[12] Through the initial efforts of the surrealists, and those of Jean Wahl he had been introduced to Hegel's work, particularly the *Logic*, after having stated his usual reads were Schelling and Nietzsche.[13] Through Hegel he discovered Marx, and along with Norbert Guterman and others in the *Philosophies* circle founded *La revue marxiste*, which was one of the first Marxist journals in France.[14] He joined the Parti Communist Français (PCF) in 1928, because, as he recalls, in abandoning the doctrines of idealism for Marxism, the practice was inseparable from the theory.[15] Lefebvre published only one piece between 1928 and 1932,[16] but it was clear through the 1930s that, as well as the extensive programme of translations and introductions that he conducted with Guterman, he was beginning to develop his own Marxist philosophical vision, often also in collaboration with Guterman, in journals such as *Avant-Poste*, *Europe* and *Commune*.

He was removed from his teaching post in 1941 during the Occupation because of his links to the PCF.[17] After this he was involved in the resistance. As Merrifield notes, Lefebvre 'wrote stinging critiques of Vichy for several communist pamphlets, helped derail enemy trains, [and] sniffed out collaborators'.[18] Although these experiences taught him much about political struggle, in his correspondence he was scathing about the gulf between the reality and the myth.[19] This time also cemented his interest in French rural life, as he was based in the Pyrenees for much of the time. After the war he worked for a while as the artistic director of a radio station in Toulouse. Although he later taught in both lycées and universities such as Toulouse, Strasbourg, Nanterre, and Paris VIII, was a part-time lecturer at the École Pratique des Hautes Études, and the head of the sociology division of the Centre National de la Recherche Scientifique (CNRS), he remained somewhat outside of the academic mainstream. Indeed he was excluded from the CNRS in 1953, ostensibly because he did not have a doctorate. Material on peasant communities in the Pyrenees solved this problem, and he was readmitted in 1954.[20] However, the reason was far more to do with his attacks on the bourgeoisie and Americanism and his Marxism, and required a union campaign to reinstate him.[21] His involvement with the PCF lasted from 1928 to 1958, and after leaving he associated with Situationists, Maoists and other leftist groups. His disputes with the Stalinist wing led to a number of his early publications, although others were censored by party officials. He was important in the setting up of a number of dissident journals, including *Voies nouvelles* and *Autogestion*. Numbering Daniel Cohn-Bendit and Jean Baudrillard amongst his students, he had a profound impact on the events of May 1968, on which he wrote an important study. Lefebvre was 67 at the time, but continued to write for over twenty more years, producing some of his most important texts during this period. As he pointed out in a 1976 interview, his work changed because the world changed.[22]

Lefebvre was married several times, his last wife being the 21-year-old member of the Communist Party who had interviewed him for the 1978 book *La révolution n'est plus ce qu'elle était*. References to his love life appear particularly in the form of the poems which punctuate some of his books. It does not seem that he was the easiest person to live with. His fourth wife

Nicole Beaurain-Lefebvre confided in Guterman that she was concerned
that she was losing her charm for him. At 34, Nicole was less than half
Lefebvre's 70 years.[23] Writing just after their return from a trip to Algeria a
month later she noted that 'Henri has already met up with his girlfriends,
platonically I believe'.[24] A few years later they had broken up. He had
several children – the oldest, Jean-Pierre, was born in 1925, the youngest
Armelle in 1964 – although he clearly did not always enjoy the family life,
once remarking that the thought of a holiday in Brittany 'made me shit [*ca
me fait chier*]'.[25]

In later life he returned to the maternal home in Navarrenx, the Maison
Darracq, which was where he had taken his holidays and where he now
continued to entertain a succession of visitors from Paris and elsewhere. As
Lourau notes, a walk with Lefebvre after a good meal at this house or a local
restaurant was almost *de rigueur* for the 'sociologists, philosophers, students,
ultra-leftists of the Situationist International' who came to visit him in the
1960s.[26] Indeed late in life Lefebvre recounts a story of taking various Situationists, those walkers of the city, deep into the countryside where they
were very much out of their element.[27] Several of the photographs in the
Guterman archive at Columbia University show the walks the old friends
took together around this time, and also reveal that Lefebvre was a committed pipe smoker. Although he returned to Paris sporadically, this was the
place he chose to spend his last years. He died in June 1991, just after his
ninetieth birthday.[28]

Through this long career, with works published from the 1920s until just
after his death, Lefebvre never stood still, showing a polymath ability in the
range of topics he discussed. There was a continual refusal to accept a
straightforward disciplinary designation. As Hess puts it, 'Lefebvre always
refused the cutting of knowledge into slices'.[29] Take, for example, the
peculiar dialogue that preceded his book on the Pyrenees, where an inter-
locutor called Olivier discusses a proposed book on the region with an
author designated by the initial 'H':

   O.   You are a philosopher.
   H.   Not exactly.
   O.   Sociologist?
   H.   Not anymore.
   O.   You toy with the unclassifiable. Have the courage to be what you are.[30]

Whilst the broad range of topics he was concerned with might be interesting and compelling, it has also created problems in his reception. Given that
he published 70 books in his lifetime, two more have appeared posthumously, and that these ranged widely from literary theory to politics, from
sociology to philosophy, from urban and rural theory to history, it is
extremely difficult to get a handle on how his work functioned as a whole.

It is worth making a few comments about these seventy-two books. Five
of these are editions of the writings of Marx, Hegel or Lenin, all co-edited

with Norbert Guterman. A couple of books are no more than new editions of old ones – *Vers le cybernanthrope: Contre les technocrates* is a slightly edited and abridged version of *Position: Contre les technocrates*, and *L'idéologie structuraliste* reprints five essays from *Au-delà du structuralisme*. Much of *L'irruption de Nan-terre au sommet* also reappears in *La survie du capitalisme*, along with some new material. Two books – *La conscience mystifiée* (with Guterman) and *La révolution n'est plus ce qu'elle était* (with Catherine Régulier) – were co-written; *Actualité de Fourier* and *Du contrat de citoyenneté* are collections of essays by a range of writers under the direction of Lefebvre; and two others are basically essays paired with ones by another writer – *Le jeu de Kostas Axelos* with Pierre Fougeyrollas; *Lukács 1955* with Patrick Tort's *Être marxiste aujourd'hui*. A num-ber of others were multi-part works – four volumes of *De l'État*, three of *Critique de la vie quotidienne*, two of *Pascal*. But even if we discount the books that are effectively edited rather than written, and *Vers le cybernanthrope* and *L'idéologie structuraliste*, we are left with a figure of over 60 books of material. And although many of Lefebvre's articles were collected into these books – *Du rural à l'urbain*, *Au-delà du structuralisme* and *Espace et politique*, for example, are all collections of essays – there are several others that only exist in edited collections or journal form, many almost impossible to find today. However even this is but a part of his writing. Many lecture courses treated topics only tangentially referred to in publications, and as he stated in 1975, 'I write a lot, and a lot more than I publish'.[31]

There are other difficulties in coming to terms with Lefebvre.[32] As anyone who has read him will attest, his was not the most fluent of styles. This is actually less apparent in English than in the original, with many translators – perhaps understandably – smoothing over his rough edges in the transition to their own language. Lefebvre sometimes used a typist to transcribe mono-logues on topics, which makes sense of the way in which his work is repeti-tive, digressive and meandering. It also perhaps explains the way he was able to produce books so quickly, some of which were written for purely financial reasons.[33] Many of these typists were 'women he desired or loved', for whom he would improvise his ideas, and he claims that his best books are ones he spoke rather than wrote.[34] Other books were written longhand and then typed, before being covered with additions and comments in Lefebvre's hand.[35] Equally much of his work is polemical and concerned with figures, debates and issues that are no longer as relevant as they were when he wrote. He is erratic in his use of references, eclectic in his examples, and almost wilful in his disregard for scholarly convention. In addition, the English-language audience has had a very narrow view of his interests, with only a few of his many books translated.

Why, then, has Lefebvre had such an extraordinary impact in the Anglo-American academy over the last fifteen years or so? In geography in particu-lar, but also in other spatially minded disciplines such as architecture and urban theory there has been a particular interest, much stemming from the translation of *The Production of Space* in 1991. The collection *Writings on Cities* developed the reception of his work in this area, showing how his broad concern with spatial politics developed from debates around the nature of urban life in France and elsewhere. Similarly his work on everyday life, of which the summary volume *Everyday Life in the Modern World* has been available in English for over three decades, has sparked much interest in fields such as cultural studies. However his key statements on this topic are in the three volume *Critique of Everyday Life*, which only started to appear in translation in 1991. In fact since *The Survival of Capitalism* these 1991 translations were the first into English for fifteen years. Given that this was also the year of his death it would not be inappropriate to recall Nietzsche's famous suggestion in *Ecce Homo* that 'some are born posthumously'.[36] For Lefebvre, in the Anglophone world at least, this would seem to be true.

In France one could make an argument along related lines. Although he played a major role in French intellectual life at various times, since his death he had been largely ignored until a recent flurry of publishing activity which has seen the re-edition of long out-of-print books including *L'existentialisme*, *Métaphilosophie* and *La fin de l'histoire*, and one that never saw the light of day in his life, *Méthodologie des sciences*.[37] None of these crucially important books is available in English, although sections of the first three are now included in the *Key Writings* collection. A colloquium in 2000 at the appropriately named *Espaces Marx* and an international conference held at Paris VIII the following year has done much to put Lefebvre back on the agenda. Perhaps in France, then, he has been reborn. Here the emphasis on his writings has been more broadly political than just his work on space, with ongoing interest in his writings on citizenship, the state and the reconfiguration of capital at a world scale. Equally, as can be seen from the re-editions, interest in his more explicitly philosophical writings is also strong.

Elsewhere Lefebvre's impact was widespread. He gave conferences across the world, advised communist politicians and travelled widely.[38] Interest was, and is, particularly strong in Germany and Japan.[39] In addition, large numbers of his books are available in Italian, Portuguese – because of his many readers in Brazil – and Spanish.[40] At one point his books were translated into more languages than any other French writer. Some books are available in Albanian, Danish, Arabic, Turkish, Swedish and Greek. His *Contribution à l'esthétique* was translated into twenty languages, and he was widely read in Yugoslavia, partly because of his links to the *Praxis* movement.

As I have argued at greater length elsewhere, one of the problems of recent appropriations and interpretations of Lefebvre in the English-speaking world is the narrowness of the reading that has been given.[41] The focus from fields of geography, urban sociology and cultural studies has largely been at the expense of interest from political theorists or philosophers.[42] This is not to say that all of the existing work in English is flawed, but that as the title of Kofman and Lebas's introduction to *Writings on Cities* suggests, there may be much 'lost in transposition'.[43] My suggestion throughout this book is that Lefebvre's work needs to be understood in the context of his Marxism and philosophy more generally. Lefebvre's writing was always theoretically informed and politically engaged. To divorce his work from either of these aspects is to do him a great disservice: his political edge is blunted and his philosophical complexity denied. Even in books that might appear entirely otherwise, these features of his work often take centre stage. It is not a simple task to compartmentalize his work into convenient academic departments, as even within single works he cuts across disciplines. As Hess puts it, 'Lefebvre always refused the cutting of knowledge into slices'.[44] The importance of politics and philosophy is especially true in his work on space, although not least among the contemporary problems is that his work on space is seen as his crowning achievement, and other interests subordinated to it. Equally a chronological approach – whilst perhaps having much to commend it – generates similar problems because themes in one book are developed and picked up years later, in a very different guise. Accordingly, this book takes a thematic approach, but one that does not fit disciplinary boundaries.

Understanding Henri Lefebvre therefore attempts to show how his work can be conceptualized as a whole – though it is certainly a multi-dimensional and irregular shape. As an introduction to understanding the whole of Lefebvre's work it aims to be fairly comprehensive, but it does not pretend to be exhaustive in its treatment – and would inevitably fail if it tried to do so. In particular there is little said about his work on linguistics and the theory of representation.[45] The issues that will take centre stage are both those that are at the forefront of his contemporary importance and those that are arguably the most central in his *oeuvre*, along with their political and philosophical underpinnings. In doing this it gives a much broader sense of his work than existing studies – in either English or French. Although I have referenced writers such as Brenner, Burkhard, Hess, Kofman, Lebas, Shields and Trebitsch where I have found their work useful, I have largely dispensed with direct challenges to existing literature. In a sense, then, this interpretation will have to speak for itself, although I would suggest that my approach is more concerned with the work itself than Hess's biography and more theoretically rigorous than Shields.[46]

The book will be divided into six chapters. Though I have sought to minimize overlap between chapters, taking a thematic approach and seeking to show how the work functions as a totality necessitates much cross-reference and linkage. This would not have surprised Lefebvre. As I will discuss at length later, he was resistant to linear teleological narratives, instead emphasizing the importance of rhythms, the repetitive, cycles and moments.

The opening chapter discusses his understanding of Marxism, both as theory and practice – the two being united.[47] It suggests that Lefebvre read Marx as a total thinker, with equal stress on the early writings and the late ones. He was interested in how concepts such as alienation were central throughout Marx's career. Contrasting his reading of Marx with other prominent French interpreters, the chapter also outlines the importance of Hegel in understanding Lefebvre's Marxism. Particular issues of concern include his understanding of dialectics and his challenge to formal logic, and his analysis of the notions of alienation and production in Marx's writings. It goes on to discuss the critique of Stalinist dogmatism, and his role as a member of the PCF until his break with it in 1958.

Chapter 2 broadens his theoretical interests by looking at his wider philosophical concerns, largely through a thinker-based approach. Lefebvre saw Marx's works as important in an understanding of the modern world, but recognized that the analysis needed to be broader based. This catholic approach was exemplified in the title of his 1975 *Hegel, Marx, Nietzsche, ou le royaume des ombres*. As well as Hegel, who was important in understanding his relation to Marx, the state, logic and dialectics, as the previous chapter will have shown, there was also Nietzsche. Nietzsche was one of Lefebvre's favourite thinkers, with his work on moments, life, poetry, music, theatre, and the extraordinary providing great inspiration. Equally his understanding of time and history, and in part his understanding of space, inform Lefebvre's own work in these areas.

But I would add one further major figure to the constellation, that of Martin Heidegger. Although Heidegger was some twelve years older than Lefebvre, their career paths were close in a number of ways. In a number of places, I suggest, Lefebvre is taking Heidegger's ideas and subjecting them to a radical critique, notably his understandings of everyday life, space, time and the political. Both thinkers wrote important works on Nietzsche in the late 1930s, with the aim of challenging National Socialist appropriations of his work. But whilst Heidegger was a card carrying member of the Nazi party at the time, Lefebvre had his book *Nietzsche* seized and burnt by the occupying army in 1940, and was later involved with the resistance. The political aspects of their relation are confronted head on, with the suggestion that though Lefebvre was generally extremely critical of Heidegger's politics he found something of enormous interest in his notion of the political. This chapter also looks at some major themes of Lefebvre's work, especially the notions of metaphilosophy, and his work on literary figures within the French tradition. It also discusses Lefebvre's relation to some contemporary writers, notably Kostas Axelos.

The aim of the first two chapters is to provide a theoretical basis upon which to understand Lefebvre's more concrete concerns with everyday life, urban and rural sociology, time, space and politics. Although these more substantive issues are the key focus of much contemporary interest, I believe that it is important to understand the conceptual underpinnings of their analysis. His is a Marxist approach certainly, but not merely a Marxist approach, with the role of Hegel, Nietzsche, and Heidegger particularly important in getting a more nuanced sense of his importance. As will be emphasized, it is significant that these are all German writers, and that Lefebvre was largely critical of French thought. Throughout the book the political context will also be noted. Events in France such as the Occupation and Liberation, the Fifth Republic and the events of May 1968 are extremely important in understanding Lefebvre's work.[48]

Chapter 3 focuses on Lefebvre's notion of everyday life, beginning with a conceptualization of the term, before moving onto some examples of his more concrete analysis. Lefebvre himself thought that his work in this area was his principal contribution to Marxism. Drawing on Marx's reworking of the Hegelian conception of alienation (particularly in the *1844 Manuscripts*) and combining it with Heidegger's notion of everydayness (*Alltäglichkeit*) in *Being and Time*, Lefebvre provided a detailed reading of how capitalism had increased its scope in the twentieth century to dominate the cultural and social world as well as the economic.

His work on everyday life can be seen as providing the foundation for his studies of urban and rural life. Chapter 4 looks at this area of his work, balancing the contemporary interest in his writings on cities with his analysis of the countryside. It was around this time that Lefebvre abandoned philosophy for sociology – at least in terms of his academic department. Lefebvre was born in the Pyrenees, and wrote his doctoral thesis on rural life. He was engaged in a number of studies throughout his life that examined the social environment, from the valley of Campan to Paris in the nineteenth and twentieth centuries. As well as analysing the historical relationship between the rural and the urban, Lefebvre also laid the foundations for an explicitly Marxist urban sociology, which looked at the key role technology played in the shaping of the urban environment. Much of this work was tied up in debates with the technocratic planning of the French Fifth Republic. As some writers have already attempted, this work bears comparison with that of Manuel Castells, whose own work is much better known in English, and with that of David Harvey.[49]

In Chapter 5 I move onto the territory which is probably most familiar to English language readers of Lefebvre, but try to put this in a rather different light. Whilst his book *The Production of Space* is indeed a remarkable study, I believe it has often been understood in a variety of ways that are not helpful in getting to the heart of his project. Often the theoretical work on space is divorced from the practical analyses it developed from – the studies of rural and urban life discussed in the previous chapter. In Lefebvre's work on space the role of Nietzsche and Heidegger is particularly important, as their analyses enable him to break with the scientific understandings of space found in modern philosophy from Descartes to Kant. They are also very important in understanding the break Lefebvre made with orthodox Marxism on the teleological principle of history. As well as re-conceptualizing space, and reinvigorating geography, Lefebvre made important contributions to the study of time and history. His work on history, moments, and rhythms will be analysed here in an attempt to broaden our understanding of Lefebvre's work.

Throughout his work Lefebvre was political in the broad sense of the term. The final chapter draws together the contribution he made to social and political theory through a detailed examination of what may be considered his major work, the four-volume *De l'État*. In this work Lefebvre both discusses Hegel, Marx, Lenin, Stalin and Mao on the state and analyses the state in the modern world, adding significantly to the literature on this topic.

De l'État also draws together his work on the urban, space, capitalism and everyday life in a broad recapitulation of the themes that dominated his work. However, Lefebvre also wrote important works on nationalism, the politics of difference, and citizenship, which are largely unknown.

This book does not have a conclusion in the usual sense. Given the inter-related nature of Lefebvre's concerns and the somewhat artificial division of material, it would seem wrong-headed to try to bring all of this together in some kind of summary statement. Instead, at the close of Chapter 6, I provide some possible openings toward future work, both on, and informed by, Lefebvre, through an examination of the question of reading thinkers politically. Given that I expect many readers will not follow the pages of the book sequentially, perhaps beginning with the chapter on the topic they are most interested in, and then (hopefully) following that with a related topic, the end of the book for them may not be its final pages. I hope Lefebvre would have appreciated this, given his stress on the cyclical. As an introduction to an understanding of Lefebvre's work, and the possibilities it provides, Lefebvre's own words on his reading of Marx are therefore appropriate:

> We interrogate these texts in the name of the present and the possible; and this is very precisely the method of Marx, which he prescribes so that the past (events and documents) lives again and serves the future.[50]

Notes

Unless otherwise stated, all references are to works by Henri Lefebvre. Dual references to French and English are given for available translations of Lefebvre's writings, although these translations have sometimes been modified. Otherwise unsourced letters are from the Norbert Guterman papers, Rare Books and Manuscript Library, Columbia University.

1 Rémi Hess, *Henri Lefebvre et l'aventure du siècle*, Paris: A. M. Métailié, 1988. Hess was Lefebvre's final doctoral student and the book was an authorized account.
2 'Connaissance et critique sociale', in Marvin Farber (ed.) *L'activité philosophique contemporaine en France et aux États-Unis – Tome Second: La philosophie française*, Paris: PUF, 1950, pp. 298–319, p. 298 n. 1.
3 'Knowledge and social criticism', in Marvin Farber (ed.) *Philosophic Thought in France and the United States: Essays Representing Major Trends in Contemporary French and American Philosophy*, New York: University of Buffalo Publications in Philosophy, 1950, pp. 281–300, p. 281 n. 1.
4 Friedrich Nietzsche, *Ecce Homo*, translated by Walter Kaufmann, New York: Vintage, 1967, p. 259.
5 *Le temps des méprises*, Paris: Stock, 1975, p. 11.
6 *La somme et le reste*, Paris: Méridiens Klincksieck, 3rd edition, 1989 [1959], p. 242.
7 Rémi Hess, 'Henri Lefebvre "philosophe" ', in *L'existentialisme*, Paris: Anthropos, 2nd edition, 2001 [1946], p. xxii.
8 See *La somme et le reste*, pp. 383–4. The question of Lefebvre's relation to Bergson is one I do not treat here, apart from some brief comments in Chapter 5, although it is an area worthy of exploration. For contrasting positions see

Rob Shields, *Lefebvre, Love and Struggle: Spatial Dialectics*, London: Routledge, 1999; and Gregory J. Seigworth, 'Banality for Cultural Studies', *Cultural Studies* 14 (2), 2000, pp. 227–68, pp. 244, 261 n. 17.

 9 'La révolution d'abord et toujours', *La révolution surréaliste* 5, October 1925, pp. 31–2.

10 Lefebvre is criticized, along with Morhange and Politzer, in André Breton, *Manifestos of Surrealism*, Ann Arbor: University of Michigan Press, 1972, p. 145. See Michel Trebitsch, 'Les mésaventures du groupe Philosophies, 1924–1933', *La revue des revues* 3, printemps 1987, pp. 6–9; 'Le groupe "philosophies", de Max Jacob aux surrealists 1924–1925', *Le cahiers de l'IHTP* 6, November 1987, pp. 29–38, pp. 33–4; 'Le groupe *Philosophies* et les surrealists (1924–1925)', *Mélusine: Cahiers du centre de recherches sur le surréalisme* XI, 1990, pp. 63–75. Lefebvre's more critical tone is found in 'André Breton, *Les vases communicants*', *Avant-Poste* 1, June 1933, pp. 75–7.

11 *L'existentialisme*, p. 42; *Key Writings*, edited by Stuart Elden, Elizabeth Lebas and Eleonore Kofman. London/New York: Continuum, 2003, p. 7.

12 On this period, see Michel Trebitsch, 'Présentation', in *Le nationalisme contre les nations*, Paris: Méridiens Klincksieck, 2nd edition, 1988 [1937], p. 8.

13 '1925', *La nouvelle revue française* 172, April 1967, pp. 707–19, p. 713; Henri Lefebvre and Michel Trebitsch, 'Le renouveau philosophique avorté des annés trente: Entretien avec Henri Lefebvre', *Europe: Revue littéraire mensuelle* 683, March 1986, pp. 29–41, p. 35.

14 See W. D. Redfern, *Paul Nizan: Committed Literature in a Conspiratorial World*, Princeton: Princeton University Press, 1972, p. 15.

15 'Georges Politzer', *La pensée* October–December 1944, pp. 7–10, p. 9.

16 The one piece was a short review, '*Verdun*, par le maréchal Pétain', *La revue marxiste* 6, July 1929, pp. 719–20.

17 Lefebvre to Guterman, 27 March 1941.

18 Andy Merrifield, *Metromarxism: A Marxist Tale of the City*, New York: Routledge, 2002, p. 72. Merrifield gives no references, but see Henri Lefebvre, Patricia Latour and Francis Combes, *Conversation avec Henri Lefebvre*, Paris: Messidor, 1991, pp. 50–1; and the discussion in Hess, *Henri Lefebvre*, pp. 108–16.

19 Lefebvre to Guterman, 7 June 1945. See Michel Trebitsch, 'Correspondance d'intellectuels: le cas de lettres d'Henri Lefebvre à Norbert Guterman (1935–47)', *Les cahiers de l'IHTP* 20, March 1992, pp. 70–84, p. 81. On the theme of military struggle more generally, see 'La pensée militaire et la vie nationale', *La pensée* 3 April–June 1945, pp. 49–56.

20 René Mouriaux, 'Un Marxisme dans le siècle', in *L'irruption de Nanterre au sommet*, Paris: Éditions Syllepse, 2nd edition, 1998 [1968], p. vii.

21 *Qu'est-ce que penser?* Paris: Publisad, 1985, p. 140; Michel Trebitsch, 'Preface: The Moment of Radical Critique', in *Critique of Everyday Life Volume II: Foundations for a Sociology of the Everyday*, translated by John Moore, London: Verso, 2002, p. xiv.

22 'Interview – Débat sur le marxisme: Léninisme-stalinisme ou autogestion?', *Autogestion et socialisme* 33/34, 1976, pp. 115–26, pp. 123–4.

23 Nicole Beaurain-Lefebvre to Guterman, 7 December 1971.

24 Nicole Beaurain-Lefebvre to Guterman, 17 January 1972.

25 Lefebvre to Guterman, undated.

26 René Lourau, 'Préface: L'espace Henri Lefebvre', in *Pyrénées*, Pau: Cairn, 2nd edition, 2000 [1965], pp. 9–13, p. 11; see *Pyrénées*, pp. 35–6.

27 'Lefebvre on the Situationists', conducted and translated by Kristin Ross, *October* 79, Winter, pp. 69–83, p. 80.

28 I have used various sources for this brief overview. They include Hess, *Henri Lefebvre*; Mouriaux, 'Un Marxisme dans le siècle'; Lourau, 'Préface'; and Michel Trebitsch, 'Lefebvre (Henri) 1901–1991', in *Dictionnaire des intellectuels français: Les personnes, les lieux, les moments*, sous la direction de Jacques Julliard and Michel Winock, Paris: Seuil, 1996, pp. 691–3; as well as Lefebvre's letters to Guterman.

29 Hess, *Henri Lefebvre*, p. 14.

30 *Pyrénées*, Pau: Cairn, 2nd edition, 2000 [1965], p. 18. The allusion is to Nietzsche's *Ecce Homo*, whose subtitle is 'how one becomes what one is'.

31 *Le temps des méprises*, p. 9. On pp. 113–14 he discusses one of these projects, on sexuality and society, based on a course at Nanterre in 1966–7.

32 See also Stuart Elden and Elizabeth Lebas, 'Introduction: Coming to Terms with Lefebvre', in *Key Writings*, pp. xi–xix.

33 An undated letter from Evelyn Lefebvre to Norbert Guterman (probably mid-1950s), talks of typing what Lefebvre was hastily writing in order to gain money to support the family. Lefebvre's father-in-law apparently compared this situation to that of Balzac. Another letter, from another wife, over ten years later, says much the same thing about the need to write. Nicole Beaurain-Lefebvre to Guterman, 13 March 1967.

34 *Le temps des méprises*, p. 11. Rob Shields, *Lefebvre, Love and Struggle* makes much of this, see particularly, pp. 6–7, 84, 97.

35 Some of Lefebvre's papers in the Guterman archive show this. See also Hess, *Henri Lefebvre*, p. 157, p. 157 n. 7 where he discusses Lefebvre's writing with pen, rather than directly with a typewriter. In a June 1988 interview cited by Hess, Lefebvre noted that 'the rhythm of the phrases is not the same'.

36 Nietzsche, *Ecce Homo*, p. 259.

37 On the renewed French interest, see Stuart Elden, 'Quelques-uns naissent d'une façon posthume: La survie de Henri Lefebvre', *Actuel Marx* 35, January 2004.

38 See, for example, *Le temps des méprises*, pp. 221–2.

39 For Germany, see most recently, 'Material zu: Henri Lefèbvre, Die Produktion des Raums', *An Architectur: Produktion und Gebrauch gebauter Unwelt*, 1 July 2002.

40 On the work in Brazil, see 'Présentation du programme d'études sur Henri Lefebvre au L.A.B.U.R. (Laboratoire de géographie urbaine) – Brésil', in *La somme et la reste: Études lefebvriennes – Réseau mondial*, 1 November 2002, pp. 6–8.

41 See Stuart Elden, 'Politics, philosophy, geography: Henri Lefebvre in Anglo-American scholarship', *Antipode: A Radical Journal of Geography* 33 (5), November 2001, pp. 809–25.

42 However, as Chapter 6 will attest, the work of Neil Brenner is of considerable importance in the first of these two areas. Bud Burkhard's *French Marxism Between the Wars: Henri Lefebvre and the 'Philosophies'*, Atlantic Highlands: Humanity Books, 2000 is also invaluable on the early part of Lefebvre's career.

43 Eleonore Kofman and Elizabeth Lebas, 'Lost in transposition – time, space and the city', in Henri Lefebvre, *Writings on Cities*, translated and edited by Eleonore Kofman and Elizabeth Lebas, Oxford: Blackwell, 1996, pp. 3–60.

44 Hess, *Henri Lefebvre*, p. 14.

45 That is *Le langage et la société*, Paris: Gallimard, 1966, and *La présence et l'absence: Contribution à la théorie des representations*, Paris: Casterman, 1980. Of the former, Lefebvre remarked that it was the work of a sociologist and not a linguist. See *Vers le cybernanthrope*, Paris: Denoël/Gonthier, p. 101 n. 1.

46 See my 'Politics, philosophy, geography', for a challenge to the readings of
   Edward Soja and Rob Shields.
47 Henri Lefebvre and Norbert Guterman, 'Préface', in *Morceaux choisis de Karl
   Marx*, Paris: Gallimard, 1934, p. 7.
48 Despite only one reference to Lefebvre, Sunil Khilnani, *Arguing Revolution: The
   Intellectual Left in Post-war France*, New Haven: Yale University Press, 1993,
   provides some useful background.
49 See, for example, Ira Katznelson, *Marxism and the City*, Oxford: Clarendon Press,
   1992, Chapter 3; and more successfully, Merrifield, *Metromarxism*.
50 *La pensée marxiste et la ville*, Paris: Castermann, 1972, p. 150.

1 Rethinking Marxism

A new reading of Marx

One of the key events in twentieth-century Marxism was the publication of Marx's *1844 Manuscripts*. They were first published in German in 1927, and Lefebvre's colleague Norbert Guterman (under the pseudonym of Alfred Mesnil) translated a few fragments in *La revue marxiste* two years later.[1] As Burkhard notes, the Russian editor of Marx, David Riazanov, had sent a package of writings to the *Revue* in 1928, which they then published in preference to their own writings.[2] These were the first translations from these works in any language.[3] For Lefebvre the *1844 Manuscripts* were the most notable of the Marxian *Nachlaß*.[4] Setting the pattern for later collaborations, Guterman's multi-lingual ability would see him undertaking the bulk of the translation, while Lefebvre took the role of commentator, claiming their importance to the Marxist canon and writing the introductions to the works.[5] The early writings were similarly featured in the 1934 anthology of Marx that Guterman and Lefebvre produced for the French audience.[6] The introduction to that volume shows just how quickly they had assimilated the importance of these writings into Marx's work as a whole. As they suggest, 'the Parisian period (November 1843–January 1845) is one of the most important and the most productive in the life and work of Marx'. It was here that he moved from being a left-democrat to being a proletarian revolutionary.[7] The works of this period are more than a stage in the development of Marx's philosophy, they are a central aspect within it.[8] In other words, they cannot be dismissed as juvenilia or early writings. Although they have elements that are indebted to Hegel, this is far from an uncritical assimilation of his work. Marx had not fully developed his mature thought, but the seeds are there.[9] Guterman and Lefebvre also edited a collection of Hegel's writings, translated Lenin's philosophical notebooks on Hegel, and together wrote the important 1936 work *La conscience mystifiée*.[10] Much later, they collaborated on a new selection and presentation of Marx's writings.[11]

It is therefore clear that by the mid-1930s Lefebvre was already fully immersed in the issue that was to dominate his philosophical thinking: Marx's relation to Hegel, and between idealism and materialism.[12] For Lefebvre, the relation between Marx and Hegel 'is a dialectical one: i.e., one full of conflict'.[13] The use of the dialectic to understand Marx's relation to Hegel, and indeed the development of Marxian thought itself, is a central theme in Lefebvre's work. The reasoning behind the arguments Lefebvre advances is that he wants to rescue Marxism from reductionist readings, which had reduced it to a single science: political economy. Marxism 'had become an economicism'.[14] Lefebvre locates a shift in Marx's work from philosophical works to works of economics and political science, but argues that the standard implication drawn from this is mistaken. 'The fact that economic science and political action had *superseded* or *subsumed* [*dépassaient*] speculative philosophy fostered the false conclusion that Marx had abandoned any conception of the philosophical world'.[15] As Lefebvre makes clear, *dépassaient* is here intended to be understood in the threefold sense of the Hegelian *Aufhebung*: negated, retained, and lifted up.[16] Philosophy is subsumed in the economic work *Capital*: subsumed but not forgotten. As Lefebvre suggests, Lenin claimed that Marxists were the first to say that human life needed to be studied in all aspects (not just including economics).[17]

A standard reading of Marx is that he alone of the left-Hegelians linked materialism with the dialectic. Bruno Bauer and Max Stirner developed a dialectical idealism, Ludwig Feuerbach a non-dialectical materialism.[18] Marx, it is argued, rescued the rational kernel of the dialectic from the mystified shell, and turned Hegel back on his feet by replacing the speculative idealism of Spirit with the concrete empiricism of materialism.[19] Lefebvre, I suggest, does not read Marx in this way. Indeed, in 1964, he described his work as 'a new reading of Marx'.[20] His is not merely another 'interpretation' – he suggests that perhaps we are suffering from an excess of conceptual equipment, an excess of interpretations[21] – but a restitution of Marx's original thought.[22] Rather than simply privileging one over the other Lefebvre is concerned with trying to understand the relationship *between* materialism and idealism. As Lefebvre notes, it was Lenin himself who suggested that nobody had properly read and understood *Capital*, because they had failed to assimilate the Hegelian dialectic.[23] In *Dialectical Materialism*, and throughout his work, Lefebvre therefore insists on the place of the dialectic in Marx's thought.

Michael Kelly usefully situates Lefebvre's arguments within their intellectual context, but accuses him of practically abandoning materialism in favour of an objective idealism, effectively reversing the direction taken by Marx and Engels.[24] However, for Lefebvre, 'in dialectical materialism idealism and materialism are not only re-united but transformed and transcended'.[25]

> Effectively it synthesises, unifies, two elements which Marx found separate and isolated in science and philosophy of his time: philosophical materialism, an already advanced science of nature – but sketched for human reality; and the dialectic of Hegel, that is a theory of *contradictions*. This denomination of 'dialectical materialism' describes the doctrine more exactly than the habitual term of 'Marxism'.[26]

Kelly essentially characterizes Lefebvre's view as seeing the dialectic as a method that is idealist or materialist depending on whether it is applied to thought or to life. Although he recognizes that the idealist/materialist distinction is, for Lefebvre, transcended or superseded,[27] he seems to miss the reason why Lefebvre is making this point: a point that would become more apparent with the practical work on the everyday and space. It is the fusion of the idealist and materialist notions, through the mechanism of the dialectic, that enable an *idealist and materialist* approach to questions of life and lived experience. This is a major claim, and one that many would take issue with. For example, Louis Althusser suggested that there is 'a total distinction between the idealist dialectic and the materialist dialectic'.[28]

In the foreword to the fifth edition of *Dialectical Materialism* Lefebvre suggests that the book is part of the struggle against dogmatism. Dogmatism, he argues, has its advantages: 'it is simple and easily taught; it steers clear of complex problems ... it gives its adherents a feeling of both vigorous affirmation and security'.[29] Dogmatic readings of Marxism do many things. One of the most important is their deep mistrust of early writings of Marx, with the notions of alienation, praxis, Total Man and social totality. Dogmatists seek to remove Hegel from Marx, and are anti-idealist, attempting a move to scientific Marxism. In doing this they formulate a simplified Marxism and materialism, with the laws of the dialectic as the laws of nature. For Lefebvre this denies the role of logic and discourse in the dialectic, but he suggests that, for the dogmatists formal, Aristotelian, logic was ideological and rooted in ancient or medieval society.[30] By making Marxism solely a political economy, sociology and psychology could be denied as being 'tainted with reformism' and 'irredeemably bourgeois' respectively.[31] In the 1930s Stalinism had denounced sociology for not being a science, and for being in the service of imperialism against the revolutionary proletariat and Marxist-Leninism.[32] For Lefebvre, not only does this deny important theoretical issues within a plural Marxism, it was politically a 'massive exercise in diversion' from the crimes of the Stalin era.[33] Equally dogmatism, for Lefebvre, manifests its stupidity through its arbitrary choices such as saying that such and such is a Marxist (such as Rosa Luxembourg), and someone else, for example Kautsky, is *not* a Marxist.[34]

It is no surprise therefore, that Lefebvre reads Marx in a variety of ways. For example, the introductory *Le marxisme* has chapters entitled 'Marxist Philosophy', 'Marxist Morality', 'Marxist Sociology or historical materialism', 'Marxist Economy' and 'Marxist Politics'.[35] To talk of a Marxist philosophy or morality is not to suggest that Marx *is* a philosopher or a moralist, but that there is a philosophy or a morality in Marx.[36] As Lefebvre notes in his 1966 book *The Sociology of Marx*, he is not trying to 'make a sociologist out of Marx'. Because of the possibility of misinterpretation he makes it explicit: 'Anyone who ascribes such a thesis to us on the basis of the title of this little book either never opened it or is acting in bad faith . . . *Marx is not a sociologist, but there is a sociology in Marxism*'.[37] This is not merely in the early works, but also in *Capital*.[38] The above chapter headings include the notion of 'Marxist Sociology or historical materialism'. Lefebvre makes this clear: historical materialism is the 'foundation of a *scientific sociology* (in fact, these two terms are equivalent and designate two aspects of the same quest)'.[39]

In their presentation of the *Oeuvres Choisis* of Marx, Lefebvre and Guterman note that they chose a chronological approach over a thematic one, and for a range of reasons. The principal reason is that it allows us to see a work in progress, work in the course of development. It also allows us to escape the idea that Marx was sometimes political, sometimes economic, sometimes philosophical. From its beginning, Marx's thought sought totality, 'where all the present and distinct aspects are nonetheless inseparable from each other'.[40] As they go on to suggest:

> It is one of the great paradoxes of our time that this thought which never stopped, which always remained open to the experiences and lessons of *praxis*, can be interpreted as an immobile and eternal dogmatism.[41]

It is also worth noting Lefebvre's insistence that Marxism should be understood in a plural sense. 'Marxism came from real collective work in which Marx's own genius blossomed.'[42] Lefebvre suggests that one day we will no longer say 'Marxism', just as we do not say 'Pasteurism' to describe bacteriology. But, he notes, we are not yet at that point.[43] Engels' contribution to Marxism should neither be passed over in silence nor thought of on a lower level. In particular, says Lefebvre, it was Engels who attracted Marx's attention to economic factors and the situation of the proletariat.[44] We might also note, as a pointer toward later concerns, that it was Engels more than Marx who looked at questions of space, in his work on the city, housing and the family.[45] Equally Marxism, as an '*open* doctrine', has not ceased to develop since Marx's death.[46] Indeed, Lefebvre suggests, certain aspects of contemporary Marxism – in 1956 he cites Stalinism and Zhdanovism – would perhaps never have been able to happen if Marx had completed his philosophical and political project.[47]

Lefebvre conceives of the relation between Marx and Hegel as dialectical – an embrace of Hegelian ideas; their rejection; and then their later reincorporation. The *1844 Manuscripts* were obviously Hegelian, but Hegel's *Logic* is particularly damned in the period when Marx is beginning to formulate the historical materialist approach, in works such as *The Holy Family*, *The German Ideology* and *The Poverty of Philosophy*. Here Marx criticizes the left-Hegelians such as Bauer and Stirner, but also the abstract analysis of Hegel himself. Hegel's *Logic*, suggests Lefebvre, is 'treated with the utmost contempt'; Marx and Engels are 'unsparing in their attacks'.[48] Marx attempts to be empirical and non-dialectical; Hegel's dialectic appears to 'damned once and for all'.[49] And yet, Lefebvre argues that the dialectic is rediscovered and rehabilitated around the time when Marx began work on *Capital* and *The Critique of Political Economy*.[50] Even where Hegel is not explicitly mentioned, Lefebvre identifies the categories of dialectic logic at work in *Capital*. Marx's

engagement with Hegel lasts over thirty-five years.[51] It is not therefore surprising that Lefebvre suggests the *1844 Manuscripts* and the *Critique of the
Gotha Programme* – 'the beginning and the end of the oeuvre' – are two of the
most important works for him.[52]

 This reading of Marx's relation to Hegel allows Lefebvre to understand
the development of Marx's thought. Indeed, he believes that the early writings help us to understand *Capital* better.[53] As Lefebvre notes, the 'ideological
authorities' within Marxism and workers' movements were concerned that,
if the early writings of Marx were read, his thought would be understood
quite differently. Lefebvre suggests they were quite right to fear this.[54] We
might note in this context the 1957 decision of the East German Institute of
Marxism-Leninism to separate the *1844 Manuscripts* from the Marx-Engels
Werke into a separate volume.[55] It is instructive to compare, albeit briefly,
Lefebvre's reading of the Marxian canon with that of Althusser and Sartre,
the two other central French Marxists of the twentieth century. For Poster,
Lefebvre was 'by far the best interpreter of Marx in France',[56] but the
divergent readings offered by Althusser, Sartre and Lefebvre help to understand their reactions to existentialism and structuralism, and the debates
around the notions of humanism and alienation. What is notable is that
whilst Lefebvre was extremely critical of both of their readings of Marx,
both praised his work in different areas: Sartre suggesting that his work on
history, sociology and dialectics was 'beyond reproach',[57] and Althusser
praising his 'excellent little book' on Lenin.[58]

The 'juvenile presumptions' of existentialism

Jean-Paul Sartre's 1943 work *Being and Nothingness* exercised a strong pull on
the French intellectual scene. This work, with its translation of the phenomenology of Husserl and Heidegger into a French context, made a number of
moves that could be identified as conflicting with Marxism. According to
Trebitsch, the PCF saw Lefebvre as the only Communist philosopher capable of stemming the tide of existentialism,[59] and Lefebvre engaged with
existentialist ideas in much of his work. Indeed, for some, the tension
between Marxism and existentialism is seen as a, if not the, constant theme
in Lefebvre's work.[60] The key text is the polemical book *L'existentialisme*,
published in 1946 at the height of Sartre's popularity.[61] Retrospectively,
Lefebvre would suggest that this book should have borne the subtitle 'the art
of making enemies'.[62]

 In *L'existentialisme* Lefebvre suggests that movements in thought often follow political upheaval: romanticism after the revolution and the Napoleonic
wars, symbolism after 1871, surrealism after World War One, and existentialism after World War Two.[63] He suggests that Sartre is making use of
arguments that he, Lefebvre, had flirted with in his youth, but that he had
become a Marxist and cured himself of this affliction. Lefebvre is particularly thinking of what he calls the *Philosophical Manifesto*, a manifesto for the
Philosophies group written in 1924, sections of which were published in

their journal *Philosophies*.[64] He argues that the ideas put forward in this were developed independently of German influences – little of Husserl's work, and none of Heidegger's, was available at the time.[65] One of the German sources that Lefebvre does acknowledge as influential to his thinking in this early period is Schelling, but he suggests that Heidegger and Sartre would reproduce the problems of Schelling, 150 years later.[66] Lefebvre is happy to dismiss the 'presumptions, ardent illusions, and displays of pedantry' found in the *Manifesto* as the work of someone in their twenties. He acerbically remarks that Sartre (in his forties in 1946) has long passed the age of juvenile presumptions and has no such excuse.[67] As Poster notes, 'in one stroke Lefebvre gave himself credit as the first existentialist, relegating Sartre to the position of a mere latecomer, and presented a self-criticism in which existentialism was exposed as juvenile'.[68]

Lefebvre does not take prisoners in his assault. As he confesses in a letter to Guterman, the reason that he hates Sartre so much is that he can see where he might have ended up, had he not given up the ideas of the *Manifesto*, 'along with the success and glory, money and women, for a hard and mediocre life, for militant thought working on real problems'.[69] He renames the movement 'excrementalism' and the earthy language is pronounced throughout.[70] More than once he likens the work to filth (*ordure*) and describes it as the 'magic and metaphysics of shit'.[71] (Interestingly, Heidegger would similarly describe *Being and Nothingness* as muck (*Dreck*).)[72] Most infamously, Lefebvre accuses Paul Nizan, another co-traveller from philosophical work to Marxism, who left the Party in the wake of the Molotov-Ribbentrop pact, and a friend of Sartre, of being a spy and traitor.[73] Given that Nizan had died in 1940, fighting Nazism, this seemed particularly unjust.[74]

Sartre locates existentialism as a humanism, one of the key points of departure for many of his commentators, and in *Search for a Method* and the *Critique of Dialectical Materialism*, attempts a fusion of existentialism with Marxism. Indeed an earlier title for *Search for a Method* was *Existentialism and Marxism*.[75] Sartre wishes to reconquer the man inside Marxism, and suggests that though there is no Marxist ethic, there can be a humanist ethic that incorporates Marxism.[76] Althusser and Lefebvre depart from this reading, though in different ways. Althusser, following the critique of Sartre in Heidegger's *Letter on Humanism*, finds a philosophical anti-humanism in Marx's works, or at least his later ones.[77] For Althusser, there is a 'theoretical disparity' in socialist humanism, in that one term, socialist, is scientific, whilst the other, humanism, is ideological (and non-scientific).[78] Althusser goes on to suggest that this anti-humanism provides 'an understanding of the necessity of existing ideologies, including humanism. Because it is a critical and revolutionary theory, it also provides an understanding of the tactics to be adopted towards them: to support them, to transform them, or to combat them'.[79]

While Althusser wishes to reject humanism entirely, Lefebvre's attitude is more nuanced. Sartre relies heavily on Marx's early works in order to find the sources for his ideas; Althusser, as has been seen, has to dismiss them to support his view.[80] Lefebvre, in reading the entire canon, arrives at an ultimately more balanced interpretation. Hess suggests that this wish to know 'the movement of his thought' characterizes Lefebvre's relation to Marx.[81] Lefebvre is not trying to inject humanism as speculative idealism into Marxism, but trying to draw out the humanism implicit in Marx's works. This humanism is not abstract and mystified, but concrete, in that it is in a constant relation with materialism. Lefebvre sees *Capital* as making the abstract concepts of 'man' and 'humanity' concrete, into *praxis*,[82] and is strongly critical of phenomenology and existentialism for their devaluation of the everyday (concrete, real, life) 'in favour of pure or tragic moments' such as anguish and death.[83] Existentialists condemn everyday life, the non-metaphysical, to triviality and inauthenticity.[84] This notion of the concrete is important, because although it means that Lefebvre's work is always in a relation with materialism, it is not confined to materialism in a crude sense. For Lefebvre, 'abstractions are very concrete' and the supreme methodological principle of dialectics is that 'the truth is always concrete'.[85] It follows that humanism is only a part of Marxism when its idealism is balanced by materialism. Marxism refuses both a metaphysics exterior to individuals *and* the privileging of the isolated individual consciousness.[86]

Existentialism is therefore viewed as a shift from the objective idealism of Hegel to a subjective idealism.[87] Lefebvre condemned Sartre as 'an idealistic subjectivist manufacturer of weapons against communism'.[88] Sartre is thus doubly damned: for being an idealist without being a materialist; and for being a subjectivist rather than an objectivist. The latter of these two points is a relatively standard criticism of Sartre's reading of Heidegger, in that if Heidegger is treated as talking about subjects he is made more Cartesian: a common move for the French.[89] Lefebvre contends that existential thought is based on 'individual consciousness, on the subject and the ordeals of subjectivity, rather than on a practical, historical and social reality'.[90] It takes notions of individual consciousness and freedom and puts them at the centre of its concerns, but conceives them as an absolute – it privileges subjectivity.[91] Sartre begins with the Cartesian *cogito*, more or less modified as an 'existential', in order to understand history.[92] If the dialectic is thought subjectively it is akin to sophistry.[93] In distinction Lefebvre was a materialist and an *objective* idealist.

Lefebvre therefore contends that Sartre gets into the same problem his own earlier work did. There is profound tension between an ideal of commitment and authenticity on the one hand, and total freedom on the other.

In 1945, as in 1924, existentialism foregrounds the speculative problem of freedom and offers two conceptions of Freedom: to be nothing (while able to become everything) and to be anything at all (after an arbitrary 'adventure'). These two propositions are equally false, but existentialism masks the contradiction by endlessly oscillating between the two; it tells those who are nothing, 'Freely become something! Choose, make yourself an essence!' To those who are already prisoners of 'something', it says, 'Free yourselves! Go back to consciousness, to existence, pure and simple.' The existentialists of 1924 staked and lost the best years of their youth on this gamble, this sterile adventure . . .[94]

Unfortunately, Lefebvre suggests, nothing can be done about this. The modern day existentialists will have to work it out for themselves. As he suggests, 'existentialists will come to a sad end, or they will break with existentialism and "overcome" themselves'.[95] He sees that possibility when he suggests that, towards the end of *Being and Nothingness*, Sartre begins to think about the objective dialectic. This brings Sartre close to 'Marxist humanism and *dialectical materialism*', but only close.[96]

Lefebvre would come to view *L'existentialisme* as not a good book, although he recognizes that the chapters on Kierkegaard and Nietzsche are probably the least bad, because they tried to say what he was actually feeling.[97] However, as will be more fully explored in the following chapter, the discussion of Nietzsche is nothing like that contained in the 1939 book on the thinker, or in the later analyses. Equally the polemical tone of the discussion of Heidegger – itself a surrogate for yet more assaults on Sartre – is not continued in later works. Most dramatically, the relationship with Sartre improved substantially, with both referencing each other's work appreciatively. From today's perspective this is not perhaps entirely surprising – Sartre moved increasingly toward Marxism and sought a rapprochement between it and his earlier thought; Lefebvre left the Party and its strictures and returned to earlier themes.[98]

Structuralism as the French ideology

After his membership of the PCF ended Lefebvre continued his engagement with contemporary modes of thought, crossing swords with structuralism, Situationism, psychoanalysis and other key intellectual trends. This was conducted simultaneously with further work on Marxism, again resistant to dogmatic readings, but now free from party constraints. In the reading of structuralism these two things come together – Lefebvre is both engaging with a particular movement, and an interpretation of Marx. Although I will argue in Chapter 2 that Lefebvre often appropriated ideas from other modes of thought, subjecting them to a critique certainly, but making use of their productive elements, there were some figures for whom he seemingly had nothing but contempt. The structuralist movement was high on this list. However, even here there may be something of worth: 'It is not a question of declaring structuralism null and void. On the contrary: it is in denouncing the abuses of the concept of structure and its dogmatic ideologisation, that one can legitimately discover its gains.'[99] He discussed structuralism in a range of places, including *Métaphilosophie, Le langage et société, Position: Contre les technocrates* and *De l'État*. He devoted a collection of essays, *Au-delà du structuralisme* to it, and reprinted many of these in a shorter work called *L'idéologie structuraliste* a few years later.[100] The essays were written over a fairly long period, with the earliest dating from 1957.

Lefebvre's argument is that structuralism is an ideology, an ideology of the dominant class, a scientific travesty of progressive thought. His criticism of this French ideology bears comparison to some of Marx and Engels' critiques of their contemporaries – at one point he suggests Dühring was a structuralist *avant la lettre*.[101] He suggests that the date of 1957 for the beginning of this work is significant, because this was the crucial moment for Marxism. Faced with the legacy of Khrushchev's denunciation of Stalin, Marxism had two options – a move toward a new democracy, or to freeze as a statist dogmatism. It was the latter, a re-established Stalinism, that won out.[102] Chapter 6 will discuss the political implications of this shift, and the attendant conception of the state, which Lefebvre thinks led both to a consolidated capitalism in the west and a stagnation in the east. A state capitalism and a state socialism – both centralizing the whole society under an authoritarian State.[103] Structuralism was, for Lefebvre, entirely in accord – not quite complicit – with this movement. Its dominance in the 1960s and early 1970s was linked to a statist bureaucracy, technocracy and statism generally. Structuralism, a knowledge which claims purity through the epistemological break from ideology, is for Lefebvre merely an ideological tool, a formal expression of the dominant ideology of the state.[104] As Eribon notes, this idea of structuralism being a reflection of Gaullist technocracy was found in the work of Lucien Goldmann and Jeannette Colombel,[105] and is developed in the writings of Jean Baudrillard on the consumer society, a term Lefebvre coins.[106]

Structuralism is therefore condemned for its scientificity. For the structuralists, this was a means of challenging the problems of humanism, a critique that was pursued in the work of poststructuralists. Like Althusser, the inspiration was often Heidegger's *Letter on Humanism*. Derrida's 'The ends of man' and Foucault's *The Order of Things* were very much in vogue at the time.[107] Lefebvre was dismissive, talking of 'best-sellers' (the reference is surely to Foucault) that cry ' "God is dead, man too" as if the death of classical humanism was that of man'.[108] For Lefebvre, such criticisms were not only flawed, but nothing new. 'Contemporary discussions of man, the human and humanism reproduce in less original terms the arguments of Marx and Nietzsche against classical humanism and its implications'.[109] Marx and Nietzsche, Lefebvre suggests, at least tried to identify solutions to the problems they perceived, while contemporary writers risk the plunge back into nihilism. Nietzsche's solution was the idea of the overman, but as Lefebvre notes, the dangers of this have since become 'cruelly evident'. The 'new man' that emerged from production and planning has been likewise shown to be problematic.[110] Rather, humanism needs to be rethought, reappropriated. In place of the old humanism – a mix of liberalism, Judeo-Christian values and the suppression of revolution – we need 'a new humanism, a new praxis, another man, that of urban society'.[111] As Lichtheim notes, when Sartre's grandiose synthesis disclosed its speculative character, the true

Marxist revisionists pursued the direction suggested by Lefebvre in his writings.[112] This renewed humanism is discussed in Chapter 3 below.

Another problem with structuralism is that it takes one concept – that of structure – and thoughtlessly privileges it above all others. Rather than recognize the relation between form, function and structure it focuses just on one. In this way it bears comparison with formalism and functionalism – all three are ideologies of one concept, giving it almost an ontological significance. They ideologize the concept, but at the same time, put it to service as an instrument.[113] Lefebvre argues that this is structural or semantic reduction: humans essentially consist in their creation of forms and significations. This ignores all sorts of other things – *praxis*, the dialectic, tragedy, emotions and passions, the individual and much of society, and of course history.[114] In *La fin de l'histoire* Lefebvre includes the privileging of formalism, functionalism and structuralism over form, function and structure as one of the problems of the modern world, along with rationalism against reason, nationalism against the nation and individualism against the individual.[115]

Lefebvre singles out a number of figures within structuralism for critique. The only figure who seems to come out well is Roland Barthes, who Lefebvre likes for his analysis of popular culture and myths.[116] Lévi-Strauss is seen as initiating much structuralist work, and Lefebvre calls his movement a new Eleatism, after the Eleatic philosophers of Ancient Greece such as Parmenides and Zeno. For the Eleatics, change and motion were inherently problematic. Most famously Zeno posed paradoxes about movement – the flight of an arrow and the race between Achilles and the tortoise – by suggesting that the stages of trajectories were distinct and discrete units. They were therefore in opposition to Heraclitus, who saw the world as flux, as becoming. 'The Eleatic analysis determines mobility as segments, instants, places, points.'[117] For Lefebvre this is what structuralism does – by cutting up time it denies history and becoming.[118] It privileges invariance to the detriment of becoming, the synchronic over the diachronic.[119] Foucault is similarly criticized, particularly concerning his book *Les mots et les choses*, translated in English as *The Order of Things*, for the lack of historical analysis.[120] For Lefebvre, structuralism 'leaps over transitions, accentuates breaks and discontinuities and tends to conceive of modes of production as coherent wholes (to the extent that the passage from one mode of production to another becomes all the more intelligible in that it signifies the disappearance of a type of intelligibility)'.[121] This was Sartre's criticism of the book too, a claim I believe is misplaced, but certainly one that had a certain currency at the time.[122]

According to Dosse, for Lefebvre

Bourdieu . . . was a 'positive sociologist', Foucault had 'eliminated critical aspects from thinking', Althusser 'made Marxism rigid and eliminated all flexibility from the dialectic . . . Althusser has the same relationship to Marxism as the Thomists do to Aristotelianism: a classification, a systematisation, but which no longer has anything to do with reality.'[123]

Lefebvre is particularly unrelenting in his critique of Althusser, whose radical interpretation of Marx gained enormous currency in the 1960s and 1970s.[124] The first point of departure is in the reading of the Marxian canon. Althusser and Lefebvre conceive of Marx's development in fundamentally different ways. For Althusser, there is a rupture, an 'epistemological break [*coupure*]' between the work of the early Marx (unscientific and Hegelian) and the later works of Marxism proper.[125] Althusser wishes to promote a scientific Marxism. To do this he must purge Marxism of its idealistic remains: 'More than ever today it is important to see that one of the first phantoms is the shade of Hegel. We need *a little more light on Marx* to send this phantom back into the night, or what is the same thing, *a little more Marxist light on Hegel himself*. We can then escape from this "inversion", from its ambiguities and confusions.'[126] This leads Althusser initially to limit mature Marx to works after 1857, and later to suggest that only the *Critique of the Gotha Programme* and the *Marginal Notes on Wagner* are '*totally and definitely exempt from any* trace of Hegelian influence'.[127] It is difficult to support Althusser's reading, as it seeks so hard to deny the Hegelianism implicit in *Capital* that it is forced to exclude the *Grundrisse* (along with several other works) and leads him to dubious readings on the issues of humanism and alienation.[128] It seems somewhat bizarre to try to rid Marx of Hegel, for aside from Marx's own acknowledgement of an influence, both Lenin and Mao identify Hegel in Marx, and they were two of Althusser's major influences. As Kelly sensibly notes, 'in laying the ghost of Hegel [Althusser] comes near to throwing out the rational kernel with the mystified shell – the Marxist baby with the Hegelian bathwater'.[129]

On the other hand, as we have seen, Lefebvre conceives of Marx's development in terms of a dialectic movement, from the Hegelian early works, to the rejection of Hegelianism, and then the rediscovery of Hegel in some of the later texts. Marxism is both a theory *of* movement and a theory *in* movement.[130] He is therefore extremely critical of Althusser's reading, and also of the notion of a break or rupture generally.[131] For Lefebvre, Althusser reading Marx is like Heraclitus seen, revised and corrected by an Eleatic.[132] Why does Althusser need to bring concepts from elsewhere into his reading of Marx? Not unfairly then, Lefebvre asks if the author of *Reading Capital* has really *read Capital*.[133] Although Althusser reflects on the idea of reading in relation to *Capital* Lefebvre argues that if he did read it, beginning with the first paragraph of the second chapter, he would realize that it is not a book that has a message that is in need of decryption, but that it is itself a decryption of the hieroglyphic text of the world of commodities.[134] Lefebvre contends that Marx is difficult, but clear. The danger is that Althusser and his collaborators on *Reading Capital* make him more obscure.[135] Unless our reading is targeted toward specific questions then it becomes mere literature, a game of writing, a scholastic exercise.[136]

The three concepts of form, function and structure, all of which are explored in *Capital*, are of '*equal* methodological and theoretical importance ... *taken together* [they] form the theoretical field in which the analysis of

Capital takes place'.[137] Narrow understandings of one are destined to reify it, to lead to narrow understandings of society as a whole.[138] One of Marx's points in *Capital* was that we needed to take the content and the form together in our analysis. The social content and the logical form went together in his work but structuralists are intent in separating them out again.[139] Althusser's reading of *Capital* is therefore akin to the structuralist move in linguistics where they eliminate the content of language – acts of communication and speech (*parole*) – in order to examine the form (*la langue*). Lefebvre calls this the structuralist reduction.[140]

Lefebvre talks of Althusser's 'cunning naivety', and suggests that his analysis of Ideological State Apparatuses (ISAs) is more useful for explaining the Eastern bloc than capitalism.[141] For Lefebvre, the ISA fits well with the State Mode of Production (SMP) in Stalin's state. We therefore need to ask the question of which apparatuses are being meant. 'The party, university, school, additional ones. Which ideology? Ideologised Marxism.'[142] Althusser's article on ISAs is thus mystificatory in a double sense: 'it masks both the ideologisation of Marxism by state apparatuses in the USSR and structuralism as the dominant ideology on the side of state capitalism.'[143] Lefebvre closely associates Althusser in particular with dogmatism, suggesting that structural Marxism (notably *For Marx*) proceeds directly from Stalinism, 'and not from Leninism as is often said':[144]

> Like Stalinism, it takes the form of a pure beginning when it prolongs both existing philosophy and the knowledge which it pretends to acquire, and already institutional political action. Neo-Stalinism saved dogmatism and Stalinist systematisation *in extremis*. Structuralism therefore accomplished a double function in the service of the State: on the capitalistic side, saving the action of structuring, and on the socialist side, saving the structured action.[145]

Elsewhere in *De l'État* he suggests that it is *Stalin* who has introduced a *philosophical break* (coupure) between pre-Marxism and Marxism, between pre-Stalinism and Stalinism. 'Philosophy, in crossing this discontinuity, passes – according to Stalinists – from idealism to materialism (dialectical)'.[146] Althusser, he suggests, in the book titled by a mystificatory antiphrasis *For Marx*, has done an inestimable service to the statist doctrine, to neo-dogmatism and neo-Stalinism.[147] Althusser is a 'neo-Stalinist ideologue';[148] structuralism is the 'ideology of the status quo'.[149] Lefebvre suggests that structuralism was decisively rejected by the student movement of 1968.[150] It is notable, of course, that the PCF, heavily indebted to Althusser's work, was very slow to support the events of May, even when the workers got involved. Such political issues will be explored further in Chapter 6, and the events of May 1968 in Chapter 4.

Lefebvre's critique of structuralism is therefore multi-faceted. He supports a revised Marxist humanism, and challenges structuralism's scientificity and lack of historicity.[151] Structuralism is not, therefore, a mere abuse of language, but a systematization, a reductive understanding of society.

Lefebvre argues that in order to understand systems the worst thing we can do is to create a systematization. 'A comparative and comprehensive science of systems requires a critical mistrust of any attempt at, or temptation by, systematisation.' Instead of an honest appraisal of the flaws and failures of Marxism, structural Marxism – Althusser – conceals them through a retreat into scientism.[152] It is another form of dogmatism because it reduces Marxism to an economicism, turns it into an epistemology that fails to recognize the role of practice, and it dismembers Marxist thought by introducing notions of a 'break'. Structuralism systematically depreciates the lived, proclaiming, in the name of an epistemological truth, the necessity and sufficiency of the conceived.[153] Structuralism is unhistorical, thinking it unscientific; it ignores the importance of the tragic in life and action; and replaces the dialectical methodology with techniques elevated to the level of method.[154] These themes will be developed in subsequent chapters – the rethinking of history in Chapter 5, the role of the tragic and the importance of Nietzsche in Chapter 2 and the dangers of technocracy in Chapter 6. For now though we turn to the importance of the dialectic. As Lefebvre notes, in seeking to deny the idealist dialectic, structuralism loses the dialectic altogether.

> The psychoanalytical structuralist lantern in hand, the poor ideologues are now searching for the lost dialectic. The dialectical movement and method, unity and struggle, transition in action, is not found either in Hegel or Marx taken in isolation, but in their confrontation and disagreement. To separate them is already to kill dialectical thought.[155]

Logic and dialectics

As was noted above Sartre suggested that Lefebvre's grasp of dialectical methodology was 'beyond reproach'. What did Sartre find so exemplary about his treatment? The use of the dialectic is found throughout Lefebvre's work, both in practical analyses – Sartre particularly cites work on rural sociology – and theorization. The key theoretical works are *Dialectical Materialism* and *Logique formelle, logique dialectique*. The latter was the projected first volume in a series of eight books called *A la lumière du matérialisme dialectique* – sometimes known as the *Traité du matérialisme dialectique*. This series, as the titles suggest, was a treatise intended to illuminate dialectical materialism, and it was conceived as a direct challenge to Stalin's understanding of diamat,[156] particularly as found in the theoretical chapter of his *History of the Communist Party of the USSR*.[157] It was first planned in the 1930s, with the attempt to provide a Marxist outline of philosophy as a whole. This was not to construct a philosophical system, but knowledge in the process of movement, moving from the abstract to the concrete; the formal (logic) to the content (*praxis*) and from the least to the more complex.[158] It could not hope to be an exhaustive analysis, which is the mark of dogmatism.[159] It was a project Lefebvre had been working on through his teaching of this decade, and with the Liberation he began to think about how it could be published.[160] Only *Logique formelle, logique dialectique* appeared and further volumes were not published, because of 'political conditions' – Stalinism and Zhdanovism.[161] The second volume was written in 1945–6, and although it was printed it was destroyed on the order of PCF censors. It did however survive in manuscript – as Hess says 'remaining for fifty years in a drawer' – and has recently been issued by Anthropos.[162]

There are various projections for the full set of eight volumes. The most fully worked out plan is in the introduction to *Logique formelle, logique dialectique*:

1. *Logique formelle, logique dialectique.*
2. *Méthodologie des sciences.*
3. A history of the dialectic, materialism and dialectical materialism, from Heraclitus to the present day.
4. A study of the relation between historical materialism and dialectical materialism.
5. On concrete humanism and the idea of the Total Man.
6. An examination of morality and the constitution of a new ethic.
7. On individuality and individual conscience.
8. An examination of aesthetics, particularly the relation between content and form.[163]

In the list of publications in some earlier works, a similar plan is found, although it appears that Volume 7 would have discussed psychology, and Volumes 3 and 4 would have been just one, with the remaining book looking at the dialectic in the study of capital and the state.[164] Although the remaining six volumes were not written in the form outlined, it is clear that many of their concerns were discussed in other places. The closest we have to one on the original plan is probably *Contribution à l'esthétique*.[165]

Many of the concerns of the first volume, and indeed some of those of future ones, had been discussed in *Dialectical Materialism*. It is worth noting that *Logique formelle, logique dialectique* has a certain didactic quality to it. For that reason, but also because of the clarity of its expression, I will use *Dialectical Materialism* as the principal guide for the following exposition. As Hirsch describes it, it 'quickly became a minor orthodox classic', yet he concedes that 'even in his orthodoxy', Lefebvre 'ran against the current'.[166] However, we should note that Lefebvre describes this book as 'only a preliminary sketch' of the project, which was 'insufficient on plenty of points, notably the relation between dialectical materialism and the sciences and their methodology'.[167] He wrote these words in 1946, before he realized that only *Logique formelle, logique dialectique* would be published. With these two books, and the newly available *Méthodologie des sciences* we can have a fair sense of the broad aims of this project.

Lefebvre suggests that traditionally there has been a clear distinction between formal logic and its content. Formal logic is only concerned with the structure and universal, analytic form of propositions and their relation. Where examples are given they are purely for illustrative purposes – they are not relevant in their own terms. Formal logic contents itself with notions of clear identity, such as: 'A is A. If A is B and B is C, then A is C'.[168] The content of such propositions is irrelevant to their formulation and relation. One of the reasons he suggests that the PCF stopped his work on logic was that 'not without some reason, I said that logic was the same in Paris, Moscow and New York. I said that $A = A$ or $(A + B)^2$ is the same formal identity in all countries, all regimes, all modes of production.'[169] This is because logic and the dialectic do not function as superstructures. Though they are historical developments they are not contained within the ideology or institution that gave rise to them.[170] That said, as will be explored in Chapter 6, Lefebvre recognizes how a particular conception of logic is adopted by capitalism as 'the philosophy of this mode of production', and how it assists its flexibility through technology, cybernetics and computing.[171]

Lefebvre however disputes that logic can so clearly be separated in form and content:

> In point of fact formal logic never manages to do without the content; it may break a piece of this content and reduce it, or make it more and more 'abstract', but it can never free itself from it entirely. It works on determinate judgments, even if it does see their content simply as an excuse for applying the form. As Hegel points out, a completely simple, void identity cannot even be formulated.[172]

To take a formal example. A logician brings in a term, 'A', and then its opposite, 'not-A'. On this basis we can assert that 'A is not not-A'. In Aristotelian logic this is the law of the excluded middle – something is either A or not-A, identity or non-identity. This logic of identity is most closely associated with the metaphysic of Being. 'Identity is seen not as a pure form but as an internal, essential and objective property of Being.' Being, and each being, is identical to itself, and thus defines itself. 'Identity is therefore taken as both form and content: its own content.' This was, Lefebvre suggests, an aspect of Aristotle's thought that was developed and taken up by thinkers throughout the Western tradition. While Aristotle himself may have also provided a 'theory of the individuality of every concrete being', this abstract aspect was the one developed in isolation by Western philosophy. 'Up until Leibniz the western mind was engaged on a heroic but vain attempt to extract the content from the form, to pass logically from thought Being to existent Being, that is to deduce the world.'[173]

For Hegel, as quoted by Lenin, 'there is no third'. The middle is excluded – identity or non-identity, A or not-A. However, Lenin, in his *Philosophical Notebooks* suggests '*There is* a third in this thesis itself. A itself is the third, for A can be both +A and −A.'[174] Lefebvre makes exactly the same point, that 'A' itself is the third term to 'plus A' and 'minus A'.[175] Lefebvre's point is that 'not A' is created, posited, only in order to vanish, in order to secure a new identity. The negation is itself negated. He suggests that therefore such judgments cannot be purely analytical, in the sense that they cannot simply be an explication of terms. As soon as we give an example, such as 'the tree is green', 'A is B' we go beyond formal logic. Formal logic is therefore always related to its content, to a concrete significance. However, it is also an attempt to abstract from that specific, to make a general assertion, and therefore buys into an ontology or metaphysics.[176] We find something similar in language, with the formal rules of grammar, which leave aside the sense, the content, the truth or falsehood of the assertion.[177]

Logic is therefore a formal expression, but without the content it is neutral. All thought has a content, an object of analysis – even mathematics.[178] Just as structuralist linguistics was criticized for stripping the content out of the form, so too with formal logic.[179] Formal logic, logic of form, like grammar, 'has only a relative scope and a limited application', it is therefore 'a logic of abstraction'. A concrete logic, a logic of content is what is needed, of which formal logic is an element within it. This is dialectical logic. Form and content are thus linked, indeed inseparable, but still different.[180] To work without content is to risk falling into formalism; but analysis without form is equally flawed.[181] Lefebvre's point is that it is content which is class based. In the case of concrete logic a class analysis is always revealed.[182] Indeed, there is a further danger if the form is over stressed – we do not end up with formal logic, but with logical formalism. As with structuralism's privileging of one element, we end up with an ideology.[183]

Formal logic therefore gets into serious difficulties for Lefebvre. How, then, are we to resolve the problem of the relation between the form and the content? Should we reverse the move, and begin with the content in order to illuminate the form? This, too, confronts major obstacles. If it is rigorous, coherent, it is destined to repeat the same terms through the syllogism. If it is useful, in that it moves from facts to laws, it is forced to introduce elements that are, logically speaking, without necessity.[184] Equally, 'if Being is what it is and never anything else, if every idea is either absolutely true or absolutely false, the real contradictions between existence and thought are excluded from thought.' Contradiction, the diverse, the fluid is, Lefebvre suggests, left to the dialectic in the old sense of the term, that is imprecise argument and sophistry. Thought defined by identity is destined to remain immobile. Reason in this sense remains ideal, rather than real; logic is isolated from the real, which finds itself in the realm of the irrational.[185]

This is why Hegel is so central to Marx, and to Lefebvre. Hegel's work is at once a response and a solution to precisely these problems. The legacy of Kant was for reason to be strictly differentiated between form and content, from our perception of the world and the thing-in-itself, the faculties of knowledge from the object of knowledge. For Lefebvre, Hegelian doctrine's central idea is 'the consciousness of an infinitely rich unity of thought and reality, of form and content, a necessary unity, implied in thought's internal conflicts'. Every conflict is a relation, but one that is fought over and transcended. This is not a negative way of thinking, but a positive, productive way, in which 'one-sided' terms are surpassed and superseded.[186] Lefebvre suggests that in real-life arguments nothing is completely or indisputably true, and equally nothing is absolutely absurd or false. If we compare the positions taken we move toward a higher unity of these seemingly conflicting positions:

> Each thesis is false in what it asserts absolutely but true in what it asserts relatively (its content); and it is true in what it denies relatively (its well-founded criticism of the other thesis) and false in what it denies absolutely (its dogmatism).[187]

The dialectic in Hegel's sense is not mere sophistry, because it does not do this simply for the sake of disruption, 'out of pure vanity', but because of the productive purpose.[188] Equally Lefebvre suggests, Hegel needed to rescue logic from the bankrupt state he found it in. The issue is precisely one of the link between form and a reality, but a fluid, diverse reality rather than static, monist one. For that reason he had to start from the content, and to extract the notions immersed in this raw material. Lefebvre cites *The Phenomenology of Spirit*: 'we must tear away the veil from substantial life', in order to raise it to the level of rationality.[189] As he importantly notes, the purpose of this aspect of his enquiry is to recapture (*reprendre*) Hegel's *Logic* 'materially'.[190]

Kant's *Critique of Pure Reason* had, in Lefebvre's mind, 'opened up a new path for logic', because of the distinction he had drawn between analytical judgments and synthetic judgments. Analytic judgments would be formal, rigorous, but sterile; synthetic judgments would add something to our knowledge, but the central question of the first *Critique* was precisely how such a thing could be possible without continual recourse to empirical validation. However, whilst Kant criticized the idea that you could have productive knowledge without reason and experience being combined, he was concerned to create the conditions of possibility for knowledge through the discovery of the categories. His synthetic *a priori* judgments were consequently 'pure, empty forms, separated from their content, as instruments of cognition indifferent in relation to their subject-matter, as subjective in relation to the object – as still conforming therefore to traditional formalism'.[191]

Therefore whilst Kant opens up a new path, he needs to be taken further. His dualism has to be transcended, even if his ideas 'prove infinitely fertile'.[192] For example Lefebvre notes that for Leibniz the proposition $1 + 1 = 2$ is purely analytical; for Kant it is synthetic. This is because Kant suggests that '2' is not simply the repetition of '1' – there is something new, a synthesis. Lefebvre's response is that because $2 = 1 + 1$ and $1 + 1 = 2$ are equivalent, $1 + 1 = 2$ is both analytic *and* synthetic.[193] We should note here that Lefebvre recognizes that as well as being crucial for identity, '1 + 1' also creates difference, because of the repetition.[194] The same point is made about $A = A$ in a number of places.[195] The second A is both the same as A and different, precisely because it is the second. Lefebvre suggests that 'repetition creates difference',[196] but contends that classical philosophy 'eludes difference',[197] a point that will be returned to in Chapter 6.

Lefebvre's point is not that Hegel discovered contradiction, but that he insists on it being there in all thought – either through outright confrontation or the reduction or exclusion of the other. As he suggests in an interview, he would always put the accent on the contradictions and not on consistency.[198] Lefebvre therefore gives Hegel credit for discovering the third term, 'which results once any determination has been enriched by its negation and transcended; it is produced rigorously whenever two terms are in contradiction, yet it is a new moment of Being and of thought'. This is not merely formal logic, but a dialectical logic that proceeds rigorously through determining a third term whenever there is a contradiction.[199] Within the third term the first is found, along with the second, but richer and more determinate. The third term is a negation of the negation of the first term, it corrects the one-sided nature of the first term, without being wholly its opposite, which would be one-sided too. 'The Third Term unites and transcends the contradictories and preserves what was determinate in them. Unity triumphs after a period of fruitful discord.'[200]

Lefebvre suggests that dialectic logic is not a replacement, an abolition of formal logic, but its transcension, because it preserves its importance whilst 'giving it a concrete significance'.[201] 'The relation of logic and dialectic is thus itself dialectical.'[202] As he notes in *La somme et le reste*, he was attacked in the *Cominform* publication on precisely this point.[203] In this early period of the Cold War various and contradictory forces were at play within France. Following from George Kennan's 'X' article, Andrei Zhdanov had given a speech at the first meeting of Cominform on 22 September 1947, where he outlined what became known as the 'two camps' doctrine. In part recognizing political reality – the Communists had been expelled from the French government in May that year – but also helping to constitute it, Zhdanov argued that there were two major camps in the post-war world: 'the imperialist and anti-democratic camp, on the one hand, and the anti-imperialist and democratic camp, on the other'.[204] You were either with one camp or against it. This was not confined to foreign policy. Zhdanovism had claimed that logic was inherently bourgeois, and entirely separate from the dialectic. Following this, the PCF had affirmed that science could be distinguished on a class basis, and that 'proletarian science against bourgeois science' would be their motto.[205] This was perhaps most painfully and erroneously played out in the debate about Lysenko's genetic theories.[206] This makes sense of the hostile reaction to *Méthodologie des sciences*. As Lefebvre remembers in *La somme et le reste*, at this time he acidly asked his comrades – 'is there a proletarian arithmetic?' The only response was a shrug of the shoulders.[207]

For Lefebvre, whilst formal logic is the logic of frozen time, of a simplified world, of abstraction; dialectical logic is the logic of history, of a subtle and nuanced world, of concrete reality. On the one hand form; on the other content. Dialectical logic 'does not reject the principle of identity, it gives it a content'.[208] If formal logic says 'A is A' dialectical logic does not say 'A is not-A' in order to contradict it, but to recognize its limitations. A tree is not *just* a tree, it is only a tree because it is a particular tree, because it has leaves, fruit and blossoms; the blossom becomes fruit, which becomes another tree in time. It is a relationship of change and becoming. To say 'A is A' is true in that it can describe and be transcended, but it is false if it is taken as an absolute, statically. Dialectical logic allows the analysis of simple *and* complex natures; it can go beyond mere classification; it can analyse becoming.[209]

Issues of quality and quantity are therefore rendered problematic. If we have a pile of sand and we remove grains one by one when does it cease to be a pile? Or two examples Lefebvre takes from Hegel: we lose the hairs on our head one by one, but at a given moment we are bald; water gets colder and colder degree by degree and then becomes solid. Changes in being are not merely quantitative, but qualitative, and the dividing line is not clear.[210]

> Becoming is a continuous development (an evolution) yet at the same time it is punctuated by leaps, by sudden mutations and upheavals. At the same time it is an involution, since it carries with it and takes up again the content from which it began, even while it is forming something new. No becoming is indefinitely rectilinear.[211]

This detailed treatment of the notion of the dialectic in Hegel is invaluable in understanding how Lefebvre works. It is also invaluable in understanding Marx. However, as is well known, Marx criticized Hegel's logic because of its mystification. What does this mean? Lefebvre suggests that Hegel continues a binary divide between the ordinary, temporal life of man in the world, and the realm of ideas, the kingdom of thought and freedom.[212]

> Thus flesh and spirit, everyday reality and thought, real necessity and ideal freedom, actual servitude and the theoretical power of the intelligence, the wretchedness of concrete life and the splendid but fictive sovereignty of the Idea, are all in conflict.[213]

Hegel also claims the position of grasping the entire content of human experience, which is contradictory. If it is infinitely rich then it cannot be entirely grasped by one thinker; if it can it cannot be infinitely rich. The content is in danger of being abstracted in order to allow its being grasped.[214] 'Inasmuch as it is a finished system, Hegelianism leads, like traditional formalism, to a sharp conflict between invention and knowledge, between fruitfulness and rigour.'[215] For Lefebvre Hegel confused action with the thought of action. Rational thought in his terms has to be rescued, like logic needed to be rescued. Hegel was not content with deepening the knowledge of the content in order to attain the form but went further and reduced it to thought, through his claims to totality. This means that truth is no longer the unity of form and content, but becomes reduced to form itself, and the identity of form with itself.[216]

The danger in all of this is that the objective content vanishes. It does in Hegel's thinking of being and nothingness, just as it does in Heidegger's analysis of the 'ontological structure' of death.[217] All of this is a 'mystical and omnipresent abyss, from which all the forces of life and matter tumble like mysterious cataracts before falling back into it again'; it becomes a 'subjective mysticism'. As Hegel's thought becomes a system, contradiction becomes a logical essence, something we find in every thing *a priori* – 'no longer the concrete unity of specific contradictions, but an absolute identity'. However, Lefebvre suggests that Hegel provides the means by which we can challenge and transcend him. The irony of Hegel's work is that whilst he recognized contradiction he attempted to resolve it, but that this contradiction necessarily existed within his own work.[218] Ultimately, 'Hegelianism is a dogma, it demands a self-discipline, a renunciation of individual experience and the vital problems of the individual'.[219]

Lefebvre claims that this 'critical examination of Hegelianism', which I have outlined here at considerable length, broadly matches that of Marx and Engels in the 1840s and 1850s. From around 1844 Marx rejects Hegel's idea that the state is the 'actuality of the ethical idea'.[220] Rather than being able to explain political and juridical forms through internal analysis or through their relation to *Geist*, they have their roots in material existence, which Hegel understands by the name of civil society. Therefore, according to Lefebvre, from this point on 'Marx will develop the content of Hegelianism (the concrete theory of civil society, of the "system of needs" and of social relations) against Hegel's fixed system and its political consequences'.[221] As was argued earlier, Lefebvre suggests that although Marx damns Hegel in his middle period, he returns to him later. The argument is made that Marx develops only a historical materialism until he re-recognizes the importance of Hegel.[222] Lefebvre argues that 'in their struggle to grasp the content – historical, social, economic, human and practical – Marx and Engels eliminated formal method'.[223] There may have been a dialectic of sorts – a dialectic of conflict – but not a dialectic that is linked to a structure of becoming. It is only later – around 1858 Lefebvre suggests – that Marx recognizes the importance of Hegel again, and this coincides with his sorting out of key concepts such as the distinction between labour and labour power, surplus value and so on.[224] Marx wants to rescue the '*rational* aspect of the method which Hegel not only discovered but also mystified'.[225] For Lefebvre, Hegelianism had something Marx wanted, and 'he wanted to save what was worth saving from the wreckage of the absolute system'.[226]

For Lefebvre this means that the dialectical method came to be added to historical materialism; that the dialectic – originally worked out in idealist form – loses its abstract, idealist form through being reworked from economic foundations. In a crucial passage Lefebvre challenges the reductive dogmatic version of Marxism, that *only* looks at economic relations to understand society: 'economic relations are not the only relations but the simplest ones'. True materialism does not look at ideas, institutions and cultures as mere epiphenomenona, a 'frivolous and unimportant superstructure'. Rather, it

> determines the practical relations inherent in every organised human existence and studies them inasmuch as they are concrete conditions of existence for cultures or ways of life. The simple relations, moments and categories are involved, historically and methodologically, in the richer and more complex determinations, but they do not exhaust them. The given content is always a concrete totality. This complex content of life and consciousness is the true reality which we must attain and elucidate. Dialectical materialism is not an economicism. It analyses relations and then reintegrates them into the total movement.[227]

Lefebvre underlines the problems that result from confusing historical materialism (dialectical) with vulgar materialism (mechanism). The latter reduces nature to being defined by mechanical properties such as volume, density, elasticity – reducing natural beings to mechanical combinations of elementary properties such as particles, corpuscles, atoms. It thinks consciousness an epiphenomenon of physical-chemical processes; reduces humans to elementary needs of drinking and eating and in reducing the complex to the simple ends up with an extremely impoverished understanding of the world and man.[228]

Lefebvre recognizes that Marx did not use the words 'dialectical materialism' and never followed up the plan of writing 'two or three sheets [i.e. printer's sheets – *Drückbogen* – of about 16 pages]' on the dialectical methodology.[229] The expression 'dialectical materialism' appears to have originated with Kautsky, and was borrowed from him by Lenin.[230] As Lenin notes in his *Philosophical Notebooks*, Marx may not have left us a *Logic* of his own, but

> He did leave the *logic* of *Capital* ... Marx applied to a single science, logic, dialectics and the theory of knowledge of materialism (three words are not needed: it is one and the same thing) which has taken everything valuable in Hegel and developed it further.[231]

Lefebvre and Guterman make a very similar claim in their introduction to Marx's writings, claiming that though he did not have the time to write the treatise on the dialectic that he planned, the dialectical worldview is enfolded in his entire work.[232] Lefebvre therefore claims that 'the elements of [Marx's] thought are undeniably those conveyed by this term' of dialectical materialism.[233] But this is undoubtedly only true if it is understood in this way rather than the dogmatism of Stalinist diamat. As Lefebvre says, a Marxist dialectician would prefer an 'intelligent idealism to a stupid materialism'.[234] We must move from the abstract to the concrete, in order to discover the whole. Rather than the concrete totality being 'the product of the concept begetting itself above perception and representation', as it was for Hegel, it is 'the conceptual elaboration of the content grasped in perception and representation'.[235] Elsewhere Lefebvre suggests that he speaks of the materialist dialectic rather than dialectical materialism precisely to avoid this spectre of a 'new systematised philosophy'.[236] Marxism is a project or a programme rather than a system.[237]

The final point that Lefebvre makes here is that the thought of the dialectic undergoes one final move in Marx's work. He suggests that this happens sometime between the 1859 Preface and *Capital* (1867).[238] The categories in 1859 appear to be abstract. But by 1867 Marx recognizes that 'there can be no pure abstraction. The abstract is also concrete, and the concrete, from a certain point of view, is also abstract. All that exists for us is the concrete abstract.'[239] Lefebvre gives a number of examples – economic categories are concrete 'historically (as moments of the social reality) and actually (as elements of the social objectivity)'.[240] An object has use-value that is concrete, and exchange-value, the simplest economic category, that is both abstract and concrete. It is an abstraction because it is the starting point for a movement of thought, but it is concrete because it is the starting point for a concrete process: that of the market economy.[241] Lefebvre discusses how this relates to fetishism, and the way other economic relations develop from exchange-value. He suggests that

> the study of economic phenomena is not an empirical one, it rests on the dialectical movement of the categories. The basic economic category – exchange-value – is developed and, by an internal movement, gives rise to fresh determinations: abstract labour, money, capital. Each complex determination emerges dialectically from the preceding ones.[242]

Applications of the dialectic

> The struggle of logic and dialectic is thus, at the theoretical level, a higher form of 'classic' struggles in thought and society.[243]

Because of his interest in the dialectic Lefebvre often tends toward working with three terms rather than the binarism of the two. Lefebvre continually stresses that the dialectic is of three terms. He notes that there have been problems in the reception of Marx's work because of the two-term opposition between bourgeoisie and proletariat, with the attendant neglect of the third aspect of land, that is the countryside and agriculture, and the subsoil, and ultimately the territory of the nation-state.[244] More generally, in his early works, Lefebvre sees the third term as being the result of the dialectic, its product, but in later works seems to conceive of the three affecting each other simultaneously – not prioritizing one term over another, and not looking for a transcension, a synthesis, a negation, but seeing the continual movement between them. The third term is a moment, an aspect of this movement.[245] The third term is *already* everywhere – 'no two without three':[246]

> A triad can be brought in as an analytic framework of the becoming of thinking ... It is no longer a matter of the thesis/antithesis/synthesis dialectic, nor of

dialectics in nature, nor the affirmation/negation/negation-of-the-negation relationship. In this perspective, dialectics allows for the analysis of becoming . . .
something that can only be conceived in three conflictual moments. This interpretation of Hegel and Marx can be supported by taking, as an exemplary case,
music, the art of time, which can only be understood in relation to three notions:
melody, harmony and rhythm. In the same way we analyse the modern world by
taking account of these three conflictual moments: the state/the nation/classes.
We could multiply the cases of becoming that can only be seized through a
dialectical triad initiated by Marx.[247]

Lefebvre's use of a third term is central to understanding his work. This is
discussed, but not well understood, in the literature. For example, Rob
Shields suggests that Lefebvre 'shifts the ground of dialectical materialism
from time to space',[248] and presents a very confusing picture of Lefebvre's
work on the dialectic.[249] Shields suggests that through his refutation of
Hegelian historicity Lefebvre places space in the dialectic, which is why his
study is subtitled *Spatial Dialectics*. Edward Soja also makes much of this
notion, and sees it as part of an argument designed to supplant the modernist binarism of the either/or with a much larger logic of 'both/and also'.[250]
He claims that this is explicitly taken from Lefebvre, and develops a notion
he calls critical thirding or thirding-as-Othering.[251] To introduce a third
term into static binarisms is seen as a postmodern critique of modernism's
dichotomies, leading Soja to propose a notion of Trialectics.

   The main reference for both of these writers is Lefebvre's notion of the
dialectique de triplicité, but this is neither a replacement of dialectical reasoning
with 'trialectics' or the introduction of space into the dialectic. As I shall
argue in more detail in Chapter 5, one of Lefebvre's problems with dialectical materialism is its tendency toward a linear, teleological picture of historical change. His book *La fin de l'histoire*, with its non-linear Nietzschean take
on progress allows the dialectic to not simply be the resolution of two
conflicting terms but a three-way process, where the synthesis is able to react
upon the first two terms.[252] The third term is not the result of the dialectic: it
is there, but it is no longer seen as a culmination.[253] This is a much more
fluid, rhythmic understanding. Lefebvre's notion of *dépassement* translates
Nietzsche's *Überwinden* (overcoming, overwinding) more than the Hegelian
or Marxist *Aufhebung* (subsumption – abolition and preservation).[254] As
Lefebvre notes, 'in Nietzsche, *überwinden* (to surmount) outweighs *aufheben* (to
carry to another level)'.[255] The fact that Lefebvre uses this understanding to
rethink the question of space – a point to which I shall return in Chapter 5 –
does not mean that the dialectic is spatialized. Rather, the non-teleological
dialectic is brought to bear on the issue of space. Shields suggests that in
Lefebvre's work this is confusing,[256] but I would claim that this is increased
by his and Soja's own presentations.

   Actually, aside from Lefebvre's own writings, to which I will turn in the
following chapters, it is actually in Sartre's *Critique of Dialectical Reason* that
one of the clearest discussions of the application of this work on dialectics

can be found. This is the discussion of the regressive/progressive approach used to balance historical and sociological study. This is found most explicitly worked out in a piece Lefebvre wrote about rural sociology, although it obviously trades on the work I have so far discussed in this chapter, and is returned to in *De l'État*. Lefebvre argues that because any given society has two levels of complexity – the horizontal level of techniques and structural relations, which are both made by and make humans, and the vertical level of historical development – a particular method is needed in order to analyse it. We will return to the way in which Lefebvre uses this mode of analysis for a rural society in Chapter 4, but for now we will confine ourselves to the theoretical model:

There are three phases:-

a) *Descriptive*. Observation, but with an eye informed by experience and a general theory. In the foreground: participant observation of the field. Careful use of survey techniques (interviews, questionnaires, statistics).
b) Analytic-regressive. Analysis of reality as described. Attempt to give it a precise *date* (so as not to be limited to an account turning on undated 'archaisms' that are not compared with one another).
c) Historical-genetic. Studies of changes in this or that previously *dated* structure, by further (internal or external) development and by its subordination to overall structures. Attempt to reach a genetic classification of formations and structures, in the framework of the overall structure. Thus an attempt to return to the contemporary as previously described, in order to rediscover the present, but elucidated, understood: *explained*.[257]

Sartre cites this and says: 'we have nothing to add to this passage, so clear and so rich, except that we believe that this method, with its phase of phenomenological description and its double movement of regression followed by progress is valid – with the modifications which its objects may impose upon it – *in all the domains of anthropology*'. Sartre suggests that he does indeed apply this method in a range of areas, to significations, individuals and relations between individuals. He adds that his only regret is 'that Lefebvre has not found imitators among the rest of Marxist intellectuals'.[258]

Lefebvre however was reluctant to accept credit for this, and his response to Sartre was dismissive. As far as he was concerned this was Marx's idea, not his – Sartre was imputing a false paternity, and should learn to read Marx.[259] Lefebvre argues that it draws upon Marx's claim that the anatomy of man is key to understanding the anatomy of the ape, that the adult is the key to the child, that bourgeois economy is the key to previous economies.[260] And yet, historical analysis helps us to make sense of the present, as Marx's own analyses attest. The successive regressive-progressive steps, Lefebvre claims, allow us to explore the possible,[261] that is both a historical analysis of the conditions of possibility for the present, and a revolutionary, progressive analysis that opens us to the future, to the possible. For Lefebvre, this is the dialectic at work, in the way that was discovered by Marx and has been

'obscured since in the heart of "Marxism" '.[262] As Lefebvre notes, some of
this was developed in the work of Engels after Marx's death, but he is
unequivocal about the right to use this: 'Engels' method does not have
anything incompatible with Marx's one'.[263] As Hess notes, this method was
also used in Freud's analyses. First an analysis of the present symptoms of
the crisis; a return to decisive moments in the patient's history; a return to
the present in the light of those moments.[264]

Lefebvre therefore believed that his work on dialectics was inherently
practical. Although this chapter has dealt with this theoretically in some
depth it is important to do so, as Lefebvre, despite doing many practical
analyses, also wrote a large number of methodological works. To read the
practical analyses without due regard for the theoretical work they trade
upon is to risk reducing Lefebvre to an empirically minded historian, geog-
rapher or sociologist. Lefebvre regularly talks of the idea of a concrete
abstraction, or a realized abstraction. As he notes in *De l'État*: 'The concept
of the *concrete abstraction* is nothing other than the concept in general, but
relativised, made dialectical, opened to becoming and social practice.'[265]
This gives us a useful lead as we follow Lefebvre's path, initially through the
concepts of alienation and production, and then through the topics of
future chapters.

Alienation

Alienation is a concept found in Marx's *1844 Manuscripts*. The concept
rarely appears by name in *Capital*,[266] and one of the key features of the
debate within Marxism is whether the concept is effectively abandoned or
retained in a different form. Lefebvre suggests that Marx's writings on alienation and its different forms are scattered throughout his work, to such a
point that their unity remained unnoticed until a very recent date.[267] Lefebvre reminds us that Marx criticizes political economy in general, and not
just classical or vulgar political economy.[268] The advantage of his work is
that it sees through the masks of ideology to the real laws of capitalist
economy. The economic works are not – to repeat – a rejection of the earlier
works, but include this philosophical approach within them. They are therefore able to see through the mystification, and go beyond mere appearance.
Political economy, as both reality and the theory of bourgeois economists, is
a form of human 'alienation'. We find this most explicitly in *Capital* in the
analysis of the fetishism of the commodity, of money, capital.[269] We must
therefore re-read Marx, especially the early writings, because they 'enable us
to restate the problems raised by his ideas and by Marxism, problems which
are still fundamentally our own ones'.[270] In the *1844 Manuscripts* Marx
rejects dialectical logic, but accepts the theory of alienation while modifying
it profoundly.[271]

Lefebvre suggests that previous interpretations of religion and metaphysics had had notions of alienation. He gives the examples of Plato and
Stoicism. The point is not simply that humans have a relation with another,

but that they depend on this 'other'; they *alienate themselves*, that is to say they become mad, raving, unhappy, absurd, and therefore inhuman or too human.[272] Alienation is also found in Hegel's writings, where humans are, like the world around them, objectified – made into objects of knowledge. Hegel gives alienation a metaphysical twist.[273] This is the notion of *Entfrem-dung*, which Lefebvre translates as *aliénation*, for want of a better term.[274] Our de-objectification, our becoming aware of ourselves, means the transcend-ing of our alienation. But this is not an individual moment; it is made possible by the activity of the whole of humanity, and presupposes the history of the human race.[275] But this, for Marx, and Lefebvre, is a very narrow view of alienation. 'The Hegelian idea is a secularised God.'[276] It suggests that the human can be replaced by consciousness: 'Hegel turns man into the man of consciousness, instead of turning consciousness into the consciousness of real men, living in the real world.'[277] This means that the concrete manifestation of humans is denied, because Hegel takes them only in their abstract form. Wealth and the state, for instance, are thought apart from their concrete existence.[278] This for both Marx and Lefebvre is yet more mystification. But this critique of Hegel is powerful, contends Lefebvre, because it 'opens the way for a positive humanism which has to transcend and unite idealism and naturalism (or materialism).'[279]

Lefebvre claims that Marx and Engels' *The German Ideology* shows how historical materialism functions. There is a philosophical problem – alien-ation, a theory of this problem and a desire to make humanism more profound and more concrete. This theory is integrated and yet transcended in historical materialism. Marx takes the Hegelian notion of alienation and transforms it into a concrete theory; giving it its dialectical, rational and positive sense.[280] Alienation is 'detached by Marx from the Hegelian system and recaptured by him in order to elucidate social practice'.[281] This theory is found in a transformed sense in the economic works and the later political writings.[282] Historical materialism – a unity of idealism and materialism – turns against the philosophy from which it came: Hegelianism, Feuerbach, philosophy in general. Philosophy is too contemplative, a mutilated and one-sided perspective, abstract, mystified. For Lefebvre, 'historical materialism fulfils philosophy by transcending it ... the three requirements of phil-osophy – efficacy, truth and the universality of its ideas – cannot be met on the philosophical plane. Speculation must be transcended'.[283] In this we see both the way in which Lefebvre will deal with philosophical ideas taken from other thinkers, and the seed of his own idea of metaphilosophy. All of these issues are discussed further in Chapter 2.

Once again, Althusser and Lefebvre illustrate the differing viewpoints. Althusser, as would be expected, rejects alienation as unscientific. Alien-ation, he argues, belongs to ideological 'problematic' of the early works. There is a rupture between this problematic and the scientific 'problematic' of *Capital*.[284] In a later essay Althusser asks 'why do so many Marxist philo-sophers seem to feel the need to appeal to the pre-Marxist ideological con-cept of *alienation* in order supposedly to think and "resolve" these concrete historical problems?'[285] For Althusser, the late Marx discovered the science of history, dropped the notion of alienation and completely redefined the notion of fetishism of commodities in such a way that the notion of alienation is no longer relevant. Lefebvre states that he finds Althusser's attitude to alienation 'ridiculous'.[286] As Colletti sensibly notes, those that suggest that Marx abandons the concept fail on two counts: first, that 'for Marx the phenomenon of alienation or estrangement and that of fetishism are one and the same thing', with fetishism and reification playing a central role in *Capital*; and second, that the terms 'alienation' and 'estrangement' appear extensively in both the *Grundrisse* and *Theories of Surplus Value*.[287]

Lefebvre likewise sees the notion of alienation present in later works, sometimes transformed into the theory of reification, of commodity fetishism, and the fetishism of money and capital.[288] This transformation is, once again, dialectical. The idealism of philosophy and the materialism of economy are dialectically fused: 'where economy and philosophy meet lies the theory of fetishism'.[289] Without the materialist input, Lefebvre agrees that alienation is an idealist concept: 'when taken *in isolation*, in other words speculatively, outside of *praxis*, the theories of alienation and totality become transformed into systems which are very remote from Marxism – into neo-Hegelianism'.[290] Lefebvre does not believe that this is what Marx does: 'The theory of fetishism demonstrates the *economic*, *everyday* basis of the *philosophical* theories of *mystification* and *alienation*'.[291] Marx largely limits *his* study of alienation to economic fetishism, but this does not mean that he, or we, should solely think it in that way.[292] For Lefebvre, this notion of alienation will become 'the central notion of philosophy (seen as criticism of life and the foundation for a *concrete* humanism)'.[293] Alienation was certainly to become a central notion in Lefebvre's work.

As Anderson and Judt have pointed out, Lefebvre's *Dialectical Materialism* and the best-seller *Le Marxisme* were 'the first outright presentation in France of Marx as a theorist of alienation'.[294] Such a reading was both novel and heretical. Judt remarks on one reason why it was viewed this way: 'Communist [i.e. Soviet, or "Orthodox"] theorists have always been deeply averse to the emphasis on alienation . . . because, having manifestly failed to end alienation in practice, they could hardly assert it as their goal in theory'.[295] Indeed, Lefebvre does make some passing remarks on alienation in socialist societies – the result of which is that it is no longer talked about.[296]

For many and obscure reasons institutional Marxism refuses to listen to talk of *alienation*. It either rejects the concept or accepts it only with reservations and provisos. The dogmatists see it merely as a staging-post in Marx's thought, quickly superseded on the one hand by his discovery of dialectical materialism as a philosophy and on the other by his formulation of a scientific political economy (*Capital*) . . . We cannot confine the use of the concept of alienation to the study of bourgeois societies. It may enable us to uncover and criticise numerous forms of alienation (of women, of colonial or ex-colonial countries, of work and the worker, of 'consumer societies', of the bourgeoisie itself in the society it has fashioned in accordance with its own self-interest, etc.), but it also enables us to uncover and criticise ideological and political alienations inside socialism, particularly during the Stalinist period. Institutional Marxists chose to reject the concept so as to avoid such risks and blunt its cutting edge.[297]

He suggests that alienation is useful to understand society, and not simply bourgeois society, though later in his life he does remark that the term can be overused, as the concept of repression borrowed from psychoanalysis often is.[298] But back in 1947, with the publication of the *Critique of Everyday Life*, Lefebvre shifted the economic alienation of Marx's writings into the social sphere. In a review of Lefebvre's work at the time, Jean Kanapa described alienation as 'the key concept in the analysis of human situations', with Lefebvre, he suggested, 'philosophy no longer scorns the concrete and the everyday'.[299]

Before this concrete application of alienation to the everyday is looked at in Chapter 3, it is worth pausing slightly in order to look at the theory of alienation found in Marx's work. Marx uses two main words to designate this concept, which he borrowed from Hegel, *Entäusserung* and *Entfremdung*. As McLellan remarks, 'Marx seemed to use the two terms indiscriminately, sometimes using both together for rhetorical emphasis'.[300] The first is closer to the idea of dispossession or externalization, the second is the idea of something being strange and alien: alienation or estrangement.[301] Whereas Hegel's notion of alienation is abstract and idealist, Marx seeks to ground it with an empirical reference, 'depicting a real situation of the worker in industrial society'.[302] Marx's understanding of alienation can be schematized as follows:

1. the alienation of workers from the product they produce: the product becomes an *objectification* of labour;
2. the alienation of productive activity itself, of the process not just the result: the work is *external* to the worker;
3. the alienation of man as species-being, from his humanity: abstraction of individual life, turned into purpose of species life;
4. the alienation of man from other men, the community: others seen by same (alienating) standards.[303]

In his *Lefebvre, Love and Struggle* Shields claims that there are usually three forms of alienation found in Marx,[304] and that it is important that Lefebvre finds four forms.[305] This is confusing because the *Economic and Philosophical Manuscripts* – to which both Lefebvre[306] and Shields refer – explicitly notes *four* forms of alienation. The reason for the confusion is that Shields conflates the first two forms of alienation Marx outlines – the alienation of humans from the product and the process of their work – thereby reducing Marx's schema to three, and splits Lefebvre's presentation of the alienation of humans from their species being into two distinct forms of alienation. Whilst this may help to summarise the various issues at stake, it is not

sufficiently different to suggest that Lefebvre outlines a new form of alienation: rather Lefebvre is simply being faithful to Marx's text.

For Marx, private property is the 'material and sensuous expression of
alienated human life;'[307] alienation is a direct result of the capitalist mode of
production. Communism, as the positive abolition of private property, is
also the abolition of human self-alienation, it is 'the return of man himself
as a *social*, i.e. really human being . . . Communism as a fully developed
naturalism is humanism and as a fully developed humanism is naturalism'.[308] Lefebvre develops this notion of alienation within capitalism to
encompass other activities than labour, and seeks to abolish this alienation
of everyday life from within a Marxist framework. This Marxist framework
is a dialectic materialism, a concrete humanism. As Lefebvre says, 'alienation may be defined philosophically as this single yet dual movement of
objectification and externalisation – of realisation and derealisation. But
this movement must be seen in its dialectical profundity. *That which realises is
also that which derealises. And vice versa.*'[309] Although it is important to
understand the place of alienation within Marx's work, the real issue for
Lefebvre is to know how this concept is useful today in understanding the
world and to see how these things can be brought to an end, to make
possible their overcoming. 'All other ways of posing the problem are
scholastic.'[310]

Production

Though Lefebvre has been accused of prioritizing the early Marx's notion
of alienation over the later idea of production, it is clear in a number of
places, not least the work on space, that the mode of production is essential
to the analysis. The human effects, whilst considered forcefully, do not dominate. For example, Lefebvre states that '*(social) space is a (social) product*'.[311]
This means that 'every society (and therefore every mode of production
with all its subvariants . . .) produces a space, its own space'.[312] This analysis
of the production of space will be examined in detail in Chapter 5. That
chapter also looks at the production of time, and the final chapter at the
State Mode of Production (SMP) outlined in *De l'État*. Whilst it is difficult to
take Lefebvre's ideas on production apart from their concrete manifestation,
it is worth spending some time on the notion of production itself here.

As would be expected given Lefebvre's distaste for dogmatic economicism
and vulgar materialism, a mechanistic understanding of Marx's 1859 Preface regarding base and superstructure is not replicated. Lefebvre does not
consider ideas, institutions and cultures as 'frivolous and unimportant superstructure' atop an economic base.[313] Rather than a crude understanding of
economic determinism, he recognizes the role of ideas in shaping society.
For example, in *De l'État* he suggests that whilst the state uses the army and
the police to control the working classes, decisions about how and why they
are used are made politically, and indirect ways – morality and even logic –
are also used.[314] Equally Lefebvre wants both to make the base/

superstructure model more subtle, and to integrate it with the other key Marxist dichotomy:

> The social is situated between the political and the economic. The political tends to absorb the social, the economic to destroy it. More precisely, the social (otherwise known as civil society) is put between the economic (the base) and the political (the superstructures).[315]

However, Lefebvre does recognize the causal efficacy of the forces and relations of production. He notes that there is a not a strict correspondence, and that sometimes things are produced by the contradictions in the mode of production. Equally, right from his earliest works he was concerned with the relation between production and *Verstand*, or understanding. The production of isolated objects, that is in separating them out, determining aspects and properties of them is an intellectual activity which isolates and defines, which defines significance. It bears comparison to the move between observing the particular and defining the general that takes place in abstract thought.[316]

By production therefore Lefebvre means both the strictly economic production of things – goods and products, but also the larger philosophical concept, 'the production of *oeuvres*, the production of knowledge, of institutions, of all that constitutes society'. This is the dual understanding found in Marx,[317] deriving from his reading of Hegel,[318] and comes close to Nietzsche's sense of creation.[319] The relation between Marx and Nietzsche's ideas in this regard will be discussed in the following chapter. But it is worth dwelling on a couple of points. First, this sense of production is not rigidly separated out into material and mental production. There is not the material production of objects and the mental production of ideas. Instead, our mental interaction with the world, our ordering, generalizing, abstracting, and so on produces the world that we encounter, as much as the physical objects we create. This does not simply mean that we produce reality, but that we produce how we perceive reality.

> By taking 'production' in its widest sense (the production of *oeuvres* and of social relations), there has been in history the production of cities as there has been production of knowledge, culture, works of art and civilisation, and there also has been, of course, production of material goods and practico-material objects.[320]

Lefebvre recognizes that though there is this dual sense of production in Marx – when he was studying capitalism he naturally emphasized the production of things – this explains but does not justify one-sided interpretations.[321] Second, and more than this, Lefebvre stresses that production is not trivial, not mere economic production. 'The creation that is pursued in the Praxis, through the sum of individual acts and existences, and throughout the whole development of history, is the creation of man by himself.'

Lefebvre quotes a passage from Marx's *1844 Manuscripts* to support this: '*the whole of what is called world history* is nothing more than the creation [or production] of man through human labour'.[322] It is therefore clear that production and alienation are closely related. If humans are merely a means toward some end, an instrument, then their condition becomes inhuman. Whilst 'some philosophers' resort to a salvation to come, in another life, Lefebvre thinks this contradiction 'between the instrumental existence of *homo faber* and human demands for freedom' must be overcome in this life.[323] As Lefebvre makes clear in his work on everyday life, humans are not merely alienated through the productive process but also through their consumption.

Lefebvre finds this anticipated in Marx's work:

A time has come 'when everything that men had looked on as inalienable has become an object of exchange or of barter, and can be alienated'. Virtue and conscience, love and knowledge, which had hitherto been passed on generously, as a gift, are now commercialised. 'It is the time of general corruption, of universal venality.'[324]

This is obviously a productive way forward into the work on everyday life. Throughout the following chapters, we find the idea of the Total Man occur and recur.

The Total Man is both the subject and object of becoming. He is the living subject who is opposed to the object and surmounts this opposition. He is the subject who is broken into partial activities and scattered determinations and who surmounts this dispersion. He is the subject of action, as well as its final object, its product even if it does seem to produce external objects. The total man is the living subject-object, who is first of all torn asunder, dissociated and chained to necessity and abstraction. Through this tearing apart, he moves toward freedom; he becomes Nature, but free. He becomes a totality, like Nature, but by bringing it under control. The total man is 'de-alienated' man.[325]

It is not therefore an either/or with alienation or production the centre of the analysis. The two are inherently related, as productive relations lead to exploitation, which demonstrates itself in a range of possible forms – slavery, serfdom, wage labour – and is therefore indissolubly linked to alienation.[326] As Lefebvre sensibly notes, we should not buy into the rhetoric of economic growth as a necessarily good thing. Economic growth and social development should be distinguished – growth is quantitative and development is qualitative.[327]

The overcoming of alienation implies the progressive overcoming and suppression of commodities, of capital and money itself, as fetishes effectively ruling over humans. It implies the overcoming of private property, not the personal appropriation of goods, but the private ownership of the means of production of goods.[328]

Outside of the narrowly defined economic realm, class relations and state power are other symptoms of this alienation. Alienation 'can be transcended but only under practical conditions'.[329] Therefore, for Lefebvre, analysis of alienation 'can be clearly defined only with reference to a possible disalienation, i.e. by showing how it can be overcome actually, by what practical means'.[330] We find this in the works on everyday life and the problems of city, among other places. The notion of the Total Man in Marx's work is transformed in his later writings to the idea of the overcoming of the division of labour.[331] As with alienation becoming the reification and fetishism of money, capital and commodities, so too is this an instance of the transition undergone by philosophical themes passing into the economic works.

The Party and beyond

What is striking about the themes explored in this chapter is the continuity of Lefebvre's ideas. From the moment when he 'became a Marxist' to his last writings he was clear about his principal intellectual context.[332] From the opening page of the *Que-sais-je?* best-seller *Le Marxisme* in 1948, which declared that 'this exposition of Marxism is the work of a Marxist',[333] to the late conference given on the centenary of Marx's death Lefebvre orientated himself around an engagement with the 'vast and complex' doctrine of Marxism.[334] This was not a position that stood still. As Martin Jay summarizes:

> Lefebvre, once on the fringes of surrealism in the 1920s, had passed through orthodox Stalinist and Marxist humanist phases, to emerge in the 1960s as a guiding light of the New Left.[335]

Although this is not entirely accurate – it is difficult to see Lefebvre as ever being Stalinist, and his relationship with official, orthodox Marxism was always far from straightforward – it is helpful to realize how much the context he was in changed. In fact more often than not it was the context rather than his own thought that changed. I have already hinted at the tension between Lefebvre's reading and dogmatic positions within the PCF, a tension that reached breaking point in 1958. Lefebvre had found himself within an increasingly untenable position – his work was criticized, censored and destroyed by a party intent on controlling the interpretation of Marx.[336] For Lefebvre, following Marx, communism was not a 'state' but a 'movement';[337] but this was always bound to lead him into problems.

Although the problems had been apparent for some time, the point of no return came with the fallout from the death of Stalin.[338] Lefebvre was in East Berlin around the time of Khrushchev's speech to the 20th Party Congress in 1956, and was given materials that outlined the crimes of the Stalin era. He recalls that he stayed up all night reading the report. On his return to France, Lefebvre was met with denial and refusal, denounced as a *salaud*, a renegade, a traitor in the service of the Americans.[339] On 18 April 1958 Lefebvre received a letter demanding he appear before the Commission Centrale de Contrôle Politique of the party, the crime being particularly the book *Problèmes actuels du marxisme*, published earlier that year. This was not entirely surprising, given the book's critique of Stalin's methodological flaws.[340] On 13 June he was suspended from the Party, initially for a year. But by July he had appeared in the pages of Sartre's journal *Les temps modernes* to put his side of the story.[341] Here he talked of his 'incriminating book', and said that he had been locked in a dilemma – 'dogmatism or revisionism'. Not being dogmatic he had clearly been revisionist. But as he notes, Lenin had 'revised' Marx; Stalin had 'revised' Lenin, Khrushchev had 'revised' Stalin.[342] Lefebvre's tactic, as stated the previous year, had been to launch a dual assault – against the adversaries of Marxism, and against the dogmatists.[343] Lefebvre followed his account with a response to one of the criticisms of this book, by Guy Besse. This response had been refused publication in *France-Nouvelle* where the original critique appeared.[344] Lefebvre is understandably angry, and does not hold back or exhibit signs of contrition. He notes that Besse mistakenly changes the title of his book to *Questions actuels du marxisme*, and wonders why he is so afraid of 'problems'?[345] For Lefebvre, as a 'professional researcher, Marxist sociologist and philosopher, the number one danger, the principal enemy, is dogmatism',[346] but as he said at the time, his was a critique from the left.[347] He says that now there are two alternatives – the concept of alienation is a useful, analytical tool and the early writings of Marx are moments of a crucial journey, an integral part of Marx's work; or they are a rejected stage, there is no more Marxist philosophy and materialism is an 'achieved' system. For Lefebvre there is no real choice: 'I take the first direction'.[348]

Realistically there was no going back, and after a period of suspension, Lefebvre left the party. As he notes, it was his choice to transform the suspension into an exclusion.[349] He recalls that he left the party from the left, rather than the right.[350] He purged himself through the confessional memoir *La somme et le reste*, which won *Les prix des critiques*,[351] and followed this with various other critiques of dogmatism and Stalin.[352] In some respects, the big question is not so much why did he leave as why did he stay so long?[353] Lefebvre remained in the party despite events such as the Nazi-Soviet pact, and the overthrow of the Nagy government in Hungary in 1956. The answer appears to have been a belief that change from inside was possible, something that seemed impossible given the reaction to Khrushchev's denunciation of Stalin. Some twenty years later, Lefebvre engaged in a discussion with a young member of the PCF, published as a collaborative book, who suggested to him that 'though you have left the Party, I don't consider you less of a Marxist for it'.[354] This rapprochement signalled more how far the Party had moved than any change on Lefebvre's part, although he did come to support Georges Marchais in the late 1970s. This is not to say that Lefebvre never changed his mind. Shortly before he left the party he declared that 'it is impossible to grasp Marx's thought except through

Lenin's thought (and work)'.[355] In the interview with the PCF member, Lefebvre returned to this issue.

> I am very worried by having written previously on Lenin in a book that your friend Althusser judged excellent, pages that today I repudiate. We are not dogmatic, are we? Dogmatists never change![356]

The communist student was Catherine Régulier, who later married Lefebvre and collaborated with him on some projects, notably writings on rhythmanalysis. The title of this book of discussions came from the rather elegiac line Lefebvre pronounced half way through – 'The revolution is not what it was, and will not be anymore'.[357]

Therefore we might argue that, in sum, unlike Sartre, who privileged Marx's earlier (humanist) works, or Althusser, who argued that only the late works were free from the vestiges of Hegel, Lefebvre saw Marx's work as a totality and was interested in how concepts such as alienation were central throughout Marx's career. Lefebvre was always concerned with the dialectical relation between the concrete and the abstract, never content with a one-sided emphasis, but always looking at the confrontation and productive clash between ideas and the material world. Marxist philosophy, or philosophical Marxism, takes concepts such as alienation or Total Man – or, we might add, numerous others as outlined in this chapter – not *in abstracto*, but only to study them in the diversity of their concrete contextual forms.[358] Such an attempt bears obvious comparison with Marx's appropriation and radical critique of Hegel's ideas. Lefebvre suggests that *Capital* and indeed Marx's thought as a whole is necessary to understand the twentieth century, but it is not sufficient. Reading his work is not an end in itself but a means, not a goal but a path, a journey.[359] If we see dialectics in the way that Lefebvre does, there is much that can be taken from the work of non-Marxist thinkers as we progress down that path, as there is inevitably something of truth in their work. Though it may be tainted with reactionary politics, mystified and abstract, and in need of being grounded in material reality in order to escape the obfuscation, this does not mean it can be dismissed out of hand. My suggestion throughout this book, but most notably in the next chapter, is that this open approach was precisely Lefebvre's attitude in his reading of Nietzsche and Heidegger. It is to these matters that we now turn.

Notes

1 Karl Marx, 'Travail et propriété privée', *La revue marxiste* 1, February 1929, pp. 7–28; 'Notes sur les besoins, la production et la division du travail', *La revue marxiste*, June 1929, pp. 513–38. See also 'Critique de la dialectique hégélienne', *Avant-Poste* 1, June 1933, pp. 33–9 and 2, August 1933, pp. 110–16. See Bud Burkhard, *French Marxism Between the Wars: Henri Lefebvre and the 'Philosophies'*, Atlantic Highlands: Humanity Books, 2000, pp. 142, 162 n. 27. For Lefebvre's

recollection see 'Les cadres sociaux de la sociologie marxiste', *Cahiers internation-aux de sociologie* xxvi, 1959, pp. 81–102, p. 92; *La somme et le reste*, Paris: Méridi-ens Klincksieck, 3rd edition, 1989 [1959], p. 40.

2 Burkhard, *French Marxism Between the Wars*, p. 107.

3 In addition, the *Revue* translated Friedrich Engels' 'De la dialectique', a previ-ously unpublished preface to *Anti-Dühring* (*La revue marxiste* 3, April 1929, pp. 257–64); 'Le testament politique de F. Engels', *La revue marxiste* 4, May 1929, pp. 285–97, and 5, June 1929, pp. 539–51; and 'Karl Marx et Pierre Lavrov', *La revue marxiste* 4, May 1929, pp. 385–97.

4 *Marx*, Paris: Gallimard, 1964, p. 19; *La somme et le reste*, p. 40. On their publica-tion and reception, see Lucio Colletti, 'Introduction', in Karl Marx, *Early Writ-ings*, translated by Rodney Livingstone and Gregor Benton, Harmondsworth: Penguin, 1973; T. B. Bottomore, 'Introduction' to Karl Marx, *Early Writings*, translated by T. B. Bottomore, New York: McGraw Hill, 1963, pp. xvii–xviii. The other major publication from the *Nachlaß* is of course the *Grundrisse*, which was not published until 1939 in Moscow, and not in a German edition until 1953. Lefebvre's most sustained reading of the *Grundrisse* is found in *La pensée marxiste et la ville*, Paris: Casterman, 1972, especially pp. 70–108. See also *La survie du capitalisme: La re-production des rapports de production*, Paris: Anthropos, 2nd edi-tion, 2002 [1973], pp. 38, 41; *The Survival of Capitalism*, translated by Frank Bryant, London: Allison & Busby, 1976, pp. 42, 45.

5 Michel Trebitsch, 'Correspondance d'intellectuels: le cas de lettres d'Henri Lefebvre à Norbert Guterman (1935–47)', *Les cahiers de l'IHTP* 20, March 1992, pp. 70–84, p. 73. An undated letter from Lefebvre to Guterman in 1936 shows Lefebvre taking the lead on the introduction. However, Trebitsch further notes that the correspondence between the two shows that Guterman played a signifi-cant role in Lefebvre's *Dialectical Materialism* and *Nietzsche*. A file of notes in Guterman's papers on nationalism (Guterman Archive, Box 8), with citations of books from numerous languages was also used by Lefebvre.

6 *Morceaux choisis de Karl Marx*, Paris: Gallimard, 1934. See also the selections included in Karl Marx, *Oeuvres choisis*, I, Paris: Gallimard, 1963 and II, Paris: Gallimard, 1966; Norbert Guterman and Henri Lefebvre, *La conscience mystifiée*, Paris: Éditions Syllepse, 3rd edition, 1999 [1936], pp. 224–9; *Marx 1818–1883*, Geneva and Paris: Trois Collines, 1947, pp. 171–4, 210–12.

7 'Préface' to *Morceaux choisis de Karl Marx*, p. 11.

8 'Préface' to *Morceaux choisis de Karl Marx*, p. 12.

9 'Avant-propos de la 2ᵉ édition', *Critique de la vie quotidienne I: Introduction*, Paris: L'Arche, 2nd edition, 1958 [1947], p. 90; 'Foreword to the Second Edition', *Critique of Everyday Life Volume I: Introduction*, translated by John Moore, London: Verso, 1991, p. 79.

10 Henri Lefebvre and Norbert Guterman, *G. W. F. Hegel, Morceaux choisis*, Paris: Gallimard, 1938; *Cahiers de Lénine sur la dialectique de Hegel*, Paris: Gallimard, 2nd edition, 1967 [1939]; *La conscience mystifiée*. On the *Cahiers*, see also *Pour connaître la pensée de Lénine*, Paris: Bordas, 1957, p. 161 n. 1. On Lefebvre and Guterman's introduction to the *Cahiers*, see Kevin Anderson, *Lenin, Hegel and Western Marxism: A Critical Study*, Urbana: University of Illinois Press, pp. 186–97.

11 Karl Marx, *Oeuvres choisis*, I and II.

12 One of the earliest and fullest expressions of this is 'Qu'est-ce que la dialec-tique?', *La nouvelle revue française* 45 (264), September 1935, pp. 351–64 and 45 (265), October 1935, pp. 527–39; superseded by the central text *Le matérialisme*

dialectique, Paris: PUF, 6th edition, 1971 [1939]; *Dialectical Materialism*, translated by John Sturrock, London: Jonathan Cape, 1968.

13 *Sociologie de Marx*, Paris: PUF, 1966, p. 20; *The Sociology of Marx*, translated by Norbert Guterman, Harmondsworth: Penguin, 1968, p. 25.

14 'Avant-propos [1961]', in *Le matérialisme dialectique*, p. 7; 'Foreword to the fifth edition', in *Dialectical Materialism*, p. 15; see *Problèmes actuels du marxisme*, Paris: PUF, 2nd edition, 1960 [1958], p. 24; *La somme et le reste*, p. 41.

15 *Critique de la vie quotidienne*, I, p. 190; *Critique of Everyday Life*, I, p. 177; see *Problèmes actuels du marxisme*, p. 14; *Marx*, p. 65; *Pour connaître la pensée de Karl Marx*, Paris: Bordas, 1947, p. 75.

16 See *Marx*, p. 37; the untitled preface in *G. W. F. Hegel, Morceaux choisis*, p. 12; *Métaphilosophie*, Paris: Éditions Syllepse, 2001 [1965], p. 40.

17 'De l'explication en économie politique et en sociologie', *Cahiers internationaux de sociologie* XXI, 1956, pp. 19–36, p. 19.

18 Michael Kelly, *Modern French Marxism*, Oxford: Basil Blackwell, 1982, p. 30.

19 See Karl Marx, 'Postface to the second edition', *Capital: A Critique of Political Economy*, I, translated by Ben Fowkes, Harmondsworth: Penguin, 1976, p. 103.

20 *Marx*, p. 46; *Sociologie de Marx*, p. 1; *The Sociology of Marx*, p. 3. For a critique, see Roger Garaudy, *Marxism in the Twentieth Century*, translated by René Hague, New York: Charles Scribner's Sons, 1970, p. 203, which describes this as one of the 'various idealist retrograde movements'.

21 *La pensée marxiste et la ville*, pp. 110–11.

22 *Au-delà du structuralisme*, Paris: Anthropos, 1971, p. 119. See *Sociologie de Marx*, p. 1; *The Sociology of Marx*, p. 3; and *Problèmes actuels du marxisme*.

23 *Logique formelle, logique dialectique*, Paris: Anthropos, 2nd edition, 1969 [1947], p. xxiii; *La pensée marxiste et la ville*, p. 110. For a discussion, see *Logique formelle, logique dialectique*, pp. 227–8.

24 Kelly, *Modern French Marxism*, pp. 46, 60, 68. See also Edith Kurzweil, *The Age of Structuralism: Lévi Strauss to Foucault*, New York: Columbia University Press, 1980, p. 5, where she describes Lefebvre as an 'idealist Marxist'.

25 *Le matérialisme dialectique*, p. 78; *Dialectical Materialism*, pp. 84–5; *Pour connaître la pensée de Karl Marx*, p. 93.

26 *Le marxisme*, Paris: PUF, 1948, pp. 21–2. See also *Diderot ou les affirmations fondamentales du matérialisme*, Paris: L'Arche, 2nd edition, 1983 [1959], p. 249, where, following Engels, he notes the important transition from an earlier mechanism to a more subtle materialism.

27 Kelly, *Modern French Marxism*, pp. 126–7.

28 Louis Althusser, 'To my English readers', *For Marx*, translated by Ben Brewster, London: Verso, 1996, p. 12.

29 'Avant-propos [1961]', p. 5; 'Foreword to the fifth edition', p. 13.

30 'Avant-propos [1961]', p. 6; 'Foreword to the fifth edition', pp. 13–14; see 'Les cadres sociaux de la sociologie marxiste', p. 94.

31 'Avant-propos [1961]', p. 7; 'Foreword to the fifth edition', p. 15; see also *Problèmes actuels du marxisme*, p. 24.

32 'Les cadres sociaux de la sociologie marxiste', p. 87.

33 'Avant-propos [1961]', p. 8; 'Foreword to the Fifth Edition', p. 15.

34 *De l'État*, Paris: UGE, 4 volumes, 1976–8, II, p. 174.

35 *Le marxisme*.

36 *Pour connaître la pensée de Karl Marx*, p. 46.

37 *Sociologie de Marx*, p. 17; *The Sociology of Marx*, p. 22.

38 'Les cadres sociaux de la sociologie marxiste', p. 81.
39 *Le marxisme*, p. 20; *Pour connaître la pensée de Karl Marx*, pp. 46, 93.
40 'Avertissement', in Marx, *Oeuvres choisis*, I, pp. 7–8.
41 'Avertissement', p. 8.
42 *Le marxisme*, p. 18.
43 *Le marxisme*, p. 18 n. 1.
44 *Le marxisme*, p. 18. Lefebvre has in mind Engels' early study of *The Condition of the Working Class in England*. See 'Préface' to *Morceaux choisis de Karl Marx*, pp. 13–14.
45 See *De l'État*, II, p. 216.
46 *Pour connaître la pensée de Karl Marx*, p. 240. See also the comments in his 'Lettre', in *Marx . . . ou pas? Réflexions sur un centenaire*, Paris: Études et Documentation Internationales, 1986, p. 23; and 'Le marxisme éclaté', *L'homme et la société* 41/42, July–December 1976, pp. 3–12, p. 5.
47 *Pour connaître la pensée de Lénine*, p. 22 n. 1.
48 *Le matérialisme dialectique*, p. 73; *Dialectical Materialism*, p. 79.
49 *Le matérialisme dialectique*, p. 74; *Dialectical Materialism*, p. 81.
50 *Le matérialisme dialectique*, p. 76; *Dialectical Materialism*, p. 83; see *Hegel, Marx, Nietzsche ou le royaume des ombres*, Paris: Castermann, 1975, pp. 107–8.
51 *Au-delà du structuralisme*, p. 329.
52 *Le retour de la dialectique: 12 mots clefs*, Paris: Messidor/Éditions Sociales, 1986, p. 13.
53 *Marx 1818–1883*, p. 147.
54 'Avant-propos [1961]', p. 6; 'Foreword to the fifth edition', pp. 13–14.
55 Reported in Colletti, 'Introduction', p. 16.
56 Mark Poster, *Existential Marxism in Post-war France: From Sartre to Althusser*, Princeton: Princeton University Press, 1975, p. 56.
57 Jean-Paul Sartre, *Critique de la raison dialectique précédé de Questions de méthode, Tome I: Théorie des ensembles pratiques*, Paris: Gallimard, 1960, p. 50; *Search for a Method*, translated by Hazel E. Barnes, New York: Vintage, 1963, p. 51.
58 Louis Althusser, *Lenin and Philosophy and Other Essays*, London: NLB, 1971, p. 33. Althusser also compliments Lefebvre's *Pour connaître la pensée de Karl Marx*, although is more critical of *Dialectical Materialism* and points to the 'serious drawback' of the unchronological *Morceaux choisis de Karl Marx*, in *The Spectre of Hegel: Early Writings*, edited by François Matheron, translated by G. M. Goshgarian, London: Verso, 1997, p. 242. See also the positive comments of Roger Garaudy, Edgar Morin, Jean Duvignaud and Pierre Hervé reported by David Caute, *Communism and the French Intellectuals 1914–1960*, London: André Deutsch, 1964, p. 267.
59 Michel Trebitsch, 'Preface' to Henri Lefebvre, *Critique of Everyday Life Volume I: Introduction*, translated by John Moore, London: Verso, 1991, p. xii. See also Poster, *Existential Marxism in Post-war France*, pp. 112–13.
60 George Lichtheim, *Marxism in Modern France*, New York and London: Columbia University Press, 1966, especially p. 87. For an extended discussion of many of these points see Poster, *Existential Marxism*.
61 *L'existentialisme*, Paris: Anthropos, 2nd edition, 2001 [1946]. This theme is pursued in *Marx 1818–1883*, where Lefebvre offers a Marxist view of concrete freedom as opposed to an abstract freedom. 'Marxism is a practical philosophy of freedom' (p. 166). See also the comments in 'Connaissance et critique sociale', in Marvin Farber (ed.), *L'activité philosophique contemporaine en France et aux États-Unis – Tome Second: La philosophie française*, Paris: PUF, 1950, pp. 298–319;

'Knowledge and social criticism', in Marvin Farber (ed.), *Philosophic Thought in France and the United States: Essays Representing Major Trends in Contemporary French and American Philosophy*, New York: University of Buffalo Publications in Philosophy, 1950, pp. 281–300.

62 *La somme et le reste*, p. 509.

63 *L'existentialisme*, p. 3. On romanticism, see also *Nietzsche*, Paris: Éditions Sociales Internationales, 1939, pp. 10–11.

64 This is discussed in more detail in Chapter 2.

65 *L'existentialisme*, p. 16.

66 *La somme et le reste*, pp. 519–20. For Lefebvre on Schelling, see particularly, 'Introduction: Le même et l'autre', in Friedrich Schelling, *Recherches philosophiques sur l'essence de la liberté humaine et sur les problèmes qui s'y rattachent*, translated by Georges Politzer, Paris: F. Rieder, 1926, pp. 7–64.

67 *L'existentialisme*, p. 20.

68 Poster, *Existential Marxism in Post-war France*, p. 115. In *La somme et le reste* he suggests that real purpose of the book was the clarification of consciences (p. 511), a phrase that echoes Marx's description of the benefit of writing *The German Ideology* ('Preface to *A Critique of Political Economy*', in Marx, *Early Writings*, p. 427). The 1940s existentialists did not refer back to those of the 1920s, although Lefebvre (*L'existentialisme*, p. 35) does note that Merleau-Ponty acknowledges Politzer in *Phénoménologie de la perception*, Paris: Gallimard, 1945, p. 194 n. 1. See Georges Politzer, *Critiques des fondements de la psychologie*, Paris: F. Rieder, 1929.

69 Lefebvre to Guterman, 31 July 1945. Cited by Trebitsch, 'Correspondance d'intellectuels', p. 81.

70 *L'existentialisme*, p. 30.

71 *L'existentialisme*, pp. 6, 30, 65; 63.

72 Hubert Dreyfus, 'Husserl, Heidegger and modern existentialism', in Bryan Magee, *The Great Philosophers*, London: BBC Books, 1987, pp. 253–77, p. 275.

73 *L'existentialisme*, p. 10. It is worth noting that the PCF supported the pact, which led to their being banned by the government. Lefebvre did nothing. See Anderson, *Lenin, Hegel and Western Marxism*, p. 284 n. 50.

74 Nizan had collaborated on *Morceaux choisis de Karl Marx*, although Lefebvre claims never to have supported his choice and organization of pieces. See *La somme et le reste*, p. 46 n. Part of the reason for Lefebvre's ire was Paul Nizan, *La conspiration*, Paris: Gallimard, 1938, which satirized the *Philosophies* group. Nizan was then unfavourably compared to Georges Politzer, who had also died a victim of the Nazis. See the obituary signed 'H.L.', 'Georges Politzer', *La pensée*, 1, October–December 1944, pp. 7–10. A defence of Nizan was mounted in 'Le cas Nizan', *Les temps modernes* 22, July 1947, pp. 181–4 by Sartre, Camus, de Beauvoir, Merleau-Ponty and others. For discussions, see Jean-Jacques Brochier, 'Avant-propos', in *Paul Nizan, Intellectuel communiste 1926–1940: Articles et correspondence inédite*, Paris: François Maspero, 1967, pp. 14–17; Michael Scriven, *Paul Nizan: Communist Novelist*, Basingstoke: Macmillan, 1988, p. 62; W. D. Redfern, *Paul Nizan: Committed Literature in a Conspiratorial World*, Princeton: Princeton University Press, 1972, pp. 199–200; and René Étiemble, *Hygiene des lettres I: Premières notions*, Paris: Gallimard, 1952, p. 123.

75 See Rémi Hess, *Henri Lefebvre et l'aventure du siècle*, Paris: A.M. Métailié, 1988, p. 183.

76 Lichtheim, *Marxism in Modern France*, pp. 99–100.

77 See particularly 'Marxism and humanism', in Louis Althusser, *Pour Marx*, Paris:

François Maspero, 1965, pp. 227–49; *For Marx*, pp. 221–47. Humanism is dismissed as a bourgeois interpretation in *Lenin and Philosophy*, p. 7. Althusser explicitly recognizes Heidegger's *Letter on Humanism* as an influence in *The Future Lasts a Long Time*, translated by Richard Veasey, London: Chatto & Windus, 1993, p. 176.

78 Althusser, *Pour Marx*, p. 243; *For Marx*, p. 236.

79 Althusser, *Pour Marx*, p. 249; *For Marx*, p. 241.

80 Althusser, *Pour Marx*, p. 249; *For Marx*, p. 241.

81 Hess, *Henri Lefebvre*, p. 261.

82 *La vie quotidienne dans le monde moderne*, Paris: Gallimard, 1968, p. 212; *Everyday Life in the Modern World*, translated by Sacha Rabinovitch, Harmondsworth: Allen Lane, 1971, p. 112.

83 *Critique de la vie quotidienne*, I, p. 98, n. 1; *Critique of Everyday Life*, vol I, p. 264, n. 95.

84 *Critique de la vie quotidienne*, I, p. 254; *Critique of Everyday Life*, I, p. 239.

85 "De l'explication en économie politique et en sociologie", pp. 32, 36.

86 *Le marxisme*, p. 9.

87 See *Logique formelle, logique dialectique*, pp. 27–8; *Marx 1818–1883*, p. 152.

88 'Existentialisme et Marxism', *Action* 40, 8 June 1945, pp. 5–8, p. 8, quoted in Ronald Hayman, *Writing Against: A Biography of Sartre*, London: Weidenfeld & Nicolson, 1986, p. 224.

89 *Qu'est-ce que penser?*, Paris: Publisad, 1985, p. 10; *Au-delà du structuralisme*, p. 202. See Dreyfus, 'Husserl, Heidegger and modern existentialism', p. 275. See also Sartre's famous formulation of existentialism as believing that 'existence comes before essence – or, if you want, that we must begin with subjectivity', which is found in *L'existentialisme est un humanisme*, Paris: Gallimard, 1996 [1945], p. 26. Heidegger takes particular issue with this formulation in the *Letter on Humanism* in *Basic Writings*, London: Routledge, 1993. I am therefore resistant to Kurzweil's suggestion in *The Age of Structuralism*, p. 57, that Lefebvre remained faithful to existential notions of subjectivity. See *Au-delà du structuralisme*, p. 86; 'What is the historical past?', in *New Left Review* 90, 1975, pp. 27–34, p. 34, for a distinction between objective and subjective within a historical study.

90 *La droit à la ville*, Paris: Anthropos, 1968, p. 41; *Writings on Cities*, translated and edited by Eleonore Kofman and Elizabeth Lebas, Oxford: Blackwell, 1996, p. 92.

91 *Le marxisme*, p. 11.

92 *Au-delà du structuralisme*, p. 348. This passage, written somewhat later, is fairly dismissive of Sartre's move toward Marxism. Lefebvre goes on to suggest that instead of renouncing existentialism for Marxism he conceives of Marxism in an existentialist way. *Au-delà du structuralisme*, pp. 348–9. See more generally, 'Critique de la critique non-critique', *Nouvelle revue marxiste* 1, June 1961, pp. 57–79; and 'Les dilemmes de la dialectique', *Médiations* 2, 1961, pp. 79–105.

93 *Problèmes actuels du marxisme*, p. 16.

94 *L'existentialisme*, pp. 44–5; *Key Writings*, edited by Stuart Elden, Elizabeth Lebas and Eleonore Kofman, London: Continuum, 2003, p. 9.

95 *L'existentialisme*, p. 50; *Key Writings*, p. 13 .

96 *L'existentialisme*, pp. 49–50; *Key Writings*, pp. 12–13. On Lefebvre's critique, see Michel-Antoine Burnier, *Les existentialists et la politique*, Paris: Gallimard, 1966, especially p. 53.

97 *La somme et le reste*, p. 511. On Sartre, see also *La somme et le reste*, pp. 516 ff.

 98 For an analysis, see Hess, in *L'existentialisme*, pp. xxx–xxxiv. Maurice Merleau-
    Ponty was another existentialist who moved into a closer position with
    Marxism, but who was critical of institutionalized communism. See his
    Adventures of the Dialectic, translated by Joseph Bien, London: Heinemann,
    1974; a book that led PCF to dispatch Lefebvre and others to critique
    him. See Roger Garaudy *et al.*, *Mésaventures de l'antimarxisme: Les malheurs de
    M. Merleau-Ponty*, Paris: Éditions Sociales, 1956. Lefebvre's piece is 'Une
    philosophie de l'ambiguïté', pp. 99–106. A longer version of this article,
    'M. Merleau-Ponty et la philosophie de l'ambiguïté', was published in *La pensée*
    68, July–August 1956, and 73, May–June 1957, pp. 37–52. For a discussion,
    see Caute, *Communism and the French Intellectuals*, pp. 270–1. More broadly, see
    Trân-Dúc-Tháo, *Phénoménologie et materialisme dialectique*, Paris: Gordon &
    Breach, 1971.
 99 *Au-delà du structuralisme*, p. 15. See also 'Le concept de structure chez Marx', in
    Roger Bastide (ed.), *Sens et usages du terme structure dans les sciences humaines et
    sociales*, The Hague: Mouton, 2nd edition, 1972 [1962], pp. 100–6. François
    Dosse, *History of Structuralism Volume I: The Rising Sign, 1945–1966*, translated by
    Deborah Glassman, Minneapolis: University of Minnesota Press, 1997, p. 174,
    suggests that in this paper Lefebvre is trying to make Marx the forerunner of
    structuralism.
100 *Au-delà du structuralisme; L'idéologie structuraliste*, Paris: Anthropos, 1975.
101 *Espace et politique: Le droit à la ville II*, Paris: Anthropos, 2nd edition, 2000 [1972],
    p. 87.
102 *L'idéologie structuraliste*, p. 7.
103 *L'idéologie structuraliste*, p. 8.
104 *De l'État*, I, pp. 23, 151; see *Au-delà du structuralisme*, p. 204. See Dosse,
    History of Structuralism Volume I, pp. 357–8; *History of Structuralism Volume II: The
    Sign Sets, 1967–Present*, translated by Deborah Glassman, Minneapolis: Uni-
    versity of Minnesota Press, 1997, p. 101; Louis Soubise, *Le Marxisme après Marx
    (1956–1965) Quatre marxistes dissidents français*, Paris: Aubier Montaigne, 1967,
    pp. 162–3.
105 Didier Eribon, *Michel Foucault et ses contemporains*, Paris: Fayard, 1994, pp. 167,
    167 n. 3.
106 See Gary Genosko, *Baudrillard and Signs: Signification Ablaze*, London: Routledge,
    1994, p. 158; Tilottama Rajan, *Deconstruction and the Remainders of Phenomenology:
    Sartre, Derrida, Foucault, Baudrillard*, Stanford: Stanford University Press, 2002,
    pp. xxi, 27, 216, 236. The key text that influenced Baudrillard was *Position:
    Contre les technocrates en finir avec l'humanité-fiction*, Paris: Gonthier, 1967. Baudril-
    lard reviewed this book as 'Henri Lefebvre: position, contre les technocrates',
    Cahiers internationaux de sociologie XLIV, 1968, pp. 176–8. Here, p. 177, Baudril-
    lard suggests that 'all thought in terms of systems tends to become systematic'.
    Of Baudrillard's work in this regard, *The Consumer Society: Myths and Structures*,
    London: Sage, 1998 [1970]; and *For a Critique of the Political Economy of the Sign*,
    translated by Charles Levin, St Louis: Telos Press, 1981 [1972] are the most
    important. In *Le temps des méprises*, Paris: Stock, 1975, pp. 115, 207–8, Lefebvre
    notes how this is an abbreviated form of his 'bureaucratic society of controlled
    consumption', hinting at the absences in the appropriations.
107 Jacques Derrida, 'The ends of man', in *Margins of Philosophy*, translated by Alan
    Bass, Hemel Hempstead: Harvester Wheatsheaf, 1982; Michel Foucault, *The
    Order of Things: An Archaeology of the Human Sciences*, London: Tavistock, 1970.

108 *La droit à la ville*, p. 118; *Writings on Cities*, p. 149; see *L'irruption de Nanterre au sommet*, Paris: Éditions Syllepse, 2nd edition, 1998 [1968], pp. 16–17; *The Explosion: Marxism and the French Upheaval*, translated by Alfred Ehrenfeld, New York: Modern Reader, 1969, p. 22; 'Au-delà du savoir', p. 14.

109 *La révolution urbaine*, Paris: Gallimard, 1970, pp. 94–5; see *Du rural à l'urbain*, Paris: Anthropos, 3rd edition, 2001 [1970], p. 153.

110 *La droit à la ville*, p. 118; *Writings on Cities*, p. 149.

111 *La droit à la ville*, p. 118; *Writings on Cities*, p. 149; see *Au-delà du structuralisme*.

112 Lichtheim, *Marxism in Modern France*, p. 101.

113 See *Au-delà du structuralisme*, pp. 22, 350; *Key Writings*, pp. 38–9; *L'idéologie structuraliste*, p. 10; *Du rural à l'urbain*, p. 223.

114 *Au-delà du structuralisme*, p. 202; *Métaphilosophie*, p. 168.

115 *La fin de l'histoire*, Paris: Les Éditions de Minuit, 1970, p. 206; see *Critique de la vie quotidienne II: Fondements d'une sociologie de la quotidienneté*, Paris: L'Arche, 1961, pp. 33–5; *Critique of Everyday Life Volume II: Foundations for a Sociology of the Everyday*, translated by John Moore, London: Verso, 2002, pp. 28–9. The problems of structuralism are discussed at length in this text. See particularly, pp. 161–5/158–62.

116 See *Au-delà du structuralisme*, p. 199; 'Les mythes dans la vie quotidienne', *Cahiers internationaux de sociologie* XXXIII, 1962, pp. 67–74; *Key Writings*, pp. 100–6; *La vie quotidienne dans le monde moderne*, p. 190 n. 1; *Everyday Life in the Modern World*, p. 99 n; and for several mentions, *Le langage et la société*, Paris: Gallimard, 1966. On this see Michael Kelly, 'Demystification: a dialogue between Barthes and Lefebvre', *Yale French Studies* 98, 2000, pp. 79–97.

117 *Au-delà du structuralisme*, p. 262; see p. 369. See also the chapter 'Sur l'ancien éléatism', in *Position*, pp. 59–76. On Lévi-Strauss, see also *La somme et le reste*, pp. 318–19, 325ff; and *Le langage et la société*, p. 52 n. 1.

118 *Au-delà du structuralisme*, p. 349.

119 *Métaphilosophie*, p. 142.

120 *Au-delà du structuralisme*, pp. 276ff, 304; see *Position*, pp. 72–3, 82–7.

121 *La fin de l'histoire*, pp. 201–2; *Key Writings*, p. 180.

122 For a discussion, see Stuart Elden, *Mapping the Present: Heidegger, Foucault and the Project of a Spatial History*, London: Continuum, 2001, Chapter 4.

123 Dosse, *History of Structuralism Volume II*, p. 109.

124 On Althusser see Gregory Elliott, *Althusser: The Detour of Theory*, London: Verso, 1988; E. Ann Kaplan and Michael Sprinker (eds), *The Althusserian Legacy*, London: Verso, 1993; Gareth Stedman Jones, 'The Rise and Fall of French Marxism', in Lisa Appignanesi (ed.), *Ideas from France: The Legacy of French Theory: ICA Documents*, London: Free Association Books, 1989. As far as I know, aside from a brief mention in Gregory Elliott, 'Preface', in Gregory Elliott (ed.), *Althusser: A Critical Reader*, Oxford: Blackwell, 1994, p. xiv – and there only to suggest that they need translation – Lefebvre's criticisms of Althusser are not discussed in the literature. More generally, see Lucien Sebag, *Marxisme et structuralisme*, Paris: Payot, 1964.

125 Althusser, *Pour Marx*, pp. 24–30, 168; *For Marx*, pp. 32ff, 167–8. See also 'The facts', in *The Future Lasts a Long Time*, p. 358. The notion of a break is borrowed from Bachelard. For a critical discussion see Etienne Balibar, 'From Bachelard to Althusser: the concept of the Epistemological Break', in *Economy and Society* 7 (3), August 1978. See *Au-delà du structuralisme*, p. 327.

126 Althusser, *Pour Marx*, p. 116; *For Marx*, p. 116.

127 Althusser, *Lenin and Philosophy*, p. 90. Here, Althusser holds to his idea that
    Capital is the work by which Marx should be judged, and defines several other
    texts – *The German Ideology*, the 1859 Preface, and the *Grundrisse* – as 'ambigu-
    ous' in their relation to Hegel. He accepts that traces of the Hegelian influence
    remain in *Capital*. As Elliott, *Althusser*, p. 212, sensibly points out, 'that only two
    short texts by Marx should have passed the Althusserian audition probably says
    more about Althusser's criteria than about Marx'.

128 See David McLellan, 'Introduction', in Karl Marx, *Early Texts*, Oxford: Basil
    Blackwell, 1971, pp. ix–xliii, pp. xxxviii–ix: 'The continuity in Marx's thought
    has been demonstrated beyond all doubt by the publication of the *Grundrisse*
    ... The *Grundrisse*, of which the *Critique of Political Economy* and *Capital* are only
    partial elaborations, is the centrepiece of Marx's work ... the Hegelian cat-
    egories in which Marx forms his work are obvious ... The *Grundrisse* then, are
    as Hegelian as the *Paris Manuscripts* and their publication makes it impossible to
    maintain that only Marx's early writings are of philosophical interest, and that
    in the later Marx specialist economic interests have obscured the early human-
    ist vision. The concept of alienation is thus seen to be central to Marx's whole
    thought, including *Capital*.' Karl Marx, *Grundrisse: Foundations of the Critique of
    Political Economy (Rough Draft)*, translated by Martin Nicolaus, Harmondsworth:
    Penguin, 1973. See also Roman Rosdolsky, *The Making of Marx's 'Capital'*, trans-
    lated by Peter Burgess, London: Pluto, 1977, p. xiii: 'The publication of the
    Grundrisse means that academic critics of Marx will no longer be able to write
    without first having studied his method and its relation to Hegel'.

129 Kelly, *Modern French Marxism*, p. 130.

130 *Pour connaître la pensée de Karl Marx*, p. 239.

131 *Au-delà du structuralisme*, especially pp. 373–5; *La production de l'espace*, Paris:
    Anthropos, 1974, p. 11; *The Production of Space*, translated by Donald Nicholson-
    Smith, Oxford: Blackwell, 1991, p. 5.

132 *Au-delà du structuralisme*, p. 325.

133 *Au-delà du structuralisme*, p. 319. See some of Althusser's comments in *The Future
    Lasts A Long Time*, especially pp. 147–8. We should of course note that the
    original French version of *Reading Capital* is longer than the English translation,
    and later French editions, including essays by other colleagues. See Louis
    Althusser, Etienne Balibar, Roger Establet, Jacques Rancière, and Pierre
    Macherey, *Lire le Capital*, Paris: François Maspero, 2 volumes, 1965.

134 *Au-delà du structuralisme*, p. 319.

135 *Au-delà du structuralisme*, p. 321.

136 *Au-delà du structuralisme*, p. 413. As early as 1933, Lefebvre was denouncing the
    dangers of scholasticism in 'Le Karl Marx de M. Otto Ruhle', *Avant-Poste* 3,
    October–November 1933, pp. 199–201, suggesting that Ruhle, like Kautsky or
    Bernstein, knew pages by heart but understood nothing.

137 *Au-delà du structuralisme*, p. 22; *Key Writings*, pp. 38–9. For a reading of *Capital* in
    this light, see *Au-delà du structuralisme*, pp. 215–18.

138 See also *Sociologie de Marx*, p. 94; *The Sociology of Marx*, p. 111.

139 *Au-delà du structuralisme*, p. 321.

140 *Au-delà du structuralisme*, p. 325; *Métaphilosophie*, p. 168. See *Le langage et la société*;
    and *Vers le cybernanthrope*, Paris: Denoël/Gonthier, 1967.

141 *De l'État*, II, p. 78. On ISAs, see Louis Althusser, 'Ideology and Ideological
    State Apparatuses (Notes towards an Investigation)', in *Lenin and Philosophy and
    Other Essays*, translated by Ben Brewster, London: NLB, 1971.

142 *De l'État*, IV, p. 339.
143 *De l'État*, IV, p. 340.
144 *De l'État*, I, p. 153.
145 *De l'État*, I, p. 153.
146 *De l'État*, I, p. 311.
147 *De l'État*, II, p. 196.
148 *De l'État*, II, p. 406.
149 *Au-delà du structuralisme*, p. 279. For a later – still critical but perhaps more balanced – view see *Une pensée devenue monde: faut-il abandonner Marx?* Paris: Fayard, 1980, pp. 59–66.
150 *L'idéologie structuraliste*, p. 9; *De l'État*, I, p. 271.
151 See J. G. Merquior, *From Prague to Paris: A Critique of Structuralist and Post-Structuralist Thought*, London: Verso, 1986, pp. 200–1. Merquior simply points out that Lefebvre's critique differed from Lucien Goldmann's: he does not suggest why, or make any inference from this difference. Lefebvre's attitude to structuralism is discussed at length in Kurzweil, *The Age of Structuralism*, though her analysis seems questionable at times. For Lichtheim, *From Hegel to Marx and Other Essays*, London: Orbach & Chambers, 1971, p. 153, Poulantzas' description of Lefebvre as a 'historicist' is the worst thing a structuralist can say of his opponents.
152 *Au-delà du structuralisme*, pp. 21–2; *Key Writings*, p. 38.
153 *De l'État*, I, p. 152.
154 *Au-delà du structuralisme*, p. 25; *Key Writings*, p. 40.
155 *Au-delà du structuralisme*, p. 329.
156 See *La somme et le reste*, p. 40.
157 J. V. Stalin, 'Dialectical and historical materialism', in *Problems of Leninism*, Peking: Foreign Languages Press, 1976, pp. 835–73.
158 *Logique formelle, logique dialectique*, p. ix.
159 *Méthodologie des sciences: inédit*, Paris: Anthropos, 2002, p. 11.
160 *La somme et le reste*, pp. 447–9.
161 *Logique formelle, logique dialectique*, p. v.
162 *Méthodologie des sciences*. For a discussion, see Rémi Hess, 'Henri Lefebvre et le projet avorté du *Traité de matérialisme dialectique*', in *Méthodologie des sciences*. The quote comes from p. xxvi. See also Rob Shields, *Lefebvre, Love and Struggle: Spatial Dialectics*, London: Routledge, 1999, p. 193.
163 *Logique formelle, logique dialectique*, p. 11.
164 See, for example, *Pour connaître la pensée de Karl Marx*, p. iv. For a brief discussion of some of the volumes, see also *Méthodologie des sciences*, p. 169.
165 *Contribution à l'esthétique*, Paris: Anthropos, 2nd edition, 2001 [1953].
166 Arthur Hirsch, *The French Left*, Montreal: Black Rose Books, 1982, p. 94.
167 *Logique formelle, logique dialectique*, p. 14.
168 *Le matérialisme dialectique*, p. 13; *Dialectical Materialism*, p. 21.
169 Henri Lefebvre and Catherine Régulier, *La révolution n'est plus ce qu'elle était*, Hallier: Éditions Libres, 1978, p. 37.
170 'Préface à la troisième édition: douze thèses sur logique et dialectique', in *Logique formelle, logique dialectique*, Paris: Terrains/Éditions Sociales, 3rd edition, 1982 [1947], pp. 3–8, p. 3; *Key Writings*, p. 57.
171 'Préface à la troisième édition', p. 8; *Key Writings*, p. 60.
172 *Le matérialisme dialectique*, p. 14; *Dialectical Materialism*, pp. 21–2; see 'Préface à la troisième édition', p. 4; *Key Writings*, p. 58.

173 *Le matérialisme dialectique*, p. 16; *Dialectical Materialism*, p. 23.

174 'Lenin's Philosophical Notebooks', in Howard Selsam and Harry Martel
     (eds), *Reader in Marxist Philosophy*, New York: International Publishers, 1963,
     p. 332.

175 *Le matérialisme dialectique*, p. 14; *Dialectical Materialism*, p. 22; *Logique formelle, logique
     dialectique*, p. vii. Lefebvre points out that 'neither Stalin nor the Stalinists liked
     the *Notebooks on the Dialectic*, which suffice to weaken the doctrinal unity of
     Leninism'; instead they prefer *Materialism and Empiro-criticism* (*De l'État*, I, p.
     181). Lefebvre suggests that *Materialism and Empiro-criticism* is indeed a central
     book but that the *Notebooks* are at least its equal. *L'existentialisme*, p. 52 n. 1; see
     Au-delà du structuralisme, p. 400; 'Introduction', *Cahiers de Lénine sur la dialectique de
     Hegel*, pp. 52–3; 'Lénine philosophe', *La pensée* 57, September–October
     1954, pp. 18–36. For a discussion, see Anderson, *Lenin, Hegel and Western
     Marxism*.

176 *Le matérialisme dialectique*, pp. 14–15; *Dialectical Materialism*, p. 22; *Logique formelle,
     logique dialectique*, p. 109; 'Préface à la troisième édition', p. 4; *Key Writings*, p. 58.

177 *Logique formelle, logique dialectique*, p. 49.

178 *Logique formelle, logique dialectique*, pp. xli–ii.

179 *Logique formelle, logique dialectique*, p. 50.

180 *Logique formelle, logique dialectique*, pp. 51–2; *Méthodologie des sciences*, pp. 43, 177.

181 *Méthodologie des sciences*, p. 3. See *Le langage et la société*, p. 76.

182 *Logique formelle, logique dialectique*, p. xlii.

183 *Logique formelle, logique dialectique*, p. 52.

184 *Le matérialisme dialectique*, pp. 16–17; *Dialectical Materialism*, p. 24.

185 *Le matérialisme dialectique*, pp. 17–18; *Dialectical Materialism*, p. 25.

186 *Le matérialisme dialectique*, p. 18; *Dialectical Materialism*, pp. 25–6.

187 *Le matérialisme dialectique*, p. 19; *Dialectical Materialism*, p. 27.

188 *Le matérialisme dialectique*, p. 20; *Dialectical Materialism*, p. 27.

189 *Le matérialisme dialectique*, p. 21; *Dialectical Materialism*, p. 28.

190 *Logique formelle, logique dialectique*, p. 12. On p. 234 of this work, Lefebvre quotes
     Lenin's discussion of Hegel's *Grand Logic*, noting that the chapter on the 'idea' is
     not really idealist, but an analysis of the dialectic as a method.

191 *Le matérialisme dialectique*, p. 23; *Dialectical Materialism*, p. 30.

192 *Le matérialisme dialectique*, p. 23; *Dialectical Materialism*, pp. 30–1. For the import-
     ance of Kant, see also *Sociologie de Marx*, p. 22; *The Sociology of Marx*, p. 27.

193 *Logique formelle, logique dialectique*, p. 92; see *Méthodologie des sciences*, pp. 53–4.

194 *Qu'est-ce que penser?*, p. 77.

195 *Métaphilosophie*, p. 262; *Hegel, Marx, Nietzsche*, p. 70.

196 *Hegel, Marx, Nietzsche*, p. 191.

197 *Le manifeste différentialiste*, Paris: Gallimard, 1970, p. 73.

198 *La révolution n'est plus ce qu'elle était*, p. 52.

199 *Le matérialisme dialectique*, pp. 23–4; *Dialectical Materialism*, p. 31; see *Logique
     formelle, logique dialectique*, pp. 269–70. See also *Nietzsche*, p. 141 for a discussion
     of how this is indebted to Nietzsche's thought.

200 *Le matérialisme dialectique*, pp. 26–7; *Dialectical Materialism*, p. 34.

201 *Le matérialisme dialectique*, p. 29; *Dialectical Materialism*, p. 37.

202 'Préface à la troisième édition', p. 7; *Key Writings*, p. 60.

203 *La somme et le reste*, p. 539. For a general discussion of these ideas in Soviet
     Russia, see 'Une discussion philosophique en U.R.S.S. Logique formelle et
     logique dialectique', *La pensée* 59, January–February 1955, pp. 5–20; and in the

Eastern bloc more generally, 'Les entretiens philosophiques de Varsovie', *Comprendre: Revue de politique de la culture* 19, 1958, pp. 237–45.

204 Zhdanov's speech appeared in *For a Lasting Peace, For a People's Democracy*, 10 November 1947. On the context, see Gavriel D. Ra'anan, *International Policy Formation in the USSR: Factional 'Debates' during the Zhdanovschina*, Hamden: Archon, 1983; and Kelly, *Marxism in Modern France*, Chapter 4. It is generally accepted now that Stalin himself was the author of this policy. See Robert C. Tucker, 'The Cold War in Stalin's time: what the new sources reveal', *Diplomatic History* 21(2), Spring 1997, pp. 273–81. See Althusser, *The Spectre of Hegel*, pp. 222, 247, for some comments on the importance of Zhdanov as a theorist.

205 *La somme et le reste*, p. 540; *Logique formelle, logique dialectique*, p. v. Lefebvre had earlier ridiculed Nazi attempts to understand Marx and Einstein on the basis of their race, with a 'Jewish science' and 'Aryan science' set up as opposites in *Pour connaître la pensée de Karl Marx*, p. 61. It is not difficult to see the same logic at play in Stalinism.

206 See T. D. Lysenko, *Soviet Biology: A Report to the Lenin Academy of Agricultural Sciences, Moscow, 1948*, London: Birch Books, n.d. For useful accounts, see A. Medvedev, *The Rise of T. D. Lysenko*, translated by I. Michael Lerner, New York: Columbia University Press, 1969; Dominique Lecourt, *Proletarian Science? The Case of Lysenko*, translated by Ben Brewster, London: NLB, 1977; and more generally, Werner G. Hahn, *Post-war Soviet Politics: The Fall of Zhdanov and the Defeat of Moderation, 1946–53*, Ithaca: Cornell University Press, 1982.

207 *La somme et le reste*, p. 541; see *Logique formelle, logique dialectique*, p. vi. For a related debate on atomic energy, see *La somme et le reste*, p. 547.

208 *Le matérialisme dialectique*, p. 30; *Dialectical Materialism*, p. 38; *Logique formelle, logique dialectique*, p. xxi.

209 *Le matérialisme dialectique*, pp. 34–5; *Dialectical Materialism*, p. 42. See also the contrast between 'pure form (logic), that of the relationship between form and content (dialectical logic), and that of social labour with its internal contradictions (dialectical movement, which includes the preceding determinations)', in *Sociologie de Marx*, p. 85; *The Sociology of Marx*, p. 101.

210 *Le matérialisme dialectique*, pp. 35–6; *Dialectical Materialism*, p. 43; *Logique formelle, logique dialectique*, p. 192.

211 *Le matérialisme dialectique*, pp. 36–7; *Dialectical Materialism*, p. 44.

212 *Le matérialisme dialectique*, p. 40; *Dialectical Materialism*, p. 47.

213 *Le matérialisme dialectique*, p. 40; *Dialectical Materialism*, p. 48.

214 *Le matérialisme dialectique*, p. 41; *Dialectical Materialism*, p. 48.

215 *Le matérialisme dialectique*, p. 42; *Dialectical Materialism*, p. 50.

216 *Le matérialisme dialectique*, pp. 43–4; *Dialectical Materialism*, p. 51.

217 *Le matérialisme dialectique*, p. 49; *Dialectical Materialism*, p. 56.

218 *Le matérialisme dialectique*, p. 50; *Dialectical Materialism*, p. 57.

219 *Le matérialisme dialectique*, p. 51; *Dialectical Materialism*, p. 58.

220 G. W. F. Hegel, *Elements of the Philosophy of Right*, edited by Allen W. Wood, Cambridge: Cambridge University Press, p. 275, § 257.

221 *Le matérialisme dialectique*, p. 53; *Dialectical Materialism*, p. 60.

222 Though see *Le marxisme*, p. 20 when he suggests it was discovered in 1844–5.

223 *Le matérialisme dialectique*, p. 75; *Dialectical Materialism*, p. 81.

224 *Le matérialisme dialectique*, pp. 75–6; *Dialectical Materialism*, pp. 81–2.

225 Letter from Marx to Engels, 16 January (14 January according to Lefebvre and some other accounts) 1858, in Karl Marx and Frederick Engels, *Collected Works*, 40, London: Lawrence & Wishart, 1983, p. 249.

226 *Sociologie de Marx*, p. 20; *The Sociology of Marx*, p. 25.

227 *Le matérialisme dialectique*, pp. 78–9; *Dialectical Materialism*, p. 85. On totality, see above all 'La notion de totalité dans les sciences sociales', *Cahiers internationaux de sociologie* XIII, 1955, pp. 55–77; and *Critique de la vie quotidienne*, II, pp. 183–96; *Critique of Everyday Life*, II, pp. 180–92.

228 *Le marxisme*, p. 107; see 'Préface' to *Morceaux choisis de Karl Marx*, p. 17. Lefebvre discusses the role of various thinkers including Diderot in overcoming brute mechanism in *Le marxisme*, p. 108; *Diderot ou les affirmations*, p. 64.

229 Marx to Engels, 16 January 1858, *Collected Works*, 40, p. 249. See Karl Marx, *Oeuvres choisis*, II, p. 345; *Pour connaître la pensée de Lénine*, p. 126.

230 *Marx*, p. 47. Engels' *Anti-Dühring* and the *Dialectic of Nature* are sometimes used to solve this problem, but as Lefebvre notes, they are not free of difficulties, notably concerning the relation between logic and dialectics. See *Pour connaître la pensée de Lénine*, p. 126. Anderson, *Lenin, Hegel and Western Marxism*, p. 15, suggests rather that the originator was Georgi Plekhanov.

231 'Lenin's philosophical notebooks', p. 361. Lefebvre cites this passage in *Pour connaître la pensée de Lénine*, p. 127.

232 'Préface' to *Morceaux choisis de Karl Marx*, p. 18. Somewhat later he would put this more strongly – if Marx had put such importance on the method, why did he not make time for its working out? Instead he suggests that it is immanent to his work on Capital. See 'Le marxisme et la pensée française', *Les temps modernes* 137–8, 1957, pp. 104–37, p. 128.

233 *Le matérialisme dialectique*, p. 79; *Dialectical Materialism*, p. 86.

234 *Problèmes actuels du marxisme*, p. 17.

235 *Le matérialisme dialectique*, p. 81; *Dialectical Materialism*, p. 87.

236 *Marx*, p. 65.

237 *Introduction à la modernité: Préludes*, Paris: Les Éditions de Minuit, 1962, p. 77; *Introduction to Modernity: Twelve Preludes*, translated by John Moore, London: Verso, 1995, p. 69. See also 'Le marxisme éclaté', p. 5.

238 The 1859 Preface is the 'Preface to *A Critique of Political Economy*', in Marx, *Early Writings*, pp. 424–8.

239 *Le matérialisme dialectique*, p. 82; *Dialectical Materialism*, p. 88.

240 *Le matérialisme dialectique*, p. 82; *Dialectical Materialism*, pp. 88–9.

241 *Le matérialisme dialectique*, p. 85; *Dialectical Materialism*, p. 91; see *Sociologie de Marx*, p. 38; *The Sociology of Marx*, p. 47.

242 *Le matérialisme dialectique*, p. 89; *Dialectical Materialism*, p. 95.

243 'Préface à la troisième édition', p. 8; *Key Writings*, p. 60.

244 *La production de l'espace*, p. 374; *The Production of Space*, p. 325. See *Éléments de rythmanalyse: Introduction à la connaissance de rythmes*, Paris: Éditions Syllepse, 1992, p. 20; *Rhythmanalysis: Space, Time and Everyday Life*, translated by Gerald Moore and Stuart Elden, London: Continuum, 2004, p. 11; *Le temps des méprises*, p. 220. A useful discussion of this topic is found in David Harvey, *The Limits to Capital*, London: Verso, new edition, 1999 [1982], especially Chapter 11.

245 *Une pensée devenue monde*, p. 194.

246 *Logique formelle, logique dialectique*, p. xxix.

247 'Toward a leftist cultural politics: remarks occasioned by the centenary of Marx's death', in Cary Nelson and Lawrence Grossberg (eds), *Marxism and the*

Interpretation of Culture, London: Macmillan, 1988, pp. 75–88, p. 86; see 'Préface à la troisième édition', pp. 4–5; *Key Writings*, p. 58; *Hegel, Marx, Nietzsche*, p. 83.

248 Shields, *Lefebvre, Love and Struggle*, p. 119.

249 Shields, *Lefebvre, Love and Struggle*, pp. 120, 160.

250 Edward W. Soja, *Thirdspace: Journeys to Los Angeles and Other Real-and-Imagined Places*, Blackwell: Oxford, 1996, p. 5.

251 Soja, *Thirdspace*, p. 60.

252 *La fin de l'histoire*.

253 Lefebvre occasionally suggests that this is the case in Marx and Hegel's own work. For various discussions, see *Le temps des méprises*, p. 220; *De l'État*, II, pp. 128, 135ff, 145–6; *La présence et l'absence: Contribution à la théorie des representations*, Paris: Casterman, 1980, p. 225; *Le retour de la dialectique*, pp. 41–2; 'Toward a leftist cultural politics', p. 86; *Éléments de rythmanalyse: Introduction à la connaissance de rythmes*, Paris: Éditions Syllepse, pp. 20–2. See also the useful discussion in Eleonore Kofman and Elizabeth Lebas, 'Lost in transposition – time, space and the city', in Lefebvre, *Writings on Cities*, pp. 9–10.

254 *La fin de l'histoire*, pp. 214–15; see *La somme et le reste*, pp. 48, 129.

255 *De l'État*, II, p. 171.

256 Shields, *Lefebvre, Love and Struggle*, pp. 150–2.

257 *Du rural à l'urbain*, pp. 73–4; *Key Writings*, p. 117. See *Le langage et la société*, p. 52 n. 1.

258 Sartre, *Critique de la raison dialectique*, p. 51 n; *Search for a Method*, p. 52 n. 8. See though René Lourau, *Le journal de recherche: Matériaux d'une théorie de l'implication*, Paris: Méridiens Klincksieck, 1988, pp. 202–3, where he finds a similar method being used in Gilles Deleuze, *Spinoza*, Paris: PUF, 1970, pp. 75–7.

259 *Le temps de méprises*, p. 144; *Du rural à l'urbain*, pp. 18–19; *La production de l'espace*, p. 79–80 n. 1; *The Production of Space*, p. 66 n. 37.

260 Marx, *Grundrisse*, p. 105. For an analysis, see *Une pensée devenue monde*, pp. 99–100.

261 *Le retour de la dialectique*, p. 47.

262 *De l'État*, III, p. 37.

263 *De l'État*, III, p. 10.

264 Hess, 'Henri Lefebvre "philosophe" ', in *L'existentialisme*, pp. xxxiv–v.

265 *De l'État*, III, p. 61.

266 For example Marx, *Capital*, I, p. 277.

267 *Le marxisme*, p. 48.

268 'De l'explication en économie politique et en sociologie', p. 24; see Dominique Lecourt, *The Mediocracy*, translated by Gregory Elliott, London: Verso, 2001, pp. 165–6.

269 'Préface' to *Morceaux choisis de Karl Marx*, pp. 22–3, see p. 18.

270 'Avant-propos [1961]', p. 12; 'Foreword to the fifth edition', p. 19.

271 *Le matérialisme dialectique*, p. 58–9; *Dialectical Materialism*, p. 65; see *Pour connaître la pensée de Karl Marx*, p. 131.

272 *Le marxisme*, p. 37.

273 *De l'État*, II, p. 187.

274 *Marx*, p. 25; see *La conscience mystifiée*, p. 151.

275 *Le matérialisme dialectique*, p. 55; *Dialectical Materialism*, pp. 61–2.

276 *Pour connaître la pensée de Karl Marx*, p. 67.

277 Marx, quoted in *Le matérialisme dialectique*, p. 55; *Dialectical Materialism*, p. 62.

278 *Le matérialisme dialectique*, p. 56; *Dialectical Materialism*, p. 62.

279 *Le matérialisme dialectique*, p. 57; *Dialectical Materialism*, p. 64.

280 *Le marxisme*, pp. 23, 37; *Pour connaître la pensée de Karl Marx*, p. 91.

281 *Hegel, Marx, Nietzsche*, p. 186.

282 *Marx*, p. 19.

283 *Le matérialisme dialectique*, pp. 66–7; *Dialectical Materialism*, pp. 72–3.

284 Althusser, 'To my English readers', p. 13.

285 Althusser, *Pour Marx*, p. 246; *For Marx*, p. 239.

286 *La révolution n'est plus ce qu'elle était*, p. 140.

287 Colletti, 'Introduction', p. 49. See *La conscience mystifiée*, p. 214, where Lefebvre and Guterman make the same point.

288 *Marx*, pp. 73–4; 'Avant-propos de la 2ᵉ édition', p. 90; 'Foreword to the second edition', p. 79; *La somme et le reste*, p. 528. See 'La notion de totalité dans les sciences sociales', p. 67.

289 *Critique de la vie quotidienne*, I, p. 192; *Critique of Everyday Life*, I, p. 178.

290 'Avant-propos de la 2ᵉ édition', pp. 88–9; 'Foreword to the second edition', p. 77.

291 *Critique de la vie quotidienne*, I, p. 193; *Critique of Everyday Life*, I, p. 179.

292 See *Critique de la vie quotidienne*, II, p. 209; *Critique of Everyday Life*, II, p. 207.

293 *Critique de la vie quotidienne*, I, p. 181; *Critique of Everyday Life*, I, p. 168, my emphasis.

294 Perry Anderson, *Considerations on Western Marxism*, London: NLB, 1976, p. 51; see Tony Judt, *Marxism and the French Left: Studies on Labour and Politics in France 1830–1981*, Oxford: Clarendon Press, 1986, p. 180.

295 Judt, *Marxism and the French Left*, p. 220; Lichtheim, *Marxism in Modern France*, p. 170.

296 'Avant-propos de la 2ᵉ édition', pp. 11, 62; 'Foreword to the second edition', pp. 5, 53.

297 'Avant-propos [1961]', pp. 8–9; 'Foreword to the fifth edition', pp. 16–17; see *Au-delà du structuralisme*, pp. 373, 377.

298 'Toward a leftist cultural politics', p. 84.

299 Jean Kanapa, 'Henri Lefebvre ou la philosophe vivante', in *La Pensée* 15, November–December 1947, quoted in Michel Trebitsch, 'Preface', p. x.

300 David McLellan, *Karl Marx: His Life and Thought*, St Albans: Paladin, 1976, p. 110 n. 2.

301 For Lefebvre's discussion of these, and other related words, see above all *Critique de la vie quotidienne*, II, p. 216; *Critique of Everyday Life*, II, p. 214.

302 Bottomore, 'Introduction', p. viii.

303 Marx, *Early Writings*, pp. 122–9.

304 Shields, *Lefebvre, Love and Struggle*, p. 40.

305 Shields, *Lefebvre, Love and Struggle*, p. 42.

306 See 'Avant-propos de la 2ᵉ édition', pp. 69–72; 'Foreword to the second edition', pp. 59–62.

307 Marx, *Early Writings*, p. 156.

308 Marx, *Early Writings*, p. 155.

309 'Avant-propos de la 2ᵉ édition', p. 82; 'Foreword to the second edition', pp. 71–2.

310 *Au-delà du structuralisme*, pp. 330–1.

311 *La production de l'espace*, p. 35; *The Production of Space*, p. 26.

312 *La production de l'espace*, p. 40; *The Production of Space*, p. 31.

313 *Le matérialisme dialectique*, p. 78; *Dialectical Materialism*, p. 85. See *Une pensée devenue monde*, pp. 223–4.

314 *De l'État*, II, p. 8.
315 *De l'État*, II, p. 198. For the most detailed discussion of structure and superstructure, see 'Le concept de structure chez Marx'.
316 *Le matérialisme dialectique*, p. 121; *Dialectical Materialism*, pp. 124–5.
317 'Bilan d'un siècle et de deux demi siècles (1867–1917–1967)', in Victor Fay (ed.), *En partant du 'capital'*, Paris: Anthropos, 1968, pp. 115–42, p. 124; *Le temps des méprises*, p. 226; *De l'État*, I, p. xxiii.
318 *La production de l'espace*, pp. 83–4, 86–7; *The Production of Space*, pp. 68–9, 71; see 'Préface: La production de l'espace', in *La production de l'espace*, Paris: Anthropos, 4th edition, 2000 [1974], p. xx; *Key Writings*, p. 208.
319 'Préface: La production de l'espace', p. xxii; *Key Writings*, p. 209.
320 *La droit à la ville*, p. 54; *Writings on Cities*, p. 102.
321 'Bilan d'un siècle et de deux demi siècles', p. 129.
322 Marx, *Early Writings*, p. 357. *Le matérialisme dialectique*, p. 126; *Dialectical Materialism*, p. 129; see *Marx*, p. 66.
323 *Le matérialisme dialectique*, pp. 126–7; *Dialectical Materialism*, pp. 129–30.
324 *Le matérialisme dialectique*, p. 153; *Dialectical Materialism*, p. 156, quoting Karl Marx, *The Poverty of Philosophy*, New York: International Publishers, 1963, p. 34.
325 *Le matérialisme dialectique*, p. 159; *Dialectical Materialism*, pp. 161–2. See also 'L'homme des revolutions politiques et sociales', *Pour un nouvel humanisme*, textes des conferences et des entretiens organisés par les Rencontres Internationales de Genève, Neuchâtel: Éditions de la Baconnière, 1949, pp. 115–35, p. 115.
326 *Au-delà du structuralisme*, p. 331.
327 'Bilan d'un siècle et de deux demi siècles', p. 124.
328 *Le marxisme*, pp. 47–8.
329 *Le matérialisme dialectique*, p. 65; *Dialectical Materialism*, p. 71.
330 *Sociologie de Marx*, p. 6; *The Sociology of Marx*, p. 9.
331 'La notion de totalité dans les sciences sociales', p. 67.
332 For a discussion of what being a Marxist meant to Lefebvre, see *La somme et le reste*, pp. 683–92; *Key Writings*, pp. 231–7.
333 *Le marxisme*, p. 5.
334 *Le marxisme*, p. 5; see 'Toward a leftist cultural politics'.
335 Martin Jay, *Downcast Eyes: The Denigration of Vision in Twentieth-Century French Thought*, Berkeley: University of California Press, 1993, p. 419.
336 See Trebitsch, 'Preface', p. xiv; and the final section of Chapter 2. A decade before Lefebvre had written a self-criticism: 'Autocritique: Contribution à l'effort d'éclaircissement idéologique', *La nouvelle critique* 4, March 1949, pp. 41–57.
337 *Pour connaître la pensée de Karl Marx*, p. 144.
338 That said, in 1974 he suggests it was due to the lack of PCF support for the Algerians. See Henri Lefebvre and Leszek Kolakowski, 'Evolution or Revolution', in Fons Elders (ed.), *Reflexive Water: The Basic Concerns of Mankind*, London: Souvenir Press, 1974, pp. 201–67, pp. 210–11.
339 *Le temps des méprises*, pp. 94–6. See also '1956', *M, mensuel, marxisme, mouvement* 1, May 1986, pp. 31–5.
340 *Problèmes actuels du marxisme*, pp. 111–17.
341 'L'exclu s'inclut', *Les temps modernes* 149, July 1958, pp. 226–37.
342 'L'exclu s'inclut', p. 232.
343 'Le marxisme et la pensée française', p. 105. This comes in the note appended in June 1957 to a text written at the end of 1956 for a Polish audience – as an

early draft of ideas that would appear in *Problèmes actuels du marxisme* it was crucial in setting up his exclusion from the Party.

344 'Réponse à camarade Besse' *Les temps modernes* 149, July 1958, pp. 238–49.
345 'Réponse à camarade Besse', p. 238.
346 'Réponse à camarade Besse', p. 241.
347 *Problèmes actuels du marxisme*, p. 3.
348 'Réponse à camarade Besse', pp. 248–9.
349 *Le temps des méprises*, p. 89.
350 *Le temps des méprises*, p. 92.
351 Evelyn Lefebvre to Guterman, 8 June 1959. However Ralph Manheim, letter to Guterman, same date, suggested that the book 'sounds idiotic. People who break with Party or Church should have a five year period of silence imposed on them.' Guterman's own view is found in his journal entry from 11 December 1939: 'Public confessions by intellectuals always disgust me; if their ideas have changed let them express the change in works' (Guterman Archive, Box 6). For a contemporary orthodox critique, see Lucien Sève, *La différence: Deux essais: Lénine, philosophe communiste; Sur* La Somme et le Reste *d'Henri Lefebvre*, Paris: Éditions Sociales, 1960.
352 See for example 'Les cadres sociaux de la sociologie marxiste', p. 87, which draws on materials given to him in 1956; and 'Avant-propos à la deuxième édition', in *Problèmes actuels du marxisme*, pp. vii–viii. In *La somme et le reste*, see particularly, p. 12.
353 See Maurice Blanchot, *L'amitié*, Paris: Gallimard, 1971, p. 100; David Caute, *Communism and the French Intellectuals 1914–1960*, London: André Deutsch, 1964, pp. 271–2; Edgar Morin, *Autocritique*, Paris: Éditions du Seuil, 2nd edition, 1970 [1959], p. 116.
354 *La révolution n'est plus ce qu'elle était*, p. 33.
355 'De l'explication en économie politique et en sociologie', p. 19.
356 *La révolution n'est plus ce qu'elle était*, pp. 103–4. See above; Althusser, *Lenin and Philosophy*, p. 33. Perhaps the most remarkable self-criticism is found in 'Retour à Marx', *Cahiers internationaux de sociologie* xxv, 1958, pp. 20–37, pp. 27–8 n. 2, where he challenges his own reading of Marx's eleventh thesis on Feuerbach. But the source for the reading – *Problèmes actuels du marxisme* – is a book from the same year. The reason, of course, is that the former, although being the subject of the Party's enquiry, was written while he was part of the Party; the second piece after he had been excluded.
357 See also *Le retour de la dialectique*, p. 124.
358 *Problèmes actuels du marxisme*, pp. 125–6.
359 *Au-delà du structuralisme*, p. 399.

2 Engaging with philosophy

Beyond Marxism

Lefebvre's view of his philosophical background is largely that, whilst he flirted with other ideas in his youth, he saw the error of his ways, and became a Marxist. Following this self-interpretation a reading of him as a Marxist is reasonably well established in the literature,[1] even if it is not always adequately acknowledged in more recent appropriations. But, to read Lefebvre *solely* as a Marxist and engaged in critique of other theories of society, is miss much of what is interesting and important about him. Lefebvre needs to be understood both within a Marxist tradition, but also beyond that. One of the key aims of this book is to show how Lefebvre's work can be profitably read as being part of a much larger intellectual tradition than simply Marxism.

It is immediately apparent from Lefebvre's writings that he did not merely criticize other currents of thought, but often incorporated insights taken from other thinkers. Lefebvre saw Marx's work as important, indeed essential, to an understanding of our times, but not something that could stand alone.[2] Marx is the 'unavoidable, necessary, but insufficient starting point'.[3] He suggests that Marx's thought today is similar to Newton's work in the light of the modern work of relativity – a stage to start from, true at a certain scale, a date, a moment.[4] In a set of programmatic theses in 1978 he suggested that 'theoreticians have only interpreted Marxism, it is now a matter of transforming it'.[5] To this purpose he regularly took ideas from elsewhere, in order to introduce some topics that Marx and Hegel did not discuss – the everyday, the urban, difference, social space, the SMP, and so forth.[6] For example in the book *Le retour de la dialectique*, he suggests that 'the works which threw their light or their shade on these pages can be counted on our fingers':

> First, the works of Marx, above all the *1844 Manuscripts* and the *Critique of the Gotha Programme* ... Then the *Logics* of Hegel. Then Heidegger's *Sein und Zeit* (around 1930) and Nietzsche's little book of philosophy (*Das Philosophen-Buch*). And Adorno, above all *Minima Moralia*. The writings of Constant Nieuwenhuis, *Pour une architecture de situation* (Amsterdam, 1953). Musil of course. And K. Axelos,

Problèmes de l'enjeu . . . Eclecticism? No. A mixture? Yes, perhaps explosive. If some subtle minds find some other traces, little importance.[7]

The previous chapter has shown how Marx's writings are central to Lefebvre's work; it also demonstrated the great importance he attributed to Hegel's *Logic*, or as he says here '*Logics*' because there are two writings – the lesser and greater *Logic*, that is the one in the *Encyclopaedia* and the stand-alone version, sometimes called the *Science of Logic*.[8] This chapter will begin with a discussion of Lefebvre's earliest writings, principally from the 1920s and early 1930s, concentrating on his relationship to a group known as the *Philosophies* and his early links to thinkers such as Schelling and Hegel. In a sense then, the first part of this chapter is a step back in Lefebvre's thought, to the period which predates the works discussed in Chapter 1. Although Schelling is only rarely mentioned after this time, and falls more into the background,[9] Hegel continues to be important, even after – or perhaps because – Lefebvre became a Marxist.

Following on the heels of Marx and Hegel, Heidegger and Nietzsche are mentioned. An examination of their relation to Lefebvre will form the centrepiece of this chapter. Lefebvre's debt to them is found in some unlikely places. For example, in the introduction he wrote to the collection of essays *Du rural à l'urbain*, Lefebvre notes that his point of departure is 'the study of philosophy and the critique of philosophy, conducted simultaneously'. He notes that he read and reread Nietzsche 'first and foremost' – 'with him it is a combat, since adolescence, the struggle between angel and demon'.[10] Lefebvre's suggestion of the writers that mattered to him included four others. They will receive less treatment here, but particularly in the examination of Heidegger, the importance of Kostas Axelos' work will be underlined; a theme that will be returned to in Chapter 6. The other three figures can only be touched upon. The relation between Lefebvre and Situationists such as Constant informs the discussions in Chapters 3 and 4;[11] references to Adorno are occasionally found in his writings, though it appears *Negative Dialectics* was as important;[12] Musil's *Man without Qualities* was for Lefebvre a powerful analysis of the Austro-Hungarian empire, employing 'a very Nietzschean irony'.[13] As Hess notes, for Lefebvre it 'was the novel of the dissolution of the modern world. The heroes of Musil spoke philosophy'.[14]

Building on the discussions of Nietzsche, Heidegger and Axelos, I then discuss Lefebvre's notion of metaphilosophy, which is an attempt to move philosophy beyond the purely speculative and into relation with everyday issues, thus forming a bridge to later chapters. The final section of the chapter discusses his writings on figures within the French intellectual tradition, such as Descartes, Pascal and Rabelais. Concerns voiced here would also reappear in a number of other places in his work.

The *Philosophies* group, Schelling and Hegel

I have already mentioned the *Philosophies* group that Lefebvre was involved with in the early 1920s. This period of his career has been dealt with in some detail in the work of Burkhard and Trebitsch, and in terms of intellectual history is the best researched part of Lefebvre's career.[15] What we find in these early writings are a number of different influences and ideas, largely as interesting snippets from a long list of planned and aborted publications. Effectively this is Lefebvre growing up in public, showing an early talent for philosophical and political work, but not entirely comfortable in his intellectual surroundings. But however much Lefebvre would retrospectively distance himself from this work, there was not a clear cut break in his turn toward Marxism, and the programme of editions of Marx, Hegel and Lenin he did with Guterman. Hegel is the most obvious link between the two periods; but many of the themes continue, albeit in transformed contexts. We can perhaps see this most clearly in *La conscience mystifiée*, a work which although avowedly Marxist, certainly bears the mark of the Hegelian influence in its content and form.

Lefebvre dates his first philosophical memory to the age of five, when, while urinating, he heard two philosophy students joke that 'I piss, therefore I am'.[16] Indeed, in his own estimation, within the *Philosophies* group he was 'probably the most philosophical, in the technical sense of the word'.[17] Lefebvre remembers that the group was something of a rival to the surrealists – 'the surrealists spoke on behalf of poetry and . . . we spoke on behalf of philosophy'.[18] Whether the others of the *Philosophies* group would have agreed with his self-characterization is of course debatable, but he certainly shows a wide knowledge of the philosophical tradition, which would prove invaluable in his later work.[19] As he later recounts, when it came to setting out their programme, it was Lefebvre who wrote the philosophical manifesto; and Morhange a literary one.[20] Some parts of these manifestos appeared in publications the young colleagues edited themselves, and Lefebvre's first major work, *Philosophie de la conscience* was also written around this time. The aim of this was to critique metaphysics, mysticism, and idealism. As he would later remember, some bits, badly edited by Morhange, also appeared in the journal *Philosophies*.[21] Much later in life, in *Qu'est-ce que penser?* Lefebvre suggested this would appear in his complete works,[22] although this has not yet happened. Another important early publication was Lefebvre's extensive introduction to Politzer's translation of Schelling's *La liberté humaine*. For Lefebvre, Schelling's work was 'certainly not true, but it is very important for the truth'.[23] As he later remembers, Politzer's response to the introduction was that though he was not sure it was Schelling, that was not important: 'this is what we have to say'.[24]

These works were actually published in part or in whole, but there was an even more extensive programme of writing which was left unpublished. In various places Lefebvre recalls the projected works – a *Déclaration des droits de l'Esprit* and a book entitled *Procès de la Chrétienté*;[25] a 'burlesque life of Jesus' in the form of a novel;[26] and, following readings of Hegel, *Capital*, *Anti-Dühring* and *Materialism and Empiro-Criticism* in 1930, a long manuscript containing a 'radical critique of philosophy'.[27] The first of these was destroyed in the late 1920s;[28] the life of Jesus was written, but like *The German Ideology* was left in an attic to the 'gnawing criticism' of mice and dust because no publisher would touch it;[29] and party censors saw off the last. Equally the back cover of the Schelling book lists a forthcoming work by Lefebvre, Morhange and Politzer, entitled *Voici ce qu'il y a* (Here is What There Is).[30] Lefebvre was also intending to write a thesis on Hegel, but was dissuaded by Brunschvicg.[31] Given Brunschvicg's view of Hegel's 'mental age, infantilism and mythology' this was perhaps to be expected.[32]

In terms of the French reception of Hegel, and not just regarding Hegel's influence on Marx, Lefebvre is of the foremost importance. This was a reading largely independent of Alexandre Kojève's famous lectures, although Lefebvre had a few conversations with him. Instead what led Lefebvre to Hegel was his links to people like André Breton and Jean Wahl.[33] In 1938 Lefebvre and Guterman presented a collection of Hegel's writings, which they introduced, edited and translated. Rather than include large pieces from his works the selections are almost aphoristic, ranging from a few lines to a few pages. The introduction attempted both to assert the importance of Hegel in the context of Marxism and fascism, but also provide a summary of Hegel's method in order to contextualize the extracts. The collection has clearly stood the test of time as a collection since it is still in print today.[34] Around the same time the colleagues published a translation of Lenin's notebooks on Hegel, which make a forceful case for the role of Hegel in Marx.[35] Many of Lefebvre's earliest writings, in journals such as *Philosophies* and *L'esprit* are explicitly Hegelian. These early essays discuss themes of representation, mystification, the Hegelian distinction between for itself and in itself (*pour soi* and *en soi*), and of course the notion of *spirit*.[36] Even after Lefebvre's reading of Marx and the direction his work subsequently took, Hegel remained key.[37] In fact, Althusser and Lefebvre first publicly clashed over Hegel – the former denouncing the 'return to Hegel' within the French academy as reactionary, the latter suggesting that Marx and Lenin, among others, all 'returned' to Hegel.[38] This relation is frequently neglected in literature on the reception of Hegel in France: for example, there is no reference to Lefebvre in Butler's *Subjects of Desire*, and Roth's *Knowing and History* only mentions Lefebvre in the bibliography.[39]

As I have suggested in the previous chapter, Hegel was central to Lefebvre's work on the dialectic and logic, but there were other interests deployed in some of his writings. *La conscience mystifiée*, published in 1936, but written between 1933 and 1934, in Paris and New York, is a good example.[40] One of the central concerns of this work is how the working classes across Europe came to embrace fascism and Nazism – Italy, Germany, Hungary and Portugal already with Spain soon to follow. In France the context is set with the rise of the *Front Populaire*, with its antifascist agenda.[41] Indeed, the book has been described as a French *History and Class Consciousness* (Lukács), 'rewritten in the context of the struggle against fascism'.[42] Lefebvre and Guterman are concerned with how consciousness has come to be mystified, how individuals come to think in particular ways. Originally this book was intended to be one of a series, entitled *La science des idéologies*, and another, more political work entitled *Le temps des dupes* was also planned,[43] along with a book on the notion of the individual. This last book, initially promised as 'Essai sur l'Individu' in their first piece in *Avant-Poste*,[44] would have treated Hume, Adam Smith and Keynes, and covered three areas:

1. The glorification of the economic individual.
2. The contradiction between the theory and practice of individualism.
3. The 'triumph' of democracy and its difficulties.[45]

The colleagues also intended editions of Engels' writings and a translation of *The Phenomenology of Spirit*,[46] but, yet again, ambition outstripped ability.

Guterman had been in New York since 1933, following his exclusion from the Communist Party in 1929. The circumstances of Guterman's expulsion – along with that of Pierre Morhange – are somewhat extraordinary, and much debated. Apparently Morhange gambled away a large sum of money, destined for *La revue marxiste*, in the casino at Monte Carlo. Guterman had no legal right to be in France, and had no papers, being a refugee from Warsaw. This is presumably why he used the pseudonym of Alfred Mesnil. With the support of the PCF withdrawn he was obliged to leave France.[47] Guterman's move to New York made further work with Lefebvre difficult at first, and then with the onset of war, impossible. Although Guterman wrote a lot himself, he was principally known as a translator, working on Adorno, Brentano, Flaubert and Schelling among others. A summary outline of the projected second volume, *La conscience privée*, written by Lefebvre alone, and dedicated to Guterman – 'reduced to silence on the other side of the Atlantic' – is found as an appendix to the recent reissue of *La conscience mystifiée*.[48] *La conscience mystifiée* was, Lefebvre contends, a 'cursed book' – it was rejected by the Soviets and French communists, and later banned and destroyed by the Nazis.[49]

Lefebvre and Guterman had done some of their research for the book in the field, visiting Germany in particular both shortly before and after Hitler's rise to power.[50] One of the benefits of Guterman's being in New York, Lefebvre recalls, was paradoxically the easier access to material about Europe – the political situation not being so highly charged.[51] Lefebvre would go on to discuss the European situation in general, and the German one in particular, in two other important works – *Le nationalisme contre les nations* and *Hitler au pouvoir*.[52] Guterman would collaborate with the Frankfurt School theorist Leo Lowenthal on a study of extremism in the United States.[53]

Lefebvre and Guterman argue that consciousness can be seen in two ways – as the consciousness of the forum, social consciousness; and private, individual consciousness. Bourgeois thought has separated the two out, marginalizing the progressive one and privileging the atomized individual, a position that bears the marks of religious thought. Philosophy has not only failed to reunite these two aspects, but has further divided them. The private consciousness is the result of a privation, the result of individuals being split apart from their society.[54]

> Taken in itself, separate and sovereign, consciousness is a lie; truth, then, is only possible in a consciousness that has surpassed that consciousness, which has re-established its relationship with all that is not consciousness, with the material world. The reality of human consciousness is the movement of human affairs. It is not the idea of man which is the truth of man, but exactly the opposite.[55]

Class, however, is not an abstraction, because it 'corresponds to the practical and everyday life' of humans in common.[56] It is an understanding of alienation – a materialist understanding – that enables us to understood the problem of consciousness; the process of mystification.[57] Fetishism, alienation and mystification are 'three almost equivalent terms, three aspects of the same event [fait]'.[58] An examination of these three together enables us to comprehend the complexities of economics and ideological foundations. Rather than a reduction of ideology to economics, the method that Lefebvre and Guterman attempt to outline is concerned with the complex birth of ideologies – such as nationalism – and their relation to social praxis, the economy of a given society.[59] Lefebvre and Guterman, who had already discussed alienation and mystification within the pages of Avant-Poste in the early 1930s,[60] were criticized for the use of these supposedly Hegelian terms, these non-scientific, non-Marxist terms. Lefebvre remarks that this criticism was there 'already' in the 1930s, suggesting implicitly that the later positions of Althusser and others were hardly new.[61]

Lefebvre and Guterman argue that nationalism is actually a homogenization, a destruction of national identity. 'We therefore have to be internationalists in the name of national culture'.[62] They argue that nationalism can have a progressive sense, when it is designed to overthrow colonial oppression, but that this cannot be the case in Europe or North America. Although the oppressive terms of the Treaty of Versailles may explain something, they ask 'in a State with well-defended frontiers, what meaning could there be in a nationalism that has to assert itself through struggle?'[63] Lefebvre is similarly scornful of any geographical essentialism – a geographical element is incontestable in a nation, but the dangers of Ratzel's geopolitics should warn us away from giving it priority. We should similarly be sceptical of the theory of 'natural frontiers' that gained a certain currency in France, following Richelieu in the seventeenth century.[64] For the nation, 'language has a more profound significance than geographical location [lieu]', but examples such as Belgium and Switzerland show that this too is problematic.[65] Despite fascist attempts to suggest that 'nature' and 'nation' share a common root, Lefebvre and Guterman are scornful of ideas that national identity has always been around. Lefebvre suggests that 'the nation is a *historical category*.[66] To go back to the late Middle Ages or the Early Modern Period would show that this is the case. In this period it is clear that class is a much stronger bond between people – the shared interests of serfs, lords or royalty. As they persuasively argue, nationalism is a bourgeois invention in the break from rule by a king. It arises when the bourgeois class realizes that its interests diverge from the aristocracy, and they therefore mobilize the nation as a whole in pursuit of their aims – in France this occurred in 1789.[67] But it is their aims, and only theirs, and the interests of the working classes are excluded from the new political settlement. We find similar hijacking of the national interest in the new forms of fascism.

> An absurd situation, you say? Evidence of a 'stupid' mentality? A lie? No, much more like the use of a form that conceals the opposite of its former content: Mystification.
> In every bourgeois nation there are two nations, said Lenin. It is perfectly legitimate to set the real nation of the working masses in opposition to the 'International' of fascist parasites and their mystifying nationalism, the enemy of the true nation.[68]

In *Le nationalisme contre les nations* Lefebvre recognizes that 'the ideology of Hitlerism is an extremely complex syncretism, whose origins are deep and remote in German thought. Sometimes it gives the appearance of a philosophy, of a *Weltanschauung*'.[69] In France the ideology is somewhat different, because it is not invented here, merely imported.[70] (It is worth noting that Lefebvre planned a project on irrationalism in French thought, but this was never completed.[71]) Lefebvre likens the German embrace of mythical roots to a potential Celtic fanaticism, promoting the 'spiritual' goal of wearing white robes and cutting mistletoe from oak trees. 'This madness is exactly that of the fascists'.[72] Fascism might appear to be a national movement, but it is effectively international – without being internationalist. The national interest is surrendered to the interests of international monopoly capitalism, and fascist propaganda is designed to fetishize the nation and create a myth, a mystification. The 'national revolution' of fascism 'is no more national than revolutionary'.[73] Whilst it mobilizes the workers, it is really in the interests of the middle classes; people who join the armed forces cease to be peasants or workers but become political soldiers; the youth of the country are used for similar aims; women are reduced to biological functionaries. Though it claims to support the nation, it actually dissolves the social and spiritual community.[74]

While many of these arguments about nationalism are today widely discussed, it must be remembered that they were written in the 1930s, long before other discussions that make similar claims. They however postdate Ernst Renan's famous discussion 'What is a nation?' which is occasionally cited by Lefebvre.[75] Lefebvre and Guterman's *La conscience mystifiée* appeared the year the *Front Populaire* took power; *Le nationalisme contre les nations* the following year, just as Hitler's planes bombed Guernica. As Lefebvre remembers, these works were, unsurprisingly, put at the top of the list of banned books when the Germans invaded France.[76] Effectively Lefebvre and Guterman are putting into practice the ideas that they had worked through in the earlier, more explicitly philosophical period. As they suggest:

> The distance between us and our selves, between our consciousness and the content of that consciousness, between the individual and the social, between the human and nature, takes place like a scission between consciousness and being – a scission determined precisely by social being and which is made from the development of that being. Schelling and Hegel perceived this scission, this internal contradiction between subject and object; but they locate it in the depths of 'Spirit' when it is a *historical and social fact*.[77]

Just as there can be a nationalism against the nation, there can be an individualism against the individual. Individualism is itself an invention of the bourgeoisie, it is one of its myths. The gulf between the notion of individualism, the promise of individualism created by a great deception, and its reality is huge.[78] That we do not realize this is due to mystification.

Somewhat later, in the light of his work on everyday life, Lefebvre would reassess his work on the private conscience. He suggested that it should not be understood solely as privation, but that it is always already social, taking into account family, neighbourhood and other interpersonal relations. The private human is already social, through needs, and individual egoism already requires relations with others – sexual, familial, friendly – but also those that are engaged in through work. That there is alienation in this sphere is undoubted, but this should not just mean that the notion is condemned.[79] In fact, Lefebvre notes that 'after having planned a work *against* the private conscience, I would rather attempt to write this study to *defend* it'.[80] Chapter 3 looks at some of the ways he did this.

Concerns with nationalism would continue to engage Lefebvre throughout his career. For example, in *De l'État* he notes the convergence of myths about race and nation with the strength of the state. 'In a sea of mud and blood emerges and then collapses first Hitlerism and Mussolini's fascism, then their opposite and enemy, Stalinism.'[81] Equally in his introduction to a book of photographs on Germany, Lefebvre notes how German national identity was forged much later than in England or France, and that this might explain something.[82] Perhaps in most detail, in the light of developments in French colonies in North Africa, Lefebvre returns to the study of the relation between class and nation in the mid-1960s.[83]

It is therefore possible to argue that Lefebvre's attitude to philosophy was not dissimilar to the way he read Marx as dealing with Hegel. In Lefebvre's earliest writings we find an embrace of a whole range of philosophies, notably Hegel. As he recounts in *L'existentialisme* and *La somme et le reste* he then became a Marxist. In the first of these books, and in other places, such as the two extant volumes of the series on dialectical materialism, Lefebvre is either silent on or critical of philosophical thought.[84] But in later works, most obviously beginning with those such as *La somme et le reste*, which were

written after he escaped the Party's censorship, the positive references return
as a flood. For example, compare the treatment of technology in *Méthodologie
des sciences* with later works, written in the light of Axelos and Heidegger's
work;[85] or equally, look at the discussion of history in that work, and compare it to the more Nietzschean *La somme et le reste* or *La fin de l'histoire*.[86] This is
not to say that in those later works – which are contemporaneous with those
for which he is best known today – that he was uncritical of the thinkers
he engaged with: far from it. But, like Marx read Hegel, there may be
something there despite the shortcomings and mystifications.

Nietzsche against the fascists

In the 1975 book *Hegel, Marx, Nietzsche ou le royaume des ombres*, Lefebvre
suggests these thinkers provide three ways to take the modern world. Hegel
thinks in terms of the state, Marx society, and Nietzsche civilization.[87] We
can therefore view the modern world as Hegelian – a political theory of the
nation-state, the state engulfing and subordinating civil society, that is social
relations; as Marxist – the relation of the working class with the nation-state,
industrial change and its consequences more important than ideas; and as
Nietzschean – an assertion of life and the lived against political and economic processes; resistance through poetry, music and theatre; the hope of
the extraordinary, the surreal and the supernatural.[88] Each of these taken
alone may not be paradoxical, he suggests, but when combined they are
inherently paradoxical. However for Lefebvre, each grasped something of
the modern world, and shaped his own reflections accordingly.[89] One of the
reasons why all these three influences are German is the deep-rooted Cartesianism of French thought, something Lefebvre, along with many of his
generation, sought to leave behind.[90] Lefebvre notes that Cartesianism
'identifies being with the conscious . . . evacuates being, the true and the *real*
from consciousness and thought'.[91] We can see this critique in many places
in Lefebvre's work, especially around the privileging of the individual
subject and the reductive understanding of space.

The term *royaume des ombres*, the 'kingdom of shadows', or the underworld,
is from Hegel's *Greater Logic*, although it is also reprised in Marx, and in *Thus
Spoke Zarathustra* Nietzsche declares that the overman appears like a shadow.
Lefebvre uses the three as epigraphs to the work.[92] This poetic aspect is
found throughout this book, Lefebvre likening the three thinkers to three
stars in the sky – three stars but one constellation:

> These three stars, in eliminating the inferior or invisible planets, revolve above
> this world moving shadows about: us. Stars in a sky where the Sun of the intelli-
> gible is no more than a symbol and which has no longer any firmament. Maybe
> these stars pass behind clouds which are hardly less dark than the night . . .
>   The kingdom of shadows, mythically, from Homeric poetry to *The Divine Com-
> edy*, had entrance and exit, journey guide and mediating powers. It had Gates,
> those of an underground city, dominated by the terrestrial City and the City of

God. Today, where are the Gates of the kingdom of shadows? Where is the exit?[93]

Lefebvre's work on Nietzsche is interesting for a number of reasons. He would acknowledge that he was not writing about Nietzsche as a specialist or philologist, but as with his reading of Pascal, he lived the ideas, he struggled with them. These were works from the heart.[94] As he would later claim, his 1939 *Nietzsche* 'was the first book written to show that Nietzsche was not at all responsible for the fascist interpretation'.[95] Though this is not strictly true – M. P. Nicolas' *De Nietzsche à Hitler* was published before it – Lefebvre was certainly ahead of the pack.[96] The introduction to the book was written around the time he was working on the books on nationalism and Hitler – that is between July 1937 and September 1938 – and these are important themes in this book too. Destroyed during the Occupation, it was indeed several years ahead of mainstream scholarship, and would bear careful comparison with, for example, Heidegger's contemporaneous lectures[97] and Kaufmann's influential study.[98] Retrospectively he would see this as a reading that disputes Georg Lukács' polemic *The Destruction of Reason*.[99] For Lefebvre, there is both a left-Nietzscheanism, and a right-Nietzscheanism,[100] something that was shown in France in the early twentieth century with the interpretations of André Gide and Drieu la Rochelle.[101] Indeed, in direct distinction to the latter, Lefebvre asserted that it was not necessary to choose between Nietzsche and Marx.[102]

According to *La somme et le reste*, the fascist use of Nietzsche was not just a theme within the book, but the very reason Lefebvre wrote about Nietzsche. Nietzsche was someone Lefebvre had returned to after some time away from his texts. This makes sense in the light of the shift away from an interest in Schelling and Nietzsche to Hegel and Marx in the late 1920s. In the mid-1930s, though, Lefebvre recalls, the writer of the *Untimely Meditations* appeared to be more current than ever.[103] Lefebvre's work on early fascism and its theorists, particularly Moeller van Bruck, alerted him to the way that this 'immense poet' was being used.[104] Why should Nietzsche be abandoned to the Hitlerians?[105] Lefebvre is critical of some aspects of Nietzsche's work – his admiration for 'dubious heroes – adventurers, condottieri and conquistadors' and the sometimes suspect nature of the will to power.[106] There is the danger – that both Dostoyevsky and Gide would also highlight – if God is dead, everything is permitted.[107] Nietzsche's embrace of Wagner is deeply problematic, as is the problem of history as a myth and some aspects of the idea of tragedy. In fact Lefebvre suggests that myth and tragedy in that sense are Wagnerian, and belong to the Wagnerian period of Nietzsche's work, which is the potentially fascist part.

However, Nietzsche's notion of overcoming, and his critiques of the state, nationalism and mass consciousness outweigh these problems.[108] Lefebvre recognizes that the will to power is not simply the will to dominate, which is merely one aspect of power, and that Nietzsche's thought is not, or at least not solely, a metaphysic of violence.[109] Indeed, in the nineteenth century

Nietzsche stands out for his emphasis on the human, the investigation of this topic instead of the idea, the unconscious, or the world. Nietzsche introduces the notion of the Total Man, who overcomes the contemporary situation, and becomes for Nietzsche the overman, but who for Lefebvre is simply the human. Nietzsche's work on the human and culture can be naturally integrated with the Marxist conception of man.[110] In sum then, the fascist interpretation of Nietzsche is a 'fanatical falsification', drawing upon selected elements only of his work, and Lefebvre therefore holds him no more responsible for Nazism than Marx is for Stalinism.[111]

It is important that Lefebvre is not just discussing Nietzsche abstractly, as an academic exercise, but is seeing how some of his ideas can be used in a practical, political way. Nietzsche's influence is found throughout Lefebvre, particularly on history, the non-linearity of time, on rhythm, space, difference and the body.[112] Nietzsche's stress on the importance of the lived, sexuality and poetry are all also important.[113] Indeed, Lefebvre remembers that reading Nietzsche from the age of fifteen, it was his stress on the lived, in distinction to Spinoza's on the conceived, which was important.[114] For Lefebvre, Nietzsche's work on power is of serious, indeed indispensable, worth.

How can we understand fascism, imperialism and neo-imperialism without the will to power? And the state-system and social hierarchy [*le pyramid sociale*]?[115]

However, the will to power, is, like the notion of being, an abstraction that needs concretization.[116] This critique of the ungrounded nature of Nietzsche's work – which will be similarly made of Heidegger – is a common theme in Lefebvre's writings. 'Well before Nietzsche, and more concretely than him because more socially, Marx had the "sense of the Earth" '.[117] Nietzsche is helpful in discerning the crisis in civilization, but for Lefebvre his failure is in not finding a way to address it, or at least to pose these problems in such a way that a solution becomes possible.[118]

For Lefebvre there is the potential for a comparison between the Nietzschean theme of *ressentiment* and Hegelian alienation. Nietzsche's notion is of alienation, but alienation through humiliation, which leads to the development of humility, but as a virtue. Because humility is a virtue, Nietzsche shows how this leads to the humiliated seeking the same and similar situations – they become victims, prey, with objects of power over them.[119] Equally many respond through brutality, the quest for dominance and the need to assert physical superiority. As Lefebvre suggests, Nietzsche's understanding of the figure of *ressentiment* is the man of the fascist masses.[120] What Nietzsche recognizes, over and above Hegel and Marx, is the longer term effect of such alienation. It is not simply something that can be overcome through reconciliation with the absolute or the reorganization of labour, because it leaves its mark in values and morals.[121] Such a pessimistic prognosis would convince Lefebvre that only a much more fundamental revolution, a revolution of everyday life, could begin to address the problems of contemporary society.

Lefebvre argues that there is also much common ground between Marx and Nietzsche – their atheism and materialism; their critique of Hegel's political theology, of language, *logos*, and the Judeo-Christian tradition; the stress on production and creation, and the body – though there is obviously much to contrast. Lefebvre suggests that Nietzsche's suggestion that 'God is dead' has tragic repercussions beyond simple atheism and naturalism; that for Nietzsche rationality is not just limited but also illusory; and that production and society are the focus for Marx, creation and civilization for Nietzsche.[122] Marx renders Hegel's dialectic materialist, Nietzsche makes it tragic.[123] Civilization, while it is here and there in Marx, is distinct from the mode of production, and is most developed in Nietzsche.[124] In Nietzsche, poetry and art take the place of knowledge, and the *oeuvre* is more important than the product.[125] Nietzsche is obviously more interested in the individual, Marx the collective.[126] Equally, for Nietzsche, it is *Überwindung* (overcoming) rather than *Aufhebung*.[127] Indeed, Lefebvre and Guterman note that to the Nietzsche's formula 'man must be overcome', the reply of Marxism is that 'man is that which overcomes'.[128]

Politically there is overlap too, with the most severe criticisms of Germany that can be found being a shared concern in their work.[129] Lefebvre therefore believed that it was absurd for Drieu la Rochelle to write 'Nietzsche against Marx . . .'[130] Although there are differences, these can be resolved in a productive manner. As Smith notes, 'what seemed to start as a Marxist critique of Nietzsche gradually develops into a Nietzschean critique of Marx'.[131] Unsurprisingly, Lefebvre was criticized for introducing Nietzschean concepts – along with Hegelian ones – into Marxism. Indeed, late in life he recalls a critical essay by his former colleague Politzer being pulled from the journal *L'humanité* at the last minute.[132] But just as Nietzsche's understanding of space is entirely different from Hegel's, so too his understanding of time has nothing in common with Marxist time.[133] This is crucial in understanding Lefebvre's rethinking of the temporal dimension of historical materialism. However, as a pointer toward themes to be discussed later, Lefebvre suggests that 'the revolutionary road of the human and the heroic route of the overhuman intersect at the crossroads of space. Do they merge there? That is another story'.[134] I have no wish to underplay the importance of Nietzsche to Lefebvre's work. However there is, as I have suggested, another thinker behind much of Lefebvre's thought, to whom little attention has been paid. Indeed I will suggest that his signposts point the way at the crossroads of space. This is Heidegger.

Heidegger and the metaphysics of the Grand Guignol

Lefebvre's relationship to Heidegger is often neglected, but I believe that it forms a key part of his theoretical armoury, and that it helps to understand what Lefebvre was doing with the concepts of everyday life and space, as discussed in Chapters 3 and 5. As Kofman and Lebas note, Heidegger was the twentieth-century philosopher with whom Lefebvre engaged most,[135] David Harvey had recently suggested that the combination of Marx and Heidegger is an area of useful future work, when he talks of 'the possibility of somehow bridging the Marxian and Heideggerian conception within a new kind of radical politic'.[136] In some respects this is what Lefebvre has already done: he appropriated a number of ideas from Heidegger, whilst subjecting them to a Marxist critique. Marx remarks of Hegel that 'the mystification which the dialectic suffers in Hegel's hands by no means prevents him from being the first to present its general forms of motion in a comprehensive and conscious manner'.[137] I believe that a similar remark might be made of Lefebvre's reading and appropriation of Heidegger. Heidegger's conservative politics and the mystifications of his ontology should not obscure the valuable ideas of everyday life, space and the political that he presents. Lefebvre declares that he is not a Heideggerian,[138] but that Heidegger was the 'most profound modern philosopher'.[139]

In *L'existentialisme* Lefebvre notes that Heidegger had remarked that Sartre does not understand the difference between him and Husserl. Lefebvre agrees with this judgement, and adds that 'it is also possible that M. Sartre does not clearly see the difference between Heidegger and Marx'.[140] Aside from its prescience, given that Marx is hardly mentioned in *Being and Nothingness*, and that the *Critique of Dialectical Reason* will be arguably concerned with precisely the articulation of this difference,[141] Lefebvre seems to be setting out the terrain on which his later work will take place. There is a difference – many differences – between Marx and Heidegger, but for Lefebvre, both are essential. As the previous chapter noted, for some writers the tension between Marxism and existentialism is a constant theme in Lefebvre's work.[142] What this misses however is that Lefebvre's interest in Heidegger is not in the Heidegger of existentialism, especially not as this was rendered in French through Sartre.

Lefebvre read Husserl in 1924 and Heidegger in the late 1920s, but, as Hess notes, was 'immediately hostile'.[143] Many years later Lefebvre would note that his rejection of Heidegger was *before* the latter's adherence to Nazism. It was because of the turn away from action toward contemplation.[144] However, throughout *L'existentialisme*, when Lefebvre is criticizing Heidegger, it is often Sartre who is his real target. Points are more often illustrated by quotation from *Being and Nothingness* than *Being and Time*. For instance, this criticism is directed at the Sartrean misreading of Heidegger rather than Heidegger himself:

> Phenomenology therefore turns to problems of the dialectic and materialism (relations of being and nothingness of being and the conscience). Theoretically, it is possible to pass from phenomenological research to dialectic materialism. With one condition: that of abandoning the pretension of achieving the 'world' by a sole conscience and of describing it exhaustively. Once speculative philosophy has been abandoned, the problem of conscience – and that of action – come up rather differently.[145]

Lefebvre makes this distinction clear in *Métaphilosophie*, suggesting that in order to understand the world we cannot base it on individual conscience (Sartre) nor on 'being' – 'a classical thesis of metaphysics, both continued and transformed by Heidegger'. However, nor can we simply understand it on the basis of *praxis*, the Marxist conception.[146] Sartre's work on the subject has neither the depth nor the radicalism of Heidegger's work.[147] For Lefebvre there is much more in Heidegger, things that may be obscured certainly, but a potential for thought. It is, for instance, the Heidegger of the critique of subjectivity – there in *Being and Time* – but found throughout his de-struction of the tradition in works throughout his career; the historical Heidegger; the Heidegger who reads the Greeks; the Heidegger who accords equal weight to issues of space that is of most interest. Heidegger's rethinking of notions of temporality and history, in Nietzsche's wake; his understandings of dwelling; and the critique of Descartes and Kant, are all valuable. As I will suggest in subsequent chapters it is particularly Heidegger's work on space and everyday life that will attract Lefebvre; but there are other points of interest, including Heidegger's conception of the political (in distinction to his politics), and his work on the rural roots of the terms *ousia* (domain or homestead) and the gathering or harvesting aspects of *logos*.[148] But Lefebvre himself, whilst acknowledging the importance of Heidegger, did not think him as important as Hegel, Marx or Nietzsche.

There are obvious reasons we might assume for this attempt to downplay a relation. One is that they were contemporaries, another is Heidegger's allegiance to the Nazi Party. In 1946 Lefebvre described Heidegger's philosophy as 'pro-fascist'.[149] He is strongly critical of the importance of death in Heidegger's work, suggesting this is a turn away from life.[150] He suggests that 'mass graves are outlined on the horizon of Heideggerianism', and describes Heidegger's philosophy as the metaphysics of the Grand Guignol (a Parisian theatre specializing in horror plays),[151] which 'can no longer be accepted now Europe has served as a field of experience for the sadists'.[152] He argues that it is not Hitler's politics or racism that is found in Heidegger's philosophy, but Hitler's 'style', that is, the S.S. For Lefebvre, in Heidegger, the Hegelian dialectic of being and nothingness, of master and slave, becomes that of executioner and victim.[153] Heideggerian existentialism, is for Lefebvre, in relation to dialectical humanism exactly as Hitler's ideology is to socialism. Both engage in mystification, and for Lefebvre, 'no indulgence is permissible for a project of this kind'.[154] Heidegger's affiliation to National Socialism at the time when it was engaged in a struggle with scientific socialism is not surprising, Lefebvre contends. Nazism needed people like him in the intellectual struggle. That after this initial period, with Marxists crushed, Heidegger was left to one side only aggravates the case, and does not whitewash him.[155]

However, in 1965, Lefebvre is content to dismiss Heidegger's politics as a 'tendency toward German nationalism'. This remarkable exculpation is all the more notable because in the previous line he had dismissed the Nazi interpretation of Nietzsche as faked, but omitted to mention Heidegger's

Party status. Indeed, he suggests that 'one would easily find the same tendencies in French works which pass for significant. Moreover, the philosophico-
political appreciation is out-of-date. It is worth no more for Heidegger than
for Kafka, Joyce or Proust.' While it is undoubtedly true that, from a political perspective, nothing is more reactionary than Heidegger's thought,[156]
for Lefebvre, the question, and the danger, of Heidegger is different. It
is one of eclecticism.[157] Notably, this is the same potential he saw in the
combination of Hegel, Marx, and Nietzsche. Consequently, there are a
number of places where Lefebvre strongly criticizes Heidegger – for his
mystification and abstraction, his ontology, his disguised theology and lack
of dialectics.[158]

For Lefebvre, Heidegger's history of being

> obscures the more concrete history of Hegel and Marx, without attaining the
> power of Nietzsche's critique of history. Heidegger's philosophy, a disguised,
> barely secularised theodicy, strives to rescue traditional philosophy without sub-
> jecting it to a radical critique. Although he touches on it, Heidegger evades the
> notion of *metaphilosophy*. He substitutes for it so-called fundamental ontology, a
> variant, whether we like it or not, of metaphysics. It is true that he offers a
> contribution to the critical analysis of modernity; he was among the first to
> perceive and foresee the dangers inherent in over-valuing technology and to
> understand that *domination* over nature (by knowledge and technology) becomes
> domination *over men* and is not the same as the *appropriation* of nature because it
> tends to destroy it . . . [However he] draws a disturbing apologia for the German
> language. This prevents his making a radical critique of the western (European)
> Logos, although he verges on it. What he says about and against Nietzsche is not
> convincing . . .[159]

To take an example, Heidegger's notion of *Dasein* is criticized for its lack
of sex, and Lefebvre suggests that the Freudian theory of the libido 'is often
richer and closer to the concrete'.[160] Heidegger's work is of 'being without
sex, without dialectic, a disguised god, playing hide and seek with that
privileged being, the human'.[161] This highlights the central tension –
Heidegger is too abstract, too philosophical for Lefebvre, never concrete
enough. These criticisms do not disappear in the later works, but more
positive references begin to appear alongside them. As Lefebvre notes in *La
somme et le reste*, from one perspective it is clear – in comparison with official
Marxists, Heidegger represents the 'opposing pole'. However, when compared to 'non-official Marxists (today called revisionists)' some parallels
begin to emerge.[162] At each stage, Lefebvre wants to ground Heidegger, to
make his analyses more *real*. Heidegger's theory needs to be related to practice, to material conditions. Like Hegel, Heidegger needs to be stood on his
feet. For Lefebvre, Heidegger shows 'the best and the worst, the archaic and
the visionary'.[163] His work on the essence of technology and its relation to
the modern world is a highpoint.[164] Therefore, despite these criticisms,
which are obviously far from minor, there are a number of areas of Lefebvre's
work that would benefit from a critical comparison with Heidegger. As

Lefebvre suggests, there is much to say about Heidegger, 'much to say for him, and even more against'.[165] We should note the second half of this, but it should not lead us to overlook the first.

In 1946 Lefebvre considers that there are a number of key issues that Heidegger does not pose. These include

1. the dialectic;
2. overcoming [*dépassement*];
3. totality;
4. what we mean when we speak of 'we'; human community;
5. the world, what this means, and the human's place in it;
6. the powers of human reality;
7. the notion of 'end' in relation to human reality, its goal, its sense, its end.[166]

Now whilst it would be an exaggeration to say that Heidegger makes good on all of these issues, it is striking just how many of them are discussed in his work after *Being and Time*. Many of these are found in lectures and discussions that were not published until after the war had ended: 'overcoming' is central to the later Heidegger's work on metaphysics; human community and reality are discussed in lecture courses on Kant; the world and human conceptions of it are key in the work on technology. Other instances could be given.

Equally interesting would be to compare their work on the notion of time critically, particularly around the issue of the moment, where both thinkers develop and critique the *Augenblick* (literally, 'blink of an eye') of Nietzsche, some of which is done in Chapter 5. Or we could examine the implications of the following passage – written by Lefebvre in the early 1940s, which is clearly related to Heidegger:

> 'Being' can be grasped in two ways, which are inseparable. In the abstract, formal sense, it is a question of being in general, undetermined . . . Being has a second sense, concrete. Being determined, rich in its complexity, a unity of differences and even of contradictions designated legitimately by the same word . . . All the work of our thought consists in following a formula of Rousseau, to give a direction to this little word 'being', but with a double sense and going unceasingly from one of these to the other: from abstract being to concrete being (content), to seize it; from concrete being (content) to abstract being, to analyse it.[167]

One of Lefebvre's last books, *Qu'est-ce que penser?*, has an almost explicitly Heideggerian title. Heidegger published a lecture course entitled *Was heißt Denken?* – 'what is called thinking?' Lefebvre argues that this assumes that there is something called thinking in the first place, and that his own enquiry, which asks 'what is thinking?' is more radical. What this misses, however, is that Heidegger's book's title is ambiguous, and also asks 'what calls for thinking', which is a rather different question, implying the sort of inquiry that Lefebvre seems to suggest is lacking.[168] However, in an interview cited by Hess, Lefebvre provides a rather different answer – instead of being, as it would be for Heidegger, for Lefebvre it is the possible.[169]

The attitude that Lefebvre has to Heidegger seems therefore to undergo a remarkable transformation. Some insight into this can be found if we examine a roundtable discussion he had with Kostas Axelos, Jean Beaufret and François Châtelet in early 1959. This dialogue was entitled 'Karl Marx et Heidegger', and was originally published in *France-Observateur*.[170] Lefebvre recalls how the previous summer – that is, the year he left the PCF – he was reading *Holzwege*, a collection of Heidegger's writings that includes 'The origin of the work of art', 'The age of the world picture' and 'Nietzsche's word: "God is dead" '.[171] Lefebvre notes that he was taken by the way Heidegger thought of the relation between humans and nature, and by his critique of technology, of power over nature. 'I think therefore that there is no antagonism between the cosmic-historical vision of Heidegger and the historic-practical conception of Marx.'[172] Lefebvre therefore poses the question – 'are there many Heideggers? The reading of *Holzwege* left me with another impression than that of *Sein und Zeit*'.[173] Although Axelos answers in the negative, and shows the continuity of Heidegger's positions, it does perhaps explain Lefebvre's position a bit better.[174]

Lefebvre was, of course, not alone in his attempt to use Heidegger to supplement and extend Marx's work, but this was not an easy issue to come to terms with. In 1960, in the *Critique of Dialectical Reason*, Sartre himself had ducked the challenge, noting that 'the case of Heidegger is too complex for me to discuss here'.[175] However he thought it important, suggesting that 'one would have to *read* him to grasp the meaning of the sentences one by one. And there is no longer any Marxist, to my knowledge, who is still capable of doing this.'[176] But there was a group of Marxists around this time, with whom Lefebvre was closely associated, who were doing exactly that. As Merquior notes, these were the thinkers of the journal *Arguments*, such as Pierre Fougeyrollas and Axelos, who had 'tried to connect and complete Marx with Heidegger'.[177] *Arguments* ran from 1956 to 1962, and had been initially set up by a number of thinkers, also including Lefebvre, Barthes, and Châtelet, many of whom had been recently expelled from the Communist Party.[178] It led to a book series of the same title with Éditions de Minuit, edited by Axelos, in which appeared many of his own books, Lefebvre's *Métaphilosophie*, *Introduction à la modernité* and *La fin de l'histoire*, and works by Eugen Fink, Deleuze, Marcuse, Trotsky, Blanchot, Bataille and Hegel.[179] Axelos was also the translator of Lukács' *History and Class Consciousness* and Heidegger's *What is Philosophy?*[180]

Lefebvre has a lot of time for Axelos, who he describes as 'one of a rare breed, if not the only one' who both studies and criticizes Marx and situates this within a wider history of thought – Heraclitus to Heidegger.[181] Rémi Hess has recently suggested that Axelos' work merits being rediscovered,[182] a point I would support, although what I can say here is far more brief than is desirable or deserved. In his 1961 book *Marx penseur de la technique* Axelos suggests how, as well as there being alienation through ideology and economics, there can be alienation through technology.[183] Marx of course discussed this through his work on the labour process, and Axelos' book ranges widely across Marx's works in order to justify this interpretation. Marx's work shows that technology conditions humans' relations to nature, the process of production of material life and by consequence social relations and ideas.[184]

> Social relations are closely bound up with productive forces. In acquiring new productive forces men change their mode of production; and in changing their mode of production, in changing the way of earning their living, they change all their social relations. The hand-mill gives you society with the feudal lord; the steam-mill, society with the industrial capitalist.[185]

However, although Axelos barely mentions him by name in *Marx penseur de la technique*, Heidegger's impact is also strongly felt throughout the study.[186] Heidegger's work on technology, deriving from his analysis of the Greek *techne*, is of central importance, and I suggest, through Axelos' interpretation, had a significant impact on Lefebvre.

> Axelos had the insight in 1961 to disengage one of the 'factors' in modern society with tendencies towards at least apparent autonomy: 'technique' and 'technicity'. He proceeds further and more boldly than Heidegger, demonstrating how Marx formulated the concept of technique and defined its importance and its role in both industry and economic growth. He employs this thesis to indicate how there is a certain order in Marx's thought and work, in the emergence and clarification of this particular concept. But having done this, Axelos cannot get beyond this impasse. His consideration of the 'problematic of reconciliation' between technique and nature, philosophy and history, thought and society, simply puts the problem of reproduction into parentheses. It leaps over the problem in one bound, going straight from capitalism to the problem of man in the world.[187]

As Poster notes, in both this work and others, such as *Vers la pensée planétaire*, Axelos 'discerned a deep flaw in Marx's thought: that Marx remained in the metaphysical tradition of philosophy since Plato, an argument that Axelos took over from Heidegger'.[188] Although Heidegger does acknowledge that both Marx and Nietzsche play a pivotal role in the endgame of metaphysics, Heidegger's own sustained treatment is of Nietzsche alone.[189] In Axelos the reverse is true: Marx plays the same role for Axelos as Nietzsche does for Heidegger. Marx is the 'last philosopher';[190] 'a great epoch of Western metaphysics, that is, of Greek, Judeo-Christian, and Modern metaphysics, reaches a culmination with Marx'.[191] For Axelos, even though Marx wants to abolish philosophy in a radical way, to materialize its instincts and direct it toward practice, he remains within the system he seeks to reverse.[192] Just as Nietzsche's reversal of Plato remains within Platonism, so too does Marx's reversal of Hegel. As Marx himself notes, 'modern philosophy has only continued work that Heraclitus and Aristotle had already begun'.[193]

For this reason then, Axelos supplemented Marx with Heraclitus in works such as *Héraclite et la philosophie*.[194] Heraclitus is the beginning of the Western tradition; Marx its culmination. But both are dialectical thinkers and Heraclitus may open up some possibilities that have been closed off since Plato. He is a thinker rather than a philosopher.[195] As Lefebvre puts it, against the new Eleatics, the Zenos of structuralism, Axelos is the 'new Heraclitus'.[196] Indeed, Lefebvre suggests that it is only really Axelos that has come even close to grasping the importance of Heraclitus' teaching of thought *of* the world and thought *in* the world, of thought that is not everything but nor is it nothing.[197] The problem with Axelos, for Lefebvre, is the analysis of the relations of production and reproduction, a theme that will be returned to in Chapter 6, and that he, like Heidegger, can be rather speculative, rather metaphysical.[198] But Axelos' merit is that he forces us to think Marx's thought in relation to 'the real problems of our times',[199] it 'situates Marx in the twentieth century'.[200] Lefebvre's work on metaphilosophy would attempt to do precisely this. In this sense it is not a question of abolishing philosophy or of putting an end to philosophy by decree. 'Philosophy is dead, long live philosophy! But is it in *the same sense*?'[201]

Metaphilosophy

Heidegger looms large in Lefebvre's work on the notion of metaphilosophy, particularly as discussed in the book of that name, which is the most detailed discussion by Lefebvre of Heidegger.[202] Indeed, in this work Heidegger is the third most oft-cited author – after Marx and Hegel, but before Nietzsche. The notion of metaphilosophy, which is one of Lefebvre's most difficult and misunderstood notions, is highly critical of Heidegger's fundamental ontology – the project of *Being and Time* – but closer to his later *thought* of the *Überwinden*, the overcoming, of metaphysics.[203] As Lefebvre argues, and Heidegger had long realized, fundamental ontology was metaphysics by another name, or at the very least, tangled within it.[204] It is in the notion of metaphilosophy that Lefebvre's rapprochement with Sartre becomes most apparent, something that has led Poster to suggest that

> Lefebvre's metaphilosophy of daily life was dependent upon Sartre's thought. The parallels between the two were striking. Metaphilosophy was explicitly a synthesis of Marxism and existentialism.[205]

Indeed, Poster pursues this claim suggesting that Axelos and Fougeyrollas 'gained their perspective on Marx from studying Heidegger', while 'Lefebvre resorted continually to Sartre's early positions in *Being and Nothingness* and his criticism of diamat'.[206] Such a characterization is not entirely wrong, but it seems to me to be rather misleading. In particular, I would put much more emphasis on the influence of Heidegger and Nietzsche, and indeed Marx, on the notion of metaphilosophy than that of Sartre.[207] Lefebvre does not exempt Sartre from some fairly fundamental criticism, and what he appears to take from Sartre could much more easily have come from Sartre's sources.[208]

The transition from philosophy to meta-philosophy has been going on for more than a century: from Marx to Nietzsche, to contemporary Marxists – that is works which are still and which are already no longer philosophical in the classic sense (Frankfurt school, Lukács, Heidegger, Axelos, etc.)[209]

Lefebvre asks what it would mean ' "to realise", "to surmount [*surmonter*]", "to overcome [*dépasser*]" philosophy?', and is concerned with how this thought prolonging traditional philosophy would relate to the world. Metaphilosophy is not a simple *after* philosophy, but is rather like a metamorphosis.[210] It aims for something more than the Marxist or Hegelian *Aufheben* and something better than the Nietzschean *Überwinden*.[211] It seeks to incorporate all philosophies from the most remote sources, from the pre-Socratics to the contemporary age, and to illuminate them, by projecting them towards the future.[212] In a sense, Lefebvre is concerned with actualizing Marx's eleventh thesis on Feuerbach.[213] How can we change the world rather than merely interpret it, but – and this is the crucial bit – how is that dependent on our interpretation? Lefebvre's notion of metaphilosophy seeks to remedy this: 'it answers the questions of the philosophers and yet it is no longer a philosophy'.[214] It is a reflection on philosophy rather than the building of a system.[215] In this respect it is a continuation of his early thinking through of dialectical materialism, which in 1947 he described as 'no longer a philosophy' and yet 'still a philosophy, it realises philosophy'.[216] The aim of these passages, Lefebvre suggests a decade later, was to seize the dialectic transformation, the passage of philosophy to something else, its overcoming. One of the advantages of Stalinism and Zhdanovism was that they brought to the surface hidden tensions, they 'exploded latent contradictions' because they 'presented dialectical materialism simultaneously as an completed philosophical system and a perfectly scientific knowledge'. But he now finds that the notion of overcoming begs the question of what it consists of – a shift from speculation to *praxis*?[217]

This is why Lefebvre thinks that Marx is important. He argues that philosophy has tended both to look down on the non-philosophical life – the lived, the everyday, common sense – but has also imposed its knowledge and wisdom upon it. Marx's notion of revolutionary practice was intended to overcome this.[218] Much of *Métaphilosophie* is taken up with an investigation of *praxis*, although Lefebvre argues that it may be too utilitarian, and draws upon the idea of *poiesis* as a 'counter-weight'.[219] Lefebvre suggests that 'it is important not to dissociate the two aspects of the creative capacity'.[220] Marx's emphasis on the economic side has neglected the other aspects of creation.[221] *Poiesis* is in some sense a balance between speculation and *praxis*, understood in a narrow sense, as it is a notion of creation, or creative production. As Lefebvre argues, 'not all creation is "*poiesis*", but all *poiesis* is creation'.[222] It is therefore based upon the insights Lefebvre drew from

Nietzsche and informed by Heidegger's analyses of ancient Greek think-ing.[223] Indeed, as Lefebvre notes, 'the examination of Marx and of Nietzsche as protagonists of metaphilosophy leads us to Heidegger'.[224] While Lefebvre praises his 'admirable studies of *Logos, Aletheia, Physis*, etc.' he suggests we need 'to study *Praxis, Techne, Mimesis, Poiesis*, etc. in the same manner'.[225] Like Lefebvre, Heidegger realized that it may not be possible to solve the problems of philosophy from within philosophy, but that some-thing else might be required. Philosophy limps behind the problems of modernity and actual praxis.[226] Struck by Nietzsche's claims that things began to go wrong at the beginning of Western philosophy, with Plato, Heidegger went back to the pre-Socratics, attempting to wrestle meaning out of the fragments of thinkers like Anaximander, Parmenides and Hera-clitus. Lefebvre's scorn for the Eleatics meant that it was to the last of these that he turned in most detail, drawing upon Heidegger and Axelos' analyses of his work, especially the suggestion (in fragment 52) that 'time is like a child playing a game'.[227]

For Lefebvre, Marx is at his most insightful when he declares that 'the world's becoming philosophical is at the same time philosophy's becoming worldly, that its realization is at the same time its loss . . .'[228] Like Axelos, Lefebvre regularly cited this as an aphorism.[229] As Poster notes, this quote is not so much the early Marx as the juvenile Marx, coming as it does from his doctoral thesis.[230] What it means is that in its becoming worldly, that is in its actualization, philosophy is transcended and overcome. Marx's early writings are wrongly called philosophical, because they already contain a critique of all systematic philosophies.[231] Lefebvre therefore describes many of his best known ideas, such as the analysis of the production of space, and the investigation into the everyday as a metaphilosophy.[232] Though effect-ively based on philosophical underpinnings, as I shall show in the following chapters, their application to concrete political problems allows these underpinnings to be transcended. Not a pure and simple abolition, nor an uncritical prolongation; not something that can be grasped by positivism or 'philosophism', nor by a philosophically systematized materialism or idealism.[233] For Labica therefore, and not without reason, *Métaphilosophie* is possibly Lefebvre's most important book, certainly a pivotal one, a turning point.[234]

Descartes and literature

As well as this engagement with significant philosophical figures, Lefebvre also wrote extensively on a range of other writers. Many of these writings were in the period between the late 1940s and the late 1950s – that is from the beginning of the Cold War, with the increasingly strict Stalinist line of the Parti Communiste Français, to his exclusion from the party. These writ-ings included books on major figures such as *Descartes* (1947), *Pascal* (two volumes, 1949 and 1954), *Diderot* (1949), and *Rabelais* (1955) and lesser known figures such as the dramatist *Musset* (1955) and the artist *Pignon*

(1956).[235] It is not insignificant that all of these figures treated in this period are French, with the exception of the 1957 book on Lenin. In 1953 he also published the more general *Contribution à l'esthétique*, a book that had originally been written four years earlier, but which had been withheld because of political reasons.[236] It covered some of the material destined for the eighth volume of *A la lumière du matérialisme dialectique*. It was finally published, in part, because of a fabricated quotation from Marx serving as an epigraph. This quotation – 'L'Art est la plus haute joie que l'homme se donne à lui-même', 'Art is the highest pleasure that man gives to himself' – was assembled from various sources, and indeed Lefebvre claims that a fairly similar phrase does appear in Marx, 'but with a much more restrained sense'. Lefebvre admits that this was a 'shameful deception', and that book was 'pretty mediocre'.[237]

The other epigraph to *Contribution à l'esthétique* was from the Soviet theoretician Zhdanov, which together with the fabrication, not only enabled the book to be published, but also led to its being translated into numerous languages including Russian. It also helps us to understand the context more clearly.[238] The two camps doctrine was applied to science and foreign policy, as was noted in Chapter 1, but equally Zhdanov had been instrumental in the establishment of the Union of Soviet Writers and broader cultural policy under Stalin, including the doctrine of socialist realism. The PCF therefore declared itself against Americanism in all its forms. Talking up its own role in the resistance was one strategy, but this was partnered by an emphasis on things French, in large part in the arts, but also through tirades against symbols of American consumerism and cultural control. Poster suggests that 'unless one were prepared to fall into the camp of the Americans with their anti-Communism – and very few French intellectuals were – Marxism had to be identified with Russian socialism without qualification'.[239] Marxists such as Louis Aragon provided readings of the great French writers within these new constraints, and, superficially at least, Lefebvre appeared to be part of the same movement. Whilst writing on figures who were not political in the most obvious sense gave Lefebvre much more freedom of expression, it would be misleading to suggest, as Poster puts it, that 'Lefebvre retreated to the relatively uncontroversial sphere of literary criticism'.[240] Lefebvre is clearly operating in a highly charged atmosphere. The fabricated epigraph from Marx and the one from Zhdanov in *Contribution à l'esthétique* are attempts to cover his tracks. We should note, too, that he occasionally puts in a complimentary reference to Stalin.[241]

In these works Lefebvre developed an explicitly Marxist sense of writing intellectual biography, which, for reasons that will become clear, was also a chance to write some intellectual history. We would be remiss though, if we did not note the specificity of the figures chosen. Many of them were writers who suffered religious or political persecution for their ideas. Descartes, for example, held back many of his works because he saw what had happened to Galileo and feared the same for himself; Diderot was imprisoned for his beliefs; Pascal defended Antoine Arnauld and Jansenism against the Jesuits;

and Rabelais' work was banned by the church for 'obscenity', which at the time meant morally and political dangerous rather than indecent.[242] The parallels with Lefebvre's own position are readily apparent.[243] Equally, Lefebvre's readings of these particular thinkers were in tension with Zhdanovist orthodoxy. As we have seen, Lefebvre eventually left the party in 1958, after a membership lasting 30 years. Undoubtedly the subterfuge concerning the fabricated Marx quotation did not help. Lefebvre remarks that several people, from various countries, asked for its source, and that some apparently read Marx's entire works searching for it![244] Lefebvre's work of this transitional period was therefore part of this appropriation of French cultural capital in opposition to Americanism and for Marxist goals; but it was also a means of resisting dominant trends within Soviet thinking. *Contribution à l'esthétique*, for example, for all its epigraphical deference to Zhdanov, and the express denial of the first lines of the book, engages with some of the central tenets of socialist realism;[245] the publication of *Diderot* was held back for a few years because it did not satisfy party censors.[246]

These writings are largely unknown to the Anglophone world. Shields' recent study only mentions the work on 'literary figures' in passing;[247] although there is a slightly longer discussion in Jameson's *Marxism and Form*.[248] Even Hess' French biography says relatively little.[249] One thing that is immediately noticeable about Lefebvre's books on these figures is how much attention is devoted to contextual background and situation of the writers in question, and how correspondingly the works themselves are of almost secondary importance. This is partly explained by my suspicion that Lefebvre was using these writers as a surrogate for other concerns, but there is a much more fundamental reason. Lefebvre argues that the history of philosophy can only be written as a chapter in the more general history of culture, ideas and knowledge. 'And this history can be nothing other than a *social history of ideas*, connected to *the social criticism of ideas*'.[250] The social history of ideas differs profoundly from a history of social ideas, which assumes 'social ideas' can be separated from other types of ideas.[251] The notion of an autonomous history of philosophy, 'badly camouflaged by vague considerations of social "milieu", of the epoch, must be rejected'. However, it should not be rejected in favour of a crude materialism.[252] Rather, we need to take ideas as historical facts themselves, 'which signifies precisely the interdependence of the ideas and the practical conditions of life and action'.[253] Much later he would ask if there is a history of philosophy that is independent of other aspects of history, such as history in general, the history of ideas, or of production? His answer would be no: each system of philosophy has an internal coherence, although we cannot absorb the history of philosophy into the history of superstructures.[254]

Lefebvre therefore believes that in order to understand a writer's work it is central to comprehend the intellectual context they were writing within. His book on Pascal, for example, situates Jansenism, Pascal's work and Christianity itself in the context of historical facts. It begins, he suggests, 'as is necessary for all Marxist studies, by situating, objectively, historically, these ideologies'.[255] Accordingly, he discusses the economic situation of France in the seventeenth century, the class divisions in the monarchical state and the opposition forces before introducing Pascal in context.[256] The political and scientific developments of the time are crucial to a proper understanding, as are economic, social and religious issues. A whole range of other thinkers, amongst them Copernicus, Galileo and Kepler, and movements such as the Jesuits supplement the argument. Political events are also crucial. Lefebvre suggests that 'the *Fronde*, and its failure, divided the "grand century", and the life of Pascal, into two distinct parts'.[257] As Lanavère puts it, Lefebvre read Pascal's *Pensées* 'as a dialectical work'; he gave it a 'coherent interpretation which was founded on the principles of a critical Marxism'.[258] Indeed, were we to put the historical sections of these books together we would have a fairly wide-ranging intellectual history of France between the late fifteenth and the eighteenth centuries.[259]

Lefebvre claims that an insufficiently historical and dialectical materialism is no better than idealism, which it can oppose only in the most sterile way. We need to recognize the balance and unity between idealism and materialism, as a dialectical movement.[260] The history of ideologies is, he argues, more complicated than it would appear to a cursory (*sommaire*) materialism, which is 'insufficiently dialectical (and by consequence insufficiently historical and insufficiently materialist!)'.[261] As he continues, 'the complete condemnation of idealism – as a block of errors – is a symmetrical error to that of idealism, which accepts it as a block of truth'.[262] Idealist arguments, such as the ontological argument for the existence of God, cannot simply be rejected, but need to be understood in their historical context.

> It requires a historical rehabilitation of idealism, which does not have anything in common with a *restoration* of idealism. Quite the contrary: the only manner of liquidating idealism is to do it justice, to explain it *as such*, and of therefore explaining the function it had in the history of knowledge, and which acquisitions were carried out *through* idealism (and not *by* idealism as such).
>
> In that way, and only in that way can idealist arguments fall![263]

The beginning of the second volume on Pascal is revealing, as Lefebvre discusses the reception of the book. His approach clearly had its critics. Although Lukács liked it, he received criticisms of his supposed sympathy to Jansenism, Jesuitism, and existentialism.[264] In response, Lefebvre suggests that the Marxist historian should move between the inside and the outside, the internal and the external, but not solely one way. The external context should both determine the reading, and be shaped and revealed by it. Pascal's *Pensées* can be read both as a product of the time, and as a producer of it. As we have seen, for Lefebvre, the base/superstructure model should not be viewed in a single direction, but in a dialectical relation. He suggests this is the same with the relation between the objective and the subjective, and that Lenin showed this at work in his notebooks on Hegel.[265]

It is important, Lefebvre contends, to recognize that we should not read later problematics into thinkers. To try to understand Descartes, for example, as an idealist or a materialist, is misleading. It is contrary to historical and dialectical materialism, because it relies on an atemporal understanding. The distinction between idealism and materialism is posterior to Descartes, and therefore does not help us to comprehend his work.[266] It is worth noting that the Zhdanovist reading of Descartes at the time reduced him to a crude mechanism, a reading Lefebvre disputes.[267] Although Descartes' work moves from the abstract to the concrete, and that concrete element is the human, this does not mean that he has transcended his time and become a Marxist two centuries before Marx. Rather, Descartes' concrete element is the human, but not the *social* human, which it is for Marx.[268]

To consider Cartesianism formally, in an abstract succession of doctrines – those of the Middle Ages, those of the Renaissance – is absurd. It is the equivalent of studying Descartes outside of his time.[269] Rather we need to understand how to analyse his work in the context of multiple, and sometimes contradictory, intellectual and social currents. For example, the *Discourse on the Method* should, Lefebvre argues, be understood as a manifesto in a triple sense: a manifesto of Western civilization, relying on myths, religion, the agrarian civilization of the Middle Ages; of industrial society, the modern human's mastery of nature and the earth – knowing, dominating and utilizing it for their own purposes; and of the ascendant bourgeoisie and liberalism.[270] All of these form the context for the work, although it seems that the last – the emergence of the bourgeoisie and liberalism – is particularly important for Lefebvre.

Why should this be so? Lefebvre underlines the emergence of the individual, with the ontological and epistemological stress of the 'I am', and the freedom of that individual. This is coupled with the sense of the rational, and together these form the rational, self-interested individual of classic, bourgeois, liberalism. Other thinkers contributed to this conception before Descartes; others following him continued it, enriching and clarifying some points, obscuring others. Of the earlier thinkers, Lefebvre notes Rabelais, Calvin, and Montaigne.[271] Pascal would surely be one of the later ones, along with more obvious figures such as Locke. All of these writers contribute to the historical role of the bourgeois classes in developing the science of nature and the techniques and forces of production. Indeed, Lefebvre suggests that the *Discourse* appears to the historian as a manifesto comparable to a manifesto which, two centuries later, inaugurated the theoretical and political ascendance of the industrial proletariat.[272] As Lefebvre and Guterman note in 1936, 'the critical work of Marx cannot be understood without his illustrious predecessors: Rabelais, Montaigne, Descartes, the *Theological-Political Treatise*, the work of Diderot'.[273]

Lefebvre underlines that Descartes needs to be read as a thinker who is at once a move toward something new, *and* as one embedded in the time he was writing. As he suggests, Descartes is not able to 'transcend' his epoch. Rather than the writers on Descartes who stress the medieval, theological, mystical aspects of his work, such as Étienne Gilson,[274] or those who see him as entirely and consistently rational,[275] we can find the 'true Descartes', which is attainable through the 'objective method of dialectical material-ism'.[276] As Lefebvre underlines, 'philosophy is a "secularisation" [*laïcisation*] of theology: it disengages from it slowly and not without difficulty'.[277] Des-cartes' work has had a wide ranging influence, in a range of extremely complicated and contradictory ways. For Lefebvre these contradictions are explained by the internal contradictions of Cartesianism, and can only be explained by way of them. But this is not simply an exercise in the *history* of ideas, because as he sagely notes, all contemporary French thinking is a bit Cartesian, even when it believes itself not to be.[278]

We find a similar quest in the book on Rabelais.[279] Rabelais' work is today often interpreted through Bakhtin's important study,[280] but as Delory-Momberger notes, though this was written in 1940, it was not published for 25 years, and only appeared in French in 1970.[281] There are a number of ways we could read Rabelais – as anticlerical atheist, a defender of royal privilege, a precursor of rationalism; or as a religious disciple of Erasmus, a humanist, a defender of a particular view of religion against the domination of Rome.[282] Romanticism also found much to applaud in Rabelais' work.[283] As with Descartes, Lefebvre claims the 'authentic figure of Rabelais'[284] is somewhere in between, he is on the cusp of the religious question, neither able fully to escape his time nor entirely embedded within it. As with the discussion of Descartes as an idealist or a materialist, to discuss Rabelais' atheism or not is to read a modern problematic back into his work. For Lefebvre, Rabelais is a 'realist visionary', with feet both in concrete reality and idealist aspiration,[285] someone who is open to a whole range of interpretations.[286]

The plan of this book is strikingly similar to the ones on Pascal and Descartes. Rather than study Rabelais thematically – the theme of giants, or the theme of the voyage – Lefebvre aims to study him according to a Marxist schema. He therefore discusses the economic and social situation of France in the sixteenth century as a prelude to Rabelais' life and finally his work.[287] Like both Pascal and Descartes, Rabelais is important because he is a transition figure – neither entirely within his own time, nor able fully to transcend it: 'The five books of Rabelais appear to us already as a *reflection* of this epoch. A *living reflection*'.[288] His work harks back to earlier literary forms, such as the epic of Homer's *Odyssey*, but looks forward toward the modern novel – particularly Balzac's *The Human Comedy*. 'Between these two great forms of literature, the work of Rabelais represents a transition. Still an epic, it is a burlesque odyssey. Already a novel, it is the novel of the first modern individual: Panurge.'[289]

There are a number of difficulties in approaching Rabelais' work, includ-ing his wide-ranging vocabulary, including technical terms, dialect, and archaisms and an abundance of word-play and comic imagery.[290] As Cohen points out, the term *Rabelaisian*, which usually refers to the scatological and sexual language, could be more properly applied to his verbosity and loquacity.[291] That is not to say that the standard sense of the word

'Rabelaisian' is misplaced. Rabelais frequently uses vulgarity, coarseness, obscenity, lewdness, cruelty, carnage and savagery for dramatic and comic effect. Equally Rabelais' sources are wide ranging, demonstrating his immense erudition. This is not simply in terms of the object of his satire, but the literary tradition he draws upon – including Celtic and other myths, religious texts, and works of literature. The story of Gargantua, for example, was popular long before Rabelais, being a name given to places, mountains and other sites; similarly Pantagruel was the name of a 'goblin, a familiar spirit [*un lutin, un elfe familier*]'.[292] In Arthurian legend, Merlin created the giants to help the King in the struggle against Gog and Magog.[293] Such a legend was the basis for the popular *Les Grandes et inestimables Croniques: Du grant et enorme geant Gargantua*, published in the same year as Rabelais's *Pantagruel*, and cited by him in its prologue.[294] To read Rabelais therefore requires some level of knowledge about the sources of his inspiration and his satire; and a recognition of the more 'vulgar' aspects of his work.[295] As Lefebvre cautions, we should not mistake his enormous richness for confusion.[296]

Lefebvre's reading of Rabelais is therefore wide ranging and historically situated. He argues that there are two major influences on Rabelais' work: the peasant life, and the emergence of a new bourgeois class, the commercial and manufacturing class, rather than the merchant bourgeoisie of the medieval cities. Rather than solely emphasize the importance of scholasticism and the Council of Trent (1545–53) – that is, the realm of ideas – we should recognize the transitions in the economic base of society, from feudalism to the emerging capitalism.[297] *Gargantua and Pantagruel* is written at the beginning of a new society, with all the future expectation and explosion of new ideas, before the stagnation and disappointment set in.[298] There is still the ability for a balance between accumulation and play; the division of labour has not set in; intellectual labour is not separated from practical, manual labour, social life, life as a whole.[299] Equally, Rabelais' work does much to illuminate the birth of the national, the formative years (*jeunesse*) of France, emerging from the Hundred Years War and the national symbol of Joan of Arc.[300] Rabelais is also central to the affirmation of the French language as a break from Latin. Latin was the language of the clergy, of nobility; French was closer to the immediate and less capable of abstraction. But Lefebvre argues that before Calvin, and well before Montaigne and Descartes, among others, Rabelais elevated the French language to one of philosophical dignity, without losing its popular character.[301] Rabelais then may be seen, on a linguistic level at least, as the French Luther.[302]

Lefebvre notes, however, that 'Rabelais, as writer and mouthpiece of the newly emergent class, is also a *peasant* writer, and indeed the greatest of these'.[303] Rabelais admires their honest simplicity and earthy language, despite his own erudition: 'He was a man intoxicated by every sort of learning and theory, who had at the same time the earthy commonsense of a peasant'.[304] As Lefebvre somewhat exaggerates: 'Only one man of this epoch can be compared to Rabelais in the extent of his knowledge and the power of his genius: Leonardo da Vinci.'[305]

Accordingly, in his analysis of Rabelais, Lefebvre provides some important discussions of rural society, of sexual behaviour and festivities, and of food and drink. These are festivities marked by a freedom and a collective intoxication (*une 'ivresse' fusionelle*), with a licence to eat as much as possible, to drink to the point of drunkenness, and through this festival to realize the communion between the members of society and nature.[306] Lefebvre uses Rubens' painting *Kermesse* (The Village Fête) as an illustration of this Rabelaisian scene, which he describes as 'floods and eddies of human flesh, frenzy, drinking, couples intertwined with an animalistic fury'.[307] The peasant festival was orgiastic, and celebrated order through the momentary disorder created when the discipline of the community came undone.[308] The carnival atmosphere was inherent to everyday life. Through this analysis of peasant life, Lefebvre is able to illuminate how collective custom is in conflict with the emerging society of production and its individualizing of morality.[309] As he importantly notes:

> Let us not forget for a moment that *paganus*, peasant [*paysan*], signifies 'pagan' [*païen*]. This simple etymology corresponds to a major historical truth in France, upon which we cannot insist too much.
>
> It clarifies whole epochs and the ideologies of the centuries of resistance to Christianity in morals and habits, heretical speech and sorcery.[310]

Let us take one example – that of sex. Lefebvre argues that sex was not a question of individual morality, but something bound by collective custom. There was not a moral conflict between instinct and individual conscience, but there were customs and rituals that had to be followed. There was considerable freedom for women before marriage, but after marriage there was a strict control of fidelity, with serious sanctions for transgression. Not, Lefebvre argues, morality in the precise sense of the word, but customs and an organization of life on the collective and familial level that is different from our own.[311] Rabelais' writings are at the cusp of the transition to a new, individualistic morality, with the breakdown of the rural community and extended family, the transition to the city and the atomization of society. New prohibitions and necessities shape a new morality, which finds particular expression in the Council of Trent, and that clashes with the old peasant custom.[312] Rabelais should therefore be seen neither as 'vulgar [*grossier*], nor as "immoral" – above all not *immoral*[313] – rather as illustrating the limit case. In a certain sense, for Lefebvre, he is a 'great moralist . . . an inventor in morality, an inventor of morality'. But this is individualistic, bourgeois, morality – at least in its nascent state, before it became more puritan.[314]

Lefebvre traces how this interrelation of pagan and peasant works in Rabelais, by showing that the agrarian myths that he draws upon were integral to the culture of antiquity as well.[315] The giants were of peasant origin, 'resulting from the Carnival, the festivals and the agrarian rites, they represent the colossal wastage at the time of the village fairs [*kermesses*] and festivals [*frairies*], at the time of sowing, the harvests and the grape harvest'.[316] The giant was not a monster, but a larger human, everything taken to excess.[317] It is in this excess that we gain more insight into the life of humans at a more ordinary, everyday level. We therefore find a whole range of influences in Rabelais – from antiquity, the Middle Ages, and the Renaissance; from peasant life, the life of the emergent bourgeoisie, from France, the King's entourage, and the Church. The books of *Gargantua and Pantagruel*, read, on the one hand, like tales of chivalry. They trace the birth of the heroes, their education and childhood, and then their heroic exploits (*prouesses*). But on the other hand, like *Don Quixote*, they are parodies: 'they "liquidate" the Middle Ages through laughter'.[318] The comparison to Cervantes' work is useful because here too we find the mix of the real and fantastic, the love of the subject of parody, and the formalistic contours of the work parodied. Like Cervantes too, the parody is in some sense more excessive than that parodied. Of course, this does not mean that they are exactly the same. In Rabelais, 'the medieval heroes become *good giants*, the Hercules and the beneficial kings who rid the earth of its monsters, installing an era of peace and the wise'.[319] As Prescott notes, 'physically, marvels and monsters were concentrated at the margins of the medieval and early modern world, but culturally they were central to the European imagination'.[320]

Brief mention should be made of Lefebvre's own attempts at artistic expression. For example, he published a collection of three plays, included poems in a number of his books, most notably *La somme et le reste*, and did the artwork for some issues of journals with which he was involved.[321] In 1937 his then wife, Henriette Valet published a novel entitled *Le mauvais temps*, which, as Trebitsch notes, Lefebvre's correspondence to Guterman suggests that he had a role in writing.[322] I will not attempt to analyse these parts of his work, though it has to be said that they were not the most successful aspect. His plays, for example, have no named characters, and include critiques of Christianity, political farces and satire of everyday life. They seem to me to be rather dated and not to have anything like the power of Sartre's work, for example.[323]

There was something of a hidden agenda in Lefebvre's work on these writers. Despite the political exigencies, Lefebvre was able to write about historical materialism, the inception of capitalism and the emergent bourgeoisie, issues of historical context and determinism, and related matters. However, it is also clear that in this work he was able to pursue topics of interest that would be more fully developed in later work. One of the most striking examples is the work in the *Descartes* book on space, a theme that is also important in his book on Pignon. These links will be elaborated in Chapter 5.[324] In *Rabelais* the discussion of the country is important to Lefebvre's writings on everyday life, and his other works on rural sociology.[325] Equally, the notion of the *fête*, the festival, is deployed regularly in

Lefebvre's work: not just in the *Critique of Everyday Life* – with which the book on Rabelais shares a startling continuity – but also in the analyses of the Paris Commune and the events of May 1968. These themes will be discussed in Chapters 3 and 4.

Notes

1 See, for example Louis Soubise, *Le Marxisme après Marx (1956–1965) Quatre marxistes dissidents français*, Paris: Aubier Montaigne, 1967; Alfred Schmidt, 'Henri Lefebvre and contemporary interpretations of Marx', in Dick Howard and Karl E. Klare (eds), *The Unknown Dimension: European Marxism since Lenin*, New York, 1972, pp. 322–41; Mark Poster, *Existential Marxism in Postwar France: From Sartre to Althusser*, Princeton: Princeton University Press, 1975; Michael Kelly, *Modern French Marxism*, Oxford: Basil Blackwell, 1982; Tony Judt, *Marxism and the French Left: Studies in Labour and Politics in France, 1830–1981*, Oxford: Clarendon Press, 1986.
2 See, for example, 'Toward a Leftist Cultural Politics: Remarks Occasioned by the Centenary of Marx's Death', in Cary Nelson and Lawrence Grossberg (eds), *Marxism and the Interpretation of Culture*, London: Macmillan, 1988, pp. 75–88, p. 76.
3 Henri Lefebvre and Leszek Kolakowski, 'Evolution or revolution', in Fons Elders (ed.), *Reflexive Water: The Basic Concerns of Mankind*, London: Souvenir Press, 1974, pp. 201–67, p. 205.
4 *Hegel, Marx, Nietzsche ou le royaume des ombres*, Paris: Castermann, 1975, p. 18.
5 Henri Lefebvre and Catherine Régulier, *La révolution n'est plus ce qu'elle était*, Hallier: Éditions Libres, 1978, p. 200.
6 *De l'État*, Paris: UGE, 4 volumes, 1976–8, IV, p. 16.
7 *Le retour de la dialectique: 12 mots clefs*, Paris: Messidor/Éditions Sociales, 1986, p. 13. In *La présence et l'absence: contribution à la théorie des representations*, Paris: Casterman, 1980, p. 7, he notes that *The Gay Science, The Genealogy of Morals*, the *Grundrisse* and Hegel's *Phenomenology* are the major texts on his work table. See Bud Burkhard, *French Marxism Between the Wars: Henri Lefebvre and the 'Philosophies'*, Atlantic Highlands: Humanity Books, 2000, p. 233 n. 28.
8 G. W. F. Hegel, *Enzyklopädie de philosophischen Wissenschaften 1*, in *Werke: Theorie Werkausgabe*, Frankfurt: Suhrkamp Verlag, 1970, Bd. VIII; translated by William Wallace as *Hegel's Logic*, Oxford: Oxford University Press, 1975; and *Wissenschaft der Logik*, in *Werke*, Bd. V–VI; translated by A. V. Miller as *Hegel's Science of Logic*, London: Allen & Unwin, 1969. See *Pour connaître la pensée de Lénine*, Paris: Bordas, 1957, p. 202.
9 See, for example, *Métaphilosophie*, Paris: Éditions Syllepse, 2nd edition, 2001 (1965), p. 66; *La présence et l'absence*, pp. 128–9. The last of these references lists five reasons why Schelling has had a significant impact on modern philosophy, and particularly notes his impact on Engels. On this see also *Le retour de la dialectique*, p. 60. Guterman's papers reveal an abiding interest. As well as editing the English translation of Schelling's *On University Studies*, he planned a book on him, and filled several A5 notebooks with drafts and ideas. Guterman Archive, Box 8.
10 *Du rural à l'urbain*, Paris: Anthropos, 3rd edition, 2001 (1970), p. 7.
11 See also Eleonore Kofman and Elizabeth Lebas, 'Recovery and reappropriation in Lefebvre and Constant', in Jonathan Hughes and Simon Sadler (eds),

Non-Plan: Essays on Freedom Participation and Change in Modern Architecture and Urbanism, Oxford: Architectural Press, 2000, pp. 80–9.

12 See *Qu'est-ce que penser?* Paris: Publisad, 1985, pp. 61–2.

13 *Hegel, Marx, Nietzsche*, p. 146; see *De l'État* I, p. 233; *La présence et l'absence*, p. 151.

14 Rémi Hess, 'Henri Lefebvre "Philosophe" ', in *L'existentialisme*, Paris: Anthropos, 2nd edition, 2001 (1946), p. xvii.

15 Burkhard, *French Marxism Between the Wars*; Michel Trebitsch, 'Les mésaventures du groupe Philosophies, 1924–1933', *La revue des revues* 3, Spring 1987, pp. 6– 9; 'Le groupe "philosophies", de Max Jacob aux surrealists 1924–1925', *Le cahiers de l'IHTP* 6, November 1987, pp. 29–38; 'Le groupe *Philosophies* et les surrealists (1924–1925)', *Mélusine: Cahiers du centre de recherches sur le surréalisme* XI, 1990, pp. 63–75. A fictionalized account appears in Paul Nizan, *La conspiration*, Paris: Gallimard, 1938. See also 'A group of young philosophers: a conversation with Henri Lefebvre', in Bernard-Henri Lévy, *Adventures on the Freedom Road: The French Intellectuals in the Twentieth Century*, translated by Richard Veasy, London: Harvill, pp. 131–8; and the brief discussion in Pascal Ory and Jean-François Sirinelli, *Les intellectuels en France: de l'affaire Dreyfus à nos jours*, Paris: Armand Colin, 1992, p. 87. More generally on this period, see Robert S. Short, 'The politics of surrealism, 1920–36', *Journal of Contemporary History* 1(2), 1966, pp. 3–26.

16 *La somme et le reste*, Paris: Méridiens Klincksieck, 3rd edition, 1989 (1959), p. 248.

17 *La somme et le reste*, p. 392.

18 'A group of young philosophers', p. 134.

19 See, for example, 'Introduction: Le même et l'autre', in Friedrich Schelling, *Recherches philosophiques sur l'essence de la liberté humaine et sur les problèmes qui s'y rattachent*, translated by Georges Politzer, Paris: F. Rieder, 1926. See also the comments in 'Une tentative métaphysique: "La dialectique du monde sensible" de Louis Lavelle', *Philosophies* 3, September 1924, pp. 241–8.

20 *L'existentialisme*, p. 16. See (Pierre Morhange), 'Billet de John Brown où l'on donne le la', *Philosophies* 3, September 1924, pp. 249ff.

21 *L'existentialisme*, pp. 16–17 n. 2; *La somme et le reste*, p. 512; see Poster, *Existential Marxism in Post-war France*, p. 115. The pieces were 'Critique de la qualité et de l'être: fragments de la philosophie de la conscience', *Philosophies* 4, November 1924, pp. 241ff; 'Positions d'attaque et de defence du nouveau mysticisme', *Philosophies* 5/6, March 1925, pp. 471–506. Two later pieces, 'La pensée et l'esprit' *L'esprit* 1, May 1926, pp. 21–69; 'Notes pour le process de la chrétienté', *L'esprit* 2, January 1927, pp. 121–47, are also from this initial project.

22 *Qu'est-ce que penser?*, p. 168 n. 1. See Hess, 'Henri Lefebvre et le projet avorté du *Traité de matérialisme dialectique*', p. xvii.

23 'Introduction: Le même et l'autre', p. 1.

24 *La somme et le reste*, p. 420. The Schelling project is discussed at pp. 415–24; *Qu'est-ce que penser?*, p. 157.

25 *L'existentialisme*, p. 30.

26 *La somme et le reste*, p. 439.

27 *La somme et le reste*, p. 441. In 1959 he mentions a future work entitled *Crise de la philosophie*, but this too never appeared. See 'Avant-propos à la deuxième édition', in *Problèmes actuels du marxisme*, Paris: PUF, 2nd edition, 1960 (1958), p. viii.

28 *L'existentialisme*, p. 41; *Key Writings*, edited by Stuart Elden, Elizabeth Lebas and Eleonore Kofman, London: Continuum, 2003, p. 6.

29 *La somme et le reste*, p. 439.

30 See *La somme et le reste*, pp. 415–16. Burkhard, *French Marxism Between the Wars*, p. 61, notes that this was to be a multi-volume project.

31 *Le temps des méprises*, Paris: Stock, 1975, p. 198. See also *L'existentialisme*, p. 16. Here Lefebvre suggests this was a version of *Philosophie de la conscience*. See Hess, 'Henri Lefebvre et le projet avorté du *Traité de matérialisme dialectique*', p. vii; *La somme et le reste*, p. 372. However, elsewhere Lefebvre suggests it was on Pascal and Jansen. See 'Divertissement pascalien et aliénation humaine', in *Blaise Pascal: L'homme et l'oeuvre*, Paris: Les Éditions de Minuit, 1956, pp. 196–224, pp. 196–7.

32 Reported in Louis Althusser, *The Spectre of Hegel: Early Writings*, edited by François Matheron, translated by G. M. Goshgarian, London: Verso, 1997, p. 174.

33 See 'A group of young philosophers', pp. 133, 138. According to Michael S. Roth, *Knowing and History: Appropriations of Hegel in Twentieth Century France*, Ithaca: Cornell University Press, 1988, which lists the participants in Kojève's seminars in an appendix, Lefebvre was not among them. For the opposing view, see the brief comment by Terry Nichols Clark, *Prophets and Patrons: The French University and the Emergence of the Social Sciences*, Cambridge: Harvard University Press, 1973, p. 229; and on the lectures, H. Stuart Hughes, *The Obstructed Path: French Social Thought in the Years of Desperation 1930–1960*, New York: Harper & Row, 1968. The reading that is most akin to Kojève is found in *Marx 1818–1883*, Genève: Éditions des Trois Collines, 1947, pp. 19–26. Further complicating the intellectual heritage is the role Heidegger plays in the thought of these thinkers. As Althusser notes, *The Spectre of Hegel*, p. 171, 'without Heidegger, as Kojève says somewhere, we would never have understood the *Phenomenology of Spirit*'.

34 G. W. F. Hegel, *Morceaux choisis*, translated by Norbert Guterman and Henri Lefebvre, Paris: Gallimard, 1938.

35 *Cahiers de Lénine sur la dialectique de Hegel*, translated by Norbert Guterman and Henri Lefebvre, Paris: Gallimard, 2nd edition, 1967 (1939).

36 See especially 'La pensée et l'esprit'.

37 I therefore take issue with Maurice Blanchot's suggestion that Lefebvre was 'not at all Hegelian'. See *L'amitié*, Paris: Gallimard, 1971, p. 98.

38 See Althusser, 'The return to Hegel: the latest word in academic revisionism', *The Spectre of Hegel*, pp. 173–84; Lefebvre, 'Lettre sur Hegel', *La nouvelle critique* 22, January 1951, pp. 99–104.

39 Judith P. Butler, *Subjects of Desire: Hegelian Reflections in Twentieth-Century France*, New York: Columbia University Press, 1987; Roth, *Knowing and History*. That said, the only references to Lefebvre in Gary Gutting, *French Philosophy in the Twentieth Century*, Cambridge: Cambridge University Press, 2001, are as a translator of Hegel (p. 113 n. 52), and as influenced by the *1844 Manuscripts* (p. 235). Of course, many of those who discuss Lefebvre's Marxism discuss the influence of Hegel too. See especially, Poster, *Existential Marxism*; Kelly, *Modern French Marxism*, 1982; and Martin Jay, *Marxism and Totality: The Adventures of a Concept from Lukács to Habermas*, Berkeley: University of California Press, 1984. The best study of Lefebvre and Hegel is found in Bruce Baugh, *French Hegel: From Surrealism to Postmodernism*, London: Routledge, 2003.

40 On the book, and particularly on its reception at the time, see Burkhard, *French Marxism Between the Wars*, pp. 213–22.

41 See James Melvin Stewart, 'Henri Lefebvre and Marxist Revisionism in France 1928–1968', PhD thesis, Boulder: University of Colorado, 1985, p. 46. On the Front Populaire, see *Introduction à la modernité: Préludes*, Paris: Les Éditions de

Minuit, 1962, pp. 81–3; *Introduction to Modernity: Twelve Preludes*, translated by John Moore, London: Verso, 1995, pp. 74–6; Henri Lefebvre and Michel Trebitsch, 'Le renouveau philosophique avorté des annés trente: entretien avec Henri Lefebvre', *Europe: Revue littéraire mensuelle* 683, March 1986, pp. 29–41.

42 Russell Jacoby, *Dialectic of Defeat: Contours of Western Marxism*, Cambridge: Cambridge University Press, 1981, pp. 108–9. For a discussion of the influence of Lukács on Lefebvre's understanding of everyday life, see Chapter 3. It can also be seen as part of a larger movement toward Hegelian Marxism, found in works such as Karl Korsch, *Marxism and Philosophy*, translated by Fred Halliday, London: NLB, 1970 (1923).

43 This work, mentioned in correspondence, was to include a critique of Hitler.

44 Henri Lefebvre and Norbert Guterman, 'Individu et classe', *Avant-Poste* 1, June 1933, pp. 1–9, p. 6 n. 1.

45 'Citations pour l'Individu', 1938, 1 p., Guterman Archive, Box 1. The Archive (Box 8) also contains a book length manuscript by Guterman on 'The individual in the French novel', sometimes titled 'The myth of the individual as revealed by the French novel'.

46 Michel Trebitsch, 'Correspondance d'intellectuels: le cas de lettres d'Henri Lefebvre à Norbert Guterman (1935–47)', *Les cahiers de l'IHTP* 20, March 1992, pp. 70–84, p. 74; Burkhard, *French Marxism Between the Wars*, p. 213.

47 Trebitsch, 'Les mésaventures du groupe Philosophies', p. 8; Armand Ajzenberg, 'A propos d'un texte retrouvé: "La conscience privée" ', in Norbert Guterman and Henri Lefebvre, *La conscience mystifiée*, Paris: Éditions Syllepse, 3rd edition, 1999 (1936), p. 235. The best account of this is Burkhard, 'The *Revue Marxiste*', *French Marxism Between the Wars*, pp. 105–32. Guterman was later investigated by the FBI and claimed that he had never officially been a Communist, having 'joined' the Party only in a very loose sense in the late 1920s. He claims never to have had a membership card and that he was not a Communist in 1933, when he moved to the US. The FBI report is in the Guterman Archive, Box 10. See also Burkhard, *French Marxism Between the Wars*, pp. 238, 243 n. 11.

48 'La Conscience privée', in *La conscience mystifiée*. A sketch of ideas for this was sent in a letter from Lefebvre to Guterman around 1938; and a 22-page manuscript under the title 'La conscience privée: Esquisse d'une phénoménologie de l'individu' can be found in the Guterman Archive, Box 6. For a discussion, see 'Préface à la 2ᵉ réédition', in *La conscience mystifiée*, p. 19. Ajzenberg, 'A propos d'un texte retrouvé', p. 235, suggests that the third volume would have been titled *La conscience sociale*. A continuation of some of these themes, though with a much more political science bent, is found in Pierre Fougeyrollas, *La conscience politique dans la France contemporaine*, Paris: Denoël, 1963.

49 'Préface à la 2ᵉ réédition', p. 19; see *La somme et le reste*, p. 452.

50 René Lourau, 'Comment cela a-t-il été possible?', in Guterman and Lefebvre, *La conscience mystifiée*, pp. 12–18, p. 13. On the trips, see *Le temps des méprises*, p. 196; *La présence et l'absence*, p. 235.

51 'Préface à la 2ᵉ réédition', p. 19.

52 *Le nationalisme contre les nations*, Paris: Méridiens Klincksieck, 2ᵉ édition, 1988 (1937); *Hitler au pouvoir: Les enseignements de cinq années de fascisme en Allemagne*, Paris: Bureau d'Éditions, 1938; and Lefebvre and Guterman's comments in 'Introduction', *Cahiers de Lénine sur la dialectique de Hegel*, pp. 8–10. Earlier pieces by Lefebvre include 'Le fascisme en France', *Avant-Poste* 1, June 1933, pp. 68–71; and 'Mussolini: le fascisme', *Avant-Poste* 3, October–November 1933, pp. 201–2.

53 Norbert Guterman and Leo Lowenthal, *Prophets of Deceit: A Study of the Techniques of the American Agitator*, Palo Alto: Pacific Books, 2nd edition, 1970 (1949). The foreword to the second edition was written by Herbert Marcuse, the introduction is by Max Horkheimer. Guterman's correspondence shows that Theodor Adorno was also a correspondent. As a point of contact between the Frankfurt School and French Marxism, Guterman was of primary importance, working with the Institute of Social Research in exile until it moved back to Germany in 1950. Indeed, in a letter to Guterman, 25 February 1947, Lowenthal notes that Horkheimer was reading Lefebvre's work. On the Frankfurt School, see also Lefebvre and Régulier, *La révolution n'est plus ce qu'elle était*, p. 35.

54 *La conscience mystifiée*, p. 70. *Privé* has this dual sense in French. On this see also *Nietzsche*, Paris: Éditions Sociales Internationales, 1939, p. 108.

55 *La conscience mystifiée*, p. 146; *Key Writings*, p. 230.

56 Lefebvre and Guterman, 'Individu et classe', p. 4.

57 *La conscience mystifiée*, p. 152.

58 *La conscience mystifiée*, p. 163.

59 *La conscience mystifiée*, pp. 163–4.

60 Lefebvre and Guterman, 'Individu et classe'; 'La mystification: notes pour une critique de la vie quotidienne', *Avant-Poste* 2, August 1933, pp. 91–107; *Key Writings*, pp. 71–83. For a criticism of the first article, see 'Autocritique', *Avant-Poste* 2, August 1933, pp. 142–3.

61 'Préface à la 2ᵉ réédition', p. 21.

62 *La conscience mystifiée*, p. 90; *Key Writings*, p. 228.

63 *La conscience mystifiée*, p. 81; *Key Writings*, p. 220. See also *Hitler au pouvoir*, pp. 18–19.

64 *Le nationalisme contre les nations*, pp. 91–2. See N. J. G. Pounds, 'France and "les limites naturelles" from the seventeenth to twentieth centuries', *Annals, Association of American Geographers* 44, 1954, pp. 51–62.

65 Much later, see *Le langage et la société*, Paris: Gallimard, 1966, p. 29. This question of the relation between a nation and space is explored in *La production de l'espace*, Paris: Anthropos, 1974, p. 132; *The Production of Space*, translated by Donald Nicholson-Smith, Oxford: Blackwell, 1991, p. 111.

66 *Le nationalisme contre les nations*, p. 92.

67 *La conscience mystifiée*, pp. 90–1; *Key Writings*, p. 228. See *Le nationalisme contre les nations*, p. 28.

68 *La conscience mystifiée*, pp. 90–1; *Key Writings*, p. 228. See *Le Marxisme*, p. 12; *Le nationalisme contre les nations*, p. 38.

69 *Le nationalisme contre les nations*, p. 70. See also *Hitler au pouvoir*, which provides a close reading of *Mein Kampf*.

70 *Le nationalisme contre les nations*, p. 71. See 'Le fascisme en France'; and discussion of this topic in *Avant-Poste* 3, October–November 1933, including contributions from André Malraux and Alain.

71 There is a manuscript entitled 'Schèma sur l'irrationalisme français', c1936, 8 pp., in the Guterman Archive, Box 1.

72 *Le nationalisme contre les nations*, p. 157; see *La conscience mystifiée*, p. 89; *Key Writings*, p. 227.

73 *Le nationalisme contre les nations*, p. 149.

74 *Le nationalisme contre les nations*, p. 158

75 For example, *Le nationalisme contre les nations*, pp. 45, 92, 106. Ernst Renan, 'What is a Nation?' translated by Martin Thom, in Homi Bhabha (ed.), *Nation and Narration*, London: Routledge, 1990, pp. 8–22.

76 *La somme et le reste*, p. 492.

77 *La conscience mystifiée*, p. 189.

78 See 'La Conscience privée', in *La conscience mystifiée*, pp. 237–8.

79 *La somme et le reste*, pp. 556–8.

80 *La somme et le reste*, p. 558.

81 *De l'État*, III, p. 246.

82 *Allemagne*, photos et notices par Martin Hurlimann, Paris: Braun & Cie, 1964, p. 11.

83 See 'Classe et nation depuis le "Manifeste" (1848)', in *Au-delà du structuralisme*, Paris: Anthropos, 1971, pp. 221–40, especially pp. 230–1; and the 1988 'Postface', in *Le nationalisme contre les nations*.

84 On the transition between these two phases of his work, see 'Du culte de "l'esprit" au matérialisme dialectique', *La nouvelle revue française* 39(231), December 1932, pp. 802–5.

85 *Méthodologie des sciences: inédit*, Paris: Anthropos, 2002, pp. 140–1; *Introduction to Modernity*, pp. 168–232.

86 *Méthodologie des sciences*, pp. 153–60, although we should note that Nietzsche does receive a brief mention here.

87 *Hegel, Marx, Nietzsche*, p. 11; *Key Writings*, p. 44. See *La fin de l'histoire*, Paris: Les Éditions de Minuit, 1970, pp. 21–2. As well as these two books, they also play a key role in *La présence et l'absence*. See especially, pp. 235–6.

88 *Hegel, Marx, Nietzsche*, pp. 9–10; *Key Writings*, pp. 42–3.

89 *Hegel, Marx, Nietzsche*, pp. 11–12; *Key Writings*, p. 44.

90 *Hegel, Marx, Nietzsche*, p. 53. See *Allemagne*, p. 18, for a discussion of the affinity between French and German thought.

91 *Éléments de rythmanalyse: introduction à la connaissance de rythmes*, Paris: Éditions Syllepse, 1992, p. 62; *Rhythmanalysis: Space, Time and Everyday Life*, translated by Gerald Moore and Stuart Elden, London: Continuum, 2004, p. 44.

92 *Hegel, Marx, Nietzsche*, p. 7. The (unattributed) quotes from Hegel and Nietzsche are *Hegel's Science of Logic*, p. 58; and Friedrich Nietzsche, *Thus Spoke Zarathustra*, in *The Portable Nietzsche*, edited and translated by Walter Kaufmann, Harmondsworth: Penguin, 1954, p. 200. (I have been unable to trace the one from Marx.)

93 *Hegel, Marx, Nietzsche*, p. 59. Lefebvre may well be borrowing from Axelos, who talks of 'the constellation Hegel-Marx-Nietzsche-Freud-Heidegger' in 'Marx, Freud et les tâches de la pensée future', *Horizons du monde*, Paris: Éditions de Minuit, 1974, p. 93. This was an article originally published in *Diogène* 72, October–December 1970.

94 *La somme et le reste*, p. 476.

95 *Hegel, Marx, Nietzsche*, p. 147 n. 5. See p. 46 n. 16; *Key Writings*, p. 261 n. 3.

96 M.-P. Nicolas, *De Nietzsche à Hitler*, Paris: Fasquelle, 1936; translated by E. G. Echlin as *From Nietzsche Down to Hitler*, London: William Hodge, 1938. For a discussion of this text, see Douglas Smith, *Transvaluations: Nietzsche in France 1872–1972*, Oxford: Clarendon Press, 1996, pp. 75–7. Georges Bataille's *On Nietzsche*, translated by Bruce Boone, New York: Paragon House, 1992, was originally published in 1945, and makes brief reference to Lefebvre's book (p. 171 n.).

97 Martin Heidegger, *Nietzsche*, translated by David Farrell Krell, Frank Capuzzi and Joan Stambaugh, San Francisco: Harper Collins, 4 volumes, 1991.

98 Walter Kaufmann, *Nietzsche: Philosopher, Psychologist, Antichrist*. Princeton: Princeton University Press, 1950.

 99 *Hegel, Marx, Nietzsche*, p. 46 n. 16; *Key Writings*, p. 261 n. 3; *La somme et le reste*, pp. 422, 478.
100 *L'existentialisme*, p. 124.
101 *Hegel, Marx, Nietzsche*, p. 145.
102 *Nietzsche*, p. 164. See Pierre Drieu la Rochelle, 'Nietzsche contra Marx', in *Socialisme fasciste*, Paris: Gallimard, 1934, pp. 63–75. Drieu la Rochelle claims Nietzsche as an inspiration for antimarxism (p. 68), and a successor, that is a surpasser of Marx (p. 69). For a contrast between Drieu la Rochelle and Lefebvre, see Pierre Boudot, *Nietzsche et l'au-delà de la liberté: Nietzsche et les écrivans français de 1930 à 1960*, Paris: Aubier-Montaigne, 1970, pp. 87–105. On Lefebvre's reading more generally, see Louis Pinto, *Les neveux de Zarathoustra: La réception de Nietzsche en France*, Paris: Seuil, 1995, especially pp. 93–4, 99–102; Smith, *Transvaluations*; Kurt Meyer, *Henri Lefebvre: Ein Romantischer Revolutionär*, Wien: Europaverlag, 1973, pp. 32–6; and Jean Granier, *Le problème de la vérité dans la philosophie de Nietzsche*, Paris: Seuil, 1966.
103 *La somme et le reste*, p. 466.
104 *La somme et le reste*, p. 467.
105 *La somme et le reste*, p. 468.
106 *Hegel, Marx, Nietzsche*, p. 48; *Key Writings*, p. 46.
107 *La somme et le reste*, pp. 468, 477–8. On the death of God, see *Nietzsche*, pp. 76–9.
108 *Nietzsche*, pp. 162–5; see Burkhard, *French Marxism Between the Wars*, p. 226.
109 *Nietzsche*, pp. 71–2. On these tensions, see also p. 103.
110 *Nietzsche*, p. 164
111 *Hegel, Marx, Nietzsche*, p. 48; *Key Writings*, p. 46.
112 For useful discussions, see Andy Merrifield, 'Lefebvre, Anti-Logos and Nietzsche: An Alternative Reading of *The Production of Space*', *Antipode* 27(3), 1995, pp. 294–303; and Eleonore Kofman and Elizabeth Lebas, 'Lost in transposition – time, space and the city', in *Writings on Cities*, translated and edited by Eleonore Kofman and Elizabeth Lebas, Oxford: Blackwell, 1996, pp. 3–60.
113 *Hegel, Marx, Nietzsche*, pp. 180, 185.
114 *Qu'est-ce que penser?*, p. 144.
115 *De l'État*, III, p. 163.
116 *De l'État*, III, pp. 164–7, 8, 9.
117 *Le marxisme*, Paris: PUF, 1948, p. 109.
118 *L'existentialisme*, p. 131. See *Nietzsche*, p. 117.
119 *Hegel, Marx, Nietzsche*, pp. 187–8.
120 *Nietzsche*, p. 163.
121 *Hegel, Marx, Nietzsche*, pp. 187–8.
122 *Hegel, Marx, Nietzsche*, pp. 212–13. See *Le langage et la société*, p. 95; *Le temps des méprises*, pp. 129–30.
123 *Nietzsche*, pp. 135–49.
124 *La pensée marxiste et la ville*, Paris: Castermann, 1972, p. 136.
125 *Hegel, Marx, Nietzsche*, pp. 212–13.
126 *Le marxisme*, p. 13.
127 *Hegel, Marx, Nietzsche*, pp. 35, 213; *La fin de l'histoire*, pp. 214–15; *La présence et l'absence*, p. 95. As an illustration of the changing position, see *Marx 1818–1883*, Genève-Paris: Trois Collines, 1947, p. 152, when he suggests that the term *dépassement* is 'contaminated by mysticism and the irrational' because it also translates the Nietzschean term.
128 'Introduction', *Cahiers de Lénine sur la dialectique de Hegel*, p. 85.

129 *Hegel, Marx, Nietzsche*, p. 53; see *Nietzsche*, p. 22.

130 *Nietzsche*, pp. 163–4. See Drieu la Rochelle, 'Nietzsche contra Marx'.

131 Smith, *Transvaluations*, p. 82.

132 Trebitsch, 'Le renouveau philosophique avorté des annés trente', pp. 38–9.

133 *La production de l'espace*, p. 31; *The Production of Space*, pp. 22–3. This is discussed further in Chapter 5.

134 *La production de l'espace*, p. 460; *The Production of Space*, p. 400.

135 Kofman and Lebas, 'Lost in Transposition', p. 8.

136 David Harvey, *Justice, Nature and the Geography of Difference*, Oxford: Blackwell, 1996, p. 312.

137 Karl Marx, *Capital: A Critique of Political Economy*, I, translated by Ben Fowkes, Harmondsworth: Penguin, 1976, p. 103.

138 *Le temps des méprises*, p. 130.

139 *Une pensée devenue monde: faut-il abandonner Marx?* Paris: Fayard, 1980, p. 40.

140 *L'existentialisme*, p. 184 n. 1.

141 See, for example, Jean-Paul Sartre, *Critique de la raison dialectique précédé de Questions de méthode, Tome I: Théorie des ensembles pratiques*, Paris: Gallimard, 1960, p. 43; 'Sartre par Sartre', in *Situations, IX: Mélanges*, Paris: Gallimard, 1972, pp. 99–134; and Jean-Paul Sartre, Roger Garaudy, Jean Hyppolite, Jean-Pierre Vigier, J. Orcel, *Marxisme et existentialisme: controverse sur la dialectique*, Paris: Plon, 1962. In a 1969 interview Sartre declares that the tension between *Being and Nothingness* and the *Critique of Dialectical Reason* is 'of course, my relationship to Marxism'. Jean-Paul Sartre, 'Itinerary of a thought', *New Left Review* 58, November–December 1969, pp. 43–66.

142 George Lichtheim, *Marxism in Modern France*, New York and London: Columbia University Press, 1966.

143 Rémi Hess, *Henri Lefebvre et l'aventure du siècle*, Paris: A. M. Métailié, 1988, pp. 54–5, 188. See Hess, 'Henri Lefebvre: Philosophe', in *L'existentialisme*, p. xix.

144 Kostas Axelos, Jean Beaufret, François Châtelet and Henri Lefebvre, 'Karl Marx et Heidegger', in Kostas Axelos, *Argument d'une recherche*, Paris: Éditions de Minuit, 1969, p. 96. This discussion shows that Heidegger's Nazism was known to and discussed by European thinkers well before the recent Farías controversy. Above all it was discussed in the pages of *Les temps modernes* in the 1940s. See also Ralph Manheim to Guterman, 9 May 1957: 'Incidentally I don't see why he [Heidegger] is forgiven so easily for his Nazism. I understand forgiving musicians and chess players, but philosophers? Repulsive fellow anyway.' Manheim was at that time engaged in translating Heidegger's *Introduction to Metaphysics*, and, judging by the correspondence, Guterman had a large hand in the final version.

145 *L'existentialisme*, p. 161.

146 *Métaphilosophie*, p. 168.

147 *Qu'est-ce que penser?* p. 161

148 On the latter, see *La somme et le reste*, p. 552. The former is discussed in Chapter 6.

149 *L'existentialisme*, p. 175.

150 *L'existentialisme*, p. 175.

151 'Guignol' is a puppet, like the French equivalent of Punch. On the Grand Guignol theatre see Mel Gordon, *The Grand Guignol: Theatre of Fear and Terror*, New York: Da Capo Press, revised edition, 1997.

152 *L'existentialisme*, p. 179; see *La conscience mystifiée*, p. 143.

153 *L'existentialisme*, pp. 180–1.
154 *L'existentialisme*, p. 176.
155 *L'existentialisme*, p. 189.
156 *La somme et le reste*, p. 141.
157 *Métaphilosophie*, p. 126. A decade earlier Lefebvre had suggested that the twin dangers to materialist and dialectical thought were dogmatism and eclecticism. See 'Une discussion philosophique en U.R.S.S. Logique formelle et logique dialectique', *La pensée* 59, January–February 1955, pp. 5–20, pp. 5–6.
158 See, for example, *La conscience mystifiée*, pp. 58, 143, 179; *La fin de l'histoire*, pp. 153–4; *Hegel, Marx, Nietzsche*, pp. 51–2; *Key Writings*, p. 49; *La présence et l'absence*, p. 239; *L'existentialisme*, pp. 175–6; *Le langage et la société*, p. 33 n. 1.
159 *Hegel, Marx, Nietzsche*, pp. 51–2; *Key Writings*, p. 49. This hints at the development Lefebvre thinks Heidegger can bring to Marx. Lefebvre suggests that 'through social practice, man appropriates nature' is an elementary thesis of Marxism. See 'Avant-propos de la 2ᵉ édition', *Critique de la vie quotidienne I: Introduction*, Paris: L'Arche, 2nd edition, 1958 (1947), p. 107; 'Foreword to the second edition', *Critique of Everyday Life Volume I: Introduction*, translated by John Moore, London: Verso, 1991, p. 96.
160 *Métaphilosophie*, p. 136; see *La présence et l'absence*, p. 239.
161 *La présence et l'absence*, p. 239; see pp. 16–17 for a more general critique on this basis.
162 *La somme et le reste*, p. 140.
163 *Métaphilosophie*, p. 133.
164 *Métaphilosophie*, p. 133.
165 *La somme et le reste*, p. 697.
166 *L'existentialisme*, pp. 175–6.
167 *Logique formelle, logique dialectique*, Paris: Anthropos, 2nd edition, 1969 (1947), pp. 139–40.
168 See *Qu'est-ce que penser?* pp. 7–9. See *Le retour de la dialectique*, p. 154, where he suggests the question is not so much what thinking is, but what remains to be thought. Heidegger's work is *Was heißt Denken?* Tübingen: Max Niemeyer, 1954, translated by J. Glenn Grey as *What is Called Thinking?* New York: Harper & Row, 1968.
169 Interview, February 1988, cited in Hess, *Henri Lefebvre*, p. 54.
170 Axelos, Beaufret, Châtelet and Lefebvre, 'Karl Marx et Heidegger'. For a discussion, see Dominique Janicaud, *Heidegger en France*, Paris: Albin Michel, 2 volumes, 2001, I, pp. 173, 178.
171 On the last, see also *Métaphilosophie*, p. 91; and 'Justice et vérité', *Arguments* 15, 1959, pp. 13–19. The article was preceded by a translation of Heidegger's essay, 'Le mot de Nietzsche "Dieu est mort" ', pp. 2–13. Lefebvre was also reading Heidegger's *Vorträge und Aufsätze*, Pfullingen: Günther Neske, 1954; *Essais et Conférences*, translated by André Preau, Paris: Gallimard, 1958; and his book on Nietzsche, which is cited in *Le langage et la société*, p. 146.
172 Axelos, Beaufret, Châtelet and Lefebvre, 'Karl Marx et Heidegger', p. 93.
173 Axelos, Beaufret, Châtelet and Lefebvre, 'Karl Marx et Heidegger', p. 96.
174 Axelos, Beaufret, Châtelet and Lefebvre, 'Karl Marx et Heidegger', pp. 98–9.
175 Sartre, *Critique de la raison dialectique*, p. 26 n; *Search for a Method*, translated by Hazel E. Barnes, New York: Vintage, 1963, p. 15 n. 9.
176 Sartre, *Critique de la raison dialectique*, p. 42; *Search for a Method*, p. 38.
177 J. G. Merquior, *Western Marxism*, London: Paladin, 1986, pp. 145–6. Axelos is

discussed below. Of Fougeyrollas' work, see above all *Le Marxisme en question*, Paris: Seuil, 1959. On this question more generally, see Janicaud, *Heidegger en France*.

178 See Eric Haviland, *Kostas Axelos: Une vie pensée, une pensée vécue*, Paris: L'Harmattan, 1995, pp. 68–74; Michel Trebitsch, 'Preface: the moment of radical critique', in *Critique of Everyday Life Volume II: Foundations for a Sociology of the Everyday*, translated by John Moore, London: Verso, 2002, pp. ix–xxix, pp. xvi–xvii.

179 See Haviland, *Kostas Axelos*, pp. 77–8.

180 Georg Lukács, *Histoire et connaissance de classe: essais de dialectique marxiste*, translated by Kostas Axelos and Jacqueline Bois, Paris: Éditions de Minuit, 1960; Martin Heidegger, 'Qu'est-ce que la philosophie?', translated by Kostas Axelos in *Questions I et II*, Paris: Gallimard, 1968.

181 *Qu'est-ce que penser?* pp. 167–8. See also *Introduction à la modernité*, p. 146; *Introduction to Modernity*, p. 392 n. 8. Lefebvre wrote a couple of reviews of Axelos' work: of *Marx penseur de la technique* in 'Marxisme et technique', *Esprit* 307, June 1962, pp. 1023–8; and 'Kostas Axelos: *Vers la pensée planétaire: le devenir-pensée du monde et le devenir-homme* [sic] *de la pensée* (Ed. de Minuit)', *Esprit* 338, May 1965, pp. 1114–17. He also collaborated with Pierre Fougeyrollas on a brief book, *Le jeu de Kostas Axelos*, Paris: Fata Morgana, 1973.

182 Rémi Hess, 'Henri Lefebvre et le projet avorté du *Traité de matérialisme dialectique*', in *Méthodologie des sciences* p. xiii n. 1.

183 Kostas Axelos, *Marx penseur de la technique: de l'aliénation de l'homme à la conquête du monde*, Paris: Éditions de Minuit, 2 volumes, 1974 (1961); translated by Ronald Bruzina as *Alienation, Praxis and Techne in the Thought of Karl Marx*, Austin: University of Texas Press, 1976. See 'Marxisme et technique', p. 1024.

184 See Ernst Mandel, 'Introduction', in Marx, *Capital*, I, pp. 11–86, p. 37.

185 Karl Marx, *The Poverty of Philosophy*, New York: International Publishers, 1963, p. 109.

186 Direct references to Heidegger are found mainly in the footnotes, but there are plenty of allusions here, and elsewhere in Axelos' writings. See particularly, *Einführung in ein Künftige denken: Über Marx und Heidegger*, Tübingen: Max Niemeyer, 1966. We should perhaps also note that the English translation of *Marx penseur de la technique* omits the 'Bibliographical itinerary' of the original, which mentions several of Heidegger's works. See volume II, p. 307.

187 *La survie du capitalisme: La re-production des rapports de production*, Paris: Anthropos, 2nd edition, 2002 (1973), p. 67; *The Survival of Capitalism*, translated by Frank Bryant, London: Allison & Busby, 1976, p. 71. See also *Une pensée devenue monde*, pp. 40–1, 55–9; *La présence et l'absence*, p. 52, and Axelos, *Le jeu du monde*, Paris: Les Éditions de Minuit, 1969.

188 Poster, *Existential Marxism in Post-war France*, p. 222. See Axelos, *Marx penseur de la technique*, I, p. 13, II, pp. 120–1; *Alienation, Praxis and Techne*, pp. 7, 246.

189 For the acknowledgement of Marx, see *What is Philosophy?/Was ist das – die Philosophie?* English-German edition, translated by William Kluback and Jean T. Wilde, London: Vision Press, 1963, p. 89; 'Letter on humanism', in *Pathmarks*, edited by William McNeill, Cambridge: Cambridge University Press, 1998, pp. 258–9. Heidegger's treatment of Nietzsche in this regard is found in *Nietzsche*, IV; *The End of Philosophy*, translated by Joan Stambaugh, London: Souvenir Press, 1975. We should not underestimate the importance of French thought on Heidegger's belated dealing with Marx – Jean Beaufret was the

recipient of the 'Letter on humanism', and had written on the relation between Marx and existentialism (see, for example, 'A propos de l'existentialisme III. Conclusion: existentialisme et marxisme', *Confluences* 7, September 1945, pp. 764–71, the sixth and final article of a series), and 'What is philosophy?' was delivered in Cerisy-la-Salle, Normandy to an audience that included Beaufret, Axelos and Jacques Lacan.

190 Axelos, *Marx penseur de la technique* II, p. 270; *Alienation, Praxis and Techne*, p. 331.

191 Axelos, *Marx penseur de la technique* II, pp. 120–1; *Alienation, Praxis and Techne*, p. 246.

192 Axelos, *Marx penseur de la technique* I, p. 13; *Alienation, Praxis and Techne*, p. 7.

193 *Rheinische Zeitung*, 14 July 1842, in *Karl Marx: Selected Writings*, edited by David McLellan, Oxford University Press, 1977, p. 19.

194 Kostas Axelos, *Héraclite et la philosophie: La première saisie de l'être en devenir de la totalité*, Paris: Éditions de Minuit, 1962. For a similar agenda, by another member of the *Arguments* group, see François Châtelet, *Logos et praxis: recherches sur la signification théorique du Marxisme*, Paris: Société d'Édition d'Enseignement Supérieur, 1962.

195 Axelos, *Argument d'une recherche*, pp. 13, 40.

196 'Au-delà du savoir', in *Le jeu de Kostas Axelos*, p. 32.

197 *Qu'est-ce que penser?* p. 13; see 'Au-delà du savoir', pp. 24–6.

198 'Interview – Débat sur le marxisme: Léninisme-stalinisme ou autogestion?', *Autogestion et socialisme* 33/34, 1976, pp. 115–26, p. 125.

199 'Marxisme et technique', p. 1028.

200 *Une pensée devenue monde*, p. 59.

201 *Qu'est-ce que penser?* p. 13.

202 See also *Critique de la vie quotidienne III: de la modernité au modernisme (Pour une métaphilosophie du quotidienne)*; Qu'est-ce *que penser?* pp. 7–9.

203 *Qu'est-ce que penser?* p. 20

204 *Hegel, Marx, Nietzsche*, pp. 51–2; *Key Writings*, p. 49. See also *Le langage et la société*, pp. 143–4.

205 Poster, *Existential Marxism in Post-war France*, p. 257. See also p. 240, where he notes Nietzsche and Heidegger beyond Sartre, and recognizes the influence of Axelos and Châtelet. See *Métaphilosophie*, p. 295 n. 1.

206 Poster, *Existential Marxism in Post-war France*, p. 222; see Arthur Hirsch, *The French Left*, Montreal: Black Rose Books, 1982, pp. 91–2.

207 See *Qu'est-ce que penser?* p. 20, which also mentions Hegel.

208 See, for example, *Métaphilosophie*, p. 79.

209 *La présence et l'absence*, p. 90.

210 *Le retour de la dialectique*, pp. 81–2; *La présence et l'absence*, p. 90.

211 *Qu'est-ce que penser?* p. 47.

212 *Le retour de la dialectique*, pp. 81–2; *Qu'est-ce que penser?* p. 21; *La révolution n'est plus ce qu'elle était*, p. 35.

213 See Georges Labica, '*Marxisme et poésie*', in *Métaphilosophie*, pp. 5–21, p. 7.

214 *Hegel, Marx, Nietzsche*, p. 177. See *Le temps des méprises*, p. 130.

215 Lefebvre and Kolakowski, 'Evolution or revolution', pp. 202–3.

216 *Descartes*, Paris: Éditions Hier et Aujourd'hui, 1947, pp. 45–6; see *La conscience mystifiée*, pp. 60–1.

217 *La somme et le reste*, p. 506. The notion of metaphilosophy is also called for in *Critique de la vie quotidienne*, II, p. 257; *Critique of Everyday Life*, II, p. 255.

218 *La présence et l'absence*, p. 93.

219 Merquior, *Western Marxism*, p. 145. A discussion is found in Pierre Lantz, 'La poièsis de la praxis: Henri Lefebvre', *L'homme et la société* 104, 1992, pp. 111–20; and for the links to Heidegger see Ulrich Müller-Schöll, *Das System und der Rest: Kritische Theorie in der Perspektive Henri Lefebvres*, Mössingen-Talheim, 1999, pp. 233–9. For a similar attempt to Lefebvre, largely concerning *logos*, but with some reference to *poiesis*, see Châtelet, *Logos et praxis*.
220 *Métaphilosophie*, p. 23; *Key Writings*, p. 22.
221 *Métaphilosophie*, p. 106.
222 *Métaphilosophie*, p. 28; *Key Writings*, p. 27.
223 See *Pyrénées*, Pau: Cairn, 2nd edition, 2000 (1965), p. 26; *Métaphilosophie*, p. 40.
224 *Métaphilosophie*, p. 126.
225 *Métaphilosophie*, p. 78. Of course, given the much wider range of Heidegger's researches now published we can see that he did indeed do much of that work.
226 *Métaphilosophie*, p. 79.
227 This is mentioned in numerous places, for example, *Au-delà du structuralisme*, p. 266 n. 6; 'Au-delà du savoir', pp. 22–3; *Qu'est-ce que penser?* p. 8. See also Poster, *Existential Marxism in Post-war France*, p. 240. Heidegger's discussion is in *The Principle of Reason*, translated by Reginald Lilly, Bloomington: Indiana University Press, 1991; Axelos' in *Problèmes de l'enjeu*, Paris: Minuit, 1979, and *Arguments d'une recherche*, pp. 195–9. On Heraclitus more generally, see *Qu'est-ce que penser?* p. 23.
228 Karl Marx, *Writings of the Young Marx on Philosophy and Society*, edited by Loyd D. Easton and Kurt H. Guddat, New York: Doubleday, 1967, p. 62.
229 In Lefebvre, see *Marx*, Paris: PUF, 1964, p. 55; *Métaphilosophie*, p. 33; 'Avant-propos [1961]', *Le matérialisme dialectique*, Paris: PUF, 6th edition, 1970 (1939), p. 10; 'Foreword to the fifth edition', *Dialectical Materialism*, translated by John Sturrock, London: Jonathan Cape, 1968, p. 17. In Axelos, it might serve as a motto for his entire work. See, for example, *Marx penseur de la technique*, I, p. 5, II, pp. 50, 162; *Alienation, Praxis and Techne*, pp. v, 202, 271.
230 Poster, *Existential Marxism in Post-war France*, p. 221. On this period of Marx's work, see 'Les rapports de la philosophie et de la politique dans les premières oeuvres de Marx (1842–1843)', *Revue de métaphysique et de morale* 63 (2–3), April–September 1958, pp. 299–324.
231 'Avant-propos', *Le matérialisme dialectique*, p. 10; 'Foreword to the fifth edition', *Dialectical Materialism*, p. 17.
232 See, particularly, *Critique de la vie quotidienne III; La production de l'espace*, p. 466; *The Production of Space*, p. 405.
233 *Métaphilosophie*, pp. 36, 39.
234 Labica, 'Marxisme et poésie', p. 7.
235 *Descartes*, Paris: Éditions Hier et Aujourd'hui, 1947; *Pascal* Vol. 1, Paris: Nagel, 1949; *Pascal* Vol. 2, Paris: Nagel, 1954; *Diderot ou les affirmations fondamentales du matérialisme*, Paris: L'Arche, 2nd edition, 1983 (1949); *Rabelais*, Paris: Anthropos, 2nd edition, 2001 (1955); *Alfred de Musset: Dramaturge*, Paris: L'Arche, 2nd edition, 1970 (1955); *Pignon*, Paris: Édition Falaise, 1956.
236 *Contribution à l'esthétique*, Paris: Anthropos, 2nd edition, 2001 (1953).
237 The epigraph appears in Lefebvre, *Contribution à l'esthétique*. It had previously appeared – without the attribution – in *Critique de la vie quotidienne* I, p. 186; *Critique of Everyday Life* I, p. 174. The discussion is found in *La somme et le reste*, pp. 536–9.
238 The second epigraph comes from A. A. Zhdanov, *On Literature, Music and*

Philosophy, London: Lawrence & Wishart, 1950, p. 72. On the use of these epigraphs, and the book more generally, see Hess, *Henri Lefebvre et l'aventure du siècle*, pp. 127–9; and 'Henri Lefebvre et l'activité créatrice', in *Contribution à l'esthétique*.

239 Poster, *Existential Marxism*, p. 38.

240 Poster, *Existential Marxism*, p. 238.

241 See, for example, *Rabelais*, pp. 25, 34, 196, 203. On the use of Stalin, and whether a single reference makes someone a Stalinist, see *La somme et le reste*, pp. 496–7.

242 Though see *Rabelais*, p. 130 where he suggests the book was charged 'not as subversive or heretical, but as obscene'. See *Méthodologie des sciences*, p. 24.

243 We should also note that in *Pour connaître la pensée de Karl Marx*, Paris: Bordas, 1947, p. 9, he discusses the way in which Marx's thought has been 'persecuted'; and that in the preface to *Morceaux choisis de Karl Marx*, he and Guterman discuss the contemporary opposition to Marx within Germany.

244 *La somme et le reste*, p. 538.

245 See *Contribution à l'esthétique*, p. 5.

246 See *La somme et le reste*, pp. 535–6.

247 Rob Shields, *Lefebvre, Love and Struggle: Spatial Dialectics*, London: Routledge, 1999, p. 84.

248 Frederic Jameson, *Marxism and Form: Twentieth-Century Dialectical Theories of Literature*, Princeton: Princeton University Press, 1971, pp. 377–8.

249 Hess, *Henri Lefebvre*, pp. 141–51.

250 *Descartes*, p. 13.

251 *Diderot ou les affirmations*, p. 9.

252 *Descartes*, p. 13.

253 *Descartes*, p. 14.

254 *La fin de l'histoire*, p. 151.

255 *Pascal*, I, pp. 8–9; see *Diderot ou les affirmations*, pp. 9–10. This is the point stressed by Jameson, *Marxism and Form*, pp. 377–8. We find something similar, though not so lengthy as these other studies, in *Nietzsche*, pp. 9–28.

256 *Pascal*, I, pp. 11–26.

257 *Pascal*, I, p. 116. The *Fronde* – literally 'the revolt' – was the period 1648–53, characterized by a range of protests during the rule of Louis XIV, from the court, nobles and the people.

258 A. Lanavère (ed.), *Pascal*, Paris: Firmin-Didot Étude/Librairie Marcel Didier, 1969, p. 154.

259 See *Rabelais*, pp. 33–115; *Descartes*, pp. 49–98; *Pascal*, I, pp. 8–150; *Diderot ou les affirmations*, pp. 9–55. Although it situates his work in the context of the time, *Alfred de Musset* does not quite treat the nineteenth century in the same way.

260 *Descartes*, pp. 16–17.

261 *Descartes*, p. 235.

262 *Descartes*, p. 235.

263 *Descartes*, p. 293.

264 *Pascal*, II, pp. 7–8. It is not entirely surprising that Lukács recognized Lefebvre's work. He too was operating under political constraints, and his work on Balzac and Goethe – written around the same time as these works of Lefebvre's – showed similar aims. For a longer discussion of Lukács, see *La somme et le reste*, pp. 559–62, 571; *Lukács* 1955, with Patrick Tort, *Être marxiste aujourd'hui*, Paris:

Aubier, 1986. See also the response to Lefebvre contained in Lukács' student Lucien Goldmann's book, *Le dieu caché: étude sur la vision tragique dans les Pensées de Pascal et dans le théâtre de Racine*, Paris: Gallimard, 1955; and their discussion in *Blaise Pascal: L'homme et l'oeuvre*, Paris: Les Éditions de Minuit, 1956, pp. 204–24. See also Henri Lefebvre and Lucien Goldmann, 'Pascal et l'ordre des *Pensées*', in Lanavère (ed.), *Pascal*, 1969, pp. 154–73.

265 *Pascal* II, p. 9; see *Descartes*, pp. 235–6.
266 *Descartes*, p. 16; see *La somme et le reste*, p. 504.
267 'Le marxisme et la pensée française', *Les temps modernes* 137–138, 1957, pp. 104–37, p. 118; *La somme et le reste*, pp. 505–6.
268 *Descartes*, p. 244.
269 *Descartes*, p. 29.
270 *Descartes*, pp. 37–9.
271 *Descartes*, pp. 36–7.
272 *Descartes*, p. 37.
273 *La conscience mystifiée*, p. 43.
274 Étienne Gilson, *Etudes sur le role de la pensée médiévale dans la formation du système cartésian*, Paris: J. Vrin, 1951. Lefebvre also cites Henri Gouhier, *La pensée religieuse de Descartes*, Paris: J. Vrin, 1924; and Jean Laporte, *Le rationalisme de Descartes*, Paris: Presses Universitaires de France, 1945.
275 Lefebvre cites Cécile Angrand, *Cours de l'Université Nouvelle*; Maxime Leroy, *Descartes: Le philosophe au masque*, Paris: F. Rieder, 2 volumes, 1929; and Gaston Milhaud, *Descartes Savant*, Paris: Félix Alcan, 1921. (I have been unable to trace the reference to Angrand's work. According to Hess, *Henri Lefebvre*, p. 142, it was an internal Party publication.)
276 *Descartes*, p. 181.
277 *Descartes*, p. 18.
278 *Descartes*, p. 303.
279 See Jean Paris, *Rabelais au futur*, Paris: Éditions du Seuil, 1979.
280 Mikhail Bakhtin, *Rabelais and His World*, translated by Helen Iswolsky, Bloomington: Indiana University Press, 1984 (1968). For a discussion see Richard M. Berrong, *Rabelais and Bakhtin: Popular Culture in Gargantua and Pantagruel*, Lincoln: University of Nebraska Press, 1986.
281 Christine Delory-Momberger, 'Avant-propos: La littérature au risqué du matérialisme historique . . . et à la lumière de Henri Lefebvre', in *Rabelais*, p. xxv.
282 For the former, see Abel Lefranc, *Rabelais: Études sur Gargantua, Pantagruel, le Tiers Livre*, Paris: Albin Michel, 1953; for the latter, Lucien Febvre, *Le problème de l'incroyance au XVIᵉ siècle: La religion de Rabelais*, Paris: Albin Michel, 1968 (1942); translated by Beatrice Gottlieb as *The Problem of Unbelief in the Sixteenth Century: The Religion of Rabelais*, Cambridge: Harvard University Press, 1982. See *Rabelais*, pp. 3–4.
283 *Rabelais*, p. 3.
284 *Rabelais*, p. 2.
285 *Rabelais*, p. 19.
286 *Rabelais*, p. 101.
287 Lefebvre outlines this plan in *Rabelais*, p. 31; and puts it into practice in the rest of the book.
288 *Rabelais*, p. 115; see p. 213.
289 *Rabelais*, pp. 31–2.
290 *Rabelais*, p. 2.

291 J. M. Cohen, 'Translator's introduction', in François Rabelais, *The Histories of Gargantua and Pantagruel*, Harmondsworth: Penguin, 1955, pp. 17–31, p. 17. I have used this text for a translation, and François Rabelais, *Oeuvres Complètes*, edited by Jacques Boulenger and Lucien Scheler, Paris: Pléiade, 1955, for the original French. It is now cited as *Gargantua and Pantagruel*, followed by book and chapter number, in roman numerals.

292 *Rabelais*, p. 28.

293 *Rabelais*, p. 63.

294 See *Gargantua and Pantagruel* II, Prologue. On the *Croniques* see *Rabelais*, p. 129; Michael J. Heath, *Rabelais*, Tempe: Medieval and Renaissance Texts and Studies, 1996, p. 16; Anne Lake Prescott, *Imagining Rabelais in Renaissance England*, New Haven: Yale University Press, 1998, pp. 13–15.

295 For an extensive treatment of the references within Rabelais, see M. A. Screech, *Rabelais*, London: Duckworth, 1979; for the coarser side, see Carol Clark, *The Vulgar Rabelais*, Glasgow: Pressgang, 1983; and Prescott, *Imagining Rabelais*, Chapter 3.

296 *Rabelais*, p. 214.

297 *Rabelais*, p. 34; see pp. 33–5; 71–115. Lefebvre cites Étienne Gilson as an example of the rejected approach.

298 See, for example, *Rabelais*, pp. 10, 24, 26, 92.

299 *Rabelais*, p. 24.

300 *Rabelais*, p. 25.

301 *Rabelais*, pp. 25–6, 124. For a critique of the abstraction of Latinate influence on French, see *Gargantua and Pantagruel* II, vi.

302 *Rabelais*, p. 209. As Lefebvre partly acknowledges, they were of course very different in numerous other ways such as on religion and Luther's polemical attitude to the peasantry. On the religious links between Rabelais and Luther, see Febvre, *Le problème de l'incroyance au XVIe siècle*. For more on the background, see John Hale, *The Civilisation of Europe in the Renaissance*, New York: Touchstone, 1993.

303 *Rabelais*, p. 27.

304 Cohen, 'Translator's Introduction', p. 17.

305 *Rabelais*, p. 79.

306 *Rabelais*, p. 58.

307 *Rabelais*, pp. 58–9; see *Gargantua and Pantagruel* I, iv–v.

308 *Rabelais*, p. 58.

309 *Rabelais*, for example pp. 42–3; 58–9; etc.

310 *Rabelais*, p. 27.

311 *Rabelais*, p. 43.

312 *Rabelais*, pp. 43–4, 159.

313 *Rabelais*, p. 43.

314 *Rabelais*, p. 188.

315 *Rabelais*, p. 27.

316 *Rabelais*, p. 28; see pp. 67–8.

317 *Rabelais*, p. 59.

318 *Rabelais*, p. 13, see p. 192; and Colette Audry, Jacques Nantet and Claude Roy, with Henri Lefebvre, *Le romantisme révolutionnaire*, Cercle Ouvert: Confrontations, Paris: La Nef de Paris, 1958, p. 8.

319 *Rabelais*, pp. 13–14; see p. 29.

320 Prescott, *Imagining Rabelais*, p. 161.

321 See *Trois textes pour le théâtre*, Paris: Anthropos, 1972; and 'Le Don Juan du Nord:
     Pièce en 3 actes', *Europe: Revue mensuelle* 28, April 1948, pp. 73–104; *La somme et
     le reste; M, mensuel, marxisme, mouvement* 2, June 1986. On the last, see Elizabeth
     Lebas, 'Politics: introduction', in *Key Writings*, pp. 218–19.
322 Henriette Valet, *Le mauvais temps*, Paris: Grasset, 1937. See Trebitsch, 'Cor-
     respondance d'intellectuels', p. 74, which references this book as *Le temps des
     méprises*. As this is Lefebvre's own 1975 book it is presumably a mistake. See also
     Shields, *Lefebvre, Love and Struggle*, pp. 19–20, 97. This work is mentioned in
     numerous letters from Lefebvre to Guterman, although it seems that *Mauvais
     temps* was also the title of a planned journal, and it is not always clear which is
     meant. Lefebvre had reviewed Valet's earlier novel, '*Madame 60 Bis*, par Henri-
     ette Valet (Grasset)', *La nouvelle revue française* 43(255), December 1934, pp. 921–
     3. They married in September 1936.
323 Lefebvre is pretty critical of Sartre's literary output, although he thinks that *No
     Exit* (Huis Clos) is his best play. See, for example, *Critique de la vie quotidienne*, I,
     p. 251; *Critique of Everyday Life*, I, p. 236; 'Avant-propos de la 2ᵉ édition', p. 44;
     'Foreword to the second edition', p. 262 n. 56.
324 See *Descartes*, pp. 144–7, 187–243; *Pignon*.
325 Lefebvre makes this link explicit in *La somme et le reste*, p. 551.

3   The critique of everyday life

Lefebvre himself thought his work on everyday life was his principal contribution to Marxism,[1] and his work in this area has been widely used, if not
always explicitly recognized. Indeed, the notion of everyday life is immanent to almost all of his work. As discussed in Chapter 1, Lefebvre was
indebted to Marx's reworking of the Hegelian conception of alienation,
particularly as found in the *1844 Manuscripts*. However, as Marx notes:

> Political economy does not deal with [the worker] in his free time, as a human
> being, but leaves this aspect to the criminal law, doctors, religion, statistical tables,
> politics and the workhouse beadle.[2]

In much of Marx's writings, therefore, it appears that alienation is something that pertains to the economic sphere. But this is not necessarily the
case, and in places Marx shows that alienation is something that can be
found in a far wider range of areas. As Lenin says, quoted by Lefebvre in the
'Foreword to the second edition' of the first volume of the *Critique of Everyday
Life*, though *Capital* is a book by a 'German Economist' it shows the 'whole
capitalist formation to the reader as a living thing – with its everyday
aspects'.[3] With some recognition of the contradiction Lefebvre argues both
that '*Marxism as a whole, really is a critical knowledge of everyday life*',[4] and that it
does not *already* 'offer a complete critical knowledge of everyday life'.[5] The
'everyday' as such may not have appeared in Marx, but his work offers us
potential for analysis.[6] Building on and going beyond this, Lefebvre provides
a detailed reading of how capitalism had increased its scope in the twentieth
century to dominate the cultural and social world as well as the economic.
In this he draws upon many of the ideas that he and Guterman had
elaborated in early essays and *La conscience mystifiée*.[7]

> 'Alienation' – I know it is there in the love song I sing or the poem I recite, in the
> banknote I handle or the shop I enter, in the poster I glance at or in the lines of
> this journal. At the very moment the human is defined as 'having possessions' I
> know it is there, dispossessing the human.[8]

As Lefebvre points out, 'workers do not only have a life in the workplace, they have a social life, family life, political life; they have experiences outside the domain of labour'.[9] The critique of everyday life must analyse the things that make us social and human beings,[10] it must look at work and leisure together, for there is 'alienation in leisure just as in work'.[11] As Trebitsch phrases it, 'alienation thus leads to the impoverishment, to the "despoliation" of everyday life'.[12] Culture has become a commodity: 'everything is for sale'.[13] Lefebvre is not intending to be critical of how Marx viewed alienation under capitalism, but that his own analyses focused on a particular aspect, and that things have developed since the time Marx was writing. The capitalist mode of production established itself in industry, and integrated industry. Then, 'it integrated agriculture, it integrated the historical city, it integrated space, and it produced what I call la vie quotidienne'.[14] In this we see how a philosophical concept, transformed through a Marxist materialist reading, can allow us access into questions of rural and urban life and the question of space. Without the understanding of everyday life our grasp of each of those aspects of Lefebvre's work is insufficient. Alienation can be economic, social, political, ideological and philosophical.[15] As Chapter 1 indicated, alienation goes beyond the economic, with everyday life the terrain of struggle, just as production is broader than that of things and encompasses all that constitutes social life.

A day in the life

Lefebvre suggests that we should undertake a vast survey of 'how we live . . . for example, a day in the life of an individual, any day, no matter how trivial'.[16] Lest this sound like a mundane exercise, Lefebvre acknowledges the importance of Hegel's dictum: 'the familiar [das Bekannte] just because it is familiar [bekannt] is not well known [erkannt]'.[17] Everyday life may be familiar to us but this does not mean that it is understood. Analysing the everyday may bring out the extraordinary in the ordinary,[18] people do not know well how they live.[19] An initial definition would be to suggest that everyday life is everything left once work is removed: 'everyday life is sustenance, clothing, furnishing, homes, lodging, neighbourhoods, environment.'[20] As a text to be read, everyday life is a perpetual palimpsest: it is continually being rewritten.[21] It is the point of contact and conflict between desire and need, the serious and the frivolous, nature and culture, the public and the private.[22]

> It concerns a level in contemporary society defined by: 1) the gap between this level and levels above it (those of the State, technology, high culture); 2) The intersection between the non-dominated sector of reality and the dominated sector; 3) transformation of objects into appropriated goods.[23]

Alternatively, instead of cataloguing a day in the life of an individual, we could pick a date at random from a calendar, and try to discover what took place on this particular day. The sources available to discover what happened on that day, are, Lefebvre suggests, fairly limited: 'Publicity . . . news items and a few marginal reports are all that is now available to reconstruct the everyday life of those twenty-four hours.'[24] Should we pick a day near the beginning of the century there is nothing to stop us imagining that it was on that day that Einstein had his first perception of relativity, or that some small decision made that day set in motion the events that triggered the world wars or revolutions.

However, if we picked 16 June 1904 we would find that James Joyce, in the novel *Ulysses*, had already given us a picture of everyday life. Lefebvre suggests that it was Joyce who 'really established the idea of daily life in literature. *Ulysses* is twenty-four hours in the life of an ordinary man',[25] it 'rescues, one after the other, each facet of the quotidian from anonymity'.[26] *Ulysses* demonstrates that a great novel can be boring, but profoundly boring, and that 'the report of a day in the life of an ordinary man had to be predominantly in the epic mode'.[27] *Ulysses* famously shows us that life is a succession of days.

The English 'everyday life' is the standard translation of *la vie quotidienne*. This is not a bad translation, but as Lefebvre himself points out, it is not perfect, as *quotidienne* refers to the repetitive nature of life.[28] To distinguish between the terms he uses, Lefebvre makes the following separation: 'The word *everyday* [*quotidien*] designates the entry of daily life [*vie quotidienne*] into modernity . . . the concept of "*everydayness*" [*quotidienneté*] stresses the homogeneous, the repetitive, the fragmentary in everyday life'.[29] 'Everyday' perhaps suggests the ordinary more than the repetition of the 'every day'. Both senses of the word should be remembered: everyday life as a concept is very close to Lukács' and the early Heidegger's notion of *Alltäglichkeit* (everydayness). However Lefebvre and Guterman were not aware of Lukács' work when they wrote *La conscience mystifiée*, but were alerted to it by a reader of the book who suggested that they had repeated many of his ideas.[30] At least, that is what Lefebvre said at the time. Twenty years later he suggests that the reason they made no reference was because they were aware of the heretical nature of Lukács' claims.[31] Most unlikely however, is the suggestion fifty years on that it was potentially Lefebvre and Guterman's discussion of everyday life that led to Lukács picking up the concept in his work![32] Actually, as Trebitsch suggests, it is more likely that it was through Heidegger – himself influenced by Lukács – that such a notion made its way into Lefebvre's work.[33]

In *History and Class Consciousness* Lukács opposes a trivial life, an inauthentic way of being, to a more fully realized and lived life. For Lukács it is capitalism that prevents the realization, and creates the conditions for this mundane, trivial life of commodity fetishism and mechanical existence.[34] It is worth noting that Lukács wrote the studies collected in this book before the discovery of Marx's *1844 Manuscripts*.[35] In *Being and Time* Heidegger too sees everydayness as the realm of inauthentic or better 'inappropriate' (*Uneigenlichkeit*) existence, an existence where humans do as one (*das Man*) does, and the authentic or 'appropriate' (*Eigenlichkeit*) way of being is not open to them.[36] Hess notes the similarity of the notions, and remarks upon

how Heidegger 'elaborated the repetitive'[37] – that is, the every day nature of
the everyday. Heidegger also stressed the ordinariness of the life he looked
at, although he does look at moments and situations of dramatic quality. For
Lefebvre, everyday life has a contradiction within it, as 'it embraces both the
trivial and the extraordinary'.[38] Lefebvre is critical of Heidegger's attribution of primitivity, triviality and anonymity to this notion,[39] and thinks that
everyday life in Heidegger is undervalued. He is similarly critical of nine-
teenth-century literature that puts such a stress on the marvellous that it
demoted and devalued 'real life, the world "as it is" '.[40] However he is
unconvincing in his denial of influence from Heidegger.[41] Lefebvre's concept of everyday life can be seen as an application of Marx's notion of
alienation to Heidegger's understanding of *Alltäglichkeit*: everyday life is such
that man is alienated.

Lefebvre argues that to investigate and examine the everyday we have to
put a critical distance between us and the object of investigation: 'it is
impossible to seize the everyday as such if we accept it, in "living" it pas-
sively, without taking a step back'.[42] The analysis must use critical knowledge
and action together,[43] theory and *praxis*: 'only the philosopher, and the sociologist informed by the dialectic, and maybe the novelist, manage to join
together the *lived* and the *real, formal* structure and *content*'.[44] This notion of
everyday life has been usefully situated between the two principal movements of post-war French theory – existential phenomenology and structuralism.[45] For Lefebvre, neither of these two approaches satisfactorily deals
with everyday life. Sartre, for example, is criticized for trying to integrate the
historical method of Marxism with the lived notions of existentialism: 'He
bends over backwards to confront them and reconcile them by linking the
two levels "dialectically" '.[46] Instead, Lefebvre sees a notion of the lived as
implicit in Marxism already. Similarly structuralism is criticized for its neglect of experience: the example Lefebvre takes is Roland Barthes. As I noted
in Chapter 1 Barthes is the one structuralist Lefebvre seemed to have any
time for. Though Lefebvre wishes to praise some of his work, he judges that
'Barthes dismisses sociology on behalf of semiology'.[47] Barthes' analysis of
fashion is first rate, but he is interested in how things works as signs, and does
not relate the signs to life itself.[48]

Lefebvre wishes to forge a different track, one that has elements of both
approaches, although this is not an integration or a fusion; rather the suggestion is that the other two approaches are lacking. Rather than the bracketing
of phenomenology, or the denial of experience found in structuralism,
Lefebvre wishes to see how the structures, signs and codes of the everyday
integrate with the biographical life.[49] Phenomenology and semiology only
cover part of the ground: only philosophy proposes a *totality*.[50] Phenomenology looks at too small a scale, removing too many of the important contextual issues and fails to see the wider picture; structuralism reifies the
structures instead of looking at their interrelation with the issues of agency,
the level of life and individuality. All this has implications for how a historical study should be undertaken. Though not neglecting the leading players,

the whole should be taken into account, with a consideration of the small details, of everyday life. He suggests that this is slowly being realized by certain historians, geographers and psychologists: 'No one so far has attempted a synthesis'.[51] It would appear that Lefebvre does.

As Trebitsch has described it, Volume II of the *Critique of Everyday Life* functions as 'a veritable "discourse on method" in sociology'.[52] Lefebvre was at the time of writing a member of the sociology section at CNRS, and had been publishing a range of studies in sociology journals. In 1958 – that is, in the preface to the second edition of the first volume – Lefebvre suggested that his original plans for the second volume had had to be rearranged because of the loss of several notebooks which he was using to plan it. Given the context of his relationship with the PCF, and the increasingly divergent line he was taking, he not unreasonably wondered if this was theft.[53] In this preface he suggests that the second volume will contain an attempt at a theory of needs; an analysis of the romantic press on the sociological level; and an analysis of class relations.[54] Elements of these three areas are found within the work, although his most sustained treatments of the question of class in relation to everyday life are found in two long articles, one of which appeared in *Cahiers internationaux de sociologie* and was reprinted in his *Au-delà du structuralisme*, the other a contribution to Georges Gurvitch's seminal *Traité de sociologie*.[55] Lefebvre notes that one of the criticisms he received of his initial inquiries from official Marxism was the neglect of the question of class, a criticism which seems wrong-footed.[56] What is perhaps more appropriate is that Lefebvre's understanding of class, following the advice of Lukács not to neglect the fractions of classes, that is the sub-classes and divisions within them, is closer to Marx in practice rather than Marxism in theory.[57] The second volume, published in 1962, anticipates many of the critical claims made about structuralism and linguistics that would be developed in later writings, although one of the central targets of those assaults, Althusser, had not yet risen to prominence. Trebitsch also claims that the book was intended to critique older, more established modes of investigation – both quantitative sociology and a participatory sociology that focused on surveys and questionnaires.[58]

There are a number of 'moments' within Lefebvre's examination of everyday life. Whereas his other multi-volume works – *Pascal* and *De l'État* – were written only a few years apart, decades separate the three instalments of the *Critique of Everyday Life* series. Volume I, already subtitled *An Introduction*, appeared in 1947, and its 1958 reissue saw the addition of a 'Foreword' which was two thirds of the length of the original book. A second volume followed in 1961, a third in 1981.[59] And yet other moments punctuate this chronology – the 1933 text published in *Avant-Poste*, *La conscience mystifiée* in 1936, *Introduction to Modernity* in 1962, *Everyday Life in the Modern World* in 1968, and *Rhythmanalysis* the year after his death, as well as a number of shorter texts. As he notes in the third volume, *Everyday Life in the Modern World* was a summary of courses he had taught at Strasbourg and Nanterre.[60] While the general thrust of the inquiry remains consistent, the different times provide historical context. The earliest texts were concerned with the rise of fascism and the crisis of the working-class conscience, the first volume has a lengthy discussion of conditions within concentration camps,[61] but is generally positive in the light of the Liberation; the second discerns the problems of new technocracy and the increasingly consumerized society; and the third discusses the putative end of modernity, advances in information technology and the knowledge economy.

A critique of the present

Lefebvre is therefore aware that the emergence of everyday life as a problematic is a historical development. Lefebvre suggests that since the establishment of capitalism in the nineteenth century its impact has slowly grown: 'From then the prose of the world spread, until now it invades everything – literature, art and objects – and all the poetry of existence has been evicted.'[62] Only after World War Two did capitalism really start to become involved in everyday life. This is obviously debatable – the workers' villages set up around factories and pits, where the gin house or pub was owned by the capitalist in order to receive wages back into the system demonstrate that control of workers' limited leisure time was apparent much earlier. But Lefebvre's point is that there has been a shift in the extent of this – with shorter working hours, labour-saving appliances in the home, and more disposable income the opportunities have increased. In a 1966 piece on urban sociology – although the example is naturally broader than that – Lefebvre talks of three kinds of time:

1. free time (leisure time);
2. required time (work time);
3. constrained time (travelling time, or time for bureaucratic formalities).[63]

These types of time have changed their balance and proportion in the twentieth century. These developments necessitate a change in emphasis. Marx saw capitalism as a mode of production where economics prevailed, so he therefore dealt with economics. Lefebvre suggests that now everyday life has taken the place of economics, and so it is this that now needs to be dealt with.[64]

In fact, he and Guterman had suggested back in the 1930s that while people are well aware of the distance between appearance and reality in the economic sphere, 'a revolutionary critique was needed in order to demonstrate these internal characteristics of bourgeois culture. All its forms reveal themselves as *alienated* and *mystified*.'[65]

> Bourgeois culture, like every ideology, has real content; it expresses and reflects something of the truth. The mystification lies in the presentation, use and fragmentation of that content; culture, taken as a whole, lives parasitically on this real content, which it has ceased to renew.[66]

As with space and time, a modern, calculative mode of understanding distances us from the more prosaic understandings. 'Everything here is cal-culated . . . money, minutes. Everything is numbered: metres, kilogrammes, calories.'[67] In sum then, we need to recognize that 'everything is suspect'.[68]

One of the key areas that Lefebvre wishes to criticize is what he called the bureaucratic society of controlled consumption.[69] His analysis of everyday life is always a critique, as is underlined in the title of the series. It is designed to be 'a radical questioning of the everyday in contemporary society: indus-trial and technological society, and so-called "consumer" society'.[70] Every-day life is both under-developed and over-organized within such a society.[71] As will be elaborated in the following chapter, one of the most striking examples of alienation in modern life is in the construction of new towns. We can also find it in the planning of leisure activities, and in the production of new needs. Following Guy Debord, Lefebvre suggests that everyday life has been 'colonized' by new technology and 'consumer society'.[72] It is there-fore the extreme point of alienation – Hegel's 'system of needs' has been shattered.[73] In fact, in distinction to the system of needs, Lefebvre suggests that what has been discovered are 'more like systems – very relative and rather fragile despite their tenacity – of *representations*, which guarantee the everyday an amount of stability even in its disappointment and drama.'[74]

An example of the manufacture of needs is lighting. Lefebvre discusses a firm which gave free paraffin lamps to Chinese peasants in order to create a market for itself in paraffin.

> And now in several million poverty-stricken Chinese households artificial light (an immense progress) shines down on muddy floors and rotten matting – because even peasants who cannot afford to buy a lamp can afford to buy paraffin . . . The 'progress' capitalism brings, like its 'generosity', is just a means to an end: profit.[75]

Lefebvre's use of Guy Debord alerts us to the links between his work of this period and that of the Situationists. Although they were to break acri-moniously around their respective work on the Paris Commune – see Chap-ter 4 – for a time their analyses coincided. Lefebvre's work on everyday life was clearly important for them, as was the idea of the festival, and their notion of the situation (spatially and temporally situated) was a development and implicit criticism of Lefebvre's notion of the moment.[76] It is plausible to suggest that this may have led to Lefebvre's response with the work on space,[77] although this would undervalue the spatial analyses found in his previous work. The theory of moments and the development to theorization of space is discussed in Chapter 5. Similarly, Lefebvre thought that Raoul Vaneigem has some interesting ideas on alienation,[78] and he was very interested in Constant's ideas on architecture.[79]

One of the most striking examples of Lefebvre at work deconstructing the myths of everyday life, exposing the mystification at work, is his reading of *Elle* magazine. In a manner reminiscent of Roland Barthes' *Mythologies*, which he cites, but also his and Guterman's *La conscience mystifiée*, he discusses fashion, home furnishing, Liz Taylor, healthy eating, love at first sight, beauty products and so on.[80] Lefebvre argues that everyday life has a more profound effect on women than men, because of the structure of societies – he is writing this in the early 1960s.[81] The initial title for the third volume – projected in 1959 – was *Situation of Women in the Modern World*.[82] The suggestion is that women work at home, using the modern technological appliances around the home, consuming the products of advertising, and hurrying to relax with the latest lifestyle magazine or romantic novel. In all these aspects of their life they are subject to alienation, but in a way that is potentially neglected by mainstream Marxist analysis.[83] There have been attempts to expand this analysis – Lefebvre is writing around the time of the emergence of second-wave feminism, and is aware of some of the literature. For example, he argues that though Simone de Beauvoir's *The Second Sex* is an important and interesting analysis of alienation as it pertains to women, it remains on the philosophical rather than the concrete sociological level.[84]

In the late 1960s, looking back at his earlier work, Lefebvre argues that the examination of the idea of everyday life in studies of different civilizations in other ages has often showed the *absence* of everyday life. 'With the Incas, the Aztecs, in Greece or in Rome, every detail (gestures, words, tools, utensils, costumes, etc.) bears the imprint of a *style*; nothing had as yet become prosaic, not even the quotidian; the prose and the poetry of life were still identical.' The style of modern life has disappeared under capitalism, it is because of this that life has become everyday. Modern life yearns for a style, but despite its attempts at resurrecting former styles a unified style eludes it.[85] This may be because seeking to implant a previous style into the modern world is doomed to rejection.

> In ancient societies, one ate, one drank, one worked; there were houses, streets and rooms, pieces of furniture, useful objects, instruments and other things. Yet there was not 'everydayness'. In the unity of ethics and aesthetics, of practice and knowledge, in a *style*, the contemporary levels [*la superposition actuelle*] of the everyday and 'culture' (high, medium, low) had neither reason, nor sense [*n'avait ni raison, ni sens*].[86]

Festival and revolution

As later chapters will demonstrate, Lefebvre's notion of everyday life is put to use in his work on urban and rural sociology, the production and use of space, and is essential to his understanding of modernity. Just as everyday life has been colonized by capitalism so, too, has its location: social space. However, Lefebvre also wished to put forward a programme for radical change, for a revolution of everyday life, so as to end alienation. Lefebvre argues that one of the many problems with Heidegger's work on everyday life is that he did not recognize the artistic and revolutionary potential of the transformation of the everyday.[87] Now, a revolution cannot just hope to change the political personnel or institutions, it must also change '*la vie quotidienne*, which has already been literally colonized by capitalism'.[88] To change the world, we must change life. The critique of everyday life that he undertakes has a contribution to make to *the art of living*, and he believes that the art of living implies the end of alienation.[89] A number of points made here need to be explained and developed.

In the first volume of the *Critique of Everyday Life*, written in 1945, Lefebvre set up the idea of the festival in rural France in opposition to the everyday. The 'festival differed from everyday life only in the explosion of forces which had been slowly accumulated in and via everyday life itself'.[90] This is because the festival and everyday life are two parts of the same whole: 'Festivals contrasted violently with everyday life, *but they were not separate from it*. They were like everyday life, but more intense; and moments of that life – in the practical community, food, the relation with nature – in other words, work – were reunited, amplified, magnified in the festival.'[91] But in the years after the writing of the first volume, the introduction to the series, capitalism expanded its scope dramatically. Looking back, Lefebvre recognizes that there was 'a simultaneous decline of Style and the Festival in a society dominated by the quotidian'. Like the festival, 'style has degenerated into culture – subdivided into everyday culture for the masses and higher culture, a split that led to specialization and decay'.[92] There is therefore no going back to the idea of the festival as found in rural France, just as there is no return to the style of previous times, but the *concepts* of style and festival can be used.

Lefebvre recognizes that for some his critique of triviality was a trivial critique,[93] but argues that 'the critique of everyday life . . . implies criticism of the trivial by the exceptional – *but at the same time* criticism of the exceptional by the trivial, of the "elite" by the mass – of the festival, dreams, art and poetry, by reality'.[94] This, again, is not a strict either/or choice or a one-way critique, but a dialectically driven process. Lefebvre's call is for us to work 'toward a permanent cultural revolution'.[95] He recognizes the obvious link with the Chinese example but does not intend to take sides or make judgements on this: 'What counts, what is significant, is the revival of a concept'.[96] This concept of cultural revolution is, he suggests, implicit in Marx, explicit in Lenin and Trotsky, and is revived by Mao Tse-Tung.[97] Lefebvre says that this is not an aesthetic revolution, not a revolution based on culture, and neither its aim nor motive is culture. Rather, it would appear to be a revolution in culture to create a style of life.

The idea of a style of life is a very obviously Nietzschean concept, and Nietzsche is similarly evident in his linking of the notions of revolution and festival: 'The revolutions of the past were, indeed, festivals – cruel, yes, but then is there not always something cruel, wild and violent in festivals? The revolution of the future will put an end to everydayness.'[98] Kristin Ross, in a Lefebvrian study of the Paris Commune shows that it was certainly no carnival – it left 25,000 dead – but, as Eagleton remarks, 'if it were not a carnival, it shared certain carnivalesque features'.[99] This notion of the revolution is necessary to restore the humanity of modern man: '*Homo sapiens*, *homo faber* and *homo ludens* end up as *homo quotidianus*, but on the way they have lost the very quality of *homo*; can the *quotidianus* properly be called a man?'[100] Lefebvre therefore calls for us to 'let everyday life become a work of art! Let every technical means be employed for the transformation of everyday life!'[101] After this transformation the 'antithesis between the quotidian and the Festival – whether of labour or of leisure – will no longer be a basis of society':[102] 'the true critique of everyday life . . . will imply a *rehabilitation of everyday life*'.[103]

In 1959 Lefebvre declared that 'I adhere to Marxism in the name of a revolutionary romanticism'.[104] As Lefebvre makes clear, the object of study is everyday life, but with the 'idea, or rather the project (the programme), of transforming it'.[105] He produced a number of texts around the idea. The first appeared two years earlier in *Nouvelle Revue Française*, entitled 'Towards a revolutionary romanticism'.[106] A lengthy discussion of this piece, with a collection of significant figures, including Tristan Tzara, Lucien Sebag and Lucien Goldmann, was organized and published by *Cercle Ouvert*.[107] The last and by far the longest of the twelve preludes in *Introduction to Modernity*, bore the title 'Towards a new romanticism',[108] and the original article was reprinted in *Au-delà du structuralisme*, with the title 'Revolutionary romanticism'.[109] Chronologically, these are all texts produced shortly before or immediately after his exit from the PCF. It should be remembered that Lefebvre entered the party in the late 1920s, following his readings of Hegel, Schelling and the surrealists. As Blanchot suggests, entering the party as a romantic, he left as a romantic.[110]

Although he draws on a range of literary and artistic figures for inspiration, Lefebvre is at pains to suggest that this is not merely an aesthetic idea, but one that has an ethical (not moral) component. This is in spite of the way in which romanticism is the substantive and revolution the qualifying adjective, rather than the other way round.[111] Ethics and aesthetics have a 'certain liaison', because 'the question of *style* concerns life as much as literature'.[112] Art is both a potentially higher creative activity and currently an alienated activity. In opposition to classicism and socialist realism the new style romanticism that Lefebvre champions continues certain aspect of old romanticism, whilst discarding others. Romanticism is traditionally associated with bourgeois thought, and as was noted in Chapter 1, Lefebvre believed that movements in thought follow the contours of political upheaval, romanticism following Napoleon. Like Heidegger, old romanticism, particularly German thought, marginalized the importance of everyday life.[113] The new romanticism would be revolutionary, that is progressive, because of its opening to the possible, for as Lefebvre argues, 'utopia today is the possible of tomorrow'.[114] Indeed, Lefebvre suggests that the term of revolutionary romantic well describes Marx's own work.[115] In this view, human fulfilment comes through everyday life, but it must certainly be through a different one to that which we live now.[116] Only a revolution of everyday life can realize the idea of the Total Man.[117]

Lefebvre's work on the everyday has been picked up and used by a number of other writers. Trebitsch has, for example, noted that Jürgen Habermas' distinction between system (specialized culture controlled by experts) and lifeworld (lived experience and everyday life) is clearly similar to Lefebvre's work.[118] As Lebas notes, 'the critique of everyday life is effectively a radical transformation of the concept of *Lebenswelt* ("the lived" or "life-world") . . . its purpose is no less than a rehabilitation and secularization of philosophy – a metaphilosophy of the everyday for a revolutionary human-ism'.[119] There are other writers who have developed Lefebvre's ideas – many of whom, like Habermas – are better known in the English-speaking world. Michel de Certeau's work, for example, explicitly acknowledges Lefebvre's influence; similarly Agnes Heller's work.[120] As I have already noted there was a push/pull relation with Situationism, both sides taking something from the other's work. These links have been explored in a number of useful works, and generally it can be said that in this area of Lefebvre's work existing English language scholarship is well advanced.[121] This is at least in part due to the availability of Lefebvre's writings in this area – by the time this book is published the third volume of the *Critique of Everyday Life* will be out, and this means that almost all of Lefebvre's significant writings in this area will be available in translation.[122] For this reason the specific analysis of this aspect has been in less depth than other parts of Lefebvre's work, but the length of this chapter is also because everyday life is implicit in almost everything Lefebvre wrote, and its problematic is treated throughout this book. The notion of everyday life provides an indispensable context for the work on urban and rural sociology, the analysis of time and space, and perhaps to a lesser extent the question of the state. These will be the topics of the following three chapters. As Lefebvre notes, 'it is the everyday that carries the greatest weight. While Power occupies the space which it gener-ates, the everyday is the very soil on which the great architectures of politics and society rise up.'[123]

Notes

1 See 'Toward a Leftist Cultural Politics: Remarks Occasioned by the Centenary of Marx's Death', in Cary Nelson and Lawrence Grossberg (eds), *Marxism and the Interpretation of Culture*, London: Macmillan, 1988, pp. 75–88, p. 78; *Qu'est-ce que penser?* Paris: Publisad, 1985, p. 133.
2 Karl Marx, *Early Writings*, translated by T. B. Bottomore, New York: McGraw-Hill, 1963, p. 76.
3 V. I. Lenin, 'What the friends of the people are', *Collected Works* I, Moscow: Progress, 1963, p. 141, quoted in 'Avant-propos de la 2e édition', *Critique de la vie quotidienne I: Introduction*, Paris: L'Arche, 2nd edition, 1958 (1947), p. 9; 'Foreword to the second edition', *Critique of Everyday Life Volume I: Introduction*, translated by John Moore, London: Verso, 1991, p. 3.
4 *Critique de la vie quotidienne* I, p. 161; *Critique of Everyday Life* I, p. 148.
5 *Critique de la vie quotidienne* I, p. 189; *Critique of Everyday Life* I, p. 176.
6 *Une pensée devenue monde: faut-il abandonner Marx?* Paris: Fayard, 1980, p. 168.
7 See, most explicitly, *Critique de la vie quotidienne* I, pp. 161–6; *Critique of Everyday Life*

I, pp. 148–53. Lefebvre suggests that the first volume completed the aborted project that they had set themselves in *Critique de la vie quotidienne II: Fondements d'une sociologie de la quotidienneté*, Paris: L'Arche, 1961, p. 273 n. 1; *Critique of Everyday Life Volume II: Foundations for a Sociology of the Everyday*, translated by John Moore, London: Verso, 2002, p. 367 n. 28.

8 *Critique de la vie quotidienne* I, p. 197; *Critique of Everyday Life* I, p. 183.
9 'Toward a Leftist Cultural Politics', p. 78.
10 *Critique de la vie quotidienne* I, pp. 160–1; *Critique of Everyday Life* I, p. 148.
11 'Avant-propos de la 2ᵉ édition', p. 48; 'Foreword to the second edition', p. 39.
12 Michel Trebitsch, 'Preface' to *Critique of Everyday Life* I, p. xxiii.
13 *Critique de la vie quotidienne*, I, p. 173; *Critique of Everyday Life* I, p. 160. Lefebvre cites Marx, *Early Writings*, p. 171 : 'The less you eat, drink, buy books, go to the theatre or to balls, or to the public house, and the less you think, love, theorise, sing, paint, fence, etc, the more you will be able to save and the *greater* will become your treasure which neither moth nor rust will corrupt – your *capital*. The less you *are*, the less you express your life, the more you *have*, the greater is your *alienated* life and the greater is the saving of your alienated being . . . [but] everything which you are unable to do, your money can do for you; it can eat, drink, go to the ball and to the theatre.'
14 'Toward a leftist cultural politics', p. 80.
15 *Critique de la vie quotidienne*, I, p. 264; *Critique of Everyday Life* I, p. 249. In *Marx 1818–1883*, Genève-Paris: Trois Collines, 1947, Lefebvre offers a parallel reading in terms of liberty. See especially pp. 90, 104, 130, 136–7, 143, 147.
16 *Critique de la vie quotidienne* I, p. 210; *Critique of Everyday Life* I, p. 196.
17 G. W. F. Hegel, *Phänomenologie des Geistes*, in *Werke: Theorie Werkausgabe*, Frankfurt: Suhrkamp Verlag, 1970, Bd. III, p. 35; *Phenomenology of Spirit*, Oxford: Oxford University Press, 1977, p. 18. Lefebvre misquotes this in 'Avant-propos de la 2ᵉ édition', p. 22; 'Foreword to the second edition', p. 15.
18 'The everyday and everydayness', in *Everyday Life: Yale French Studies* 73, Fall 1987, pp. 7–11, p. 9.
19 *La somme et le reste*, Paris: Méridiens Klincksieck, 3rd edition, 1989 (1959), p. 605.
20 *La vie quotidienne dans le monde moderne*, Paris: Gallimard, 1968, p. 46; *Everyday Life in the Modern World*, translated by Sacha Rabinovitch, Harmondsworth: Allen Lane, 1971, p. 21; for a succinct summary see 'The everyday and everydayness'.
21 For the idea of everyday life as a social text, see *Critique de la vie quotidienne* II, pp. 306–12; *Critique of Everyday Life* II, pp. 306–12; and *Du rural à l'urbain*, Paris: Anthropos, 3rd edition, 2001 (1970), pp. 94–5.
22 'Les mythes dans la vie quotidienne', *Cahiers Internationaux de Sociologie* XXXIII, 1962, pp. 67–74, p. 67; *Key Writings*, edited by Stuart Elden, Elizabeth Lebas and Eleonore Kofman, London: Continuum, 2003, pp. 100–6.
23 'Les mythes dans la vie quotidienne', p. 67; *Key Writings*, p. 100.
24 *La vie quotidienne dans le monde moderne*, pp. 7–8; *Everyday Life in the Modern World*, p. 1.
25 'Toward a leftist cultural politics', p. 79.
26 *La vie quotidienne dans le monde moderne*, p. 9; *Everyday Life in the Modern World*, p. 2.
27 'Avant-propos de la 2ᵉ édition', p. 35; 'Foreword to the second edition', p. 27.
28 'Toward a leftist cultural politics', p. 78.
29 'Toward a leftist cultural politics', p. 87 n.
30 Lefebvre to Guterman, 17 February 1936.
31 See *La somme et le reste*, p. 452; and for a discussion, Russell Jacoby, *Dialectic of*

Defeat: Contours of Western Marxism, Cambridge: Cambridge University Press, 1981, pp. 108–9.

32 Henri Lefebvre and Patrick Tort, 'Entretien liminaire', in *Lukács 1955 / Etre Marxiste aujourd'hui*, Paris: Aubier, 1986, p. 15. On p. 20 of this same interview, Lefebvre suggests that *La conscience mystifiée* was actually a critique of Lukács' position, and that his later support for Lukács was a political and strategic decision, rather than a mark of intellectual affinity. See, for example, his 'Lukács 1955', in this work – a lecture that the PCF prevented from being published. In *La somme et le reste*, p. 76 n. 1, he recounts that this was 'an absolute prohibition on pain of expulsion'. For the difference, see also Henri Lefebvre and Catherine Régulier, *La révolution n'est plus ce qu'elle était*, Hallier: Éditions Libres, 1978, p. 141.

33 Trebitsch, 'Preface', p. xviii; see his 'Le groupe "philosophies", de Max Jacob aux surrealists 1924–1925', *Le cahiers de l'IHTP* 6, November 1987, pp. 29–38, p. 30. However, see 'Le quotidien (mise au point)', *M, mensuel, marxisme, mouvement* 11, May 1987, p. 9, where he suggests the concept was being discussed as early as 1925.

34 Georg Lukács, *History and Class Consciousness: Studies in Marxist Dialectics*, translated by Rodney Livingstone, London: Merlin, 1971.

35 See Lukács, 'Preface to the new edition' (1967), in *History and Class Consciousness*, p. xxxvi, where he recounts reading the *Manuscripts* in Moscow in 1930, and how they challenged the fundamental outlook of his work.

36 On the link between Lukács and Heidegger, see above all, Lucien Goldmann, *Lukács and Heidegger: Towards a New Philosophy*, translated by William Q. Boel-hower, London: Routledge & Kegan Paul, 1977.

37 Rémi Hess, *Henri Lefebvre et l'aventure du siècle*, Paris: A.M. Métailié, 1988, p. 53.

38 'Avant-propos de la 2ᵉ édition', p. 28; 'Foreword to the second edition', p. 20.

39 See *Critique de la vie quotidienne* I, p. 137; *Critique of Everyday Life* I, p. 124; *Critique de la vie quotidienne* II, pp. 27–30; *Critique of Everyday Life* II, pp. 22–4; *Critique de la vie quotidienne III: De la modernité au modernisme (Pour une métaphilosophie du quotidienne)*, Paris: L'Arche, 1981, pp. 23–4; *Métaphilosophie*, Paris: Éditions Syllepse, 2ᵉ édition, 2001 (1965), p. 132.

40 *Critique de la vie quotidienne* I, p. 117; *Critique of Everyday Life* I, p. 105. On the transformation, see Maurice Blanchot, *L'entretien infini*, Paris: Gallimard, 1969, p. 356.

41 *Critique de la vie quotidienne* III, p. 23. This is not to downplay the differences, many of which are usefully explored in Peter Osborne, *The Politics of Time: Modernity and Avant-Garde*, London: Verso, 1995.

42 *La vie quotidienne dans le monde moderne*, p. 56; *Everyday Life in the Modern World*, p. 27.

43 *Critique de la vie quotidienne* I, p. 202; *Critique of Everyday Life* I, p. 189.

44 'Avant-propos de la 2ᵉ édition', pp. 105–6; 'Foreword to the second edition', p. 94.

45 Alice Kaplan and Kristin Ross, 'Introduction to *Everyday Life*', *Yale French Studies* 73, Fall 1987, pp. 1–4, p. 3.

46 *Introduction à la modernité: Préludes*, Paris: Les Éditions de Minuit, 1962, p. 246; *Introduction to Modernity: Twelve Preludes*, translated by John Moore, London: Verso, 1995, p. 250.

47 *La vie quotidienne dans le monde moderne*, p. 308; *Everyday Life in the Modern World*, p. 166.

48 *La vie quotidienne dans le monde moderne*, p. 190 n.; *Everyday Life in the Modern World*, p. 99 n. There would seem to be some interesting avenues opened here. Barthes

and Lefebvre were close friends and colleagues, and Poster suggests that the 1957 work *Mythologies* may have influenced Lefebvre. See Mark Poster, *Existential Marxism in Post-war France: From Sartre to Althusser*, Princeton: Princeton University Press, 1975, p. 313; Roland Barthes, *Mythologies*, translated by Annette Lavers, London: Vintage, 1993; Michael Kelly, 'Demystification: a dialogue between Barthes and Lefebvre', *Yale French Studies* 98, 2000, pp. 79–97.

49 See *Critique de la vie quotidienne* II, pp. 60–2; *Critique of Everyday Life* II, pp. 55–7.

50 *La droit à la ville*, Paris: Anthropos, 1968, pp. 41–2; *Writings on Cities*, translated and edited by Eleonore Kofman and Elizabeth Lebas, Oxford: Blackwell, 1996, p. 92.

51 *Critique de la vie quotidienne* I, pp. 149–50; *Critique of Everyday Life* I, pp. 136–7.

52 Michel Trebitsch, 'Preface: the moment of radical critique', in *Critique of Everyday Life* II, p. x.

53 'Avant-propos de la 2ᵉ édition', p. 109 n. 1; 'Foreword to the second edition', p. 265 n. 103.

54 'Avant-propos de la 2ᵉ édition', pp. 108, 109–10; 'Foreword to the second edition', pp. 97, 99. The initial subtitle of the second volume was to be *Theory of Needs*. See *La somme et le reste*, p. 609.

55 See 'Sociologie de la bourgeoisie', in *Au-delà du structuralisme*, Paris: Anthropos, 1971, pp. 165–93; 'Psychologie des classes sociales', in Georges Gurvitch (ed.), *Traité de sociologie*, Paris: PUF, 2 volumes (1958–60) II, pp. 364–86.

56 *La somme et le reste*, p. 613.

57 Report of a conversation with Lukács in Budapest, 1950, in *La somme et le reste*, p. 571. Lukács claimed that this was one of the reasons he moved away from the positions of *History and Class Consciousness*.

58 Trebitsch, 'Preface: the moment of radical critique', p. xi.

59 In *Everyday Life in the Modern World*, p. 26, the third volume is listed as forthcoming – thirteen years before it actually appeared.

60 *Critique de la vie quotidienne* III, p. 15.

61 *Critique de la vie quotidienne* I, pp. 254–61; *Critique of Everyday Life* I, pp. 240–6.

62 *La vie quotidienne dans le monde moderne*, p. 61; *Everyday Life in the Modern World*, p. 29.

63 *Du rural à l'urbain*, p. 198; *Everyday Life in the Modern World*, p. 53.

64 *La vie quotidienne dans le monde moderne*, p. 360; *Everyday Life in the Modern World*, p. 197.

65 Norbert Guterman and Henri Lefebvre, 'La mystification: notes pour une critique de la vie quotidienne', *Avant-Poste* 2, August 1933, pp. 91–107, p. 95; *Key Writings*, p. 74.

66 'La mystification', p. 96; *Key Writings*, p. 75.

67 *La vie quotidienne dans le monde moderne*, p. 45; *Everyday Life in the Modern World*, p. 21.

68 'La mystification', p. 104; *Key Writings*, p. 81.

69 *La vie quotidienne dans le monde moderne*, pp. 117, 133–207; *Everyday Life in the Modern World*, pp. 60, 68–109. On this see Chapter 1, note 106 above, and Alain Touraine, *The Post-Industrial Society: Tomorrow's Social History, Classes, Conflicts and Culture in the Programmed Society*, translated by Leonard F. X. Mayhew, New York: Random House, 1971.

70 'Les mythes dans la vie quotidienne', p. 74; *Key Writings*, p. 106.

71 *Vers le cybernanthrope*, Paris: Denoël/Gonthier, 1967, p. 18.

72 See Guy Debord, 'Perspectives for conscious alterations in everyday life', in *Situationist International Anthology*, edited and translated by Ken Knabb, Berkeley:

Bureau of Public Secrets, 1981, pp. 68–75, p. 70. This was a lecture recorded on a tape, and presented to Lefebvre's seminar at the CNRS. It originally appeared in *Internationale Situationniste* 6, August 1961.

73 *Critique de la vie quotidienne* II, pp. 16–17; *Critique of Everyday Life* II, p. 11.

74 *Critique de la vie quotidienne* II, pp. 65–6; *Critique of Everyday Life* II, p. 61. See *Critique de la vie quotidienne* III, p. 70; and above all, *La présence et l'absence: Contribution à la théorie des représentations*, Tournai: Casterman, 1980.

75 *Critique de la vie quotidienne* I, pp. 244–5; *Critique of Everyday Life* I, pp. 229–30. See also *Du rural à l'urbain*, p. 93 n. 2 on the 'need' to smoke and its relation to advertising.

76 See, for example, Guy Debord, *Society of the Spectacle*, Detroit: Black & Red, 1983; and *Comments on the Society of the Spectacle*, London: Verso, 1988. For a discussion, see 'Lefebvre on the Situationists', pp. 70, 72.

77 David Harvey, 'Afterword', in *The Production of Space*, translated by Donald Nicholson-Smith, Oxford: Blackwell, 1991, p. 430. See also the discussion in Hess, *Henri Lefebvre*, p. 216.

78 *Au-delà du structuralisme*, p. 316. Of Vaneigem's work, see especially *Traité de savoir-vivre à l'usage des jeunes generations*, Paris: Gallimard, 1967.

79 See, for example, *Critique de la vie quotidienne* III, pp. 28–9. On the Situationists generally, with some comments on their relationship with Lefebvre, see the essays in Stewart Home (ed.), *What is Situationism: A Reader*, Edinburgh: AK Press, 1996; Sadie Plant, *The Most Radical Gesture: The Situationist International in a Postmodern Age*, London: Routledge, 1992, pp. 63–4. More detailed analysis is found in Eleonore Kofman and Elizabeth Lebas, 'Recovery and reappropriation in Lefebvre and Constant', in Jonathan Hughes and Simon Sadler (eds), *Non-Plan: Essays on Freedom Participation and Change in Modern Architecture and Urbanism*, Oxford: Architectural Press, 2000, pp. 80–9; Martin Jay, *Downcast Eyes: The Denigration of Vision in Twentieth-Century French Thought*, Berkeley: University of California Press, 1993, pp. 418–20; and Edward Ball, 'The great sideshow of the Situationist International', in *Everyday Life: Yale French Studies* 73, Fall 1987, pp. 21–37. Some interesting links are made in Greil Marcus, *Lipstick Traces: A Secret History of the Twentieth Century*, London: Secker & Warburg, 1989. Lefebvre discusses them most fully in 'Lefebvre on the Situationists', conducted and translated by Kristin Ross, *October* 79, Winter 1997, pp. 69–83.

80 'Les mythes dans la vie quotidienne', pp. 68–70; *Key Writings*, pp. 101–2.

81 *Critique de la vie quotidienne* II, pp. 17, 83–91; *Critique of Everyday Life* II, pp. 11–12, 79–87; see *La vie quotidienne dans le monde moderne*, p. 142; *Everyday Life in the Modern World*, p. 73.

82 *La somme et le reste*, p. 609. In *Le temps des méprises*, Paris: Stock, 1975, pp. 206, 208, Lefebvre notes that this volume was 'not without difficulties', but that it would discuss issues such as sexuality and society, desire, need, *jouissance*.

83 See *Critique de la vie quotidienne* II, p. 19; *Critique of Everyday Life* II, p. 13; 'Les mythes dans la vie quotidienne'; *Key Writings*, pp. 100–6.

84 *La somme et le reste*, p. 121. See also the comments on Kate Millett and Betty Friedan in *La survie du capitalisme: La re-production des rapports de production*, Paris: Anthropos, 2ᵉ édition, 2002 (1973), pp. 54 n. 1, 69–70; *The Survival of Capitalism*, translated by Frank Bryant, London: Allison & Busby, 1976, p. 73 (the first French reference is not in the translation); and the passing reference to Germaine Greer in *La présence et l'absence*, p. 59. *La présence et l'absence* contains perhaps the most sustained discussion of feminism pp. 147ff.

85 *La vie quotidienne dans le monde moderne*, p. 60; *Everyday Life in the Modern World*, p. 29.

86 *La fin de l'histoire*, Paris: Les Éditions de Minuit, 1970, p. 155.

87 *Métaphilosophie*, p. 132.

88 'Toward a leftist cultural politics', p. 80.

89 *Critique de la vie quotidienne* I, p. 213; *Critique of Everyday Life* I, p. 199; see *Qu'est-ce que penser?* p. 134.

90 *Critique de la vie quotidienne* I, p. 216; *Critique of Everyday Life* I, p. 202.

91 *Critique de la vie quotidienne* I, p. 221; *Critique of Everyday Life* I, p. 207.

92 *La vie quotidienne dans le monde moderne*, p. 73; *Everyday Life in the Modern World*, p. 36.

93 'Avant-propos de la 2ᵉ édition', p. 13; 'Foreword to the second edition', p. 6.

94 *Critique de la vie quotidienne* I, p. 266; *Critique of Everyday Life* I, p. 251.

95 *La vie quotidienne dans le monde moderne*, pp. 355ff; *Everyday Life in the Modern World*, pp. 195ff. On this see also *Le retour de la dialectique: 12 mots clefs*, Paris: Messidor/Éditions Sociales, 1986, pp. 126–8. This phrase is echoed in Bruce Brown, *Marx, Freud, and the Critique of Everyday Life: Towards a Permanent Cultural Revolution*, New York: Monthly Review Press, 1973.

96 *La vie quotidienne dans le monde moderne*, pp. 362–3 n. 1; *Everyday Life in the Modern World*, p. 198 n.

97 *La vie quotidienne dans le monde moderne*, p. 370; *Everyday Life in the Modern World*, p. 203.

98 *La vie quotidienne dans le monde moderne*, pp. 73–4; *Everyday Life in the Modern World*, p. 36.

99 Terry Eagleton, 'Foreword', to Kristin Ross, *The Emergence of Social Space: Rimbaud and the Paris Commune*, Basingstoke: Macmillan, 1988, pp. vi–xiv, p. ix.

100 *La vie quotidienne dans le monde moderne*, p. 354; *Everyday Life in the Modern World*, p. 193.

101 *La vie quotidienne dans le monde moderne*, p. 372; *Everyday Life in the Modern World*, p. 204.

102 *La vie quotidienne dans le monde moderne*, p. 74; *Everyday Life in the Modern World*, pp. 36–7.

103 *Critique de la vie quotidienne* I, p. 140; *Critique of Everyday Life* I, p. 127.

104 *La somme et le reste*, p. 671. Kurt Meyer takes this as the main theme of his *Henri Lefebvre: Ein Romantischer Revolutionär*, Wien: Europaverlag, 1973.

105 *Critique de la vie quotidienne* II, p. 8; *Critique of Everyday Life* II, p. 2.

106 'Vers un romantisme révolutionnaire', *Nouvelle revue française* 58, 1957, pp. 644–72.

107 Colette Audry, Jacques Nantet and Claude Roy, with Henri Lefebvre, *Le romantisme révolutionnaire, Cercle Ouvert: Confrontations*, Paris: La Nef de Paris, 1958.

108 *Introduction à la modernité*, pp. 235–373; *Introduction to Modernity*, pp. 239–388.

109 *Au-delà du structuralisme*, pp. 27–50.

110 Maurice Blanchot, *L'amitié*, Paris: Gallimard, 1971, p. 99. See *Le temps des méprises*, p. 109.

111 *Le romantisme révolutionnaire*, p. 2.

112 *Au-delà du structuralisme*, p. 29.

113 *Critique de la vie quotidienne* III, pp. 23–4.

114 Lefebvre and Régulier, *La révolution n'est plus ce qu'elle était*, p. 200; see 'Lettre', in *Marx . . . ou pas? Réflexions sur un centenaire*, Paris: Études et Documentation Internationales, 1986, p. 21.

115 See *La somme et le reste*, pp. 399–402. As early as *La conscience mystifiée*, Paris: Éditions Syllepse, 3rd edition, 1999 (1936), p. 67, he and Guterman had suggested that there could be two humanisms – a revolutionary and a bourgeois one. See also pp. 68–72; and 'L'homme des revolutions politiques et sociales', *Pour un nouvel humanisme*, textes des conferences et des entretiens organisés par les Rencontres Internationales de Genève, Neuchâtel: Éditions de la Baconnière, 1949, pp. 115–35, p. 135.
116 *Métaphilosophie*, p. 225.
117 *La somme et le reste*, pp. 587ff.
118 Trebitsch, 'Preface', p. xxviii. See particularly, Jürgen Habermas, *The Theory of Communicative Action, Volume 2, Lifeworld and System: A Critique of Functionalist Reason*, translated by Thomas McCarthy, London: Polity Press, 1987.
119 Elizabeth Lebas, 'The Critique of Everyday Life: Introduction', in *Key Writings*, pp. 69–70, p. 69.
120 Michel de Certeau, *The Practice of Everyday Life*, translated by Steven Rendall, Berkeley: University of California Press, 1984; Michel de Certeau, Luce Giard and Pierre Mayol, *The Practice of Everyday Life Volume 2: Living and Cooking*, translated by Timothy J. Tomasik, Minneapolis: University of Minnesota Press, 1998; Agnes Heller, *Everyday Life*, translated by G.L. Campbell, London: Routledge & Kegan Paul, 1984.
121 See, for example, Mike Featherstone, 'The heroic life and everyday life', *Theory, Culture and Society* 9 (1), 1992, pp. 159–82; Osborne, *The Politics of Time*, pp. 189–96; Neil Maycroft, 'Marxism and Everyday Life', *Studies in Marxism* 3, 1996, pp. 71–91; Maycroft, 'Henri Lefebvre: Alienation and the Ethics of Bodily Reappropriation', in Lawrence Wilde (ed.), *Marxism's Ethical Thinkers*, London: Palgrave, 2001, pp. 116–43; Michael E. Gardiner, *Critiques of Everyday Life*, London: Routledge, 2000; Gregory J. Seigworth, 'Banality for cultural studies', *Cultural Studies* 14(2), 2000, pp. 227–68; Roger Silverstone, *Television and Everyday Life*, London: Routledge, 1994.
122 That is, the three volumes of the *Critique of Everyday Life*, *Everyday Life in the Modern World*, and *Introduction to Modernity*. Two important essays appear in *Key Writings*.
123 *Le survie du capitalisme*, p. 85; *The Survival of Capitalism*, pp. 88–9.

4   From the rural to the urban

In the *Grundrisse*, which it should be remembered was available in a German edition only as late as 1953,[1] Marx gives an outline of how a materialist approach should proceed:

> When we consider a given country politico-economically, we begin with its population, its distribution among classes, town, country, the coast, the different branches of production, export and import, annual production and consumption, commodity prices, etc.[2]

In his *Le Marxisme*, published in 1948, Lefebvre both anticipates and extrapolates on this theme. For Lefebvre, scientific sociology:

> considers an ensemble, a concrete whole for a given country. This concrete ensemble immediately appears in a range of aspects: distribution of population among towns and the country, production and consumption, importation and exportation, etc. A simple description, for example of lifestyle, or work, or human geography provides certain sociological insights into this country. But it does not go very far. It does not show the history, the formation. It does not penetrate the economic-social structure, that is, the essence of the phenomenon that it describes. To deepen our insight, we must analyse.[3]

From these quotations it is possible to take a number of things. The most immediate is the importance of the issue of the town and the country, analysed by Marx in part, but not in nearly as much depth as questions of export and import, production, consumption and prices. This chapter looks at Lefebvre's contribution to the analysis of location. The means of conducting that analysis is also important. As Lefebvre makes clear, a simple description can never be sufficient. A sociological account must be supplemented by a historical analysis, and the two together will also provide insight into the structural whole. As was discussed in Chapter 1, the regressive-progressive methodology for examining the relation between history and sociology within historical materialism was originally outlined in a study of rural sociology. What is of interest here is how Lefebvre put this into practice in relation to matters of the rural and the urban.

Although Lefebvre spent much of his life in cities such as Paris and

Strasbourg, it should not be forgotten that he was born in the Pyrenees and always remained very attached to that region. During the War he retreated to a village in the mountains, and used the time and the archives he discovered to write a thesis on the subject of peasant communities in the Pyrenees, which gained him a doctorate in 1954. The secondary or complementary thesis was later published as *La vallée de Campan* in 1963.[4] In 1972 he published a collection of three plays, one of which was set in a spa town resort in the mountains.[5] Lefebvre's last few years were also spent in this region, in his family's old house at Navarrenx. The *Groupe de Navarrenx* who collaborated on the last book published in his lifetime, *Du contrat de citoyenneté*, used to visit him here. Lefebvre published other studies about country matters, including an analysis of the Pyrenees and a collection of essays on the theme, and intended others – including an ambitious history of rural France to be written with Albert Soboul, and a *Manuel de sociologie rurale*, which was stolen from a car in a late draft.[6] According to Hess, who recalls a conversation with Lefebvre on this book, it contained material on rents, land revenues, their distribution, and the relation between rents and markets; a section on agrarian reform (both theoretical and practical) along with historical analysis of this reform in various countries such as Mexico, Spain and Iran and regions such as the Pyrenees, southern Italy, and Tuscany. This manual, Hess notes, was never rewritten because Lefebvre moved onto other concerns,[7] though of course some of the topics are discussed in shorter pieces Lefebvre wrote around the same time.[8]

From the mid-1960s Lefebvre wrote less on these topics, but instead turned his attention to the urban social environment. Lefebvre recounts that it was the developments in his homeland that led him to this work. In the 1950s the area around Lacq was developed because of the natural gas and oil deposits, and a new town called Mourenx built nearby. Lefebvre wrote several analyses of this town and of bigger cities such as Paris, Tokyo, Kyoto and New York,[9] but his work also developed into more general meditations on urbanization, political and economic questions with regard to the city, and an attempt to conceive of the changes in theoretical terms. It led directly to his work on the politics of space. As well as analysing the historical relationship between the rural and the urban, Lefebvre also laid the foundations for an explicitly Marxist urban sociology, which looked at the key role technology played in the shaping of the urban environment. Much of this work was tied up in debates with the technocratic planning of the French Fifth Republic, although there was also a historical interest in Paris.

This chapter moves through four stages. In the first, I consider Lefebvre's discussion of the historical relationship between the country and the city. Second, I outline Lefebvre's work on the rural, particularly concentrating on the methodological innovations and his work on the Pyrenees. Third, I move to consider his work on the urban. This is the longest section of this chapter, and considers a number of political issues, looking at relations of centre and periphery, technocracy and the right to the city. It also discusses Lefebvre's analysis of Mourenx. It was in his work on the urban that Lefebvre developed many of the theoretical innovations that would find their fullest expression in *The Production of Space*. Finally I draw upon two of his historical analyses – the events of Paris in 1871 and 1968 – in order to show how these historical analyses demonstrate the crucial importance of 'urban phenomenon'. In their balance between questions of temporality and spatiality, between history and geography, I read them as illustrations of what I have called elsewhere spatial history.[10] This leads into the next chapter of this study, which examines the more theoretical works on history and space that were written after, almost as culminations of, the practical analyses.

The town and the country

Until relatively recently Lefebvre was best known in English for the book *The Sociology of Marx*, which takes as its central claim the idea that though 'Marx is not a sociologist . . . there is a sociology in Marxism'.[11] As before, Lefebvre is trying to rescue Marx from the reductionist reading of econonomicism. A number of different sociological studies are present in Marx's work, of the family, of classes, knowledge, the state and society, and of the town and the countryside.[12] The relationship between the town and the countryside is, for Lefebvre, a historical relationship, with the mediating role being played by technology. Until the late nineteenth century, suggests Lefebvre, the town was conceived in opposition to the countryside: the countryside was situated between the town and nature. This is a relationship of three terms.[13] In the twentieth century, however, this opposition was reversed and the country is now seen and conceived in relation to the City: 'the specific weight of each term has altered'.[14] The three terms in existing reality are rurality, urban fabric and centrality.[15] Lefebvre notes that the period in which he wrote the studies collected in *Du rural à l'urbain* – from 1949 to 1969 – the period in which France entered into modernity.[16]

The separation of the town and country is, Lefebvre contends, one of the most fundamental divisions of labour, along with age, sex (the biological division of labour), and tools and skills (the technical division).[17] But unlike Dühring, who thought this separation was a permanent feature of society, Marx and Engels recognized its historical development.[18] The shift in the relative position of the town over the country is located in the rise of industrialization and the advance of technology. The industrial society has, Lefebvre argues, been supplanted by urban society. This was only just beginning in Marx's time, so it is therefore understandable that he failed to perceive that 'the *production of the city* was the end, the objective and the meaning of *industrial production*'.[19] In his book *La pensée marxiste et la ville*, Lefebvre attempts a thematic reading of Marx and Engels' work, a synthesis of their various pronouncements. Indeed, as Lefebvre somewhat grandly proclaims

One can therefore think, following Marx, that *Weltgeschichte*, worldwide history, was born with the city, of the city and in the city: the oriental, ancient, medieval city.[20]

It is worth spending a little more time examining these changes, which Lefebvre discusses at most length in *La révolution urbaine*.[21] Lefebvre suggests that we can draw an axis from 0 to 100 per cent, along which we can plot the extent of urbanization. At one end we have 'pure nature', nature left to the elements; at the other the achievement of the process. Of course, neither pole is likely to be seen, but the mapping of the process along this line may have certain benefits.[22] Of course, such a one dimensional measure seems rather crude, and he recognizes that it is only one aspect of this story, with an admittedly abstract and arbitrary cutting up of time,[23] and no real recognition of the development of related concepts such as nature (*physis*) or *logos* (reason).[24] However, what is important is that Lefebvre notes that 'this axis is at the same time temporal and spatial: spatial, because the process extends in space, which it modifies; – temporal because it develops in time, initially a minor aspect and then predominant in practice and history'.[25] The establishment of a political town, what might generally be called a city state like the Greek *polis* or the Roman city, is Lefebvre suggests very near the start of this line, this process. They arose around the same time or soon after the establishment of an organized societal life, of agriculture and the village. From Lefebvre's description it appears that this applies to his understanding of almost all forms of communal life until the late Middle Ages, that is, until the beginning of industrialization. While the political town administered, protected and exploited the surrounding territory, which was often a huge geographical area, and organized things such as drainage and irrigation to work the land, this was of another order to what happened in the ensuing period.[26] For long periods, Lefebvre suggests, the city was parasitic on the countryside, only providing 'non-productive functions – military, administrative, political', and it was only with the advent of capitalism that 'the city supplants the countryside in respect of productive work'.[27]

What is important to note is that this development is not a strict linear progression, although Lefebvre's 0 to 100 per cent schema can suggest that. It is essential to realize that there was in a certain sense a regression from antiquity, which came from the town, to the Middle Ages (understood as a European or Western European phenomenon), which came from the country.[28] It was with the breakdown of the Roman empire and its conquest by Germanic tribes, which were both primitive communities and military organizations that led to a reorganization of these relations. 'The feudal property of land is the outcome of the dissolution of this sovereignty (city, property, relations of production). Serfs replace slaves.' The European Middle Ages 'begin from the countryside'.[29] Lefebvre dates the start of the real transition to a new urbanization, in Europe, in the fourteenth century. At this time the town ceased being the exception, the urban island in the ocean of the countryside, opposed to the nature of the village or country, but it emerged as a term of equal importance to the country, so that it made sense to talk of the town–country relation. The country became no more than 'the "environment" of the town, its horizon, its limit'. Equally the villagers became no longer workers on behalf of territorial lords, but producers for the town, for the urban market. Of course, this transition was accompanied by the rise in the importance of the state.[30]

It is also linked into broader cultural and sociological changes, including the rise of capitalism, and the scientific revolution. As both Lefebvre and Heidegger realize, the importance of mathematical, calculative science has an impact far beyond the narrow confines of the laboratory. For Lefebvre, 'the rationalism which culminated with Descartes accompanied the upheaval which replaced the primacy of the countryside with the priority of the urban'.[31] In this new reason, urbanity (cultivated) is opposed to rusticity (naïve and brutal).[32] However, in distinction from structuralism, Lefebvre cautions that the break (*coupure*), that is, a relative discontinuity, between the urban and its antecedents is not an epistemological or philosophical break, but a political or historical one.[33] This took us to about the middle point on this line of measurement. Further developments through industrialization, building programmes and so on push us further along this line.

In this increasingly industrialized society, agricultural life loses its autonomy, its independence. Local particularities are lost in the spread of uniformity. '*The urban fabric* proliferates, extends itself, corrodes the residues of agrarian life.'[34] Lefebvre's term 'urban fabric' is actually, as he acknowledges, closer to a 'net of uneven mesh', which allows some areas or villages to escape control. However, generally it means that 'urban society and life penetrate the countryside'. This would include services such as water and electricity, the car and the television.[35] As Lefebvre notes, at the time of Marx only England had capitalist agriculture, but today agricultural production has become an aspect of industrial production, that is capitalist.[36] Although the notion of an *agroville* is a Soviet concept, we find much the same thing happening across the world. 'In the United States, except for certain regions of the south, the peasantry has virtually disappeared; only islands of peasant poverty exist, next to islands of urban poverty.'[37] This is not a localized phenomenon, nor is it confined to the national level. As Lefebvre recognizes, 'the *urban problematic* imposes itself on the world scale',[38] 'in sum, the *virtual object* is nothing other than the planetary society and the "world town" '.[39] This has important methodological issues, because it means that 'urban space cannot be defined differently in socialist countries than in other countries'. Again we see Lefebvre's insistence that not all things are conditioned by the mode of production. For Lefebvre, 'the urban problematic, urbanism as ideology and institution, urbanism as a global tendency, are worldwide facts. The urban revolution is a planetary phenomenon.'[40] Analysing urban problems in the capitalist mode of production, requires us to illuminate the contradictions of the urban phenomenon within the global process.[41]

Lefebvre's schema can therefore be portrayed in the following way:

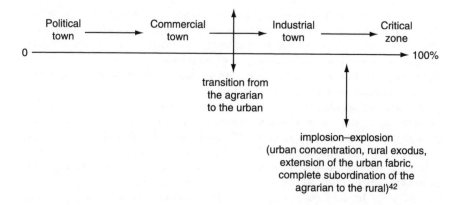

Later chapters of *La révolution urbaine*, notably Chapter IV, 'Levels and dimensions', complicate the linearity of the initial presentation, because they recognize the three levels of the global, the mixed and the private.[43] The transition from rural to industrial to urban is the diachronic, the three levels of the urban period introduce the synchronic. The global brings into focus the power of the state, the mixed is the level of the urban proper, and the private that of dwelling, of individual domestic life.[44] The notion of dwelling, which owes much to Heidegger, is more fully discussed in Chapter 5.[45] Lefebvre adds in three 'dimensions' to go with these levels of the synchronic. These are abstract social relations such as economic or legal forms projected onto the urban, making urban phenomena 'concrete abstractions'; urban phenomena as the site and terrain of social struggle; and urban practice. There are also conceptual oppositions such as the distinction between the public and the private and the open and the closed.[46] The diagram becomes still more complicated:

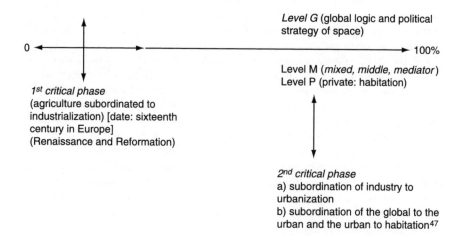

Writing in 1968, Lefebvre suggests that 'the great event of the last few years is that the effects of industrialisation on a capitalist society of production and property (superficially modified but conserving the essential) have produced their results: a programmed *everydayness* in its appropriate *urban setting*. Such a process was favoured by the disintegration of the traditional town and the expansion of urbanism.'[48] What this has produced, and therefore what must be examined, is an urban environment. Lefebvre suggests that this expression is better than 'technological environment', 'since technology only produces an "environment" in the city and by the city; outside the city technology produces isolated objects: a rocket, a radar station'.[49]

This is, of course, questionable, as it would seem to be self-evident that the advances of technology in, for example, farming, have sculpted the 'rural' as much as parallel developments have the urban. When Lefebvre does discuss this, his work is again similar to that of Heidegger.[50] Like Heidegger, Lefebvre recognizes that modern technology dominates nature, rather than working with it. As he suggests in *La pensée marxiste et la ville*:

> The countryside disappears, and this in a double way: by industrialisation of agricultural production and the disappearance of peasants (and therefore of the village) on one hand, on the other by the ruination of the earth and the destruction of nature.[51]

As urbanization extends into the countryside, it creates peripheries of towns and destroys old villages. This is an urbanization that is degraded and degrading.[52] Nature is challenged by this domination, which is not a mere appropriation.[53] Both Lefebvre and Heidegger trace this back to the scientific revolution, and in particular Descartes, with the shift in the understanding of the world. Lefebvre acknowledges the importance of Heidegger in this regard,[54] but develops his insights in more concrete analyses. As an example of the tension between technicity and nature consider this passage about the French Alps:

> Try the following experiment: go to Chamonix and take the cable car for the Aiguille du Midi. There are all kinds of people in the cabin with you: babies, old men, foreigners enjoying the ease and comfort of the trip like the experienced travellers they are. Are you fascinated by heights? Soon the séracs, glaciers and vertiginous rock faces start parading past you like so much cardboard, and the scenery of Mont Blanc begins to look not a little stagey. Near the Vallée Blanche, if you're lucky enough to spot some climbers roped together for the difficult and dangerous ascent, you may become conscious of a strange feeling. These men's lives are absorbed in this climb, their bodies accomplish it; for them the mountain represents pure nature, whereas you are being effortlessly lifted to the summit by modern technology. They make you seem pathetic. But then, you make *them* seem pathetic too. Why bother to make the effort? What's the point? Surely it's as ludicrous as wanting to live in a shepherd's hut, as old-fashioned as a paraffin lamp?[55]

It is essential to note that Lefebvre sees a distinction between the production of *oeuvres* – works, or works of art – in the rural and the production of products in the urban.[56] The latter are results of industrialization, the capitalist mode of production and the rage for mechanism and calculation. Lefebvre notes that of course the city existed before industrialization, but that it has clearly changed as a result. He argues that 'the most eminent urban creations, the most "beautiful" *oeuvres* of urban life ... date from epochs previous to that of industrialisation'.[57] With the advent of industrialization the production of products replaced the production of *oeuvres* and the social relations attached to them, of which the city is an obvious example.[58] This does not mean that the situation is irretrievable. Lefebvre suggests that the city can be a work in the sense of a work of art, because it is not simply organized and instituted, but can also be modelled and appropriated.[59] This can happen through its appropriation by the people, through challenges to the dominant system and political arrangements. The events of May 1968 and 1871 are examples of how this might happen. As well as being revolutions in the urban, they were revolutions of the urban.

This is one end of the scale, but it is important to note that the term 'nature' is itself misleading:

> One says *nature* for the *countryside*, for cultivated, worked earth, the producer of wealth, of use-value (exchangeable via the market). The idea of nature, inasmuch as it substitutes for the earth, for agricultural production, revenues and land rents, plays a role in the great mystification which unites history, the nation, and the state under its dark wing.[60]

The myth of pure nature is as misleading as one of pure technicity.[61] It should also not be forgotten that the urban environment is, of course, directly affected by state planning. This is another development of relatively recent times. As Lefebvre remarks, the state 'is actively involved in housing construction, new towns, urbanisation. What we call "urbanism" is part of both ideology and the would-be rational practice of the state.'[62] As a good example of how he sees technological developments working, consider this passage from *Introduction to Modernity*:

> Fixed and artificial, electric lighting makes the city and its monuments, roads and streets stand out sharply against the natural environment: countryside, sky, space. Electric lighting emphasises the features of the urban landscape more starkly than gaslight (which had played a significant role in forming the nineteenth century myth of the city).[63]

We shall return to the *perceptions* of urban and rural space: for now it is enough to consider, with Trebitsch, how, as Lefebvre 'moved from rural sociology to urban sociology, his thinking on the everyday was to become inseparable from his thinking about modernity'.[64] This understanding of the shift from the rural to the urban – both in historical terms, and in his own work – enables Lefebvre to escape the accusations that suggest that there is a strong urban bias in much continental theory. Margaret Fitzsimmons castigates Marx and Weber for this, and sees the bias continue in the more recent work of Althusser, Foucault, Derrida and Lacan. Only Lefebvre escapes her damning condemnation of 'their obsession with *la vie urbaine, la vie parisienne*, as the only civilised manifestation of *la vie quotidienne*'.[65] Lefebvre's understanding of the rural and urban together rather than in isolation is one of his key points: the over-emphasis of the urban is one of his criticisms of the Situationists;[66] whilst the neglect of the problems of urbanization is seen as a fault with Marcuse.[67]

A sack of potatoes

Rather than Marx's dismissive attitude, with his praise of the way bourgeois urbanization had 'rescued a considerable part of the population from the idiocy of rural life',[68] and his suggestion that the homogeneity of the peasant classes, villages and departments meant they were as isomorphous as 'a sack of potatoes',[69] Lefebvre both appreciated and understood the rural. Little of his work in this area has been translated into English, except for an essay in *Key Writings* and a chapter in the first volume of the *Critique of Everyday Life*. The essay, 'Perspectives of rural sociology', discusses some methodological concerns, and the chapter shows his work in use. However, Lefebvre's work is much broader than that. His first writing on this topic was published in 1949 in the *Cahiers Internationaux de Sociologie* – a house journal of the *Centre National de la recherche scientifique* of which Lefebvre was director of the sociology section – in which he would publish a number of his articles.[70] Some of these articles – as in this case – were less polemical; others were very explicitly anti-Stalinist. Presumably publishing in a non-party journal gave him much more freedom of expression. In this particular essay he identified some of the principle problems of rural sociology – both in terms of its subject matter and its methodology. These were pursued in a number of other articles, most of which are collected in *Du rural à l'urbain*. Although many of the specific issues he was concerned with are of little importance or relevance to us today, over half a century later, the general questions are worth a little attention.

    Lefebvre notes that because rural life and agriculture preceded the 'modern' life of cities and factories, there is a temptation to believe that it is more simple. This would be misleading.[71] When it was the dominant form of life it was largely neglected, and has only really become an object of investigation 'from the moment it posed *practical* problems'.[72] One of the central concerns is that of the relation between a sociology of the rural and its history. While it might not be immediately apparent, the history of the region is inscribed in its present. Sometimes, like in a city, many of the buildings show the marks of the past – medieval manors or Roman remains juxtaposed with the contemporary ones – but in the rural landscape the history can remain much more hidden. Rural sociology though, which is a study of the present moment, cannot exist without a recognition of history. History persists and acts in the present moment.[73] Equally, even within France, there is a great deal of difference between a village in the north-east and one in the Midi. When a village from France is compared to one from Italy or Spain the differences become even greater.[74] To study a village then, will require a combination of history, geography and political economy within sociology.[75]

Lefebvre bemoans the lack of materials for such a study, but recognizes that there has been much written about the topic in the USA and USSR. In the USA, he suggests that it has become a distinct science, a branch of general sociology which is taught in universities. He suggests that this is partly because of the problems faced by American agriculture, and he recognizes that it is both descriptive and normative. However this empirical, descriptive approach is non-historical, because it deals with contemporary reality as if it had no past, they approach it without historical depth. In the USSR, rural studies are largely concerned with the transformation of the existing system. Economic and political theory are used to define what should happen. Of course, this means that practicality is often substituted for doctrine, but historical work has been more apparent in this area.[76] One of the things that Lefebvre thinks Lenin has contributed, and therefore should be added to the positive side of his balance sheet, is the theorization of the agrarian question.[77]

In the initial piece from 1949 Lefebvre recognizes three principal stages or issues to be investigated:

1. problems of origin;
2. problems of filiation, succession, sociological causation;
3. historical problems: the interaction of forms.[78]

However, these are not very fully worked out, and it is not entirely clear how they might be balanced. Four years later, in the more theoretically, more developed 'Contributions to rural sociology', he outlined and employed the regressive-progressive method discussed in Chapter 1. Lefebvre argues that, in France, rural life was largely studied by historians and human geographers. This work, he suggests, can be continued, but it needs to be made concrete and integrated within an overall structure of sociology – 'the study of the totality of the social process and its laws'.[79]

The rural world therefore has complexity of two kinds – *horizontal complexity*, and *vertical complexity*. The former demonstrates the issues within a given historical period, where differences within space and the levels of the structure are important; the latter looks at the juxtaposition of different historical developments within the same place. Lefebvre gives a number of examples, including mass mechanized agriculture side by side with hand ploughs and other more archaic forms of cultivation.[80]

> The two kinds of complexity – the one we call *horizontal* and the one we call *vertical* but could call *historical* – intertwine, intersect and interact; hence a confused mass of facts that only a sound *methodology* can disentangle. We have at the same time to determine the objects and objectives of rural sociology – and to define its relationship with its ancillary fields and disciplines: human geography, political economy, ecology, statistics, etc.[81]

The problem, therefore, is the '*relationship between sociology and history*'.[82] This should not mean that sociology is absorbed by history, but that the sociologist first has to engage in a historical analysis in order to explain. History is therefore 'an ancillary, subordinate science in the study of the social process *as a whole*'.[83] The method – with its three stages of descriptive, analytico-regressive and historico-genetic – has been discussed in Chapter 1. What is worth noting is that, as well as incorporating sociology and history into a methodology, this also avoids one of the most significant problems of structuralism. While structuralism in its classic French sense either avoided history deliberately or unintentionally, but was precisely developed because of the lack of geographical and structural analysis in standard research, Lefebvre's work here allows the incorporation of the synchronic with the diachronic.[84]

The study of rural life involves more than simply the investigation of political economy and a narrowly sociological approach. It is important to take into account questions of folklore and mythology,[85] and we can learn from literature such as the work of Balzac or Rabelais. Equally, in an initial glimpse of later concerns, Lefebvre suggests that the organization of the rural community is both '*in time* (calendar of work and festivals) *and in space* (distribution of plots and lots; distribution of works of general concern)'.[86] In his study of the Pyrenees, Lefebvre suggests that to do such a topic justice would require an interdisciplinary team – geographers, historians, anthropologists, sociologists and linguists – and that his own work's only merit is to indicate the way.[87] As he recognizes, the study of the rural is not merely to illuminate its own subject matter, but also human life more generally: 'In sum, we propose *to consider the historico-sociological study of the peasant community as one of the leading threads to follow in the entanglement of human reality*'.[88]

Reading rural spaces

Lefebvre's work on the rural, although almost unknown in the English-speaking world, predates much of the existing literature. Cloke and Thrift have noted how work on the rural, in the wake of Raymond Williams' *The Country and the City*, has followed four overlapping phases. These are a functional approach; one based on political economy; a sense that rurality is a social construct; and a deconstructive approach to rural 'texts'.[89] Whilst it is clear that the first and second have been deployed in Lefebvre's work, although subsumed in the playing out of the third, the fourth is perhaps harder to see in what has already been said. (This is not to suggest that Lefebvre was a 'poststructuralist' or that he practised 'deconstruction', but that some of his work anticipates their themes. This is not entirely surprising given that some key people were students or assistants of Lefebvre.)[90]

In the first volume of the *Critique of Everyday Life*, Lefebvre suggests that we should consider 'how many times have we all "strolled" through the French countryside without knowing how to decipher the human landscape before our eyes!' Straightforward things like the ploughs being used or the

shape of fields evade our understanding.[91] For Lefebvre, there is the potential to learn how to decipher the landscape: this is to use the dialectical
method, the Marxist method, to facilitate a critique of everyday life, which
will enable us to 'look at the irksome and incomprehensible mumbo-jumbo
of our towns and villages, our churches and our works of art, and read them
out loud, like an open book'.[92] This, of course, prefigures much of the
expanded understanding of the notion of 'text' to include such things as
architecture and events. Such 'texts' are then critically 'read'.[93] At least at
this point in his work Lefebvre is sympathetic to the idea of 'reading' landscapes, although later he does become more critical of the idea, mainly
because of its abuse by others.

In 1947 Lefebvre simply notes that the comparison between landscapes
and books is not completely exact: 'a book signifies, whereas town and rural
areas "are" what they signify'. Rural areas, he suggests, tell us about 'the
dislocation of primitive community, of poor technical progress, of the
decline of a way of life which is much less different from that of ancient
times than is generally believed'.[94]

In his introduction to the book of photographs on Germany, Lefebvre
makes this explicit:

> The historian interests himself in all that he sees; the past emerged, sprung up,
> and transfixes the present; a stone, a wall, a fragment of a book piques his
> curiosity and stimulates his imagination. He reads the Modern Times [*les Temps
> Modernes*] on a page of *Confidences* or *Elle*, and the history of Gaul in the walls of a
> village.[95]

Important readings of rural landscapes in Lefebvre's work include the
chapter in the *Critique* entitled 'Notes written one Sunday in the French
countryside', and the work on the valley of Campan. Lefebvre's 'Notes'
begin with the extended meditation on the role of the festival in peasant life
that was considered in Chapter 3 above, but go on to consider the sociology
of rural space. Lefebvre suggests we take an ordinary village in France as an
example:

> The network of roads and paths, fences and hedgerows, encloses a land which is
> by no means unworkable . . . Scattered farms and then, around the church and
> the graveyard, a few houses grouped together, the village. A green land;
> meadows, their brooks full with autumn rain.[96]

One of the clearest parts of Lefebvre's discussion is of the village church,
a reading that is clearly influenced by Nietzsche's remarks on the spaces of
churches.[97] Like Nietzsche, Lefebvre identifies the power of the symbols in
the church: 'for me this space can never be just like any other space'.[98] The
discussion then side-steps into one on the alienating power of religion,
which little furthers the purpose here. What is evident, even in this initial
sketch, is that Lefebvre has appropriated the Nietzschean notion of power in

space: 'Castles, palaces, cathedrals, fortresses, all speak in their various ways of the greatness and the strength of the people who built them and against whom they were built'.[99] As Lefebvre notes in his study of the Pyrenees, the church is extremely important as a focus for rural communities, because it is often the sole public space. Official notices are placed on its walls, it houses the post box, and the municipal council meets there. As well as being a religious centre it is also a political and social hub.[100]

We find a more rigorous study in *La vallée de Campan*. As noted above, this was assembled on the basis of documentary material found during the War. Indeed the first part of the book is devoted to the presentation of and commentary on that material.[101] Whilst some of this draws upon published sources, there are also extensive unpublished records, dating back to the eleventh century, which Lefebvre catalogues until they become too numerous in the seventeenth.[102] The second half of the book is entitled 'a study of historical sociology'. The book as a whole is subtitled 'a study of rural sociology', and the interrelation of these terms is, as discussed above, crucial to understanding this period of his work. The study is both historical and sociological, and Lefebvre notes that the term 'historical sociology' 'indicates a dialectical movement between research structured concerned with history and that concerned with sociological reality'.[103] Much of the second half of the book is devoted to a detailed historical study of the area, drawing upon the documentary sources, but incorporating geographical material as well. It is clear that the intent is to go back through the region's history in order to illuminate its present. To take an early example:

> The village itself is only about five kilometres from Bagnères-de-Bigorre, a thermal spa dating from the Romans, a market town situated at the opening of the mountains to the plain. As a result, the valley of Campan presents a remarkable juxtaposition of the laws of custom and written laws (Roman), of mountain traditions and the influences which dissolved them.[104]

Although it was later incorporated fully into France, Campan remained almost independent for quite some time, a 'quasi-autonomous veritable pastoral republic', an example of the little Pyrenean states of an earlier period of which Andorra is the sole surviving example.[105] As Lefebvre notes in his book on the Pyrenees, the mountains both separate and link France and Spain, they are both bridge and barrier.[106]

It is this linkage between the valley and the nascent state that is perhaps the most important and prescient part of the study. The central chapter here is Chapter 2 of the second part, entitled 'The struggle for the integrity of the territory'. In microcosm, the valley saw a struggle similar to that of peoples and nations, a struggle to occupy the space within its 'natural frontiers'. Over centuries, perhaps even millennia, the members of the community wanted to be the masters of their valley, but also to go beyond these frontiers, to invade their neighbours – what Lefebvre calls a 'sort of imperialism of the agri-pastoral community'.[107] The notion of a 'natural frontier', like in larger scale history, is important and politically charged because it is partly based upon material reality and partly arbitrary, and only has sense through an economic structure and a well-defined politics.[108] As he comments elsewhere, the Pyrenees frontier is a political and juridical fiction.[109] Lefebvre notes that the oldest document in the archive, dating from 1083, although it is probably apocryphal, is nonetheless of interest. It, and the other early documents, show an effort to establish a *march*, boundaries and land around them, on behalf of the inhabitants.[110] As Lefebvre notes, the struggle for the integrity of the territory is simultaneously a struggle for the protection of liberties and customs.[111]

Most of the rest of the historical material is only really of specialist interest, and I do not intend to say anymore about it. However, it is worth noting that Lefebvre thinks that one of the principal reasons to be interested in Campan, or indeed any other village, is its proximity to a past that is often more distant.[112] Elsewhere he describe the situation in the Pyrenees as one of 'sociological fossils'.[113] In other words Campan can illuminate other parts of France, and possibly elsewhere, because here – because of historical and geographical conditions – the past is better preserved, even if often juxtaposed with contemporary farming techniques. We find a similar claim in the work on Germany, where Lefebvre claims that villages still show something of the organization of primitive huts, the organization of clans and tribes. Of course, as Lefebvre recognizes, the tapping into a barbarian past was central to Aryan mythology, but he suggests that there is a positive side to this primitivity in its purity and sensitivity.[114]

Lefebvre is noticeably uninterested in the landscape of the Pyrenees for its own sake, but much more in the relationship between the land and its people. It is not a case of describing a region, but of 'outlining the contours of a culture bruised by historical events, dying, living again'. It is therefore history, rather than geographical description or the picturesque quality that is important.[115] This unique experience is in danger from a range of causes, notably tourism, modern agriculture and industrialization.[116] The society of leisure requires the creation of resorts, something that Lefebvre would discuss in more detail as one of the elements of the production of space. Equally the south-west of France is becoming the 'corn belt' for the rest of the country, and the creation of Lacq-Mourenx symbolizes the industrialization of the region.[117]

The spectre of the urban

The creation of the new town had a positive side effect, because it led Lefebvre to study the process of urbanization in detail. His interest in this topic coincided with a return to the idea of everyday life, with the publication of the second volume of the series and the reissuing of the first, with the lengthy foreword. Indeed, Lefebvre's work on the urban environment is even more extensive than his work on the rural. More than half of *Du rural à l'urbain* is devoted to the town and the city, and he wrote several books dedicated to the topic. These include *Position: Contre les technocrates*, which was re-edited four years later as *Vers le cybernanthrope; Right to the City*, with a second volume *Espace et politique; La révolution urbaine* and *La pensée marxiste et la ville*. Kurzweil suggests that Lefebvre decided, 'convinced that urbanism is the cancer of modern life, that a Marxist research of its space might be the cure'.[118] In *La fin de l'histoire* the stress of *urbanism* – that is, the ideology of town planning – over the urban is one of the problems of the modern world.[119] This research is begun by the establishment of the *Institut de Sociologie Urbaine*, and the journal *Espaces et Société*, of which the first article of the first issue was Lefebvre's 'Reflections on the politics of space'.[120] Readings of urban spaces are found in several other places in his work, notably the seventh prelude in *Introduction to Modernity*, which analyses Mourenx, and the discussions of the events of Paris in 1871 and May 1968. Quite a bit of this work on urban sociology is now available in English, especially given the 1996 translation of the collection *Writings on Cities*, which includes the whole of *Right to the City* and a couple of essays from *Espace et politique*. In the 1970s a collection of Lefebvre's urban writings was planned with Guterman as translator.[121] We can only speculate on how English language urban studies would have changed had this ever appeared. *Key Writings* contains one essay from *Du rural à l'urbain*, an excerpt from *La révolution urbaine* and a journal piece on Paris from 1974. *La révolution urbaine* has recently appeared in a full translation.[122] However, as before, Lefebvre's work is more detailed than even this would suggest.

Although Marx and Engels had quite a bit to say about the relationship between the town and the country, they said less about specifically urban problems. Lefebvre suggests that at their time of writing, 'the city did not yet pose major problems, except for the question of housing (which was treated by Engels)'.[123] Today, though, 'the problem of the city is immensely greater than that of housing'.[124] However, as Lefebvre notes, there are some scattered reflections on the town and urban problems, but these are usually unsystematic and within the context of a wider discussion.[125] As he notes in respect of Engels, the housing question was a subordinate aspect of the wider question of the relations between town and country.[126] In this respect then, Lefebvre is forging new concepts within a Marxist framework, as the existing work of Marxism is inadequate to the task. This was only belatedly recognized by two other writers on these issues – Manuel Castells, whose own work is much better known in English, and David Harvey. Castells had been a student of Touraine and Lefebvre at Nanterre, although his principal influence was Althusser.[127]

Castells and Harvey's early work looked at the interlinked nature of spatial or urban forms and social processes, applying a radical political economy to the themes of modern geography. These were largely structuralist readings: Althusser being the principal focus for Castells; Piaget for Harvey.[128] Castells' aim was to examine the current practice of the French state towards urban questions. However, as Soja has noted, this was Marxist geography as a geography informed by Marxism. The standard themes of

geography were given an explicitly Marxist reading, with attention being paid to the distinction between exchange and use value, the role of class struggle, and the superstructural forms resulting from the changes in the mode of production. Lefebvre's work was more radical – it disrupted many of the assumptions of Marxist theory. But in doing this Lefebvre was criticized by Castells and Harvey for elevating space to the level of causal efficacy, rather than being an expression of the relations of production. As Soja notes, in attempting to be good Marxists, Castells and Harvey established boundaries beyond which spatial analysis should not pass. For them, Lefebvre fell foul of the charge of spatial fetishism. There was a danger of spatial or territorial conflict replacing class conflict as the mover of social transformation. Soja suggests that the criticisms of Castells and Harvey miss the (dialectical) point. The choice is not an either/or: *either* space as a separate structure affecting the social, *or* space as an expression of social relations, but space as a component of the relations of production – simultaneously social and spatial.[129]

Both Castells and Harvey had second thoughts concerning Lefebvre, and their own work. Harvey in particular, in probably his most important book, *The Limits to Capital*, attempts to fill the 'empty boxes' of Marx's thought, the elements he did not complete himself concerning spatial processes. He is concerned with steering a middle course between 'spatial fetishism' and space as a 'mere reflection of the processes of accumulation and class reproduction'.[130] He pursued this not only in the theoretical *The Limits to Capital*, but also in *Consciousness and the Urban Experience* and *The Urbanization of Capital*.[131] In doing so he radically develops what Marxism is. Castells has in recent years moved away from Marxist thought entirely, but in *Class, City and Power* suggested that 'the focus should have been the historical transformation of the urban, rather than the conceptual deployment of Marxist theory'.[132] As Merrifield notes, this is almost an 'undoing of his indictment of Henri Lefebvre';[133] it is certainly a distancing from Althusser.[134] Castells continues to be critical of Lefebvre, though this has been from the basis of its lack of empirical grounding. This was a criticism of Lefebvre's philosophical style, not his ideas. For Castells, metaphysics does not help too much:

> The ideas of Lefebvre were so powerful that, in spite of the fact that he had not the slightest idea about the real world – not at all: he didn't know anything about how the economy works, how technology works, how the new class relations were building – but he had a genius for intuiting what was really happening. Almost like an artist . . . I don't think it has any research foundation to it . . . So he was not a researcher, but he was probably the greatest philosopher on cities we have had.[135]

This can clearly be related to Lefebvre's criticisms of philosophers such as Hegel, Nietzsche and Heidegger – that their work was abstract and not rooted in materiality. Castells' criticism here, while not entirely accurate, is

perhaps more applicable in the work on the urban than on the rural, which
was underpinned by extensive archival work in Campan. That said, as I will
show, his work on Paris was also grounded on observation and historical
background. We should note, though, that, in distinction to Lefebvre's positive view of rural life, and the elegiac tone of much of his writings on it, his
view of the city was much more critical. Urbanization had played a significant role in the ascendancy of the bourgeoisie, of bourgeois thought and the
attendant exploitation and alienation of the proletariat.

> Towns tell us of the almost total decomposition of community, of the atomisation
> of society into 'private' individuals as a result of the activities and way of life of a
> bourgeoisie which still dares to claims that it represent 'the general interest'.[136]

Instead of the spectre of communism, it is the spectre of the urban, the
shadow of the city that now haunts Europe.[137] What this means is that urban
questions are extremely important, and cannot be ignored in studies of
quite diverse topics.[138] There are questions about the political economy of
the urban – rent and the distribution of living space – and questions about
the politics of the urban – questions of centre-periphery relations, marginalization, ghettoization, segmentation, the organization of its space and the
power relations that course through it. It is therefore no real surprise, as
Lefebvre notes, that 'large modern towns are poorly thought of. We can
scarcely mention them without according them a pejorative or defamatory
epithet: monstrous or tentacular towns, moloch-cities, etc.'[139]

We should note at the very outset that Lefebvre's term 'urban society',
which he regularly abbreviates to simply 'the urban', has a particular meaning. Rather than simply any society structured around a town or a city –
such as the Greek *polis*, the oriental or medieval town, a commercial or
industrial city or anything from a small town to a megalopolis – Lefebvre
means more specifically a society that results from complete urbanization.
In 1970 he suggests that this is virtual, but expects that in the future it will
become real.[140] This is the society that is born of industrialization, a society
that dominates and absorbs agricultural production. Literature at the time
he was writing names this society in various ways – industrial or post-
industrial society, technical society, society of abundance, leisure or consumption. Lefebvre prefers 'urban society' to these denominations, which
contain some empirical or conceptual truth but also some exaggeration or
extrapolation. For Lefebvre, 'urban society', a society born of and succeed-
ing industrialization, designates 'a tendency, an orientation, a virtual state of
affairs, rather than a *fait accompli*'.[141] As was noted in Chapter 3 above, this is
the 'bureaucratic society of controlled consumption'.[142]

His is a Marxist analysis, so we might wonder how this fits with existing
Marxist concepts. For Lefebvre, urbanism is a superstructure of the neo-
capitalist society – a capitalism of organization rather than organized capitalism. 'Urbanism organises a sector which seems free and available, open to
rational action: inhabited space. It directs the consumption of space and

habitat.'[143] One of the problems of much existing analysis is, according to Lefebvre, that it does not recognize that this superstructural quality must be distinguished from practice, social relations, from society itself. Urbanism and the 'urban' must not be confused – there is a separation between urban practice and the urban phenomenon. Pseudo-marxists have advanced the claim that the urban phenomenon is merely a superstructure – thereby confusing practice with ideology, social relations with the institutional. It is this double aspect that must be examined – it is this that shows how urbanism constitutes space (seemingly neutral and non-political) as an object.[144]

We would be misled, therefore, if we saw urban reality as a superstructure – that is as the result of changes in the economic system. Urban reality equally modifies the relations of production, although it is not able to transform them.[145] In other words, though the economic might be determinant 'in the last instance', this does not mean that there is a top-down or one-way effect. Productive forces do not merely operate within space but on space, and space equally constrains them. As Lefebvre says – and this will be examined in greater detail in Chapter 5 – 'space and the politics of space "express" social relations, but also react upon them'.[146] The city itself was born out of relations of production, that is the contradictions within them – not from the mode of production, nor superstructures or ideology, nor productive forces themselves.[147] The modern city is not simply the passive place of production or the place where capital is concentrated, but 'urban phenomena profoundly reshape the apparatuses of production: productive forces, relations of production, contradictions between productive forces and relations of production'.[148]

There is a very specific politics to Lefebvre's work, particularly as a challenge to what he called technocracy. The power of technique, or technology, a mechanized, calculated, controlled, measured way of operating was one of the central problems that Lefebvre identified in modern society. It was this, as an offshoot of capitalism, which extended control from the economic to the cultural and social spheres of our existence. As Goldmann suggests, technocrats need to be 'distinguished very clearly from the bureaucrats'. While bureaucracy, as elaborated by Weber is

> a mechanism with precise and abstract rules which functions independently of any individual intervention which, on the contrary, is presented as a cause of disturbances. Technocracy is essentially different. Here we are concerned with a group which monopolizes the decision-making; a group capable, by its very decisions, of avoiding all bureaucratisation, of adapting itself, of making effective decisions beyond abstract rules. Outside this group and its powers, the whole of society is fundamentally reduced to being a mere passive performer.[149]

This is a very helpful summary of the understanding Lefebvre uses. It is interesting that the above description from Goldmann comes in his discussion of Lukács and Heidegger, who, as we saw in the previous chapter, were instrumental in shaping Lefebvre's conception of everyday life. This interest in technology is also paralleled in Heidegger's work, as was mentioned in Chapter 2.

As far as urban space is concerned, the technocrats have their influence principally through urbanism or town planning (*urbanisme*) and architecture. There is a division of labour between architects who are concerned with the level of dwelling and urbanists who are concerned with the level of society as a whole.[150] In a number of places Lefebvre argues that the space of urbanists and architects is perceived as geometrical.[151] For this mindset, everything is seen as calculable and quantifiable, and decisions can be made in a 'programmable' way. Within the urban there is a recourse to geometry, symmetry and system.[152] We find this exhibited particularly in the notion of the plan. This is not simply planning (*planification*), though this is naturally included within it, but what Lefebvre calls 'plan-measuring' (*planimétrie*).[153] In the sixteenth and seventeenth centuries we see the beginning of plans for towns in Europe, notably the first plans for Paris. These go beyond mere abstract plans, 'a projection of urban space within a space of geometric coordinates', but provide 'a mixture of vision and conception, works of art and science, they show the town from above and afar, in perspective, at the same time painted, depicted, described geometrically'.[154] It is because urbanism is able to portray the space it creates as objective, scientific and neutral that it is able to hide its repressive character.[155] In a formula which could equally be found in Heidegger, for Lefebvre, 'the generalised terrorism of the quantifiable accentuates the efficacy of repressive space'.[156]

Lefebvre argues that technocracy is a myth, because these administrators, and bad administrators at that, rarely use much actual technology. However, they have an ability to persuade the people as a whole that because these are technological decisions they should be accepted. In other words, a large part of Lefebvre's criticism is not that technocrats *are* technocrats, but that they are precisely the opposite. Technology should be put at the service of everyday life, of social life rather than being precisely the condition of its suppression and control. Urbanism, for example, is an ideology that operates under the cover of this myth of technocracy.[157]

One of the most obvious examples of the change in the understanding of the city can be found by comparing cities designed before the advent of cars and those after. Striking examples can be found by juxtaposing US cities on the East Coast with those on the West, for instance. Lefebvre notes that the invasion of cars into cities, and the pressure put by this industry – the car lobby – has turned parking into an obsession, circulation the primary objective. But for Lefebvre, the road should not simply be a means of passage and circulation, but is central to social and urban life. The road is a meeting place, and both links up the other meeting places such as cafés and halls and makes them possible. These meeting places animate the street, which is a spontaneous theatre, where we are both spectator and spectacle.[158] The street has an informative function, a symbolic function, a ludic function.[159]

One optimises information and communication into a model. This technocratic and systematized planning, with its myths and its ideology (namely, the primacy of technique), would not hesitate to raze to the ground what is left of the city to leave way for cars, ascendant and descendant networks of communication and information. The models elaborated can only be put into practice by eradicating from social existence the very ruins of what was the city.[160]

We find a similar critique of technocracy in Lefebvre's discussion of le Corbusier and his urban plans. For Lefebvre, le Corbusier 'gets rid of the city and replaces it by gigantic houses where everything is given over to circulation'. In his assessment, le Corbusier was 'a good architect but a catastrophic urbanist, who prevented us from thinking about the city as a place where different groups can meet, where they may be in conflict but also form alliances, and where they participate in a collective *oeuvre*'.[161] There is a danger that through this functionalization the town simply becomes a dormitory,[162] and the car strikingly illustrates the conquest of human life by technology.[163] There will come a time, Lefebvre suggests, where we will need to limit the rights and powers of the car,[164] because there is a danger that we lose what is unique about the city.

> What are the reasons for this loss? We know them: cars, offices and the rule of bureaucracy, specialisation and functionalisation of places, the primacy of profit, the embourgeoisification of the city, the desertification of the elegant quarters and the gentrification of old quarters, etc.[165]

As noted above, three broad stages can be discerned in the historical development of society: the rural, the industrial, and the urban.[166] Each of these has its own organization of space-time. In the rural stage time is cyclic and organization is orientated around local particularities. Years and seasons, local issues and specificities are important, and the broader temporal scope and spatial situation relatively unimportant. In the industrial period there is a tendency towards homogeneity, towards rational unity and planning of both time and space. Urban space-time, though it is a product of industrial rationality and homogeneity, actually appears as the *differential*.

> Each place and moment has no existence except within the ensemble, by the contrasts and oppositions which link them to the other places and moments they are distinguished from.[167]

This means that in the urban environment there is a tension, a dual nature to many places and times. One the one hand they are homogeneous and organized, on the other utterly distinct. Lefebvre therefore introduces the concepts of *iso-topia* and *hetero-topia* to partner the more common term of *u-topia*. *Iso-topias* are the same place – neighbourhood and immediate environs; *hetero-topias* are places that are other, or other places (*le lieu autre ou l'autre lieu*), places that are different in type or location, or indeed places of the other (*le lieu de l'autre*). The contrasts within the uniformity allow us a sense of the subtleties of urban space, the contradictions, the dialectical relations.[168] '*Isotopias* are defined at each level: political, religious, commercial, etc. space. In relation to these isotopias, other levels are uncovered as *heterotopias*'.[169] Compared to rural space, Lefebvre suggests that all urban space is heterotopic.[170] It does not make sense to talk of urban space in the singular, but rather of 'urban spaces, lots of differentiated spaces'.[171] To understand a modern city we need to deploy all three conceptions of places, all three *topias*.[172]

There is therefore a profound tension between conceptions of space, which view it as abstract space, tending toward homogeneity (quantitative, geometrical and logical space) and the various perceptions of space, which accentuate differences.[173] As is well known, Lefebvre distinguishes further a way in which we live space, which is further removed from the abstractions of technocracy and planning. Social space, space as we experience and live it, is not like geometrical space and is also distinct from standard geographical ways of viewing it.[174] This distinction is further developed in Lefebvre's more theoretical work on space, which emerges from these reflections on the urban environment.

Reading urban spaces

The reading of a rural landscape that Lefebvre employed in analysing Campan and the Pyrenees more generally is also applied to the urban. A straightforward sociological description is inadequately historical; likewise he does not think that a simple geographical reading of these landscapes is sufficient. It might be necessary to describe the land, the relation of different human groups to that land and the physical environment, but this does not go far enough.[175] Lefebvre deploys the same regressive-progressive methodology. He suggests that his work in *La révolution urbaine* is not historical in the standard sense of the term.

> We have taken the object of the 'town' to describe and analyse its genesis, its modifications, its transformations, but only in appearance. In truth, we have first posed a virtual object; which permits us to trace the spatio-temporal axis. The future illuminates the past, the virtual permits the examination and situation of the accomplished. It is the industrial town, or rather the explosion of the pre-industrial and pre-capitalist town under the impact of industry and capitalism, which allows us to understand its conditions, its antecedents – that is the commercial town. This, in its turn, allows us to grasp the political town which it surpasses.[176]

Likewise, bourgeois society – however complex and opaque it might seem – allows us to understand more transparent societies such as the ancient or medieval world, rather than the contrary.[177] This is a double movement – regressive first, going from the virtual to the actual (*l'actuel*), the present (*l'actuel*) to the past; the progressive next, from the overcome and the finished to the movement that produces this end, which initiates and gives birth to something new.[178] Lefebvre uses in this his reading of Marx generally, but on the city he intends to extend Marx's thought to a topic that is not explicitly examined. To do this, one must first restore the thought[179] – that is, outline and synthesize its insights.

However, Lefebvre does not confine his study to this way of analysis. In a later work Lefebvre returns to this theme of reading urban spaces, and, drawing upon work from semiology, clarifies his sense.

> The city can be read because it writes, because it was writing. However, it is not enough to examine this without recourse to context. To write on this writing or language, to elaborate the *metalanguage of the city* is not to know the city and the urban. The context, what is *below* the text to decipher (everyday life, immediate relations, the *unconscious* of the urban, what is little said and of which even less is written), hides itself in the inhabited spaces – sexual and family life – and rarely confronts itself, and what is *above* this urban text (institutions, ideologies), cannot be neglected in the deciphering . . . The city cannot therefore be conceived as *a* signifying system, determined and closed as a system. The taking into consideration the *levels* of reality forbids, here as elsewhere, this systematization.[180]

Around the time that Lefebvre began to be concerned with urban issues he was also engaged in an ongoing debate about semiotics and structuralisms. In numerous places in his work, but particularly in *Vers le cybernanthrope* and *Le langage et la société*, we find discussions of systems of signs and early forms of structuralism (such as Jakobson and Hjemslev, and Chomsky's early writing).[181] However Lefebvre argues that the suggestion that the town and urban phenomena can be read as a 'system' is a dogmatic thesis. The phenomena cannot be reduced to a system of signs or a semiology.[182] It therefore follows that whereas it might be able to learn something from it, critical analysis cannot restrict itself to semiology and methods taken from linguistics.[183] Analysis can also learn from literature on the town – Victor Hugo (symbolic dimensions), Baudelaire (paradigmatic), Gérard de Nerval, Lautréamont, Rimbaud (syntagmatic).[184]

Therefore, whilst we can conceive of semiology of the urban on the one hand, or a *phenomenological* description of urban life on the other, what we really need is a philosophical analysis in the broad scope, because for Lefebvre

> [o]nly philosophy and the philosopher propose a *totality*, the search for a global conception or vision. To consider 'the city' is it not already to extend philosophy, to reintroduce philosophy into the city or the city into philosophy? It is true that the concept of *totality* is in danger of remaining empty if it is only philosophical. Thus is formulated a problematic which does not reduce itself to the city but which concerns the world, history, 'man'.[185]

This is, of course, yet another example of Lefebvre's ability to bridge opposed positions, of how his analysis of everyday life is, in some sense, situated between structuralism and phenomenology.

Like the 'Notes' on the countryside, one of Lefebvre's best pieces is his

'Notes on the new town', which is one of the preludes of his *Introduction to Modernity*. In this piece Lefebvre contrasts a village like the one discussed above with the 'new town' a few kilometres away. This is the town of Mourenx, which was constructed in the Pyrenees close to the oil, gas and sulphur deposits at Lacq that provided the central industry.[186] Lefebvre recalls that the arrival of the bulldozers to level the trees and start building the new town was a significant moment in his life and career.[187] Regarding the village, which is his home of Navarrenx, he claims that he knows every stone: 'In these stones I can read the centuries, rather as botanists can tell the age of a tree by the number of rings in its trunk.' In contrast, Mourenx is without a past.[188] Lefebvre likens Navarrenx to a seashell – a structure slowly secreted by a living organism: in contrast the new town is very much a *planned*, rather than a natural, development. Though in certain respects the new town has a lot going for it, in terms of the aesthetics of its design and the comforts it provides its inhabitants, Lefebvre claims to be filled with dread when he sets foot in it, terrified by the 'machines for living in' that fill it.[189]

Elsewhere, Lefebvre suggests that capitalism has developed towards an organization of both the working life, and of the private life, of leisure:

> The *new town* was the typical significant phenomenon in which and on which this organisation could be *read* because it was there that it was *written*. What, apart from such features as the negation of traditional towns, segregation and intense police surveillance, was inscribed in this social text to be deciphered by those who knew the code, what was projected on this screen? The organisation of the everyday, neatly subdivided (work, private life, leisure) and programmed to fit a controlled, exact time-table . . .[190]

Will the people be compliant, wonders Lefebvre, 'and do what the plan expects them to do, shopping in the shopping centre, asking for advice at the advice bureau, doing everything the civic centre offices demand of them like good, reliable citizens?'[191] The town has some strange demographics. Most of the adults are aged between 28 and 45; their children up to 10 years old. There are therefore no adolescents or young people, and no old ones either. Social structures of child care and leisure therefore work in different ways.[192] In a telling metaphor, Lefebvre suggests that there are not many traffic lights in this town, but that effectively 'the place is already nothing but traffic lights: do this, don't do that'. The town is a closed system, its text totally legible. But it is not legible like a novel, revealing surprises or possibilities, but as clear and direct as a propaganda leaflet. There is no history to read here.[193]

Lefebvre talks a lot about the boredom of this programmed, everyday life; the triumph of technocracy and planning.[194] The derricks and new tower blocks are awkwardly placed in this agricultural region. Despite the talk of it being a *pôle de croissance* – a focus for economic growth – the region still owes more to corn than oil.[195] It is the private capitalist firms and Paris that benefit from the wealth being created in this region. The level of technology used allows the extraction of vast amounts of resources – 1.2 million tonnes of sulphur; almost a tenth of France's total consumption of oil – which is exported to developed regions and large cities. Béarn furnishes them with energy and raw materials. Like other peripherial regions such as Brittany and Alsace, surplus value is extracted. It is, in a sense, a new form of colonialism.[196] Economic colonialism therefore, and political control of the citizens' everyday life. Instead, we can imagine a town where everyday life is completely transformed, where people are the masters of it.[197]

For Lefebvre, Paris was more than a place where he lived and worked. Like the Pyrenees, it was also a place where he did fieldwork, a place in which he saw many contemporary events played out and new developments in urbanism occurring. Although he discussed Paris in a range of texts, here I will focus on three main areas: his analysis of 'the other Parises' made for a short film,[198] supplemented by his discussions of the right to the city; his reading of the events of May 1968, written soon after the event and from a particularly close vantage point;[199] and his discussion of the Paris Commune written a few years before the events of 1968, and, if some accounts are to be believed, a central inspiration for the later episode.[200]

Paris is a place that is open to multiple readings. This is what Lefebvre intends with his reading of 'the other Parises'. There is a straightforward Paris, available as a conventional representation and produced for our consumption, but this is only the surface, or the veneer. Paris can be viewed in terms of its monuments, as a political city or a military city, a Paris of academic production of knowledge or commercial production of wealth.[201] Walking the streets, viewing the buildings and decoding the planning can tell us much about the city – and Lefebvre's piece, designed to be seen along with visuals, opens up new possibilities for its understanding. But much of Paris remains hidden beneath the surface, inscribed in its history.

In terms of the production of modern Paris, one figure above all stands out. This is Baron Haussmann (1809–91), Prefect of the Seine under Napoleon III, who rebuilt and reorganized much of Paris. His wholesale destruction of working-class neighbourhoods, with their crowded housing and winding streets, led to the broad boulevards Paris is famed for today. Although we may now be grateful for his opening of Paris up to traffic, this was not the intent. Nor was it for the beauty of views. These streets were partly designed for easy movement of troops and artillery, and he built barracks in strategic places to control the working classes. Sordid working-class quarters were replaced with bourgeois ones.[202] As Lefebvre notes, the 'victorious bourgeoisie carved up the existing space and quartered, shattered and rearranged it to suit its own requirements . . . this process has not stopped since, but still continues today'.[203] More recent developments would include the rebuilding of Les Halles and the construction work out at La Défense. Much of this feeds into Lefebvre's analysis of the right to the city. Much of the planning work has marginalized the workers, driving rents higher and the workers out into far flung parts of the city. As he aphorizes:

'On the walls of Marais can be read class struggle and the hatred between classes, a victorious meanness.'[204]

Urban space is therefore not just the place where political struggles happen, but increasingly the very object of that struggle. Just as a battlefield is the site of conflict but also part of the territory over which conflicts are often initiated, the city plays a similar role. One of the crucial issues is that of the relationship between the centre and the periphery. For Lefebvre, the call for a right to the city is a right to centrality.[205] The importance of centrality can be found in different forms in the cities of each kind of society, each mode of production. In the oriental city, the palace of the prince is at the centre, a place from which armies leave to protect or oppress the surrounding areas:

> In the Greek and Roman antique city, centrality is attached to an empty space, the agora and the forum. It is a place for assembly. There is an important difference between the agora and the forum. Prohibitions characterise the latter and buildings will quickly cover it up, taking away from its character of open space . . . For its part the medieval city soon integrated merchants and commodities and established them in its centre; the marketplace. A commercial centre characterised by the proximity of the church and the exclusion of the enclosure – a heterotopy of territory. The symbolism and the functions of this enclosure are different from that of the oriental or antique city. The territory belongs to the lords, peasants, vagrants and plunderers. Urban centrality welcomes produce and people. It forbids its access to those who threaten its essential and economic function, thus heralding and preparing capitalism.[206]

Increasingly in contemporary times, the city is the centre of consumption,[207] but is also a place from which people are excluded, economically or otherwise. For Lefebvre, the frontier line of the new antagonisms 'does not pass between *town* and *country*, but through the interior of the urban phenomena between the dominated periphery and the dominating centre'.[208] Economic changes and transformation of techniques of production accompany important movements of population. In earlier periods of urbanization this was generally a move toward cities but today, on the contrary it is often a movement of workers to the edges of cities – a shift from concentration to decentralization.[209] These issues, understandably have important relations to class. In two of the essays in *Espace et politique*, Lefebvre examines the relation between the bourgeoisie on the one hand and the proletariat on the other, to space.

These issues of marginalization or regionalization are crucial. Segregation and discrimination should not remove people from the urban.[210] As we shall see, one of the central claims in Lefebvre's analysis of the Paris Commune was the way in which it could be read as a reclaiming of the urban centre by the marginalized masses. In the contemporary period, Lefebvre wishes to free people from the monotony of tube-work-sleep (*metro-boulot-dodo*).[211] We find similar arguments in Britain today with the call for affordable housing for key workers, particularly in London. The working of any place is dependent on there being people to run it. For Lefebvre:

> The right to the city manifests itself as a superior form of rights: right to freedom, to individualism in socialization, to habitat and dwelling. The right to the *oeuvre*, to participation and *appropriation* (clearly distinct from the right to property), are implied in the right to the city.[212]

However, it is not a simple centre-periphery relation – important though that is. Lefebvre talks of an underground Paris in a number of senses – in a physical sense of the sewers and catacombs, in the Dostoyevskian sense of 'the Paris of the unconscious and the unconscious of Paris', but also:

> first and foremost, the city of poverty, of the deserving and undeserving poor. Marginal Paris? Those words mean nothing. There are many kinds of poverty in a big city, and many poor areas in the larger Paris. Metaphors like 'marginality', or 'underground life' help to disguise what someone wants to hide.[213]

At times, and this is a point that will be revisited, Lefebvre seems to be writing a history, or worse, a description, of space(s). It would be a relatively straightforward task to write a history of Paris as a space, analysing the way in which the city grew from early settlements, the draining of the Marais, the expansion into new areas, the emergence of new suburbs and the recoding of industrial areas to residential and so on. 'Les Autres Paris' covers much of this ground, as do parts of *La révolution urbaine*.[214] Edifying though that would doubtless be, in terms of the relation between time and space, history and geography, it continues the predominance of the first of each pair. Change through time is looked at as the most important aspect; space becomes another attribute to be historically analysed.

This was one of the arguments of my previous book on Heidegger and Foucault, where I outlined the way in which I thought that Foucault's work, when read through Heideggerian lenses, demonstrated the possibility of what I called spatial history. As I argued there, spatial history would be a reading of events with attention to spatial perspectives – space as a tool of analysis instead of merely an object of it. There have been criticisms that the book does not really deliver on this claim, and that what would be a spatial history is unclear.[215] These criticisms seem to me to be misconceived. It was not my intention to spend the first half of the book outlining a method and then applying it myself; rather to suggest that two of Foucault's major projects – the history of madness and the history of discipline – were spatial histories, and that they needed to be read in that way. In short, if you want to see what a spatial history might be, read *Histoire de la folie* or *Discipline and Punish*.

In Lefebvre's work, there is relatively little explicit history written – at least, much of what history he does write is intellectual history, the history of ideas or concepts.[216] When he does write histories of events, the importance of spatial elements is evident, but not perhaps as much as in his more political writings. One of the central texts is the short analysis of the events of May 1968 – an analysis that accords special status to 'urban phenomena' – another is the study of the 1871 Paris Commune, which is sometimes looked at as a key inspiration of the student movement. It is to this history of the Commune that I will turn first.

Lefebvre's analysis of the Commune as an event, a situation, is one which is close to the work of the Situationists.[217] Indeed, he had discussed many of the issues in the book with them, and thanks Guy Debord and Michèle Bernstein in the introduction.[218] However, the book – or more specifically, an initial statement of its position in the journal *Arguments* in 1962 – was accused of plagiarism by the Situationists, who believed that Lefebvre had insufficiently acknowledged their input and stolen ideas from their 'Theses on the Paris Commune'.[219] Lefebvre argues that the ideas had been thrashed out in group discussions at his base in the Pyrenees, and that only a few ideas from this made their way into his book.[220] In any case the notion of the festival is something that he had discussed at some length in earlier works such as the first volume of the *Critique* and *Rabelais*. It is somewhat ironic that the Situationists, who loudly proclaim that their journal has 'no copyright', and that their texts 'may be freely reproduced, translated or adapted, even without mentioning the source', should have been so bothered about this. However, it is certainly true that around this time Lefebvre developed the temporal 'moment' to a temporal-spatial 'situation' or 'event'. As he argues in the conclusion of the study, history can be seen as a succession of static periods, times of stagnation and relative balance, separated by creative bursts and revolutions – the 'events'. But these cannot be separated, because each lies as a germ in the heart of the other. Lefebvre suggests that though a historian cannot grasp all of this in its becoming, its development, the cooperation of a historian, a sociologist, an economist, a theoretician of ideas and a psychologist can push us toward a total history.[221] The plural approach is, as I have already suggested, characteristic of Lefebvre's work as a whole.

Lefebvre's central claim is the marginalization of the working classes within Paris. In the 1860s several areas outside of Paris became *arrondisse-ments*, incorporating large numbers of industrial workers into its population. At the same time, many previously central enterprises moved to the outskirts of the city or the suburbs. This was coupled with a dramatic reduction in worker numbers due to increased mechanization.[222] The uneven development of Paris is a significant issue behind the situation. Workers often lived in slum dwellings, with ever increasing rents, owned little other than the clothes they wore, and struggled to provide bread for their families. Wages improved slightly, but the cost of living rose quicker. Haussmann's plans displaced tens of thousands of workers from the central parts of the city. They truly had little to lose but their chains.[223] The city had become dominated by industrialization on the economic level and the state on the political; as a capital it was a monstrous head on a body that was no longer the body of that head. The Parisian insurrection was a reassertion of the liberty which along with reason and law was born with the city, in the imposing of rational order on the chaos of nature. Liberty, for Lefebvre, only had meaning in the city.[224] Despite the Parisian proletariat not being conscious of this

full situation, and their leaders only having an incomplete sense of it, this –
for Lefebvre – is the background.

The festival – which is how Lefebvre describes the events – was a spontaneous reaction against the programming and control of their life.[225] The
Situationist theses had also described this as a festival, but the analysis is
more based on Lefebvre's ideas of the peasant festival, where the festival of
the city amplifies rural traditions of transgression and disorder.[226] The
organized space of Haussmann's boulevards is challenged by the barriers
erected, by the use of the road, the café and the festival, which constitute the
social space of the poor.[227] It was, for Lefebvre, the first urban revolution,[228]
understood, as I suggested, not merely as a revolution in an urban setting,
but one that had the potential to challenge that context fundamentally. The
people of Paris come into the streets, into all the quarters of the city. They
flood (*inonde*) the streets, they drown out the existing power.[229] The workers
reappropriate the space from which they had been excluded by Bonapartism
– and therefore the Commune demonstrates the contradictions of space,
and not simply the contradictions of historical time.[230]

Elsewhere in this study we find discussion of transport networks of roads
and rivers within France;[231] of the siege of Paris;[232] of the strategies and
tactics taken during the Commune and the 'bloody week' (21–27 May 1871)
when Paris was retaken by the government in exile in Versailles; the placing
of the cannon that had initially sparked the proclamation.[233] There is a
detailed map of the city showing the opposed forces and the reoccupa-
tion,[234] and some remarkable pictures of the barricades. For Lefebvre it is
essential to grasp this revolutionary event both in its singularity – without
reducing it to its antecedents and consequences – and in terms of the
elements that made it up and the conditions that made it possible. Economic
conditions provide a necessary condition. A proletarian revolution supposes
a proletariat; but a simple analysis of the economic situation does not
explain the fullness of the situation they found themselves in. Similarly the
historical events leading up to the Commune are important – the disintegration of the Second Empire, the loss of the war – but not in themselves
sufficient. Social and urban factors are also crucial to understanding the
event; the interaction of groups of heterogeneous people creating spontaneous goals; ideological currents of the time and so on. It is only this kind
of multi-faceted analysis that can recognize the conflicting influences and
causes of this event.[235] As Lenin indicated, it is the conjunction of objective
and subjective elements that make a revolutionary event.[236]

The most explicit reading of the situation is perhaps actually found in the
book about May 1968, where he draws parallels between the events:

> In 1871, the people were armed; the entire people took to the streets, festival and
> battle; the bourgeoisie had already left the capital or was preparing to do so. It
> was not therefore a marginal category of 'citizens' who intervened in abolishing
> the divisions. However, an analogy remains. In March 1871 as in May 1968, the
> people come from the periphery, from the outside where they had been driven,

where they only found a social vacuum, assembled and headed toward the urban centres in order to reconquer them.[237]

What we find is this passage is manifold. As well as a class analysis we might expect from a Marxist, there is also a recognition of both the conflictual and festive aspects of the irruptions. However, most important, is the spatial analysis inherent in this work. There is a recognition of the relation between the centre and periphery, the class relations that this spatializes, and the emptiness of the peripheral life. What Lefebvre called the right to the city is clear here, with the challenge to dominant power structures on the urban scene. The workers return to the centre, reconquer the city.

Lefebvre's study of May 1968 follows similar contours. There is much background material on the contemporary status of capitalism and the French state – indeed much of the book would be reused in *La survie du capitalisme* a few years later. In the analysis of the events proper, Lefebvre looks first at the Faculty of Letters at Nanterre, an area just outside Paris where he taught, and where the movement began. (It is worth noting, with Lourau, that despite Lefebvre's extreme proximity to the events – he taught Daniel Cohn-Bendit for example, and signed a manifesto in *Le Monde* in solidarity with the movement – of contemporary analyses his reads today as one of the most calm and measured.)[238] Nanterre is close to *la Défense*, which at the time was filled with commercial buildings and truck depots, proletarian housing and misery, but which Lefebvre suggests may be an urban centre by 1980. It is in this 'curious context and desolate landscape' that the Faculty 'conceived in terms of the concepts of the industrial production and productivity of neo-capitalist society' is based. Instead of living up to its intent, Lefebvre suggests that the buildings and environment reflect the real nature: the production of 'mediocre intellectuals and "junior executives" for the management of this society'.[239] Lefebvre emphasizes the alienating aspects of this habitat, which is segregated both functionally or socially – a ghetto of students – and industrially – the students are on an extra-urban site due to their non-productive status. Small prohibitions and regulations become intolerable – not because of their small effects – but because they symbolize repression generally. This ghettoization is a generalized tactic in the metropolis – suburbs, foreigners, factories and students are all segregated and congregated. New towns have something akin to colonial towns.[240]

The buildings of the faculty exhibit the purpose for which they were designed; the site is marginalized because of its purpose, and the segregation is an experience as well as a physical reality; anomie becomes the norm; and decisions are made for rather than by the students.[241] The functional nature of the buildings – vast amphitheatres, smaller rooms, administration blocks – underlies the tensions.[242] The students from Nanterre are being trained for these junior positions in education, industry and bureaucracy; ready for a life of worry about 'slow promotion, bills, transfers, apartments and cars', and for them 'this image of everydayness is far from appealing'.[243] Nanterre is therefore what Lefebvre describes as a 'heterotopia',[244] although here he opposes it to the utopia of the inner city, rather than the isotopia he would later introduce.

The initial economic objectives of the uprising led to questions of ideology and values,[245] which coincided with the arrival of the Nanterre students in the Latin Quarter. Lefebvre suggests that there was 'a dialectical interaction between marginality and urban centrality'. Though the movement originated in Nanterre, a focus was needed, and the action came to the centre in the Sorbonne. Lefebvre sees the Occupation of the Latin Quarter as a re-appropriation of a space that had been taken from them. During the demonstrations, Lefebvre argues that Paris changed and was restored: 'the views, the streets, the Boulevard Saint-Michel which, rid of automobiles, again became a promenade, became a forum . . . the old Sorbonne hung with black and red flags took on a transfigured symbolic dimension'.[246]

Lefebvre notes that it was in the streets that the demonstrations took place, it was there that 'spontaneity expressed itself – in a social area not occupied by institutions'.[247] This demonstrates the importance of urban phenomena – 'the streets have become politicised areas . . . social space has assumed new meaning . . . political practice transferred to the streets side-steps the practice (economic and social) which emanates from identifiable places'. The streets become political areas, political places.[248] This stress on the location of the struggle is important, because not only are spatial relations – marginalization and centrality, uneven development, ghettoization and so on – political in themselves, politics is played in a spatial field. What is important in the movement being on the streets is that groups who are normally kept apart – such as students and workers – are able to meet.[249]

Sorbonne is the utopia to Nanterre's heterotopia, and within this 'concrete utopia',[250] new mechanisms of power and space become apparent. Lefebvre argues that the events allowed speech that had previously been repressed to 'burst forth in the crowded lecture halls, courtyards, on the square, in the vast forum'. Previous boundaries were crossed, as people who before had never dared cross 'the gates of this sanctuary, a place consecrated to private knowledge, mysterious writings, and class-marked scientificity' now did.[251] This was, it would seem, an instance of the revolution of everyday life he was calling for. We should note that his own *Right to the City* was published right at the beginning of 1968.[252] Indeed, he does relate the movement to notions of the festival we have already discussed in relation to everyday and peasant life: 'Festival and struggle – this ambiguity characterises certain urban phenomena. It is a condensation and intensification of what has happened in the villages over the centuries.' Laughter and speech, humour and songs characterize this urban experience.[253]

As an anticipation of later themes, which will be much more fully explored in Chapter 6, Lefebvre notes that 1968 can be seen as a fundamental challenge to the state. This is not just in Paris, but also in the Prague Spring of the same year, which also saw a challenge to the dominant regime. For Lefebvre, the events in Paris were an attack against state capitalism, those in Prague against state socialism.[254] They are part of a wider concern with a challenge to the power of the state – what might be best illustrated today, despite suggestions that globalization is itself a challenge to the power of the state, in anti-globalization movements. Lefebvre's suggestion – again one that will be elaborated later – is that the movement 'sketches a project of generalised *autogestion* and in this sense involves a *social practice*'.[255] *Autogestion* is a movement for self-management, or workers' control – a revolt against control and management from above. The same themes are found in the analysis of 1871. Lefebvre also reads this struggle as one against the state, against its bureaucracy and military, against the police, judicial, fiscal and financial institutions,[256] and suggests that we can see it as the first attempt in history to achieve the *autogestion* of public services.[257] This is not only at the level of production, but of territory, of urban communities.[258] The desire is to achieve the *autogestion* of urban life by the people of the city. This is what is meant by the dictatorship of the proletariat – the democratic power of the armed people, destroying the state apparatus, and its organs – bureaucratic, military and police.[259] It is the conquest of political power by the working class, but more fundamentally than a simple transfer of power, it also a transition of the sense of power. As Marx argues, it puts the social and society above the political.[260] It is clear that Lefebvre's critique of urbanism is central to his critique of the state and politics.[261] For Lefebvre, Marxist theory is founded on the French experience of the Commune, the ideology of French socialism, rather than the ideology of state socialism found in Germany particularly in Lassalle's vision.[262]

It is therefore clear that Lefebvre believed that the issues he was analysing in relation to the rural and the urban were explicitly political issues, as well as raising more general theoretical issues concerning space and time.

> In the course of this vast process of transformation, space reveals its nature, what it always was: a) a political space, site and object of strategies; b) a projection of time, reacting on it and allowing its domination, and as a consequence, today of its exploitation to death.[263]

Lefebvre's work therefore combines two key strategies of understanding – the radical critique of urbanism, of its ambiguities, contradictions, variants (both those it confesses and those it hides); and the elaboration of the science of the urban phenomena. The work on the rural – interesting enough in itself – is important in understanding what has been changed and indeed lost in the transition. Equally there are three key political strategies – to recognize the importance of urban problems as a question of the first order; a programme of generalized *autogestion*; and 'the introduction within the contractual system (enlarged, transformed, concretised) of a "right to the city" (that is the right not to be excluded from the centrality and its movement)'.[264] The theoretical issues will be developed in the following chapter; the political ones in Chapter 6.

Notes

1 See Martin Nicolaus, 'Foreword', in Karl Marx, *Grundrisse: Foundations of the Critique of Political Economy (Rough Draft)*, translated by Martin Nicolaus, Harmondsworth: Penguin, 1973, p. 7 n. 1, who notes that although there was an earlier edition in two volumes in 1939 and 1941, this was a limited edition. Nicolaus cites Roman Rosdolsky, *Zur Entstehungsgeschichte des Marxschen Kapital: Der Rohentwurf des Kapital, 1857–8*, p. 7 n. to the effect that only three or four copies made it to the Western World. See Roman Rosdolsky, *The Making of Marx's 'Capital'*, translated by Peter Burgess, London: Pluto, 1977, p. xi n. 1.

2 Marx, *Grundrisse*, p. 100.

3 *Le marxisme*, Paris: PUF, 1948, p. 32.

4 As the book notes, *La vallée de Campan: Étude de sociologie rurale*, Paris: PUF, 1963, p. 220, was written in Bagnères-de-Bigorre in 1941 and Paris in 1952. For the background, see *La somme et le reste*, Paris: Méridiens Klincksieck, 3rd edition, 1989 (1959), p. 263 n. 1; René Mouriaux, 'Un Marxisme dans le siècle' in *L'irruption de Nanterre au sommet*, Paris: Éditions Syllepse, 2nd edition, 1998 (1968), p. vii. See also 'La communauté villageoisie', *La pensée* 66, March–April 1956, pp. 29–36.

5 *Trois textes pour le théâtre*, Paris: Anthropos, 1972, pp. 63–100.

6 See Rémi Hess, *Henri Lefebvre et l'aventure du siècle*, Paris: A. M. Métailié, 1988, pp. 114, 165–70; Michel Trebitsch, 'Preface' in Henri Lefebvre, *Critique of Everyday Life Volume I: Introduction*, translated by John Moore, London: Verso, 1991, p. xxv. The *Manuel* is sometimes named as the *Traité de sociologie rurale*.

7 Rémi Hess, 'Présentation de la troisième édition', in *Du rural à l'urbain*, Paris: Anthropos, 3rd edition, 2001 (1970), pp. xxii–iii.

8 See, for example, 'Les classes sociales dans les campagnes: La Toscane et la "mezzandira classica" ', *Du rural à l'urbain*, pp. 41–62, on Tuscany; and 'Théorie de la rente foncière et sociologie rurale', *Du rural à l'urbain*, pp. 79–87, on rents and revenues.

9 See *Le temps des méprises*, Paris: Stock, 1975, p. 223.

10 Stuart Elden, *Mapping the Present: Heidegger, Foucault and the Project of a Spatial History*, London/New York: Continuum, 2001.

11 *Sociologie de Marx*, Paris: PUF, 1966, p. 17; *The Sociology of Marx*, translated by Norbert Guterman, Harmondsworth: Penguin, 1968, p. 22.

12 *Sociologie de Marx*, p. 19; *The Sociology of Marx*, p. 24.

13 *La droit à la ville*, Paris: Anthropos, 1968, p. 76; *Writings on Cities*, translated and edited by Eleonore Kofman and Elizabeth Lebas, Oxford: Blackwell, 1996, p. 118.

14 *La vie quotidienne dans le monde moderne*, Paris: Gallimard, 1968, p. 219; *Everyday Life in the Modern World*, translated by Sacha Rabinovitch, Harmondsworth: Allen Lane, 1971, pp. 115–16.

15 *La droit à la ville*, p. 76; *Writings on Cities*, p. 118.

16 *Du rural à l'urbain*, p. 1.

17 *La droit à la ville*, p. 34; *Writings on Cities*, p. 87; see *Sociologie de Marx*, p. 56; *The Sociology of Marx*, p. 67.

18 *Espace et politique: Le droit à la ville II*, Paris: Anthropos, 2nd edition, 2000 (1972), p. 87. We should note that the utopian socialists Fourier and Owen believed that this opposition could be overcome, as did Engels following them. See *Espace et politique*, p. 84. For Lefebvre on Fourier, see his introduction to *Actualité de*

Fourier: Colloque d'Arcs-et-Senans sous la direction de Henri Lefebvre, Paris: Anthropos, 1975; and *Critique de la vie quotidienne* II: *Fondements d'une sociologie de la quotidienneté*, Paris: L'Arche, 1961, p. 289; *Critique of Everyday Life* II: *Foundations for a Sociology of the Everyday*, translated by John Moore, London: Verso, 2002, p. 288.

19 *La vie quotidienne dans le monde moderne*, p. 356; *Everyday Life in the Modern World*, p. 195; see also *La droit à la ville*, pp. 1ff, 92; *Writings on Cities*, pp. 65ff, 130.

20 *La pensée marxiste et la ville*, Paris: Castermann, 1972, p. 102. In *La fin de l'histoire*, Paris: Les Éditions de Minuit, 1970, p. 137, Lefebvre similarly draws upon the town–country relation as central to the understanding of history.

21 See also Monique Coornaert and Henri Lefebvre, 'Ville, urbanisme et urbanisation', *Perspectives de la sociologie contemporaine: Hommage à Georges Gurvitch*, sous la direction de Georges Balandier, Roger Bastide, Jacques Berque et Pierre George, Paris: PUF, 1968.

22 *La révolution urbaine*, Paris: Gallimard, 1970, pp. 14–15.

23 *La révolution urbaine*, pp. 15, 36.

24 *La révolution urbaine*, p. 37.

25 *La révolution urbaine*, pp. 14–15.

26 *La révolution urbaine*, pp. 16–17, see 18–21; *La pensée marxiste et la ville*, pp. 37–8.

27 *Sociologie de Marx*, p. 35; *The Sociology of Marx*, p. 43.

28 *La pensée marxiste et la ville*, p. 37.

29 *La droit à la ville*, p. 37; *Writings on Cities*, p. 89. See also 'La communauté villageoisie', pp. 30–1.

30 *La révolution urbaine*, pp. 20–1.

31 *La révolution urbaine*, p. 21.

32 *La révolution urbaine*, p. 22.

33 *La révolution urbaine*, p. 163.

34 *La révolution urbaine*, p. 10; see *Du rural à l'urbain*, p. 243.

35 *La droit à la ville*, pp. 10–11; *Writings on Cities*, p. 71.

36 *Espace et politique*, p. 149.

37 *La révolution urbaine*, p. 11.

38 *La révolution urbaine*, p. 25, see p. 220.

39 *La révolution urbaine*, p. 28.

40 *La révolution urbaine*, p. 152, see pp. 184, 220.

41 *La pensée marxiste et la ville*, p. 146.

42 *La révolution urbaine*, p. 26; for an earlier schema, see *La droit à la ville*, p. 81; *Writings on Cities*, p. 123. See Derek Gregory, *Geographical Imaginations*, Oxford: Blackwell, 1994, p. 371, for an alternative diagram of 'Lefebvre's urban revolution'.

43 *La révolution urbaine*, pp. 105–6; *Key Writings*, edited by Stuart Elden, Elizabeth Lebas and Eleonore Kofman, London: Continuum, 2003, p. 136.

44 *La révolution urbaine*, p. 106; *Key Writings*, p. 136.

45 See *La révolution urbaine*, pp. 110–11.

46 *La révolution urbaine*, pp. 117–18; *Key Writings*, p. 140.

47 *La révolution urbaine*, p. 135; *Key Writings*, p. 148.

48 *La vie quotidienne dans le monde moderne*, pp. 126–7; *Everyday Life in the Modern World*, p. 65.

49 *La vie quotidienne dans le monde moderne*, p. 98; *Everyday Life in the Modern World*, p. 50.

50 See, for example *La droit à la ville*, pp. 76, 93–4; *Writings on Cities*, pp. 118, 131; *Espace et politique*, p. 56. See particularly Martin Heidegger, 'The question concerning

technology' in *The Question Concerning Technology and Other Essays*, translated by William Lovitt, New York: Harper & Row, 1977.

51 *La pensée marxiste et la ville*, p. 122.

52 *La pensée marxiste et la ville*, pp. 143–4.

53 *La pensée marxiste et la ville*, p. 152; *Pyrénées*, Pau: Cairn, 2nd edition, 2000 (1965), p. 128.

54 *Hegel, Marx, Nietzsche ou le royaume des ombres*, Paris: Castermann, 1975, p. 52; *Pyrénées*, p. 26.

55 *Introduction à la modernité: Préludes*, Paris: Les Éditions de Minuit, 1962, p. 97; *Introduction to Modernity: Twelve Preludes*, translated by John Moore, London: Verso, 1995, p. 90.

56 Elsewhere Lefebvre suggests that there were *oeuvres* in the urban environment before industrialization. See *La droit à la ville*, pp. 1–3; *Writings on Cities*, pp. 65–6; *La proclamation de la commune*, Paris: Gallimard, 1965, p. 31.

57 *La droit à la ville*, p. 2; *Writings on Cities*, p. 65. The distinction draws upon that of Heidegger's 'The origin of the work of art', in *Basic Writings*, edited by David Farrell Krell, London: Routledge, revised edition, 1993.

58 *La droit à la ville*, p. 5; *Writings on Cities*, p. 67.

59 *Espace et politique*, p. 74.

60 *De l'État*, Paris: UGE, 4 volumes, 1976–8, I, p. 233. Lefebvre criticizes Marx's abstract vision of nature as 'an atoll in the Pacific' in *Le manifeste différentialiste*, Paris: Gallimard, 1970, p. 130.

61 *Introduction à la modernité*, p. 97; *Introduction to Modernity*, p. 90.

62 *L'irruption de Nanterre au sommet*, p. 42; *The Explosion: Marxism and the French Upheaval*, translated by Alfred Ehrenfeld, New York: Modern Reader, 1969, p. 46.

63 *Introduction à la modernité*, p. 180; *Introduction to Modernity*, pp. 180–1.

64 Trebitsch, 'Preface', p. xxvi.

65 See Margaret Fitzsimmons, 'The Matter of Nature', in Trevor Barnes and Derek Gregory (eds), *Reading Human Geography: The Politics and Poetics of Inquiry*, London: Arnold, 1997, pp. 183–94, especially p. 188. It is worth noting that while most continental theorists are blamed for the emphasis on the urban, Heidegger, whose work privileges the rural, has been criticized for his nostalgic celebration of poetic dwelling and, more seriously, of adopting the ideologically loaded (Nazi) notions of blood and soil.

66 *Introduction à la modernité*, p. 336; *Introduction to Modernity*, pp. 345–6.

67 *L'irruption de Nanterre au sommet*, p. 27; *The Explosion*, p. 33. For a more generalized critique of Marcuse, see *L'irruption de Nanterre au sommet*, pp. 19–27; *The Explosion*, pp. 24–33; *Vers le cybernanthrope*, Paris: Denoël/Gonthier, 1967, p. 38 n. 1; *La survie du capitalisme: La re-production des rapports de production*, Paris: Anthropos, 3rd edition, 2002 (1973), pp. 112–13; *The Survival of Capitalism*, translated by Frank Bryant, London: Allison & Busby, 1976, pp. 114–15.

68 Karl Marx and Friedrich Engels, 'Manifesto of the Communist Party', in *Revolutions of 1848: Political Writings Volume 1*, edited by David Fernbach, Harmondsworth: Penguin, 1973, p. 71. On Marxism's dismissal more generally, see *Une pensée devenue monde: Faut-il abandonner Marx?* Paris: Fayard, 1980, pp. 179–81.

69 Karl Marx, 'The eighteenth Brumaire of Louis Bonaparte', in *Surveys from Exile: Political Writings Volume 2*, edited by David Fernbach, Harmondsworth: Penguin, 1973, p. 239. For a more positive appreciation of the changes in the countryside, see Karl Marx, *Capital: A Critique of Political Economy* I, translated by Ben Fowkes,

Harmondsworth: Penguin, 1976, pp. 637–8. For a discussion, see Andy Mer-rifield, *Metromarxism: A Marxist Tale of the City*, New York: Routledge, 2002, pp. 22–3.

70 See Michel Trebitsch, 'Preface: the moment of radical critique', in *Critique of Everyday Life* II, p. xii.

71 *Du rural à l'urbain*, p. 79.

72 *Du rural à l'urbain*, p. 64; *Key Writings*, p. 111.

73 *Du rural à l'urbain*, p. 22.

74 *Du rural à l'urbain*, p. 79.

75 'De l'explication en économie politique et en sociologie', *Cahiers internationaux de sociologie* XXI, pp. 19–36, p. 35. For a discussion of some of these issues, see Kurt Meyer, *Henri Lefebvre: Ein Romantischer Revolutionär*, Wien: Europaverlag, 1973, pp. 19–24.

76 *Du rural à l'urbain*, pp. 26–8; see pp. 64, 66–7; *Key Writings*, pp. 111–12, 113–14.

77 *De l'État* II, p. 357; see *Du rural à l'urbain*, pp. 82–4, 218; *De l'État* IV, pp. 171–2. In contrast, he notes that Trotsky underestimates the peasant movement, *De l'État* II, p. 391.

78 *Du rural à l'urbain*, pp. 34–8.

79 *Du rural à l'urbain*, p. 64; *Key Writings*, p. 112.

80 *Du rural à l'urbain*, pp. 65–6; *Key Writings*, pp. 112–13.

81 *Du rural à l'urbain*, p. 66; *Key Writings*, p. 113.

82 *Du rural à l'urbain*, p. 69; *Key Writings*, p. 115; see *La vallée de Campan*, p. 83; *Du rural à l'urbain*, p. 80.

83 *Du rural à l'urbain*, p. 72; *Key Writings*, p. 116.

84 See also *La proclamation de la commune*, p. 31; *Au-delà du structuralisme*, Paris: Anthropos, 1971, pp. 211, 319; and the diagram in *Le langage et la société*, Paris: Gallimard, 1966, p. 50.

85 *Du rural à l'urbain*, p. 39; *La révolution urbaine*, p. 139.

86 *Du rural à l'urbain*, p. 33.

87 *Pyrénées*, p. 175.

88 *Du rural à l'urbain*, p. 39.

89 Paul Cloke and Nigel Thrift, 'Introduction: refiguring the "Rural"', in Paul Cloke *et al.*, *Writing the Rural: Five Cultural Geographies*, London: Paul Chapman Publishing, 1994, pp. 1–5.

90 At Nanterre, for example, Lefebvre had Jean Baudrillard, Alain Touraine and René Lourau as his colleagues. On this department, see François Dosse, *History of Structuralism Volume II: The Sign Sets, 1967–Present*, translated by Deborah Glassman, Minneapolis: University of Minnesota Press, 1997, pp. 109–11.

91 *Critique de la vie quotidienne* I, p. 145; *Critique of Everyday Life* I, pp. 131–2.

92 *Critique de la vie quotidienne* I, p. 238; *Critique of Everyday Life* I, p. 224.

93 In Lefebvre's own work, above all see *Critique de la vie quotidienne* II, pp. 306–12; *Critique of Everyday Life* II, pp. 306–12. In others, see, for example, Gaston Bachelard, *The Poetics of Space*, translated by Maria Jolas, Boston: Beacon, 1969; Paul Carter's outstanding *The Road to Botany Bay: An Essay in Spatial History*, London: Faber & Faber, 1987, especially p. 247, where he talks of 'reading' landscapes; and Salman Rushdie's description of Edward Said as someone who 'reads the world as closely as he reads books', in Edward Said, 'On Palestinian identity: a conversation with Salman Rushdie', in *New Left Review* 160, November/December 1986, pp. 63–80.

94 *Critique de la vie quotidienne* I, p. 248; *Critique of Everyday Life* I, p. 233.

95 *Allemagne*, Paris: Braun & Cie, 1964, p. 7.

96 *Critique de la vie quotidienne* I, p. 224; *Critique of Everyday Life* I, p. 210.

97 *Critique de la vie quotidienne* I, pp. 228ff; *Critique of Everyday Life* I, pp. 213ff. See, for example, Friedrich Nietzsche, *Thus Spoke Zarathustra*, in *The Portable Nietzsche*, edited and translated by Walter Kaufmann, Harmondsworth: Penguin, 1954, pp. 203–4, and *Human All-too-Human*, translated by R. J. Hollingdale, Cambridge: Cambridge University Press, 1986, p. 69.

98 *Critique de la vie quotidienne* I, p. 228; *Critique of Everyday Life* I, p. 214.

99 *Critique de la vie quotidienne* I, p. 247; *Critique of Everyday Life* I, p. 232. For a discussion of Nietzsche's comments on space and power, see Elden, *Mapping the Present*, pp. 49–51.

100 *Pyrénées*, pp. 59, 115. We should note that the original edition of this book, *Pyrénées*, Lausanne: Éditions Rencontre, 1965, is fully illustrated.

101 *La vallée de Campan*, pp. 1–82.

102 *La vallée de Campan*, pp. 31–4.

103 *La vallée de Campan*, p. 83 n. 1.

104 *La vallée de Campan*, p. 84.

105 *La vallée de Campan*, p. 84; *Pyrénées*, p. 36. In *Pyrénées*, p. 36, Lefebvre also gives the example of Llívia, an enclave, a little Spanish city in the middle of French territory.

106 *Pyrénées*, pp. 29, 35. Lefebvre briefly mentions the importance of this area as a way out of occupied Europe during World War Two on p. 35. This was the place where Walter Benjamin committed suicide in 1940. See Merrifield, *Metromarxism*, p. 68.

107 *La vallée de Campan*, p. 96.

108 *La vallée de Campan*, p. 97. See also *Le temps des méprises*, p. 223.

109 *Pyrénées*, p. 36. The border between France and Spain, set in the 1659 Treaty of Pyrenees following the war between them was the first modern border in Europe. See *Pyrénées*, pp. 181–2; and Peter Sahlins, *Boundaries: The Making of France and Spain in the Pyrenees*, Berkeley: University of California Press, 1989.

110 *La vallée de Campan*, pp. 97–9.

111 *La vallée de Campan*, p. 103.

112 *La vallée de Campan*, p. 116.

113 'Structures Familiales Comparées', in Georges Friedmann (ed.), *Villes et campagnes: Civilisation urbaine et civilisation rurale en France*, Paris: Armand Colin, 1953, pp. 327–62, p. 327; see *Pyrénées*, p.190.

114 *Allemagne*, p. 13.

115 *Pyrénées*, p. 101.

116 *Pyrénées*, p. 175.

117 *Pyrénées*, pp. 175–7.

118 Edith Kurzweil, *The Age of Structuralism: Lévi Strauss to Foucault*, New York: Columbia University Press, 1980, p. 78. Lefebvre critically reflects on his work on space in 'An interview with Henri Lefebvre', translated by Eleonore Kofman, *Environment and Planning D: Society and Space* 5(1), 1987, pp. 27–38.

119 *La fin de l'histoire*, p. 206.

120 'Réflexions sur la politique de l'espace', *Espaces et Société* 1, 1970, pp. 3–12; reprinted in *Espace et politique*, pp. 49–70; 'Reflections on the politics of space', *Antipode* 8 (2), 1976, pp. 30–7.

121 Theodore D. Tieken, Maarovfa Press to Guterman, 15 February 1977.

122 *The Urban Revolution*, translated by Robert Bononno, Minneapolis: University

of Minnesota Press, 2003. This appeared after this book was written, hence references are to the original only.

123 *Une pensée devenue monde*, p. 149; see *La droit à la ville*, p. 92; *Writings on Cities*, p. 130; 'Bilan d'un siècle et de deux demi siècles (1867–1917–1967)', in Victor Fay (ed.), *En partant du 'capital'*, Paris: Anthropos, pp. 115–42, p. 129. See, for example, Friedrich Engels, *The Housing Question*, Moscow: Foreign Language Publishing House, 1955; *The Condition of the Working Class in England*, Oxford: Basil Blackwell, 1958. For Lefebvre's discussion of Engels' work in this area see *La pensée marxiste et la ville*, pp. 9–26; *Espace et politique*, pp. 81–97. See also Mario Rui Martins, 'The theory of social space in the work of Henri Lefebvre', in R. Forrest, J. Henderson and P. Williams (eds), *Urban Political Economy and Social Theory: Critical Essays in Urban Studies*, Aldershot: Gower, 1982, pp. 160–85, pp. 161–3.

124 *La droit à la ville*, p. 92; *Writings on Cities*, p. 130.

125 *La pensée marxiste et la ville*, p. 7.

126 *Espace et politique*, p. 83.

127 Though see Manuel Castells, 'Citizen movements, information and analysis: an interview with Manuel Castells', *City* 7, 1997, pp. 140–55, pp. 144–5.

128 Manuel Castells, *La question urbaine*, Paris: François Maspero, 1972; *The Urban Question: A Marxist Approach*, translated by Alan Sheridan, London: Edward Arnold, 1977; David Harvey, *Social Justice and the City*, Oxford: Basil Blackwell, 1988 (1973) (especially pp. 287, 288–9, 297, 299, 302). Noting the change of title from Lefebvre's urban *revolution* to Castells' urban *question*, Soja and Hadjimichalis suggest this demonstrates the less radical nature of Castells' work. See Edward W. Soja and Costis Hadjimichalis, 'Between geographical materialism and spatial fetishism: some observations on the development of Marxist spatial analysis', *Antipode* 11(3), 1979, pp. 3–11. For a contextual discussion, particularly showing the range of French perspectives, see Elizabeth Lebas, 'Urban and regional sociology in advanced industrial society: a decade of Marxist and critical perspectives', in *Current Sociology* 30(1), Spring 1982, pp. 1–130.

129 Edward W. Soja, *Postmodern Geographies: The Reassertion of Space in Critical Social Theory*, London: Verso, 1989, pp. 77–8, see, pp. 69–70; Kristin Ross, *The Emergence of Social Space: Rimbaud and the Paris Commune*, Basingstoke: Macmillan, 1988, p. 9. Neil Smith, *Uneven Development: Nature, Capitalism and the Production of Space*, Oxford: Basil Blackwell, 2nd edition, 1990, p. 91, praises Soja for having 'endorsed, refined and developed the basic ideas in Lefebvre's vision; at the same time he attempts to correct what he sees as a systematic misinterpretation of Lefebvre in the Anglo-American [tradition]'. On Castells on Lefebvre and spatial fetishism, see also Andy Merrifield, 'Henri Lefebvre: a socialist in space', in Mike Crang and Nigel Thrift (eds), *Thinking Space*, London: Routledge, 2000, pp. 167–82, p. 169.

130 David Harvey, *The Limits to Capital*, London: Verso, new edition, 1999 (1982), p. 374.

131 David Harvey, *Consciousness and the Urban Experience: Studies in the History and Theory of Capitalist Urbanization*, Oxford: Basil Blackwell, 1985; *The Urbanization of Capital: Studies in the History and Theory of Capitalist Urbanization 2*, Oxford: Basil Blackwell, 1985.

132 Manuel Castells, *Class, City and Power*, translated by Elizabeth Lebas, London: Macmillan, 1978, p. 12.

133 Merrifield, *Metromarxism*, p. 124.

134 See Castells, 'Citizen movements, information and analysis', p. 145.

135 Castells, 'Citizen movements, information and analysis', pp. 146–7. This is discussed in Merrifield, *Metromarxism*, p. 114. On Castells' work of this period, see Peter Newman, 'Urban political economy and planning theory', in R. Forrest, J. Henderson and P. Williams (eds), *Urban Political Economy and Social Theory: Critical Essays in Urban Studies*, Aldershot: Gower, 1982, pp. 186–202; Lebas, 'Urban and regional sociology in advanced industrial society'; and Peter Saunders, *Social Theory and the Urban Question*, London: Hutchinson, 2nd edition, 1986. On Harvey, see John L. Paterson, *David Harvey's Geography*, London: Croom Helm, 1984. For a discussion of Castells and Harvey, see Kian Tajbakhsh, *The Promise of the City: Space, Identity, and Politics in Contemporary Social Thought*, Berkeley: University of California Press, 2001. Their relation to Lefebvre is usefully brought out in Merrifield, *Metromarxism*; and M. Gottdiener, *The Social Production of Urban Space*, Austin: University of Texas Press, 2nd edition, 1997 (1985). For a contemporary analysis, see the essays in Michael Harloe (ed.), *Captive Cities: Studies in the Political Economy of Cities and Regions*, Chichester: John Wiley & Sons, 1977. Another discussion of the three together is Ira Katznelson, *Marxism and the City*, Oxford: Clarendon Press, 1992, Chapter 3, although this is somewhat restricted in his reading of Lefebvre himself, particularly in the peculiar claims that in this work he departed from Marxism. There are some useful directions in Soja, *Postmodern Geographies*, which I discuss in more detail in 'Politics, philosophy, geography: Henri Lefebvre in Anglo-American scholarship', *Antipode: A Radical Journal of Geography* 33 (5), November 2001, pp. 809–25, pp. 813–14.

136 *Critique de la vie quotidienne* I, p. 248; *Critique of Everyday Life* I, p. 233.

137 *La droit à la ville*, p. 109; *Writings on Cities*, p. 142.

138 See, for example, *De l'État* II, pp. 390–1.

139 *Du rural à l'urbain*, p. 110.

140 *La révolution urbaine*, p. 7.

141 *La révolution urbaine*, pp. 8–9.

142 *La révolution urbaine*, p. 9, see *Vers le cybernanthrope*, pp. 19–20; *De l'État* IV, pp. 184–5.

143 *La révolution urbaine*, p. 217.

144 *La révolution urbaine*, p. 217.

145 *La révolution urbaine*, p. 25, see pp. 185, 220.

146 *La révolution urbaine*, p. 25.

147 *La pensée marxiste et la ville*, p. 58.

148 *La révolution urbaine*, p. 220; see *La droit à la ville*, p. 65; *Writings on Cities*, p. 110.

149 Lucien Goldmann, *Lukács and Heidegger: Towards a New Philosophy*, translated by William Q. Boelhower, London: Routledge & Kegan Paul, 1977, p. 87.

150 *Du rural à l'urbain*, p. 219.

151 *Du rural à l'urbain*, p. 233.

152 *La révolution urbaine*, p. 160.

153 *La révolution urbaine*, p. 22.

154 *La révolution urbaine*, p. 22.

155 *La révolution urbaine*, p. 239.

156 *La révolution urbaine*, p. 244.

157 *Du rural à l'urbain*, pp. 220–1; *Vers le cybernanthrope*. On technocrats more generally,

see *Vers le cybernanthrope*, pp. 19, 22, 192–3, 196–7, 200–1, 209; *La somme et le reste*,
pp. 754–5; *Métaphilosophie*, Paris: Éditions Syllepse, 2nd edition, 2001 (1965),
pp. 158–9.

158 *La révolution urbaine*, p. 29; see *Du rural à l'urbain*, pp. 98–100.

159 *La révolution urbaine*, p. 30; see *Du rural à l'urbain*, p. 224. On the ludic see also *La
présence et l'absence: Contribution à la théorie des représentations*, Paris: Casterman,
1980, p. 194, where Lefebvre suggests his principal inspirations on this topic
are Heidegger, Axelos and Eugen Fink.

160 *La droit à la ville*, p. 29; *Writings on Cities*, p. 84.

161 *Writings on Cities*, p. 207.

162 *La révolution urbaine*, p. 30.

163 *Vers le cybernanthrope*, pp. 13–15; see *Writings on Cities*, p. 207.

164 *La révolution urbaine*, p. 29.

165 'Les autres Paris', *Espaces et sociétés* 13–14, October 1974–January 1975,
pp. 185–92, p. 192; 'The other Parises', in *Key Writings*, pp. 151–9.

166 *La révolution urbaine*, p. 41.

167 *La révolution urbaine*, pp. 53–4, see pp. 167–8.

168 *La révolution urbaine*, pp. 54–5, 172.

169 *La droit à la ville*, p. 69; *Writings on Cities*, p. 113.

170 *La révolution urbaine*, p. 173.

171 *Du rural à l'urbain*, p. 224.

172 *La révolution urbaine*, pp. 174–5; see also *Espace et politique*, p. 79; *Logique formelle,
logique dialectique*, pp. xxix–xxx, xl, xlvii–viii. The notion of heterotopia is also
used by Michel Foucault in a 1966 lecture, although this was not published
even in French until 1984. See 'Des espaces autres', in *Dits et écrits 1954–1988*,
edited by Daniel Defert and François Ewald, Paris: Gallimard, 4 volumes,
1994, IV, pp. 752–62; 'Of other spaces', translated by Jay Miskowiec, *Diacritics*
16 (1), Spring 1986, pp. 22–71. For various discussions of the term, see Soja,
Postmodern Geographies; John Marks, 'A new image of thought', *New Formations*
25, Summer 1995, pp. 66–76; Kevin Hetherington, *The Badlands of Modernity:
Heterotopia and Social Ordering*, London: Routledge, 1997; and Elden, *Mapping the
Present*, pp. 116–18.

173 *La révolution urbaine*, p. 221.

174 *Du rural à l'urbain*, pp. 213, 224.

175 *Du rural à l'urbain*, p. 145.

176 *La révolution urbaine*, p. 35.

177 *La révolution urbaine*, p. 35.

178 *La révolution urbaine*, pp. 35–6.

179 *La pensée marxiste et la ville*, p. 151.

180 *La droit à la ville*, p. 63; *Writings on Cities*, p. 108.

181 See *Du rural à l'urbain*, p. 245.

182 *La révolution urbaine*, pp. 70–1, 71ff.

183 *La révolution urbaine*, pp. 115–16, *Key Writings*, p. 139.

184 *La révolution urbaine*, p. 145. These terms are most fully elaborated in *Le langage et
la société*. See, for example, pp. 266, 288–93. For a discussion and application,
see René Lourau, *L'analyse institutionnelle*, Paris: Éditions de Minuit, 1970,
pp. 272–4.

185 *La droit à la ville*, pp. 41–2; *Writings on Cities*, p. 92.

186 Lefebvre also analyses this town in *Pyrénées* and various essays in *Du rural à
l'urbain*.

187 'Lefebvre on the Situationists', conducted and translated by Kristin Ross, *October* 79, Winter, pp. 69–83, p. 76.

188 *Introduction à la modernité*, p. 121; *Introduction to Modernity*, p. 116.

189 *Introduction à la modernité*, p. 123; *Introduction to Modernity*, p. 118. For a discussion, see Merrifield, *Metromarxism*, pp. 82–3.

190 *La vie quotidienne dans le monde moderne*, p. 115; *Everyday Life in the Modern World*, p. 59. On the social text in the urban, see also *Le langage et la société*, pp. 296–7.

191 *Introduction à la modernité*, p. 123; *Introduction to Modernity*, pp. 118–19.

192 *Du rural à l'urbain*, pp. 124–5.

193 *Introduction à la modernité*, p. 124; *Introduction to Modernity*, p. 119.

194 *Introduction à la modernité; Introduction to Modernity; Vers le cybernanthrope*, p. 28.

195 *Pyrénées*, p. 72; *Du rural à l'urbain*, p. 116.

196 *Pyrénées*, pp. 121–2, 177; see *De l'État* IV pp. 179–80.

197 *Du rural à l'urbain*, pp. 151–2.

198 'Les autres Paris'; *Key Writings*, pp. 151–9.

199 *L'irruption de Nanterre au sommet; The Explosion*.

200 Lefebvre recalls a student at Nanterre telling him this in *Le temps des méprises*, p. 120. See Didier Eribon, *Michel Foucault et ses contemporains*, Paris: Fayard, 1994, pp. 79–80. However, the Situationist text 'The beginning of an era', in *Situationist International Anthology*, edited and translated by Ken Knabb, Berkeley: Bureau of Public Secrets, 1981, pp. 225–56, which originally appeared in *Internationale Situationniste* 12, Septembre 1969, disputes this. There, pp. 227–8, they repeat the suggestion that he plagiarized their work on the Commune, but worse, that he failed to recognize that such an event was imminent. For Lefebvre's suggestion that the events of 1871 would not repeat, including a critique of the Situationists, see *Position: Contre les technocrates en finir avec l'humanité-fiction*, Paris: Gonthier, 1967, p. 195. For a discussion, see Merrifield, *Metromarxism*, pp. 86–7.

201 See also 'Lefebvre on the Situationists', p. 80

202 *La proclamation de la commune*, p. 32; *La droit à la ville*, pp. 17–18; *Writings on Cities*, p. 76.

203 'Les autres Paris', p. 187; *Key Writings*, p. 154.

204 *La droit à la ville*, p. 16; *Writings on Cities*, p. 75.

205 *La révolution urbaine*, p. 179 n. 1. For a discussion, see Ash Amin and Nigel Thrift, *Cities: Reimagining the Urban*, Cambridge: Polity, 2002, pp. 142–3.

206 *La droit à la ville*, pp. 147–8; *Writings on Cities*, p. 169.

207 *La droit à la ville*, p. 148; *Writings on Cities*, pp. 169–70.

208 *La révolution urbaine*, p. 152; *La pensée marxiste et la ville*, p. 46.

209 *Du rural à l'urbain*, p. 109.

210 *Espace et politique*, p. 22; *Writings on Cities*, p. 195.

211 Reported in Martins, 'The theory of social space in the work of Henri Lefebvre', p. 183. The nearest formulation to this that I have found in Lefebvre's work is *La droit à la ville*, p. 133; *Writings on Cities*, p. 159.

212 *La droit à la ville*, p. 155; *Writings on Cities*, pp. 173–4. See also 'Le droit à la ville', *L'homme et la société* 6, October–December 1967, pp. 29–35.

213 'Les autres Paris', p. 189; *Key Writings*, p. 157.

214 *La révolution urbaine*, pp. 169–71.

215 See, for example, David Cunningham and Jon Goodwin, 'Spacey', *Radical Philosophy* 114, July/August 2002, pp. 38–40.

216 See the discussion in Chapter 2.

217 See *La proclamation de la commune*, p. 21.

218 *La proclamation de la commune*, p. 11 n. 1.
219 See, for example, *Aux poubelles de l'histoire*, Paris: IS, 1963, reprinted in *Internationale Situationniste* 12, September 1969; and 'Les mois les plus longs (février 1963–juillet 1964)', *Internationale Situationniste* 9, August 1964.
220 'Lefebvre on the Situationists', pp. 77–8, 79–80; *Le temps des méprises*, p. 159. See their text, 'Theses on the Paris Commune', signed by Guy Debord, Attila Kotányi, Raoul Vaneigem, in *Situationist International Anthology*, pp. 314–17; and Lefebvre's 'La signification de la commune', *Arguments* 27–8, 1962, pp. 11–19.
221 *La proclamation de la commune*, p. 410. See also the SI text 'La théorie des moments et la construction de situations', *Internationale Situationniste* 4, June 1960.
222 *La proclamation de la commune*, pp. 73–4.
223 *La proclamation de la commune*, pp. 76–7.
224 *La proclamation de la commune*, p. 32.
225 *La proclamation de la commune*, pp. 20–1; *Key Writings*, pp. 188–9; *La proclamation de la commune*, p. 40.
226 See also Arthur Hirsch, *The French Left*, Montreal: Black Rose Books, 1982, p. 145, where he suggests that Lefebvre's earlier work on the festival was influential for the Situationists.
227 *La proclamation de la commune*, p. 124.
228 *La fin de l'histoire*, p. 137.
229 *La proclamation de la commune*, p. 126.
230 *Espace et politique*, p. 168.
231 *La proclamation de la commune*, p. 70.
232 *La proclamation de la commune*, pp. 173ff.
233 *La proclamation de la commune*, p. 234.
234 *La proclamation de la commune*, pp. 412–13.
235 *La proclamation de la commune*, pp. 407–8.
236 *La proclamation de la commune*, p. 409.
237 *L'irruption de Nanterre au sommet*, p. 107; *The Explosion*, pp. 117–18.
238 Pierre Cours-Salies, René Lourau and René Mouriaux, 'Prolongements . . .' in *L'irruption de Nanterre au sommet*, pp. xxiii–xxx, p. xxiii. The Manifesto appeared on 10 May 1968, and was signed by Lefebvre, Sartre, Blanchot, Lacan, Klossowski and others. It appears in Michel Contrat and Michel Rybalka, *Les écrits de Sartre: Chronologie, bibliographie commentée*, Paris: Gallimard, 1970, p. 464. Lefebvre was apparently asked by the authorities which of his students were likely militants, and claims to have answered 'I am not a cop'. 'Lefebvre on the Situationists', p. 82.
239 *L'irruption de Nanterre au sommet*, pp. 95–6; *The Explosion*, p. 104.
240 *L'irruption de Nanterre au sommet*, p. 85; *The Explosion*, p. 93.
241 *L'irruption de Nanterre au sommet*, p. 96; *The Explosion*, p. 104.
242 *L'irruption de Nanterre au sommet*, p. 97; *The Explosion*, p. 106.
243 *L'irruption de Nanterre au sommet*, p. 98; *The Explosion*, p. 107.
244 *L'irruption de Nanterre au sommet*, pp. 96, 107; *The Explosion*, pp. 105, 118.
245 *L'irruption de Nanterre au sommet*, p. 101; *The Explosion*, pp. 110–11.
246 *L'irruption de Nanterre au sommet*, pp. 107–8; *The Explosion*, p. 118.
247 *L'irruption de Nanterre au sommet*, p. 66; *The Explosion*, p. 71.
248 *L'irruption de Nanterre au sommet*, p. 66; *The Explosion*, p. 72.
249 *L'irruption de Nanterre au sommet*, p. 91; *The Explosion*, p. 98.
250 *L'irruption de Nanterre au sommet*, p. 108; *The Explosion*, p. 118.

251 *L'irruption de Nanterre au sommet*, p. 108; *The Explosion*, p. 119.

252 Cours-Salies, Lourau and Mouriaux, 'Prolongements . . .', p. xxvi.

253 *L'irruption de Nanterre au sommet*, p. 107; *The Explosion*, p. 118. For an analysis of the events generally, with some reference to Lefebvre, see Kristin Ross, *May '68 and its Afterlives*, Chicago: University of Chicago Press, 2002.

254 *De l'État* I, pp. 271–2, 336–8.

255 *L'irruption de Nanterre au sommet*, p. 111; *The Explosion*, pp. 122–3.

256 *La proclamation de la commune*, p. 161, see p. 131.

257 *La proclamation de la commune*, p. 307.

258 *La fin de l'histoire*, p. 218.

259 *La proclamation de la commune*, p. 309; see *Pour connaître la pensée de Karl Marx*, Paris: Bordas, 1947, pp. 173–4. It is clear that this analysis derived from Marx's reflection on 1871. See 'The Civil War in France', in *The First International and After, Political Writings Volume 3*, edited by David Fernbach, Harmondsworth: Penguin, 1974. On *autogestion* and the city, see also *La révolution urbaine*, p. 199.

260 *La proclamation de la commune*, p. 391. See Marx, 'The Civil War in France', p. 211.

261 *La révolution urbaine*, p. 216.

262 *La proclamation de la commune*, p. 391; *Le manifeste différentialiste*, p. 154.

263 *La révolution urbaine*, p. 63.

264 *La révolution urbaine*, p. 199.

5 Space and history

Lefebvre sometimes played the role of a historian. We can see this in his readings of Paris in 1871 and 1968, as demonstrated in Chapter 4, and in the intellectual histories of figures in the French literary tradition discussed in Chapter 2. But not only did Lefebvre write history, he also thought about it in a more abstract sense. Lefebvre was concerned with the methodological assumptions behind history, and as previous chapters have shown, this was not simply through historical materialism. The most obvious development for which Lefebvre was responsible was the enormous emphasis he put on questions of spatiality, best known in the English world through his work on the production of space. This is a book that has had an significant impact in the discipline of geography. However, I contend that this has been understood in some less than helpful ways, and that ultimately it gives a misleading view of Lefebvre's work. It is essential to realize that the theoretical work on space was the culmination of previous work – particularly the work on rural and urban landscapes discussed in the last chapter – rather than a programme of future study. Similarly, the role of Nietzsche and Heidegger is central to understanding his project. But perhaps most importantly, the stress on the work on space occludes the rethinking of questions of temporality and historicity that was also carried out in Lefebvre's work.

In this respect, I am concerned here with challenging the accepted wisdom, that, as Michael Dear puts it, 'most social theorists are by now aware that Lefebvre's project is aimed at a reorientation of human inquiry away from its traditional obsession with time and toward a reconstituted focus on space'.[1] It might be assumed that when it came to questions of temporality and historicity that Lefebvre would fall back on Marxism, as Marxism as a whole can be understood as historical materialism, in other words a meditation on the understanding of history. However, as Kofman and Lebas suggest in their introduction to *Writings on Cities*, here too he incorporates the insights of Nietzsche and Heidegger.[2] How he does this is less well explored. In the discussion of Nietzsche in Chapter 2, following Kofman and Lebas, and Merrifield, it was suggested that it was particularly in terms of history, the non-linearity of time, and rhythm that Nietzsche had an impact.[3] As Lefebvre notes in *The Production of Space*, Nietzsche's understanding of time is entirely opposed to Marxist time.[4] Just as we will see with space, time needs to be grasped in a range of complementary and yet contradictory ways. In other words, Lefebvre did not replace temporal with spatial analysis, but thought the relation between space and time, and in the process rethought both concepts. It is crucial to remember that they must be thought together, and yet cannot be reduced to the other.[5] Space and time are the indispensable coordinates of everyday life, and therefore a rethinking of them essential to that overall project.[6]

This chapter therefore moves through four stages. In the first two, I discuss Lefebvre's work on questions of time and history – particularly concentrating on his analysis of moments, and his book *La fin de l'histoire*. *La fin de l'histoire* is in some sense a forerunner of *Hegel, Marx, Nietzsche ou le royaume des ombres*, and the three figures of the later book play an important role in this earlier work, as does Heidegger.[7] Nietzsche and to a lesser extent Heidegger enable Lefebvre to break with Hegel and orthodox Marxism on the teleological principle of history. In the third stage, I provide a rereading of *The Production of Space*, in the light of the earlier studies of the country and the city, and with emphasis on the two terms in the title. I argue that the stress on the term 'production' shows Lefebvre's Marxism at work, and that it gives the lie to suggestions that he was more interested in the earlier Marx on alienation than the later Marx on political economy. In the analysis of the term 'space', I show how Lefebvre politicized and radicalized many of Heidegger's analyses, particularly around his understanding of the notion of dwelling or inhabiting. This was particularly important for Lefebvre, as Heidegger's work is central in the break from traditional philosophical understandings of space. In the final stage of this chapter I provide a reading of Lefebvre's work on rhythms. Although the concern with rhythm was found throughout his career, it was only very late on that he developed his insights in any real detail. The work on rhythmanalysis, which examines change through time *and* space, is both the culmination of the work on everyday life and a return to the analysis of urban landscapes. Philosophically sound and politically aware, it was a fitting end to his career.

Time and moments

The events of 1871 and 1968 are examples of what Lefebvre would call moments, instants of dramatic change and disruption to everyday routine. One of the most significant moments in Lefebvre's own life was a vision he had as a young man in the mid-1920s, in the Pyrenean countryside. On a walk one day he saw a church cross with a circle surrounding it. 'They had crucified the sun!'[8]

> I no longer saw the cross of Christ wreathed in solar glory or surrounded by the crown of thorns, as had been explained to me, but the darkened sun, marked by a black sign, nailed to the Christian cross. The sun was youth, brilliant [*l'éclatante*], my own, but overcast, pinned down by mental, sexual, and social misery; it was the heat of vitality, the ardour of energies fallen into the coldness of the void and

its sign. Even in the research bearing the name which had appeared so beautiful to me for a long time: philosophy.[9]

Lefebvre's understanding of the symbol of the crucified sun gives us a sense of the 'tormented, rebellious, anarchistic' youth he had had, and of his adolescent battle with Catholicism.[10] It was a crucial moment, and was the beginning of his work on the abandoned *Procès de la Chrétienté* – the trial of Christianity – a work inspired by Nietzsche.[11] This was a struggle of intellectual and personal freedom, and he suggests that his early work on Jansen and Pascal can be understood in this context.[12] The 'solar cross – or the crucified sun'[13] is a symbol he would use in numerous works, the first being an article for *Les temps modernes* in 1959, a piece that became part of the autobiographical *La somme et le reste*.[14] As Lefebvre recalls, this was a time of considerable distress in his life – the CNRS exclusion and re-admission, followed by the suspension and then expulsion from the PCF. For Lefebvre, in *La somme et le reste*, 'the crucified sun was a symbol of destiny. The revolution is also the crucified sun.'[15]

> The crucified Sun is the symbol of division, humiliation, failure and hopelessness. The Sun bears evidence of its own contradiction and denial; it bears its death and the instrument of death. Black lines, rigid and intersecting at right angles, brand the image of the source of fire with a funereal blazon. Its message is no longer the joy of passionate reason. Crucified, the sun loses its nature under the imprint of the cross which eclipses its splendour. The cross proclaims an end to the cosmic cycle, the cosmic cycles of creative love whose repetitions are never in vain because they spread its seeds throughout space and time. It is the multiple symbol of lost and blighted youth, of Revolution darkened by the shadow of its own history, of a generation, of an era, of passionate countries scarred by slavery and wars, and the destiny of their own liberation, the countries of the Orient, of Asia, of Africa.[16]

It is not a fascist symbol – though Lefebvre notes it appeared as graffiti in Paris – nor is it a merely a juxtaposition of pagan and Christian symbols.[17]

> The Sun symbolises the Father; the Cross indicates the Word, signs, languages, conflicts, .choices, mutilations, death. The crucified Sun, a duality of symbols, shows man and announces for man the expectation and the possibility of reconciliation.[18]

Instead, for Lefebvre, the sun represents all that is vital and full of potential, the cross, the repression and alienation of life. The important moment of realization was also a realization of the importance of moments. As Lourau poetically puts it, 'beyond structures and structuralisms . . . and of the almost Bergsonian flux of the phenomenological "*accomplissements*", the "moment" is, under the sign of the immanence of the everyday, like the caress of an angel's wing, a passing fling with transcendence'.[19] This moment and its thinking through was important to Lefebvre's work on time more generally, because it forced him to come to terms with some aspects of Nietzsche's work. In Nietzsche's *Thus Spoke Zarathustra* the true task of Zarathustra is to accept his role as the teacher of the eternal return, a cyclical understanding of temporality and history. The crucial image of the eternal return is a gateway with the word *Augenblick* – blink of an eye, or moment – inscribed above it. This is the place where past and future collide in the present moment.[20] Indeed, in Nietzsche's writings he talks of the moment where the thought of the eternal recurrence came to him, a moment that is also explicitly situated: August 1881, during a walk along the lake of Silvaplana, at a 'powerful pyramidal rock not far from Surlei'.[21] Thinking about the moment got Lefebvre interested in questions of time and space, and the rhythms of life and death, and also led him, following Nietzsche, to affirm life.[22] Nietzsche's work was also important for Lefebvre in thinking about the tension between memory and becoming; questions of rhythm and style, energy and force.[23]

Lefebvre's work on moments is not intended to be epistemology or ontology, or a critique of ontology, but a study of everyday reality 'at a *sociological* level, at which the individual is not separate from the social'.[24] For Lefebvre, the moment is 'the attempt to achieve the total realisation of a possibility'.[25] Moments are

> limited in number, although the list cannot be declared closed: play, love, work, rest, struggle, knowledge, poetry . . . If the number proved unlimited, they would no longer be moments. However, we cannot stop enumerating them, since it is always possible to discover or to constitute a 'moment', in principle, at least, and since there are perhaps 'moments' in individual life. Theory ought, if it is to be consistent, to declare a criterion. What is a 'moment'? What is not? It is not obliged to undertake the task of making an exhaustive list. In order for it to present a coherence that would make it acceptable, it is better to indicate and emphasise a few general characteristics of these 'moments'.[26]

Lefebvre goes through these in some detail. A moment 'defines a form and is defined by a form', it has 'a certain constancy over time, an element common to a number of instants, events, situations and dialectical movements (as in "historical moment", "negative moment" or "moment of reflection")'.[27] Questions of form and content – as explored in Chapter 1 – are important; moments raise questions about the relation of social life and nature; and disrupt a simplistic boundary between nature on the one hand and society or culture on the other. They demonstrate that the individual cannot be separated apart from society. Moments similarly challenge strict divisions between sociology and philosophy: it is crucial to look at these issues from a social perspective, but this is inadequate alone. 'Sociology studies the formation of "moments"; rather than moments, it deals with the groups who create them. "Moments" and the theory of moments are on another level, that of philosophy.'[28] Moments are 'social relationships and forms of individualised consciousness', and in a return to a theme discussed earlier, 'the theory of moments thus repeats with a new meaning the theory of the "Total Man" '.[29]

The theory of moments is therefore important in understanding Lefebvre's work for a range of reasons. Although it owes much to Nietzsche, Lefebvre also recognizes that Hegel is important.[30] A sociologically grounded notion, it nonetheless claims philosophical status; it is important in thinking the every day nature of the everyday, that is the temporal dimension and the importance of repetition; and although explicitly temporal is transformed in the analysis of the event, a more situated concept. For Lefebvre, however, the moment is not the same as a situation, but it creates them. Lefebvre is concerned with moving away from a rationalist understanding of an event, which sees it as 'a privileged instant, that of a crisis. When there was a revolutionary event, that decisive moment enabled the leap forward, the hour of birth through (more or less brutal) violence. In all cases and all situations, the event was conceived of as an end result.'[31] This is the Marxist understanding, which tends to think of it in terms of its progress toward economic growth or increases of productive forces, even if these explanations are lost on the actors, who think that they operate 'for liberty, for peace, against oppression'. If the event is historical, 'it will leave traces. And we are going to become attached to this henceforth privileged phenomenon: the trace. And we shall try to understand the so-called historical event in terms of a series of things, revealed by traces'.[32] Equally, as will be shown later in this chapter, the work on rhythmanalysis is in germ in the earlier work on the theory of moments.[33]

> The 'moment' thus conceived of has its memory and specific time. Repetition is an important aspect of this 'temporality'. The repetition of moments forces us to refine the concept of repetition. It frees itself from psychology or metaphysics. It is no longer repetition of an 'ontic' or ontological nature; nor it is any more a repetition copied to the letter from the phenomena of memory, pushed as far as they will go. The re-presentation of a form, rediscovered and reinvented on each occasion, exceeds previous conceptions of repetition. And furthermore, it includes them; because it also involves the return and reintegration at a high level – individual and social – of elements of the past and the surpassed.[34]

Lefebvre therefore challenges abstract reductive understandings of time just as he does space. The application of the notion of 'measure' to time requires the privileged instrument of the clock. The measure of time is no longer time, just as the measure of work is no longer work. Time is thus a representation, but it is not entirely abstract, because it requires 'the clock, a material object, as a means and as a support'.[35] As with space, the concept of time has a distance from the actual time that we live. There is therefore a fundamental difficulty with the concept of time, in that it removes all reference to *praxis* and thereby descends into speculative metaphysics. 'The mental is separated from the social.'[36] However, we should be cautious in abandoning a concept of time altogether, lest we eliminate history. We need to retain an abstract sense of time *alongside* examinations of 'lived time'. Along with this mental grasping of time there must come a range of other times. Social, biological, physical and cosmic time, played out in cycles or linear progressions, demonstrate that time is something which is already plural and differential.[37]

Nietzsche's constant example for time, and one Lefebvre would use again and again, is music. (It is worth noting that Lefebvre played the piano.) 'Nietzsche knew that music transformed the real, that is the triviality of the everyday.'[38] In music all is repetition, and rhythm, harmony and melody appear from the repetition of vibrations, intervals, timbres and themes.[39] 'The structure [*texture*] of becoming no longer appears in the same way', it is illuminated by music, understood through repetition, the deployment of time, space shot through with rhythm. Appearance and disappearance, and both in each other, along with surface and depth, manifestation and latency demonstrate the relation between the same and the other, repetition, and the genealogy of difference.[40] What we find in Nietzsche is a replacement of philosophical rationality and scientific historicity with art, particularly tragedy and music. Art is at the centre of knowledge.[41] And yet, mathematical thought and physics are born, like philosophy, like tragedy, 'out of the spirit of music'.[42] As with the importance of painters like Pignon and Picasso to the understanding of space – discussed later in this chapter – here too an aesthetic medium shows the power and limits of representation.

> Music shows the appropriation of time, painting and sculpture that of space. If the sciences discover partial determinisms, art and philosophy show how a totality grows out of partial determinisms.[43]

To understand music, we need to think about melody, harmony and rhythm together. The neglect of the last is Lefebvre's criticism of Douglas Hofstadter's otherwise 'remarkable book', *Gödel-Escher-Bach*.[44] Indeed, Lefebvre suggests that this is a neglected area of musical study more generally.[45] Lefebvre claims that rhythm can be separated from melody only by an abstraction.[46] One of the things interesting about music, Lefebvre contends, is that sound occupies a space, and there music perhaps 'presupposes a unity of time and space, an alliance'.[47]

Lefebvre notes that Beethoven and Schumann are his favourite composers, but although he finds the work of modern composers such as Webern, Schönberg and Boulez interesting, he is resistant to the dogmatism that attends some of these new ways of thinking. Lefebvre argues that there is a link between music and philosophy. This is most obvious with Bach and Leibniz, and Wagner and Nietzsche, but is also shown in the way the break with previous notions of musical tone parallels developments in other aesthetic and representative issues.[48] Schopenhauer and Bergson are also mentioned in relation to their philosophies of temporality.[49] As well as music, Lefebvre notes that poetry also shows the use of repetition – the use of assonance, rhyme, words or clauses – and rhythm through the role of metre.[50] And, in a French twist to the standard modern myth, he suggests that a monkey with a typewriter will eventually produce the *Comédie humaine* of Balzac.[51]

Nietzsche was therefore central, but Lefebvre was also inspired by Proust's work on time, a time he suggests can be reduced neither to Bergsonian nor Heideggerian time. Time is not simply something lost, but time is loss itself. 'Proust's time cannot be reduced to fluidity, nor to the juxtaposition of states with determined contours, nor to irreversibility or reversibility.' Time, in Proust, is something regained, but never entirely: we can recall our youth, childhood, and memories, but without returning there. This time is more 'polyvalent and more contradictory than that of philosophy. Lived time allows memory and art.'[52] Lefebvre therefore recalls that it was reading Proust and other novelists around the same time he had the experience of the crucified sun that led to the development of the 'theory of moments'. This was in 1925, while he was part of the group of young philosophers.[53] What is important to note is that this was a theory of time developed before Lefebvre encountered Marxism. It therefore illustrates how his understanding of historical materialism, though Marxist, exceeded and critiqued Marx on some points, notably on the question of time and the concomitant understanding of history.

History

As Hess remarks in his note to the second edition of *La fin de l'histoire*, we should remember the subtitles of some of Lefebvre's books. *Introduction to Modernity* talked of 'preludes', *Métaphilosophie* of 'prolegomena' and *La fin de l'histoire of 'épilégomènes'*.[54] This untranslatable word – save for a neologism like *epilegomena* – is obviously a play on prolegomena, and has a sense of both an epilogue and a recapitulation. This use of language is important with regard to this book. Whilst the most obvious translation of the title is *The End of History*, 'end' here must be understood in the sense of both goal and conclusion. The Kantian term of the 'kingdom of ends' can be reappropriated – not without some irony – to describe Marxist thought. 'In Marx, Hegelian theory does not disappear. It is transformed. The end of history becomes the history of ends.'[55] These would include the end of religion, philosophy, of 'man', ideologies and abstract 'truth', of the state, of representation, political economy, blind or unquestioning historicity, and classes themselves. It is worth noting that a number of those are apparently more Nietzschean than Marxist. These would be replaced – in Marx – by a range of alternatives and strategies. Religious alienation, abstract anthropology and the state would be transformed by the enriching of social relations; abstract truth would be displaced by concrete truth, practical and social, rather than class-bound ideology; and so on.[56] As Lefebvre notes in *La somme et la reste*, he did not enter the PCF to do politics, but because Marxism announced the end of politics.[57]

Equally *histoire* has the sense of a story, a *récit*, a narrative.[58] The book could be translated as *The End of the Story*. The content of the book makes it clear that the former is the predominant sense, but this does not mean it is the only one. There is certainly something in Lefebvre's analysis that calls into question the broad-scale interpretations of history, what Lyotard would later call grand or meta-narratives, *les grands récits*.[59] Lefebvre notes that 'the end of history, end of the sense of history, sense of the end of history' are three interlaced themes within the book.[60] However, *le sens de l'histoire* has a secondary meaning of the direction of history, as well as the well-known ambiguity in *sens* – sense or meaning.[61] The notion of the end of history has, Lefebvre notes, a paradoxical ring or an internal contradiction. There will always be events; we will always arrive at something; time does not end. Because time and history go together, history cannot end. This, for Lefebvre, is to misunderstand the matter at hand. History is not simply unlinked events. The surface marks of history (*des traces*), or the consequences of these minor details, do not make history, although historical events leave traces. We can therefore attempt to define history by historical time, but although this is implicitly the case, it rests upon a tautology. There is a plurality of times, of physical, biological, social, cyclical and linear times, which overlap and conflict in various ways. But to say this is to risk being unable to define history at all. If there is nothing fundamental about historical time then history is a fiction, or an abstraction. For Lefebvre, we must define history in terms of an end. This does not merely give history a sense, a direction, but outside of this sense history cannot be defined and has no sense. Without *end* history is chaos.[62]

Lefebvre's book can be seen both as a challenge to Daniel Bell's *The End of Ideology*,[63] and as an anticipation of critiques of Francis Fukuyama's 1989 article, and the subsequent bestseller that shares Lefebvre's title.[64] Rather than Fukuyama's irony-bypass and casual optimism Lefebvre looks at the notion of 'end' with a much more progressive sense, and realizes the problems of Nietzsche's 'last man'. Lefebvre claims that it is not so much a question of purely and simply liquidating history as empiricists or structuralists wish, nor of prolonging historicity as those who cling to 'historical truths' desire, but of evading both of these dogmatisms.[65] In order to achieve this, the book follows a particular path:

1. an examination of the formation of historical thought in Hegel and Marx, and the criticism of it in Nietzsche;
2. the question 'what is history?' is replaced by that of 'what was history?' in its *belle époque*, what was it waiting for, and how did it conclude;
3. an examination of the end of history and its meaning. 'If it is true that the founders of history defined it in terms of an end, it is time to discern the sense of that end and not of history.'[66]

This notion of an end is of course central to Hegel and Marx's work. A finality in history does not require that the goal is fixed and actually represented, but that time, becoming, has a direction, and is determined by that term. There are a number of conceivable ends to history. For Hegel, history

is defined by the realization of philosophy in a political system, the state; for
Marx industrial praxis, the proletarian revolution, by the mastery of social
man over nature. But Lefebvre argues that neither of these has happened in
the way their originators thought, and that perhaps the 'end' of history
'does not coincide with the finalities envisaged by the creators of historical
thought'.[67] For that reason Lefebvre turns to Nietzsche. While Hegel, Marx
and others like them thought that a post-historical period would be born
from history, Nietzsche thought that a *civilization* different from our own
would be born. We will remember that civilization was, for Lefebvre, the
central aspect of Nietzsche's understanding of the modern world (see
Chapter 2). It would be different

> Because it would be born through a repudiation of history, historicity, the his-
> toric, the past and its knowledge as useless excess, burdens on the memory, more
> and more sterile inventories of the accomplished. The birth of this civilisation
> implies a radical break, a total discontinuity, a renewal of methods of knowledge,
> and a repudiation of historical thought.[68]

The advantage that this has is that the end of history is radically altered.
It is not an end in the Hegelian or Marxist sense of a progression; but
history will either end or has ended already, in contradiction, under the
weight of knowledge and historical cultures. The last of three meanings of
the end of history – 'the end of history, end of the sense of history, sense of
the end of history'[69] – is therefore the most important, as the sense of history
is to finish, to end. It ends in decline, in a withering away (*dépérissant*). History
does not end as much as we exit it, we leave it behind and this should be
seized in terms of an overcoming. This is a surpassing or overcoming
(*dépassement*) of history, in the sense of *aufheben*, but also, and more centrally,
in the sense of *überwinden*, surmounting (*surmonter*).[70] *Aufheben* is central to the
work of Hegel and Marx, and has a famous or notorious range of meanings,
including 'to lift up', 'to preserve' and 'to cancel', which purport to explain
dialectical transformation. *Überwinden* is a term much used by Nietzsche
which is usually translated as 'overcoming'. As Lefebvre later underlines, he
understands *dépassement* more as *überwinden* 'rather than by a sober, calm
[*sage et tranquille*] *aufheben*'.[71]

It is significant that the question of the end of history contains another
question: the relationship between the state and history.[72] For Marx, Lefebvre
argues, Hegel was wrong about the relation between history and the state.
The state was not the final moment of history, but an obstacle in its way. If
history continued then the state would move toward its end; if the state was
able to remain, to consolidate itself, then Hegel would be right and history
would have ended. The state, Marx suggested, was not an end in itself, but a
power, a means, only an instrument for other forces.[73] However Lefebvre
notes that history is born at the same time as the state, in Ancient Greece.
'Just as the City makes itself a State, history emerges from insignificant tales
[*du récit anecdotique*], annals, and epic poems to talk of this constitution, to tell

of the struggles of the city-state (a limited but real democracy).'[74] This is important, because it suggests that history did not emerge just to tell any story, but a particular story, that of the state and its challenges. This is found in the work of Herodotus and Thucydides. We clearly find a related parallel in Hegel's work with the consequences of the French Revolution and the Napoleonic Wars.[75] Marx's thought of the withering away of the state is therefore concomitant with the end of history.[76]

As we have seen in the examination of the town and country relation, Lefebvre believes we can break things into three main periods – the agrarian, the industrial, and the urban. Particular political forms accompany these understandings of the modes of production. The second stage is the one in the writings of Hegel and Marx; the third is the new period that requires us to think beyond their writings. New conceptions of time and space arise along with this shift in the organization of production. Lefebvre cautions that this theoretical separation does not preclude the need for the study of transitions, conflicts and so on between the stages. For Lefebvre, the urban inaugurates the trans-historical.[77] This is coupled with a transition in the sense of history itself. Hegel and Marx both talked of world-history (*Weltgeschichte*). Lefebvre cautions that 'we should not forget that worldwide history is also the making-worldly [*mondialisation*] of history'. This is not simply a continuity. There are two main phases – one of homogenization, characterized by the primacy of technology, growth, economics and the destruction of nature; and one of divergence or differentiation. These are in some sense complementary, and the second is certainly a response to the first.

> Phase I is linked with the process of industrialisation. Phase II (it is also the theoretical hypothesis) would be linked with the process of urbanisation (at first subordinate to industrialisation, then coming into the foreground and tending to form urban society).
>
> If the hypothesis is proved correct, there is now an intense, though unconscious, struggle between the forces of homogenisation and the forces of differentiation.
>
> Phase I is historical, even today. Phase II, although originating in history, would be trans-historical.[78]

'*The transitional period – is the end of history.*' This does not mean that we are abolishing history, that history will be unimportant or abandoned. Rather it is something like Marx's comments about religion. There will come a time when people have no need of the opium of religion, likewise today, 'in the midst of tragedy, genocide and huge massacres . . . religion and morality are coming to an end. And history. And, doubtless, the State.'[79] The end of history is therefore not defined by a frontier to be reached but by an exit. The exit from history is a transitional period, it is still history and is already no longer history. 'Becoming continues but is changing', it moves from the historical to the trans-historical, from particularities to differences, and from homogenization to differential practices.[80]

As Lantz notes, the distinction between three types of history – the monumental, the antiquarian and the critical – in Nietzsche's second *Untimely Meditation* is central to Lefebvre's work, but also to Heidegger's *Being and Time*. Lefebvre's use of the regressive-progressive approach follows Nietzsche's injunction that history must be made to serve life, for a present critical purpose. Although Heidegger and Lefebvre would ultimately do rather different things with it, both were also interested in the notion of repetition.[81] 'The study of repetition, [is] for Nietzsche, the point of departure, the foundation.' Repetition is not something that we find here or there, but covers the whole of experience, from the real to the rational. 'It is concerned as much with logic and mathematics as with aesthetics and morals, physics and so called "philosophical" theory of knowledge, abstract thought and practice.'[82] One of the reasons that Lefebvre was so interested in Nietzsche's notion of repetition is the problematizing of ideas of the same and the other which it brings with it.

Nietzsche's notion is of the eternal recurrence of the same, and yet something other occurs. As Lefebvre phrases it: 'From the beginning then, a paradox: the generation of difference through repetition.'[83] In Chapter 1 I noted how Lefebvre recognized that a simple identity such as A = A is already producing difference, because the second A is both the same, and different, because it is the second.[84] This is crucial to understanding Lefebvre's work on the politics of and the right to difference, which will be more fully discussed in Chapter 6. Lefebvre argues that the true consequence of the eternal return is not history beginning again, but the announcement of its end.[85] In other words, history (as we understand it) requires linearity and a cyclical understanding disrupts it. If we can conceive of pre-historical time and historical time, we can also conceive of post-historical time.[86] Finally then:

> Nietzsche has his position of eminence. It is he who inaugurated thinking on and pursuit of the different, who proclaimed the diversity of values and meanings, and who in consequence opens the way to affirmation within difference . . . The Same cannot affirm itself without the Other; the Other (the different and the elsewhere) reveals itself through the Same, and attains itself by passing through the Identical. The struggle to differ starts but will not end with history.[87]

If the arguments of the previous chapters are to be believed, we might expect Heidegger to play a role here. Did Heidegger's work on history and the fundamental work he did on time not influence Lefebvre? What about the work on difference and his notion of *Ereignis*, the event of appropriation?[88] Most fundamentally, what about the discussions of Nietzsche's understanding of the moment that we find in Heidegger's 1961 book *Nietzsche*, based on a range of lecture courses he gave in the 1930s and 1940s?[89] There are some important comparisons and issues, but the standard Lefebvrian criticism of Heidegger continues. While he acknowledges the importance of his thinking on difference and appropriation, and recognizes that using his model we can say 'the urban follows technology on the path of being and its development', he acknowledges that 'one may object that these still philosophical propositions are not of great importance in throwing light on praxis . . .'[90] Equally, as was noted above, Lefebvre's work on time dates back to the 1920s, before his engagement with Heidegger. Given that Lefebvre's initial reaction was one of hostility, and that he had already independently thought about many issues concerning time through Proust and Nietzsche, it was not surprising that his understanding of time owes little to Heidegger.

One particular point of contrast is that whilst Heidegger opposes the two terms *Geschichte* and *Historie* as history as it happens and as it is written respectively, Lefebvre describes them precisely the other way round – the former as historicity, the latter as the knowledge of becoming, *devenir*. Lefebvre argues that the accord between these two, as postulated by Hegel and accepted by Marx is challenged by Nietzsche, because of his suggestion that historical knowledge can be destructive.[91] It is difficult to resist the temptation to say that Lefebvre merely got the German opposition the wrong way round. If the terms are reversed and *Geschichte*, which has a direct relation to words concerned with happening and destiny, is viewed as the notion of becoming, we have an understanding that is actually very close to Heidegger's. Indeed, Lefebvre argues that one of the problems of the modern world, is the stress on historicism over becoming (*le devenir*).[92] However, we can begin to see the problem if we read further into Lefebvre's criticisms of Heidegger. Lefebvre characterizes Heidegger as suggesting that history is nothing other than the history of being, which has nothing in common with the history of the historians. Despite some of the insights of his history of being, Lefebvre has a problem with Heidegger's suggestion that historical destiny, history, *Geschichte*, is that which is sent (*geschickt*) by destiny (*Schicksal*). 'The play of these words illuminates the situation of Being because it is Being which gathers them.' There is, according to Heidegger, pre-history (Nature) – history (*logos* and technology) – post-history (the uncovering of Being). Lefebvre does not believe that this allows us to define historicity in a satisfactory way. Essentially it evades the crucial point, that the history of being implies a being of history. It is precisely this that is in question.[93]

On the question of history Lefebvre is therefore much closer to Nietzsche than to Heidegger, and notably draws upon Deleuze for the sense of genealogy.[94] Genealogy, for Lefebvre, is concerned with 'filiations, concrete encounters, detours and *détournements*, influences, etc.'[95] Like Foucault it is concerned with the emergence and descent of concepts, but these tend to be more flexible and less tied to specific systems of thought.[96] Rather than the Heideggerian Nietzscheanism that I have found in Foucault's work on history, in Lefebvre we have a version of Nietzschean history, of genealogy, that is somewhat less monolithic. The regressive aspect of the regressive-progressive methodology – though explicitly Marxist – is implicitly Nietzschean.[97] Therefore, although Nietzsche and Marx are opposed on temporality, on some aspects of the question of history they coincide. For example, Lefebvre sees both of them challenging Hegel on the notion of world history: 'is it necessary to underline the convergence between this critique [Nietzsche's] and that of Marx and Engels? Nietzsche goes further and hits harder',[98] but the point of departure – the critique of Hegelianism and particularly left-Hegelianism – is shared.[99]

> We can thus arrive at an objective relativism, or rather a theory of a deeper objectivity which does not exclude a certain relativity. *The past becomes present (or is renewed) as a function of the realisation of the possibilities objectively implied in this past.* It is revealed with them. The introduction of the category of the Possible into historical methodology permits us to conceive the objectivity – while yielding its due to the relativity, novelty and inexhaustibility – of history, without collapsing into pure relativism. It restores historical actions and personages to the effective movement of history, without falling into subjectivism.[100]

The production of space

In recent years within social theory there has been a noticeable shift from questions of temporality to those of spatiality. As Frederic Jameson asks, 'why should landscape be any less dramatic than the event?'[101] Several of the reasons for the importance Lefebvre gives to location can be located in the questions that he was asking about the change from the rural to the urban, and the situation of everyday life. Lefebvre's work on a plural Marxism also gives reasons why this importance should be so stressed. As he argues in *La fin de l'histoire*, among the material causes of change are such things as economics, production, geopolitics and geographical 'factors'.[102] Issues of space are therefore central to a material analysis. In the book *Espace et politique*, a work that collects a number of essays and that sits between the work on the urban and the more explicit theorization, Lefebvre suggests that 'research on the city and the urban refer to that concerning space which will be the object of a work to be published under the title *The Production of Space*. This theory of social space encompasses on the one hand the critical analysis of urban reality and on the other that of everyday life.'[103]

As David Harvey has phrased it, 'the whole history of territorial organisation, colonialism and imperialism, of uneven development, of urban and rural contradictions, as well as of geopolitical conflict testifies to the importance of such struggles within the history of capitalism'.[104] One of the reasons why capitalism has survived into the twentieth century is because of its flexibility in constructing and reconstructing the relations of space and the global space economy. Just as everyday life has been colonized by capitalism, so too has its location – social space.[105] Indeed, in 1989 Lefebvre suggested to his interviewers that courses in history and sociology that leave aside urban (spatial) questions seem ludicrous, in that they lack their very substance.[106] The production of space is a theme that has explicit political aspects, and is related to developing systems of production within capitalism.

Although the production of space is treated here, it will be revisited with an explicitly political slant in the following chapter.

However, one of the most significant sources for Lefebvre's work on space is – as far as I can tell – never mentioned.[107] It is his essay on Édouard Pignon, which was published as a book along with a chronology of the painter's career and several reproductions in 1956. The book was reissued in 1970, with more illustrations, but with an unchanged text.[108] Pignon was a member of the PCF and a contemporary of Picasso. His often political painting ranged from ones concerned with grape and olive harvests in Mediterranean France to a series known as *L'Ouvrier mort* which were situated in Northern industrial zones. In his analysis of Pignon, in broad strokes, and albeit in somewhat tenuous fashion, Lefebvre outlines many of the key concerns of his later work.

Lefebvre traces Pignon's work back to Cézanne, and even back as far as Tintoretto, and suggests that their painting acts as a means of challenging the geometric representation of space.[109] In his own analysis, Pignon also draws upon precisely these antecedents.[110] In Cézanne, and the cubists following him, what is painted is not so much reality as the act of perceiving reality. Cubism dispenses with the unified viewpoint of a sedentary observer, and shows movement through time in a spatial frame. Space – in the eyes of the observer – becomes differentiated, heterogeneous.[111] Cubism therefore both renders the abstract space of three dimensions perceivable (*sensible*), and makes the perceivable abstract.[112] Apparently absent, the observing human is there in Cézanne's canvas, and those that followed him.[113] In distinction, the observer was excluded from the paintings of the strict classicists.[114] As Lefebvre notes, space and time in themselves may not change, but our perceptions of them do – they become more fine, more subtle, more profound, more differentiated.[115] Cézanne's paintings of Mont Sainte-Victoire break with the measures and rules of 'classic' perspective and the mountain looms toward us, enormous and disproportionate, and therefore becomes more real, for us and with us.[116] Lefebvre notes the way in which in strictly representative painting geometric rules add to the anomie of the subjects, in this case workers, and how Pignon seeks to break out of that representation. Against the mechanism of capitalist technology, Pignon posits a more organic, physiological world. Pignon shows an organic whole against the fragmented world of solitary humans, alienated both from nature and other people.[117]

One of Pignon's most recent canvases, at the time of Lefebvre's writing, is concerned with the installers of electrical power cables. There is, for Lefebvre, a crucial relation between the bodies of the workers and the technology.

> On the pylons, separately or in groups, in clusters, the bodies of the workers hang on and move about in an organised manner. They lift up the parts, unwind the cables, tighten the nuts. Their muscles tighten, their bodies twist; they lean over the void, risking a fall and giving us vertigo. They stand out in the space, the air

and the light. Electric lines and pylons 'structurally' divide space, as well as the lines of the small hills. This hard labour unfolds in a landscape, in immediate contact with and naturally assimilated into a group of houses, hills, olive trees and pines.[118]

What we find in the analysis of Pignon is therefore both an interest in space as an aesthetic experience, and an understanding of how it is always related to questions of temporality.[119] Equally, a number of themes such as alienation, new technology and the relation between this and nature are discussed. Such themes would concentrate many of Lefebvre's efforts in subsequent work. Lefebvre's interest in space is also found in some of his early writings like *Méthodologie des sciences*. Here we find a discussion of ancient geometry and physics, as well as later developments in François Viète, Descartes and Kant. Lefebvre works through some of the issues around quantity and calculation that would be important in later analyses, and shows that he is more than familiar with the classic positions, as well as contemporary writings on non-Euclidean geometry.[120] Reading these last writers alerted him to the way in which modern mathematics 'did not study space, but a multiplicity of spaces'.[121]

Alternatively, we can again use *Ulysses* as an example. For Lefebvre, the novel 'has a referential or "place", a topical (toponymical and topographical) ensemble: Dublin, the city with its river and its bay . . .'.[122] Just as novels must bear in mind space, Lefebvre provides a reason why considerations of events must take into account the social, the temporal and the spatial. He considers a simple sentence: 'I bought this chair in the Faubourg Saint-Antoine'. This, Lefebvre argues, is a statement that involves a *context* that is not only linguistic but also practical and social. We cannot situate or define a thing, the object 'chair', the reality 'road', or the French language, without an understanding of French society and specifications of space and time.[123] Similarly he argues that the city is 'written on mapped space and graduated time'.[124]

It is important to note that Lefebvre argues that space is the ultimate locus and medium of struggle, and is therefore a crucial political issue. As he aphorizes, 'there is a politics of space because space is political'.[125] For instance, where the space of town planners is seen as a scientific object, as pure and apolitical, Lefebvre argues that has been shaped and moulded by historical and natural elements, through a political process.[126] Lefebvre and Heidegger both realize the Cartesian understanding of space as calculable and controllable allows social and technological domination.[127] Following Heidegger, Lefebvre suggests a distinction between the domination and appropriation of nature, with domination leading to destruction. This conflict takes place in space.[128] Space is not just discovered by humans and occupied, but in the process it is transformed. As was noted in the previous chapter, nature is challenged by this domination. Urbanization is one aspect of this 'colossal extension'.[129] Space is not just the place of conflict, but an object of struggle itself. There is therefore work to be done on an understanding of space and how it is socially constructed and used. Space is a social and political product. This is clearly why Lefebvre's main work on space is entitled *The Production of Space*. There are two terms in this title, both need to be critically examined.[130]

Chapter 1 discussed the importance of Marx's understanding of production to Lefebvre's work. This is particularly evident in the writings on space. As was noted above, Lefebvre states that '*(social) space is a (social) product*'.[131] Space needs to be understood in the context of the mode of production of a particular epoch. Despite Lefebvre's attention to the role of ideas, he does recognize the importance of forces and relations of production. Spaces are sometimes produced by the contradictions of the mode of production such as the medieval town, which was produced out of feudalism, but eventually emerged victorious.[132] But Lefebvre goes further than according space an important role as a product. In the strict Marxist tradition social space would be considered part of the superstructure, but for Lefebvre it enters into the forces of production, the division of labour, and has relations with property. Social space and space itself escape the base-structure–superstructure model.[133]

It is worth stressing again what is meant by production in Lefebvre's work.

> The term *production* acquires a more forceful and a wider significance, when interpreted according to Marx's early works (though still bearing *Das Kapital* in mind); production is not merely the making of products: the term signifies on the one hand 'spiritual' production, that is to say creations (including social time and space), and on the other material production or the making of things . . .[134]

Production, then, is broader than the economic production of things (stressed by Marx) and includes the production of society, knowledge and institutions. The production of things is but a narrow sense of the wider sense of the production of *oeuvres*.[135] These other aspects – while allowed for in Marx's conception – are less often treated in his work as such. Production in Lefebvre's sense – deriving from Marx, Hegel, and Nietzsche's notion of creation – needs to be grasped as both a material and mental process. An analysis of production in the modern world shows that 'we have passed from the production of things *in space* . . . to the production *of space* itself'.[136] Both of these need to be considered.[137] There is however, something of a tension in Lefebvre's work on the production of space. On the one hand he is anxious to point out that 'a social space is not a *socialised* space',[138] that is, it did not exist beforehand as a non-social space, as a natural space, but is produced by social forces. On the other hand, he notes that

> Productive forces permit those who dispose of them to control space and even to *produce* it. This productive capacity extends to the whole of the earth's space, and beyond. Natural space is destroyed and transformed into a social product by an ensemble of techniques, particularly physics and information science.[139]

One of the key factors is therefore technology, another area that bears comparison with Heidegger.[140] Scott Kirsch has pointed out that this is sometimes neglected in an analysis of Lefebvre's work: 'In addition to its significance to production *in* space, technology also plays a mediating role in the production *of* space.' Lefebvre's critique of technocracy surfaces again here.

> The thought of technocrats oscillates between the representation of an empty space, quasi geometric, occupied only by concepts, by logics and strategies at the highest rational level – the representation of a space finally filled, occupied by the results of these logics and strategies. They do not perceive that in the first place all space is *produced*, and consequently that this product does not come from conceptual thought that is not immediately a productive force. Space, considered as a product, results from the relations of production taken in charge or in hand by an effective group.[141]

Kirsch also cautions against 'resorting to the rather cartoonish shrinking world metaphor', which risks losing sight of the complex relations between capital, *technology*, and space. Space is not 'shrinking', but must rather be perpetually recast.[142] We might wish to modify and rephrase this last sentence. Space is not shrinking, it is being perpetually recast, but we *perceive* it to be shrinking.

This highlights an important point. Lefebvre not only corrected the modernist imbalance of time over space, but also, *contra* Kant, emphasized the historicality of their experience. No longer the Kantian empty formal containers, no longer *categories* of experience, time and space could be experienced *as such*, and their experience was directly related to the historical conditions they were experienced within. For Lefebvre, of course, these historical conditions are directly linked to the mode of production: hence the *production* of space.[143] Lefebvre therefore wished to make two main moves in his work. First to put space up with and alongside time in considerations of social theory, and in doing so correct the vacuity of the Kantian experiential containers. Spatiality is as important as, but must not obscure considerations of, temporality and history: 'space and time appear and manifest themselves as different yet inseparable'.[144] Secondly he wished to use this new critical understanding to examine the (modern) world in which he was writing. This is accomplished through an analysis of how space is produced, and how it is experienced. Space is produced in two ways, as a social formation (mode of production), and as a mental construction (conception).

As many of the commentators on Lefebvre have pointed out, Marxism is not particularly noted for its attendance to questions of space. Soja attributes to Marx the view that history was important, and geography an 'unnecessary complication', though he fails to give a reference for this quotation – if indeed it is a quotation.[145] Similarly, Richard Peet suggests that 'Marxism has little to say about relations with nature and sees events occurring on top of a pin rather than in space.'[146] The fairness of these claims is

moot – we might suggest such critics look at the second volume of *Capital* on
the circulation of capital, passages on the scarcity of space, the analyses of
the town/country relation, and of the military, amongst others[147] – though it
is certainly true that the analyses never claim centre stage. This is partly due
to what Marx published in his lifetime of the overall plan for *Capital*. As he
notes in the *Grundrisse*:

> *Circulation proceeds in space and time.* Economically considered, the spatial condition,
> the bringing of the product to the market, belongs to the production process itself
> . . . this spatial moment is important insofar as the expansion of the market and
> the exchangeability of the product are concerned with it.[148]

In his 1980 summary of the current state of Marxism, Lefebvre noted
that 'space presented itself to Marx only as the sum of the places of production, the location [*territoire*] of the various stages'.[149] We have seen how
Lefebvre recognizes the limitations of Marx and Engels' work on the city in
Chapter 4, but also how he recognizes that this was understandable given
the context in which they were writing. One way that has been advanced as
a solution to this apparent neglect is to suggest that 'although space is not
analysed in *Capital*, certain concepts, such as exchange value and use value,
today apply to space'.[150] Political economy has become a political economy
of space.[151]

Some Marxists have made use of spatial metaphors but have often failed
to analyse space itself. A classic instance is Althusser, who uses such terms as
field, terrain, space, site, situation, position, but whilst the metaphors in
Nietzsche, Heidegger and Foucault are wedded to practical analyses,
Althusser seems to rely on language alone.[152] This charge could be levelled
at many of the Structuralists, whose language was often overtly spatialized.
Lefebvre calls this a fetishism of space, in part because of the neglect of
questions of historicity. Questions of space must not be separated apart
from questions of time.[153] Equally whilst the use of spatial language for
metaphor should not be knocked, an understanding of *why* this language is
so useful should perhaps be appended. Much spatial language deals with
contestation, struggle and productivity. This is precisely because it mirrors
the actual uses and experiences of space.

As Massey sensibly warns, 'space' and 'spatial' are regularly used as if
their meaning was clear, but writers generally fail to realize that they have
many different interpretations. She accepts that Lefebvre realized this, and
that he is fairly explicit in his understanding of these problematic terms.[154]
The French word *espace* has, of course, a wider range of meanings than the
English 'space'. In English these different meanings could be understood as
close to our terms of 'area', 'zone' or even 'place'.[155] Lefebvre begins *The
Production of Space* by suggesting that up until recently one view of space
dominated. This was the view of space based on the division Descartes
established between *res cogitans* and *res extensa*. Space was formulated on the
basis of extension, thought of in terms of coordinates, lines and planes, as

'Euclidean' geometry. Kant further complicated the picture by conceiving of space and time as *a priori* absolute categories, structuring all experience.[156] We have already seen how Lefebvre's emphasis on the production of space historicizes this experience; the critique of Cartesian formulations still needs to be achieved.

As early as 1939, Lefebvre had described geometric space as abstractive, and had likened it to clock time in its abstraction of the concrete.[157] In his 1947 investigation of Descartes, Lefebvre notes that in the middle of the fifteenth century, Nicolas Oresme used a system of rectangular coordinates (latitude and longitude).[158] This forms a necessary prelude to Descartes' work on the mathematization of nature, which Lefebvre dwells on at length.[159] Descartes' distinction between *res cogitans* and *res extensa* means that the fundamental ontological determination of substance, material being, is that it is extended in three dimensions. Descartes importantly suggests that all problems in geometry can be reduced to the length of some straight lines, to the values of the roots of the equations,[160] thereby turning space into something that is quantitatively measurable, calculable, numerical. Descartes reduces all physics and even physiology to geometric mechanism.[161] What is interesting for Lefebvre in Descartes is that there is not simply a paradox in his work, but a 'very precise contradiction'.[162] On the one hand Cartesian space is reduced to a simple *thought* – a thought of quantity separated from a sensible quality. The experience of space is removed, and replaced with the abstract, scientific quantification. The scholastic understanding of quality is reduced to quantity – 'simpler, more abstract, more general, more malleable [*maniable*]', quantity or size is reduced 'in its turn to length, which is itself reduced to *order*'. Order is effectively the *order* of succession of values of a variable x, and its *relation* to another variable y, and is sufficient to understand everything in analytical geometry. On the other hand, and following from this, space is a *reality*, outside of thought, the thought of the *Cogito*. Space is *res extensa*, which is entirely other than *res cogitans*.[163]

This position is, of course, untenable. If space is an 'extended thing' entirely other than thought, then thought is unable to comprehend it; if space is nothing other than a thought, knowledge of space is without content. For Lefebvre, Descartes fluctuates between two contradictory positions, the reduction of geometric space to thought; the 'realization' of space outside all thought. Space, for Descartes, is therefore, he suggests, not properly speaking 'paradoxical', but comprised of two contradictory attributes. But because Descartes did not realize the contradiction as such, he was content to oscillate between these two contradictory theses.[164] Although Lefebvre's presentation here is rather inchoate, it is clearly a prefiguring of his later argument that space needs to be understood not in two ways – as conceived, abstract thought of space, or perceived, concrete reality of space – but in three ways, with the additional of space as *lived*, which resolves the conflicts between the previous two, without being reducible to either. Lefebvre notes that 'in traditional metaphysics, we find the (well known) hypothesis that intelligible space has nothing in common with real space. Intelligible space is not extensive.'[165] Lefebvre's point is that it is an abstraction to think 'real' space in this way too, and that it is precisely an intelligible form of space imposed over the material world.

This can be usefully related to Heidegger's critique of geometric space in *Being and Time* and other works. It is no easy task to summarize Heidegger's contribution to our understanding of space. I have tried to discuss this, in much greater detail, elsewhere.[166] Here, I will provide only a brief summary. Although in his early works Heidegger is more concerned with an analysis of time, he does occasionally make some penetrating remarks about understandings of space. In later works, beginning from around the mid-1930s, Heidegger starts to redress the balance and to treat questions of spatiality as equally important to those of temporality. The principal thrust of his argument is that space, like time, has been understood in a narrow, calculative, mathematical sense, which is divorced from our experience of space in our everyday dealings with the world. In a number of striking examples – walking into a lecture room, the uses of a kitchen table, a bridge over a river – Heidegger takes issue with such a reductive analysis. Instead, he suggests that we deal with the world as a matter of concern, acting with and reacting to objects within it in a lived, experiential way, instead of abstracting from them in a Cartesian grid of coordinates. From his earliest works Heidegger refused the separation of mind and matter, and analysed what he called being-in-the-world.[167] Lefebvre notes the importance of Heidegger's analysis of world – as image, symbol, myth and place.[168] For Heidegger, in a way similar to our dealings with equipment, we encounter space geometrically only when we pause to think about it, when we conceptualize it.[169]

Heidegger's later work introduces a term known as 'poetic dwelling', which derives from his lecture courses on Hölderlin in the 1930s and 1940s,[170] and is fully elaborated in later essays.[171] In a late poem, Hölderlin suggested that 'poetically, man dwells on the earth'.[172] For Heidegger, this notion of dwelling, *wohnen*, is precisely this way of inhabiting the world in a lived, experienced manner instead of one of calculative planning.[173] Indeed, this notion of dwelling is the direct opposite of the understanding of technology that Heidegger thinks holds sway in the modern world. Technology, taking the world as a substance which can be ordered, planned, and worked upon – instead of worked with – is a direct consequence of Cartesian metaphysics, and is the condition of possibility for modern science, mechanized forms of agriculture, the holocaust, nuclear weapons and other modern forms of control. Heidegger's critique of Nazism, such that it is, is principally grounded upon it being a continuation of, instead of a challenge to, this metaphysical understanding of the world.[174]

It could be contended that there are two principal things missing from Heidegger's work on space. Whilst he is exceptionally interesting in a historical reading of the philosophical tradition, he is less good on historical detail, with the illustrations often merely passing references. Equally, while he is penetrating in his analysis of the spatial aspects of the Greek *polis*, he often neglects the more explicitly political aspects of modern appropriations of space. As I have tried to show in *Mapping the Present*, Foucault is extremely important in taking Heideggerian ideas forward in an analysis of the relation between history and space. Here, I want to cover the other side of the matter. Lefebvre, building upon Heidegger's philosophical critique, is exceptionally powerful in looking at the relation between politics and space, especially in relation to modern capitalism. He does this through an analysis of the *production* of space. The bringing in of a Marxist concept, with all the political issues that implies, is tremendously important in understanding Lefebvre's distance from Heidegger, even as the emphasis on 'space' is indebted to him. Lefebvre's work *The Production of Space* should be read between Marx and Heidegger.

For Lefebvre, absolute space has dimensions, but these are left and right, and high and low rather than the dimensions of abstract, geometric, space.[175] Indeed, Lefebvre argues that one of the questions is 'how to construct a left and a right, a high and a low, corresponding to gestures, to movements, to the rhythm of bodies'.[176] Like with Heidegger, our mode of reaction to space is not geometric, only our mode of abstraction is. There is an opposition established between our *conception* of space – abstract, mental and geometric – and our *perception* of space – concrete, material and physical. The latter takes as its initial point of departure the body, which Lefebvre sees as the site of resistance within the discourse of Power in space.[177] Abstract, decorporalized space is, he suggests, still another aspect of alienation. This, again, is tied up with the power of the technocrats. Space is available for them, it is 'the place of their future exploits, the terrain of their victories'.[178]

Lefebvre therefore introduces a distinction between concrete and abstract space. Concrete space is the space of gestures and journeys, of the body and memory, of symbols and sense. This concrete content, of time inscribed in a space, is misunderstood by reflexive thought, which instead resorts to the abstract space of vision, of geometry.[179] 'Abstract space is measurable.'[180] Architects and urbanists work with this abstract space, this paper space of drawings, and are divorced from the level of the 'lived' in a dual sense. This is because, as well as abstracting from it in their understanding, they then project this understanding back onto the lived level.[181] As Lefebvre notes, the plan does not rest innocently on paper – on the ground it is the bulldozer that realizes these 'plans'.[182] 'Space has long ceased to be a passive geographic or empty geometric milieu. It has become *instrumental*.'[183]

In order to make progress in understanding space, we need to grasp the concrete and the abstract together. As Lefebvre argued in *Dialectical Materialism*, if only one is grasped and turned into an absolute, a partial truth becomes an error: 'By rejecting a part of the content it gives sanction to and aggravates the dispersion of the elements of the real.'[184] Just as Lefebvre described the state as a 'realized abstraction',[185] space too is a realized (in both senses of the word) abstraction. Here there is a balance struck – a dialectical relation – between idealism and materialism. Space is a mental

and material construct. This provides us with a third term between the poles
of conception and perception, the notion of the lived. Lefebvre argues that
human space and human time lie half in nature, and half in abstraction.
Socially lived space and time, socially produced, depends on physical and
mental constructs.

It is from this that Lefebvre derives his conceptual triad of spatial practice; representations of space; and spaces of representation.[186] Space is
viewed in three ways, as perceived, conceived and lived: *l'espace perçu, conçu,
vécu*. This Lefebvrian schema sees a unity (a Marxist totality) between physical, mental and social space. The first of these takes space as physical form,
real space, space that is generated and used. The second is the space of *savoir*
(knowledge) and logic, of maps, mathematics, of space as the instrumental
space of social engineers and urban planners, of navigators and
explorers.[187] Space as a mental construct, *imagined* space. The third sees
space as produced and modified over time and through its use, spaces
invested with symbolism and meaning, the space of *connaissance* (less formal
or more local forms of knowledge), space as *real-and-imagined*.[188]

It is here perhaps above all, that we can see Heidegger's influence. The
spatial notion of poetic dwelling, a notion of lived experience of everyday
life is enormously important. Lefebvre's use of *habiter*, which we might trans-
late as 'to inhabit', or 'to dwell', is a direct translation of Heidegger's *wohnen*,
which is usually translated as 'to dwell', or, in French, as *habiter*.[189] Indeed, in
a number of places, Lefebvre cites Hölderlin's 'poetically man dwells', and
mentions Heidegger's discussion positively.[190] Heidegger and Gaston Bachelard are cited for their meditations on the Greek city and the temple and the
poetics of the house.[191] Lefebvre's suggestion that inhabiting (*habiter*) has
been reduced to the notion of habitat (*habitat*) parallels Heidegger's notion
of a crisis in dwelling.[192] Lefebvre's distinction is important, because he
suggests that the space of dwelling, of *habiter* is not separated from urban
and social space, whereas *habitat* is merely a box, a *cadre*. *Habiter* is an activity,
a situation, whereas *habitat* is a function, a brutal material reality.[193] As
Lefebvre notes, explicitly following Heidegger, this crisis 'springs from a
strange kind of excess: a rage for measurement and calculation';[194] qualified
space is replaced by quantified space.[195]

However, it should be borne in mind that the previously reliable referentials of the last century, Euclidean (or, rather, Cartesian) three-dimensional
space and clock time, have, since the last *fin de siècle*, been in occasional
crisis. Lefebvre sees this as particularly evident in the sphere of aesthetics:
'perspective changed, the vanishing point, a token of geometric space,
vanished; it was the same with the tonal system in music, where the key-
note is a token of fixity granted to the section of sound continuum thus
limited'.[196]

At the beginning of the 20th century, the referentials collapsed, from perceived
and conceived space (Euclidean space, space of classical perspective) to lived
time, from the horizon line to tonality, from the city to history.[197]

We could make too much of this: most people still do not paint like Picasso, and most people do not hum twelve-tone melodies. What it does show, however, is that space and time have become, despite the attempts of some to forestall this, relative. There are many spaces and many times, as Einstein has shown in physics. In this view of lived space, Cartesian-Kantian notions of space are not necessarily wrong – they can be perfectly reasonable approximations – but they are approximations.[198] To repeat, they are approximations that begin at the level of abstraction, crucially one level away from the initial level of lived reaction. Dwelling has a more directly rooted understanding of space or place, one that is closer to lived reaction.

Lefebvre is critical of Heidegger and Hölderlin's concept of dwelling. For one thing he notes that for centuries this idea would have had no meaning outside the aristocracy.[199] This is clearly a criticism of the politics of the idea, suggesting that it is elitist and class based. Heidegger is also censured for his reliance on the rural,[200] though in response, as we have seen in Chapter 4, in making this notion more relevant to modern, urbanized capitalism, Lefebvre did not solely concentrate on the city. Also, as would be expected, he suggests that Heidegger's notion is insufficiently concrete:[201]

> Heidegger, now, shows us a world ravaged by technology, that through its ravages leads towards another dream, another (as yet unperceived) world. He warns us: a lodging built on the basis of economic or technological dictates is as far removed from dwelling as the language of machines is from poetry. He does not tell us how to construct, 'here and now', buildings and cities.[202]

However, as he suggested in *La révolution urbaine*, 'even if this "poetic" critique of "habitat" and industrial space appears as a critique from the right, nostalgic, "old-fashioned [*passéiste*]", it did nothing less than inaugurate the problematic of space'.[203]

The construction, or production, of spaces therefore owes as much to the conceptual realms as to material activities. An example of a space that incorporates both mental and material constructs is a cloister, where 'a gestural space has succeeded in grounding a mental space – one of contemplation and theological abstraction – thus allowing it to express itself, to symbolise itself and to come into practice'.[204] As Lourau notes, there can be 'no institution without a space of legitimation',[205] a phrase that is quoted by Lefebvre without the last two words.[206] In doing so, he twists Lourau's suggestion of an intellectual into a material grounding. Another example shows how constructs are experienced in a modern city. A park is *conceived*, designed and produced through labour, technology and institutions, but the meaning of the space, and the space itself, is adapted and transformed as it is *perceived* and *lived* by social actors and groups.[207] But this notion of space as lived is on its own not sufficient. Another of Lefebvre's criticisms of Heidegger is that he failed to understand the notion of production in sufficient detail. Heidegger's conception of production is seen as 'restrained and restrictive', as he envisages it as a 'making-appear, an arising [*un surgissement*] which brings forth a thing, as a thing present among things already-present'.[208] What is involved, therefore, is a *social* and *political* production of space. It is to Marx that he turns to make sense of the problematic, particularly in terms of the notion of production.

Lefebvre suggests that in the past there were shortages of bread, and never a shortage of space, but that now corn is plentiful (at least in the developed world), whilst space is in short supply: like all economies, the political economy of space is based on the idea of scarcity.[209] There are a number of passages in *Capital* that are concerned with this issue.[210] Lefebvre suggests that 'the overcrowding of highly industrialised countries is especially pronounced in the larger towns and cities'.[211] Indeed, in *The Production of Space*, Lefebvre argues that it only makes sense to talk of spatial scarcity in urban *centres*.[212] We therefore need a more nuanced approach than simply one of scarcity. As Lefebvre notes, it does not make sense to say that scarcity has disappeared with the shift to a world scale. Whilst advanced – that is industrialized, urbanized – countries have overcome the shortage, this has necessarily been at the expense of others. New types of organization have overcome those historically bound to scarcity.[213] Social space is allocated according to class, social planning reproduces the class structure. This is either on the basis of too much space for the rich and too little for the poor, or because of uneven development in the quality of places, or indeed both. There are also important issues around marginality and segregation. For Lefebvre, 'today more than ever, the class struggle is inscribed in space'.[214] 'Space permits the economic to be integrated into the political.'[215] There are at least two ways to take this forward – either to develop a political economy of space, where space is yet another commodity examined or in thinking through a politics of space.[216]

Time, space and rhythm

How then should an analysis of space proceed? Despite his earlier use of the idea of 'reading' space, Lefebvre now suggests that space is produced, and then lived in, a 'reading' can only follow. 'This space was *produced* before being *read*; nor was it produced in order to be read and grasped, but rather in order to be *lived*.'[217] This is fairly clear, but verges on the banal. What Lefebvre seems to miss is that 'reading' a space is not like reading a book, but more like *critically* reading a book, understanding intent, power relations and context. To force Lefebvre's argument to its logical conclusions, books are written (produced), not to be critically examined (read), but to be read (lived). It would be a strange thesis that suggested that critical reading of books is therefore invalid. As Lefebvre argues, reading a space cannot help us to 'predict' future spaces. Maybe not, but crucially it can help us to understand those we 'live' in. David Harvey has helpfully separated out two conflicting, though often conflated, terms, which may enable us to make more sense of Lefebvre's meaning. He argues that to suggest various tactics of, for example, deconstruction, can be used on 'texts' is useful, but to suggest that the world is nothing but a text waiting to be deconstructed is not.[218]

Whether we call it reading or whether we call it analysing, space still needs to be understood. It is perhaps only because the notion of reading has been used so uncritically and poorly that it has fallen into disrepute. One thing is clear, the importance of space. Just as the social is historically shaped, so too is it spatially shaped. Equally the spatial is historically and socially configured. The three elements of the social, spatial and temporal shape and are shaped by each other. 'Social relations, concrete abstractions, only have real existence in and through space. *Their support is spatial.*'[219] And yet space is not merely 'the passive locus [*lieu*] of social relations'.[220]

Searching for a name for this new approach, Lefebvre toys with spatio-analysis or spatio-logy, but accepts there is a problem with these, as we need an analysis of the *production of space*.[221] As he had said the previous year, 'not a science of space, but a knowledge (a theory) of the production of space'.[222] David Caute has given Lefebvre credit for developing a satisfactory method of integrating sociology and history within the perspective of historical materialism, a remark that clearly draws on the regressive-progressive methodology.[223] Given the work that Lefebvre produced after the publication of Caute's book, we may feel tempted to add 'spatiology' as the third term. An analysis of the *production* of space, given that this is clearly informed by Lefebvre's reworking of dialectics and historical materialism would be a useful step in taking Lefebvre's work forward. Lefebvre does not see the analysis of space as a replacement of other analyses, but rather as a supplement to them, and recognizes that we also need to look at the production of population and class structure.

It was suggested above that Lefebvre made two main moves in his work: an assertion of the importance of space in tandem with that of time, and an analysis of the spaces of the modern age. In particular, as I have shown here and in other chapters, much of his work is tied up within French debates about technocratic planning. The explicit role of the state in planning and producing space will be discussed in detail in the next chapter. Whilst in Lefebvre's subtle and nuanced work this distinction is clear and useful, in the hands of less adroit writers this all too often descends into a heavy-handed examination of the postmodernization of, for example (though it is depressingly regularly the only example), the Los Angeles cityscape.[224]

As Chapter 4 noted, Lefebvre's work was initially read by Castells as a kind of spatial fetishism. It was felt that the prioritizing of space was injurious to historical materialism, which of course marginalized space, and privileged time and history. It has been convincingly argued that this is a misreading of what Lefebvre is doing.[225] Lefebvre inhabited the limits of Western Marxism/historical materialism, but was still trying to further an explicitly Marxist analysis. Given the imbalance previously found within historical materialism, some over-prioritization of space – in order to redress the balance – was perhaps to be expected. Had space not been thrust to the fore it would probably have been ignored. More recently Lefebvre has been championed as the 'original and foremost historical and geographical materialist',[226] and his work has become key in the debates looking to introduce a spatial element into Marxism. Soja is one who has followed this path, though it has been noted that while he hopes to spatialize history, and put time 'in its place', he seems largely unaware that Lefebvre's work is a historicism of sorts.[227] This is a key issue: does Lefebvre spatialize history, historicize space, or simply spatialize sociology? Whilst I believe that Lefebvre, working with three continually relating terms, was attempting to do all these and more, it can appear that he is writing a *history of space*, and not a *spatial history*.[228] As I have tried to show in Chapter 4, with the analysis of Paris in 1871 and 1968 this can be misleading. There is a danger of crowning space at the expense of an impoverished historical understanding, a problem that is exacerbated by the way in which Lefebvre's work on time and history is still largely unknown in English. Although the first part of this chapter analysed this work it is not exactly clear how the two might be balanced together. In this regard, his late work on rhythmanalysis may provide some leads.

Indeed, in the closing pages of *The Production of Space*, Lefebvre opens up this possibility and explicitly points out the importance of this work. An analysis of rhythms, a rhythmanalysis, 'would complete the exposition of the production of space'.[229] Analysis of space must also be historical – it is not something static,[230] it must take into account rhythm, through the human body.[231] 'The history of time, and the time of history, should include a history of rhythms, which is missing.'[232] But this is not solely a temporal bias, rather, space and time are interrelated and dependent on each other.[233] As Lefebvre noted as early as 1968, his analyses had shown him the extreme importance of the relation between space and time.[234] But where rhythmanalysis comes into its own is its possibility of exceeding a history of space, because it would also be a step forward in the project of a spatial history. The key difference between a spatial history and a history of space is that in the former the concept of space – neglected in much social and political theory – becomes not simply an object of analysis, but a constituent part of the analysis itself.[235]

Although *Elements of Rhythmanalysis* was his last book, Lefebvre had been concerned with these ideas for some time. His early study of Nietzsche had noted the importance of human and social rhythms, and in *Contribution à l'esthétique*, for example, he notes the importance of rhythm and measure for grasping human life, and counts them superior to biological laws.[236] Earlier in this chapter, in the discussion of time, I showed how music was for Lefebvre a privileged glimpse into the importance of rhythm for the break from simply linear understandings of time. In addition, as well as being a way of thinking through issues of spatiality and temporality together, *Elements of Rhythmanalysis* explicitly continues the project of the *Critique of Everyday Life*. Indeed, Ajzenberg has convincingly suggested that it should be seen as the fourth volume of that occasional series,[237] and in the second volume Lefebvre expressly promises this work – 30 years before it actually appeared.[238] The third volume again stresses the importance of these themes, and suggests that the pages within it which look at 'elements of rhythmanalysis' return to an unexplicated thesis of the first volume.[239] Lefebvre provides here a snapshot of the work that he would undertake over the last years of his life, much of it in collaboration with his last wife, Catherine Régulier. The collaborative work comprised an essay on 'The rhythmanalytical project' and one on the rhythms of Mediterranean cities.[240] These were followed by the short book *Elements of Rhythmanalysis*, which only bears Lefebvre's name on the title page and that appeared after his death, edited by René Lourau.[241] The first essay is available in *Key Writings*; the second in *Writings on Cities*, which also includes a chapter from the book.[242] All of these writings are included in the volume *Rhythmanalysis: Space, Time and Everyday Life*. The term rhythmanalysis, as Lefebvre acknowledges, is taken from Gaston Bachelard's *Dialectic of Duration*, and Bachelard himself takes it from the work of Dos Santos. Bachelard's work on poetics and elemental imagery – especially *The Psychoanalysis of Fire* – was important to Lefebvre here, just as *The Poetics of Space* was to his other writings.[243]

Rhythmanalysis is, for Lefebvre, a new science, a new field of knowledge. This does not mean that it has not been anticipated in various places at various times, but that rhythm has only recently taken on a specific developed form.[244] However – and in a sense this tension runs throughout his work – it is not a separate science, because it must continually be related to practice.[245] These two comments bookend his study of rhythms. What then is rhythm? How does Lefebvre understand it? The question of rhythms raises a number of other questions – 'difference and repetition – interaction and composition – cyclical and linear – frequency and measure ... eurhythmia, arrhythmia, polyrhythmia . . .'[246] Lefebvre's main aim is show how there is a contrast between natural rhythms, those of the body, for example, and those of mechanism and machines. The latter are more properly known as movements, a sequence of programmed 'acts' rather than organic gestures.[247] On the one hand we have 'logical categories and mathematical calculation', and on the other the 'visceral and vital body'.[248] This distinction was perhaps less obvious with earlier forms of mechanism – such as steam engines with their cylinders, pistons and jets – and modern electric locomotives that obscure the movement in boxes.[249]

The notion of the rhythmic in social, biological and psychological senses is also discussed by Lefebvre in some detail in an interview with Kostas Axelos from 1972. Here too he notes the importance of the repetitive, but recognizes that there can be both linear repetition and cyclic repetition.[250] We might analyse these separately, but they coexist in all sorts of practical situations. The cyclic, as we have seen, comes from the cosmic, from nature, but the linear comes from social practice.[251] As Lefebvre notes – and in this he also bears comparison to Heidegger – the issue with linear time is that it dissects indefinitely. Just as Cartesian geometry allowed the division of a line into mathematical coordinates, so too does the division of temporality into fragments of time. In this instance Lefebvre contrasts repetition with rhythm: the working practices of modern labour disrupt and break natural rhythms because they begin and end at any time.[252] The rhythm of capital is that of production and destruction. The former is both the production of things and human life more generally; the latter is the destruction through war, 'progress' and invention.[253]

Studying rhythms requires attention to the small details of the everyday, particularly in light of the stress on the every day repetition.[254] In various places he makes references to the importance of understanding the temporal and rhythmic elements of the everyday. It is only through relating this work to that on the everyday that Amin and Thrift's admonition that Lefebvre is 'frustratingly elusive' about the tools of rhythmanalysis can be addressed.[255] Linear temporalities of technology and industrial production are contrasted with the cyclical time of our cosmic and biological origins. For Lefebvre, 'the link between the everyday with the cyclic and cyclical time, that of days and nights, of weeks and months, seasons and years, is obvious'.[256] In fact, as he notes, for a long time this was the understanding of time that humans had. It is only with the advent of different mechanisms for calculating and measuring time that a distance has been created. 'Social man had not yet dominated nature, that is, he had not separated himself from it.'[257] The cyclical, rhythmic nature of the lived is therefore often contrasted with the linear, repetitive time of the technical and the social. Using the same contrast he marshalled in the understanding of space, this is the conceived.[258]

The point of cyclical time is that there is no beginning and end; that new cycles are born from previous ones; and that time is shot through with repetition. 'However, in cyclic time, repetition is subordinated to a more "total" body rhythm which governs the movements of the legs and arms, for example.'[259] This clearly shows the importance of the body to Lefebvre's understanding – just as it was to his work on space. While I have continually stressed the resistance of Lefebvre's thinking to calculation and measurement, it is important that he notes that some numbers are important. Above all, twelve, because of hours, months, divisions of a circle, notes of the musical scale, which is continued in notions of a dozen, for example eggs or oysters.[260] Indeed, Lefebvre suggests that twelve, with its relation to the cosmic and cyclic can be usefully opposed to the linear homogeneity of ten.[261] Lefebvre notes that repetition is not exact – these are not closed or vicious circles that admit no change. As has been noted above, Nietzsche taught Lefebvre about the creation of difference through repetition.

This is not to say that rhythms of cyclical nature do not coexist with modern ones. Lefebvre notes that we still largely sleep and eat according to natural timescales.[262] And yet, capitalism increasingly affects these parts of our lives, taking up time in hours of darkness, and, as various social and animal experiments have shown, creates problems through the disruption to circadian rhythms.[263] As early as 1939 he had realized the importance of these: 'it is obvious ... that the human rhythms (biological, psychological and social time-scales – the time-scale of our own organism and that of the clock) determine the way in which we perceive and conceive of the world and even the laws we discover in it'.[264] Our biological rhythms of hunger, sleep and excretion are conditioned through our family and social existence. We train ourselves to keep our bodies under control, and if we get used to eating at certain times, we will grow hungry at those same times.[265] This is the time of work, the way in which capitalist production has affected the lives of people.[266] This is a concept Lefebvre treats at some length in an analysis of the notion of dressage.[267]

This puts an important stress on the body, as the point of collision as it were, of the social and biological, which needs to be grasped in all its elements, as a totality.[268] Indeed, he later suggests that the body is the first point of analysis for the rhythmanalyst, because it is here that we are closest to rhythms, and can thereby use them as a basis for the external rhythms of the world. Our body serves us as a metronome.[269] The body has been largely neglected in philosophy, left to physiology and medicine, and the poor relation of the mind-body dualism. The rhythmanalyst will draw on all their senses – breathing, circulation of the blood, the beat of the heart and metres of their speech.[270] The body is a 'bundle of rhythms', which when they coexist in harmony is a state known as eurhythmia.[271] There is a necessary tension in their coexistence with the rhythms of social life, leading to the problems of arrhythmia. Dressage – a term also used by Foucault in *Discipline and Punish* – looks at the way in which these social rhythms and the time of work and production is imposed over the physical rhythms of human life. The model, as it is for Foucault, is the military.[272]

Lefebvre therefore argues that

The critique of everyday life studies the persistence of rhythmic time scales within the linear time of modern industrial society. It studies the interactions between cyclic time (natural, in a sense irrational, and still concrete) *and linear time* (acquired, rational, and in a sense abstract and antinatural). *It examines the defects and disquiet this as yet unknown and poorly understood interaction produces. Finally, it considers what metamorphoses are possible in the everyday as a result of this interaction.*[273]

Drawing on the rhythms of rural life, and harking back to both his work on France and the writings of Rabelais, Lefebvre talks of the way a young farmer is affected by different time scales.[274] Somewhat later Lefebvre notes how global forces and processes have shaped urban space and the city. 'Indeed, if they have influenced urban rhythms and spaces, it is by enabling groups to insert themselves, to take charge of them, to *appropriate* them; and this by inventing, by sculpting space (to use a metaphor), by giving themselves rhythms.'[275] The rhythmanalyst needs to be attentive to questions of time when examining the spaces of the urban – time over space perhaps here, but not omitting the space.[276] We can see this in practice in two remarkable parts of his work on rhythms – the analysis of Paris as 'seen from the window', and the work he and Régulier did on Mediterranean cities.[277]

In the work on rhythmanalysis, at the very end of his life, Lefebvre returns to several of his earlier themes – everyday life, the rural and the urban – and rethinks them through the notion of rhythm. Rhythms are 'historical, but also everyday', they are 'at the heart of the lived'.[278] His insistent point is that the rhythmanalytical project continually underlines the importance of grasping space and time together, despite the way they are often kept quite separate.[279] 'No rhythm without repetition in time and space, without *reprises*, without returns, in short without *measure [mesure]*'.[280] As he stresses, at no point has the analysis lost sight of the body.[281]

Notes

1 Michael Dear, 'Postmodern bloodlines', in Georges Benko and Ulf Strohmayer (eds), *Space and Social Theory: Interpreting Modernity and Postmodernity*, Oxford: Blackwell, 1997, pp. 49–71, p. 49. A much more convincing reading of the role of history in Lefebvre's work on space is found in Derek Gregory, *Geographical Imaginations*, Oxford: Blackwell, 1994, pp. 348–416. Although Gregory draws upon a number of neglected texts, he does not look at Lefebvre's explicit work on history itself.

2 Eleonore Kofman and Elizabeth Lebas, 'Lost in transposition – time, space and the city', in Henri Lefebvre, *Writings on Cities*, translated and edited by Eleonore Kofman and Elizabeth Lebas, Oxford: Blackwell, pp. 3–60, p. 27.

3 Andy Merrifield, 'Lefebvre, Anti-Logos and Nietzsche: An Alternative Reading of *The Production of Space*', *Antipode* 27(3), July 1995, pp. 294–303.

4 *La production de l'espace*, Paris: Anthropos, 1974, p. 31; *The Production of Space*, translated by Donald Nicholson-Smith, Oxford: Blackwell, 1991, pp. 22–3.

5 See *La présence et l'absence: Contribution à la théorie des representations*, Paris: Casterman, 1980, pp. 44–5; *Une pensée devenue monde: Faut-il abandonner Marx?* Paris: Fayard, 1980, p. 157. Henri Bergson in works such as *Time and Free Will: An Essay on the Immediate Data of Consciousness*, translated by F. L. Pogson, New York: Macmillan, 1910, was concerned with trying to free time from spatial representations. For a discussion see Keith Ansell Pearson and John Mullarky, 'Introduction', in Henri Bergson, *Key Writings*, edited by Keith Ansell Pearson and John Mullarky, London: Continuum, 2002, pp. 1–45. The early Heidegger tried to do this to such an extent that he founded spatiality on temporality. See Martin Heidegger, *Being and Time*, translated by Edward Robinson and John Macquarrie, Oxford: Blackwell, 1962, especially §70. The late Heidegger recognizes this attempt is a failure in *On Time and Being*, translated by Joan Stambaugh, New York: Harper & Row, 1972, p. 23. For an extended reading of how this problematic works through Heidegger's career, see Stuart Elden, *Mapping the Present: Heidegger, Foucault and the Project of a Spatial History*, London: Continuum, 2001, Chapters 1 to 3.

6 See, for example, *Critique de la vie quotidienne III: De la modernité au modernisme (Pour une métaphilosophie du quotidienne)*, Paris: L'Arche, 1981, p. 8.

7 See *Une pensée devenue monde*, p. 31, where he cites these four in relation to history.

8 *La somme et le reste*, Paris: Méridiens Klincksieck, 3rd edition, 1989 (1959), p. 252. The use of the sun behind the trinity is also found in the onion domes of Russian churches.

9 *Qu'est-ce que penser?* Paris: Publisad, 1985, p. 139; see *La somme et le reste*, pp. 252–3.

10 'Connaissance et critique sociale', in Marvin Farber (ed.), *L'activité philosophique contemporaine en France et aux États-Unis – II: La philosophie française*, Paris: PUF, 1950, pp. 298–319, p. 298 n. 1. See *La somme et le reste*, p. 251.

11 *La somme et le reste*, pp. 254–5. See also the brief mention of this in Chapter 2.

12 *La somme et le reste*, p. 380.

13 *Pyrénées*, p. 103.

14 'Le soleil crucifié', *Les temps modernes* 155, January 1959, pp. 1016–29; *La somme et le reste*, pp. 251–64.

15 *Qu'est-ce que penser?* p. 140. For a discussion, see Kurt Meyer, *Henri Lefebvre: Ein Romantischer Revolutionär*, Wien: Europaverlag, 1973, pp. 24–7, 36–40.

16 *Introduction à la modernité: Préludes*, Paris: Les Éditions de Minuit, 1962, p. 102; *Introduction to Modernity: Twelve Preludes*, translated by John Moore, London: Verso, 1995; *Introduction to Modernity*, p. 96.

17 *Introduction à la modernité*, p. 102; *Introduction to Modernity*, p. 96.

18 *Pyrénées*, Pau: Cairn, 2nd edition, 2000 (1965), p. 151.

19 René Lourau, 'Lefebvre, "parrain" de la Maffia "Analyse institutionnelle" ', in *La somme et le reste*, p. xiii.

20 See Friedrich Nietzsche, *Thus Spoke Zarathustra*, in *The Portable Nietzsche*, edited and translated by Walter Kaufmann, Harmondsworth: Penguin, 1954, especially pp. 269–72. For a discussion of the moment in Nietzsche, and Heidegger's reading of it, see Elden, *Mapping the Present*, Chapter 2.

21 Friedrich Nietzsche, *Ecce Homo*, translated by Walter Kaufmann, New York, Vintage, 1967, p. 295; see *Nietzsche*, Paris: Éditions Sociales Internationales, 1939, p. 61.

22 *La somme et le reste*, pp. 256, 481; see *Nietzsche*, pp. 140–1. For a suggestion that – at least in Engels – there is the possibility of reconciling Marxism with notions of the eternal return, see *La somme et le reste*, p. 401.

23 *Nietzsche*, pp. 51, 57, 71, 148.

24 *La somme et le reste*, pp. 642–3; *Key Writings*, edited by Stuart Elden, Elizabeth Lebas and Eleonore Kofman, London: Continuum, 2003, p. 166.

25 *Critique de la vie quotidienne II: Fondements d'une sociologie de la quotidienneté*, Paris: L'Arche, 1961, p. 348; *Critique of Everyday Life Volume II: Foundations for a Sociology of the Everyday*, translated by John Moore, London: Verso, 2002, p. 348.

26 *La somme et le reste*, p. 648; *Key Writings*, p. 170.

27 *La somme et le reste*, p. 648; *Key Writings*, p. 170.

28 *La somme et le reste*, p. 651; *Key Writings*, pp. 172–3.

29 *La somme et le reste*, p. 652; *Key Writings*, p. 174. On the theory of moments see also *Critique de la vie quotidienne* II, pp. 340–57; *Critique of Everyday Life* II, pp. 340–58.

30 *Critique de la vie quotidienne* II, pp. 343–4; *Critique of Everyday Life* II, pp. 343–4; see Henri Lefebvre and Catherine Régulier, *La révolution n'est plus ce qu'elle était*, Hallier: Éditions Libres, 1978, p. 52.

31 *La fin de l'histoire*, p. 195; *Key Writings*, p. 178. See Lefebvre and Régulier, *La révolution n'est plus ce qu'elle était*, p. 178.

32 *La fin de l'histoire*, p. 196; *Key Writings*, p. 178.

33 Lourau, 'Lefebvre', p. xiii.

34 *La somme et le reste*, p. 653; *Key Writings*, p. 174. There is a useful discussion of moments in Rob Shields, *Lefebvre, Love and Struggle: Spatial Dialectics*, London: Routledge, 1999, pp. 58–60.

35 *La présence et l'absence*, p. 29. See *Une pensée devenue monde*, pp. 167–8; *Le retour de la*

dialectique: 12 mots clefs, Paris: Messidor/Éditions Sociales, 1986, p. 118. See *Critique de la vie quotidienne* III, p. 85; Henri Lefebvre and Catherine Régulier, 'Le projet rythmanalytique', *Communications* 41, 1985, pp. 191–9, p. 191; *Rhythmanalysis: Space, Time and Everyday Life*, translated by Gerald Moore and Stuart Elden, London: Continuum, 2004, p. 73. For a discussion, in relation to the city, see Ash Amin and Nigel Thrift, *Cities: Reimagining the Urban*, Cambridge: Polity, 2002, pp. 96–7.

36 *La fin de l'histoire*, Paris: Les Éditions de Minuit, 1970, p. 190; *Key Writings*, p. 177.
37 *La fin de l'histoire*, p. 191; *Key Writings*, pp. 177–8. See *Le manifeste différentialiste*, Paris: Gallimard, 1970, pp. 92–3.
38 See *Le manifeste différentialiste*, p. 79.
39 *Le manifeste différentialiste*, p. 81; *La fin de l'histoire*, p. 85. On the repetitive in Nietzsche, see also *Hegel, Marx, Nietzsche*, pp. 190–1, 192ff.
40 *La fin de l'histoire*, p. 85.
41 *La fin de l'histoire*, p. 79. See *Hegel, Marx, Nietzsche*, p. 83.
42 *Logique formelle, logique dialectique*, p. xxii; see xxvi–viii. See *Le manifeste différentialiste*, p. 79.
43 *La droit à la ville*, p. 130; *Writings on Cities*, p. 157. For some additional discussion of music, see also *Le langage et la société*, pp. 275–86; *La fin de l'histoire*, pp. 81ff; *Une pensée devenue monde*, pp. 200–4. In an article on the relation between music and semiology, Lefebvre extends these themes. See 'Musique et sémiologie', *Musique en jeu* 4, 1971, pp. 52–62.
44 *Éléments de rythmanalyse: Introduction à la connaissance de rythmes*, Paris: Éditions Syllepse, 1992, p. 24; *Rhythmanalysis*, p. 14. See Douglas R. Hofstadter, *Gödel, Escher, Bach: An Eternal Golden Braid*, New York: Basic Books, 1979.
45 *Éléments de rythmanalyse*, pp. 79–80; *Rhythmanalysis*, pp. 57–8.
46 *Le manifeste différentialiste*, p. 87.
47 *Éléments de rythmanalyse*, pp. 82–3; *Rhythmanalysis*, p. 60.
48 *Qu'est-ce que penser?* pp. 65–6; *La somme et le reste*, pp. 279–81; *Au-delà du structuralisme*, p. 247. See also the discussion in *Critique de la vie quotidienne* II, pp. 126–7; *Critique of Everyday Life* II, pp. 122–4.
49 *Éléments de rythmanalyse*, p. 88; *Rhythmanalysis*, p. 64.
50 *Logique formelle, logique dialectique*, p. 50.
51 *Hegel, Marx, Nietzsche*, p. 211 n. 22.
52 *La somme et le reste*, pp. 381–2.
53 *La somme et le reste*, p. 382. He explicitly distances it from Bergson in *Critique de la vie quotidienne* II, p. 342; *Critique of Everyday Life*, II, p. 342, citing Georges Politzer's 1928 work *Le bergsonisme* as another expression of this, see Politzer, *La fin d'une parade philosophique: le bergsonisme*, Pauvert: Paris, 1967.
54 Rémi Hess, 'Note de l'éditeur', in *La fin de l'histoire*, Paris: Anthropos, 2nd edition, 2001 (1970), p. v. We should perhaps also note that these are the three books Lefebvre published in Axelos' *Arguments* series. On the meaning of 'preludes' – a fragmentary rather than systematic inquiry – see *Introduction à la modernité*, p. 11; *Introduction to Modernity*, p. 3.
55 *La fin de l'histoire*, p. 42. See *Une pensée devenue monde*, p. 40.
56 *La fin de l'histoire*, p. 43; see *La somme et le reste*, pp. 741ff; *Marx*, Paris: PUF, 1964, p. 52; *Au-delà du structuralisme*, Paris: Anthropos, 1971, p. 330; *La présence et l'absence*, p. 23; and *Qu'est-ce que penser?* p. 18.
57 *La somme et le reste*, p. 671. See also 'Lettre', in *Marx . . . ou pas? Réflexions sur un centenaire*, Paris, Études et Documentation Internationales, 1986, p. 21.

58 See Pierre Lantz, 'Présentation de la seconde édition', in *La fin de l'histoire*, 2nd edition, pp. ix–x.

59 Jean-François Lyotard, *The Postmodern Condition: A Report on Knowledge*, translated by Geoff Bennington and Brian Massumi, Manchester: Manchester University Press, 1984.

60 *La fin de l'histoire*, p. 173.

61 The theme of the direction of history is particularly played out in Jean Baudrillard, *The Illusion of the End*, translated by Chris Turner, Cambridge: Polity Press, 1994.

62 *La fin de l'histoire*, pp. 12–13.

63 Daniel Bell, *The End of Ideology: On the Exhaustion of Political Ideas in the Fifties*, Illinois: Free Press of Glencoe, 1960. For explicit critiques of Bell, see *La fin de l'histoire*, p. 10; *L'irruption de Nanterre au sommet*, Paris: Éditions Syllepse, 2nd edition, 1998 (1968), pp. 5–6; *The Explosion: Marxism and the French Upheaval*, translated by Alfred Ehrenfeld, New York: Modern Reader, 1969, p. 9.

64 Francis Fukuyama, 'The end of history?' *The National Interest* 16, Summer 1989, pp. 3–18; *The End of History and the Last Man*, Harmondsworth: Penguin, 1992.

65 *La fin de l'histoire*, p. 16.

66 *La fin de l'histoire*, p. 18.

67 *La fin de l'histoire*, p. 14.

68 *La fin de l'histoire*, pp. 14–15.

69 *La fin de l'histoire*, p. 173.

70 *La fin de l'histoire*, p. 15. For a discussion, see Kostas Axelos, 'La question de la fin', *Horizons du monde*, Paris: Éditions de Minuit, 1974, pp. 101–27.

71 *La fin de l'histoire*, p. 215; *Key Writings*, p. 182; see *La fin de l'histoire*, p. 214; *Hegel, Marx, Nietzsche ou le royaume des ombres*, Paris: Casterman, 1975, p. 35; *La présence et l'absence*, p. 95. On overcoming and Hegelian subsumption see *La fin de l'histoire*, pp. 73–4; *Logique formelle, logique dialectique*, Paris: Anthropos, 2nd edition, 1969 [1947], pp. 211–16.

72 *La fin de l'histoire*, p. 225; *Key Writings*, p. 184.

73 *La fin de l'histoire*, pp. 51–2.

74 *La fin de l'histoire*, p. 106. See François Châtelet, *La Naissance de l'histoire: La formation de la pensée historienne en grèce*, Paris: Éditions de Minuit, 1962, p. 405.

75 *La fin de l'histoire*, p. 106.

76 *La fin de l'histoire*, p. 107.

77 *La fin de l'histoire*, p. 112.

78 *La fin de l'histoire*, pp. 200–2; *Key Writings*, pp. 179–80.

79 *La fin de l'histoire*, p. 202; *Key Writings*, p. 180.

80 *La fin de l'histoire*, p. 155.

81 Lantz, 'Présentation de la seconde édition', pp. x, xix. See Friedrich Nietzsche, 'On the uses and disadvantages of history for life', in *Untimely Meditations*, translated by R. J. Hollingdale, Cambridge: Cambridge University Press, 1983, pp. 59–123; Heidegger, *Being and Time*.

82 *La fin de l'histoire*, p. 84.

83 *La fin de l'histoire*, p. 85.

84 See also *Éléments de rythmanalyse*, p. 16; *Rhythmanalysis*, p. 8.

85 *La fin de l'histoire*, p. 91.

86 *La fin de l'histoire*, p. 24.

87 *La fin de l'histoire*, pp. 228–9; *Key Writings*, pp. 186–7.

88 See Heidegger, *Being and Time; Identity and Difference / Identität und Differenz*, English–

German edition, translated by Joan Stambaugh, New York: Harper & Row, 1969; *Contributions to Philosophy: From Enowning*, translated by Parvis Emad and Kenneth Maly, Bloomington: Indiana University Press, 1999.

89 Martin Heidegger, *Nietzsche*, translated by David Farrell Krell, Frank Capuzzi and Joan Stambaugh, San Francisco: Harper Collins, 4 volumes, 1991.

90 *La fin de l'histoire*, pp. 212–13; *Key Writings*, p. 182.

91 *La fin de l'histoire*, p. 72.

92 *La fin de l'histoire*, p. 206.

93 *La fin de l'histoire*, pp. 154–5. See Lantz, 'Présentation de la seconde édition', p. xix.

94 See *La fin de l'histoire*, p. 88, where he draws upon Gilles Deleuze, *Nietzsche et la philosophie*, Paris: PUF, 1965.

95 *La présence et l'absence*, p. 55.

96 Of Foucault's work, see notably 'Nietzsche, genealogy, history', in *Language, Counter-Memory, Practice*, edited by Donald F. Bouchard, Oxford: Basil Blackwell, 1977, pp. 139–64.

97 For a brief account, see Kofman and Lebas, 'Lost in Transposition', p. 9.

98 *La fin de l'histoire*, p. 84.

99 *La fin de l'histoire*, p. 68.

100 *Au-delà du structuralisme*, p. 86; 'What is the historical past?', *New Left Review*, 90, 1975, pp. 27–34, p. 34.

101 Frederic Jameson, *Postmodernism, or, The Cultural Logic of Late Capitalism*, London: Verso, 1991, p. 364.

102 *La fin de l'histoire*, p. 140.

103 *Espace et politique: Le droit à la ville II*, Paris: Anthropos, 2nd edition, 2000 (1972), p. 7; *Writings on Cities*, p. 185.

104 David Harvey, *The Condition of Postmodernity*, Oxford: Blackwell, 1989, p. 237.

105 Kristin Ross, *The Emergence of Social Space: Rimbaud and the Paris Commune*, Basingstoke: Macmillan, 1988, pp. 8–9, goes so far as to suggest that social space is a synonym of everyday life – that everyday life is primarily (though not entirely) a spatial concept.

106 *Writings on Cities*, p. 215.

107 For example, except in their bibliographies of Lefebvre's work, Rémi Hess, *Henri Lefebvre et l'aventure du siècle*, Paris: A. M. Métailié, 1988; and Meyer, *Henri Lefebvre*, do not mention him at all. Shields' only reference, *Lefebvre, Love and Struggle*, p. 73, mistakes this book for one on a writer. Pignon is briefly discussed in David Caute, *Communism and the French Intellectuals 1914–1960*, London: André Deutsch, 1964, especially pp. 342–3, which includes a reference to Lefebvre's book on the painter, but this is not concerned with the theorization of space.

108 *Pignon*, Paris: Édition Falaise, 1956; *Pignon*, Paris: J. Goldschmidt, 2nd edition, 1970. All references are to the first edition. There is also a brief discussion of Pignon along with Picasso in 'Connaissance et critique sociale'; 'Knowledge and social criticism', in Marvin Farber (ed.), *Philosophic Thought in France and the United States: Essays Representing Major Trends in Contemporary French and American Philosophy*, New York: University of Buffalo Publications in Philosophy, 1950, pp. 281–300. Picasso takes on a major role in *La production de l'espace*, pp. 346–9; *The Production of Space*, pp. 301–3, where Pignon is not mentioned at all. On the importance of Picasso to Lefebvre's work on space, see Gregory, *Geographical Imaginations*, pp. 393–4.

109 *Pignon*, pp. 10–11.

110 See, for example, Édouard Pignon, *La Quête de la réalité*, Paris: Denoël, 1966, pp. 91–101, 107–9. For a retrospective on Pignon's career, see Philippe Bouchet *et al.*, *Édouard Pignon en pleine lumière*, Arles: Actes Sud, 1999.

111 *Pignon*, pp. 10, 36.

112 *Contribution à l'esthétique*, Paris: Anthropos, 2nd edition, 2001 (1953), p. 12 n. 1.

113 *Pignon*, p. 14.

114 *Pignon*, p. 36.

115 *Pignon*, p. 21.

116 *Pignon*, p. 12.

117 *Pignon*, pp. 38–9.

118 *Pignon*, p. 47.

119 On this see also *Contribution à l'esthétique*, p. 70.

120 See, for example, *Méthodologie des sciences: Inédit*, Paris: Anthropos, 2002, pp. 52, 62–3, 65, 73, 79–80.

121 *Méthodologie des sciences*, p. 73.

122 *La vie quotidienne dans le monde moderne*, Paris: Gallimard, 1968, p. 13; *Everyday Life in the Modern World*, translated by Sacha Rabinovitch, Harmondsworth: Allen Lane, 1971, p. 4.

123 *La vie quotidienne dans le monde moderne*, p. 210; *Everyday Life in the Modern World*, p. 111.

124 *La vie quotidienne dans le monde moderne*, p. 155; *Everyday Life in the Modern World*, p. 155.

125 *Espace et politique*, p. 59.

126 *Espace et politique*, pp. 50–1.

127 *La pensée marxiste et la ville*, Paris: Casterman, 1972, p. 152; *Marx*, p. 35; *Le manifeste différentialiste*, pp. 127–8.

128 *La production de l'espace*, p. 396; *The Production of Space*, p. 343; see *Hegel, Marx, Nietzsche*, p. 52.

129 *La pensée marxiste et la ville*, p. 152.

130 *La production de l'espace*, p. 83; *The Production of Space*, p. 68. An early version of part of the introduction appeared as 'La production de l'espace', *L'homme et la société* 31–32, January–March 1974/April–June 1974, pp. 15–32. The first extensive use of Lefebvre's work in this area in English was M. Gottdiener, *The Social Production of Urban Space*, Austin: University of Texas Press, 2nd edition, 1997 (1985). For a French reception of this aspect of his work, see the essays in the special issue 'Actualités de Henri Lefebvre', presented by Monique Coornaert and Jean-Pierre Garnier, *Espaces et sociétés* 76, 1994, pp. 3–145.

131 *La production de l'espace*, p. 35; *The Production of Space*, p. 26.

132 'An Interview with Henri Lefebvre', translated by Eleonore Kofman, *Environment and Planning D: Society and Space* 5(1), 1987, pp. 27–38, p. 31; see *La production de l'espace*, p. 65; *The Production of Space*, p. 53.

133 'Préface: La production de l'espace (1986)', in *La production de l'espace*, Paris: Anthropos, 4th edition, 2000 (1974), p. xxi; *Key Writings*, p. 209.

134 *La vie quotidienne dans le monde moderne*, pp. 62–3; *Everyday Life in the Modern World*, pp. 30–1.

135 *La survie du capitalisme: La re-production des rapports de production*, Paris: Anthropos, 3rd edition, 2002 (1973), p. 16; *The Survival of Capitalism*, translated by Frank Bryant, London: Allison & Busby, 1976, pp. 21–2.

136 *Espace et politique*, p. 105, see p. 154.

137 *La production de l'espace*, p. 244; *The Production of Space*, p. 212.
138 *La production de l'espace*, p. 220; *The Production of Space*, p. 190.
139 *La survie du capitalisme*, p. 80; *The Survival of Capitalism*, p. 84.
140 See for example, Martin Heidegger, *The Question Concerning Technology and Other Essays*, translated by William Lovitt, New York: Harper & Row, 1977.
141 *La révolution urbaine*, Paris: Gallimard, 1970, p. 204.
142 Scott Kirsch, 'The incredible shrinking world? Technology and the production of space', *Environment and Planning D: Society and Space* 13(5), 1995, pp. 529–55, pp. 533, 544. The critique of the shrinking world metaphor is expressly directed at David Harvey's work, specifically *The Condition of Postmodernity*. Kirsch suggests that the metaphorical space of the shrinking world takes material space out of geography, and is therefore akin to a fetishism of space. It is suggested that Lefebvre's space, a concrete abstraction, cannot be divorced from its materiality. On these issues more generally, see Erik A. Swyngedouw, 'Territorial organization and the space/technology nexus', *Transactions of the Institute of British Geographers* 17 (NS), 1992, pp. 417–33.
143 On this see Jameson, *Postmodernism*, pp. 364–5.
144 *La production de l'espace*, p. 204; *The Production of Space*, p. 175.
145 Edward W. Soja, *Postmodern Geographies: The Reassertion of Space in Contemporary Social Theory*, London: Verso, 1989, p. 32. The source for Soja is almost certainly David Harvey's use of the phrase in quotation marks, in *The Urbanization of Capital: Studies in the History and Theory of Capitalist Urbanization 2*, Oxford: Basil Blackwell, 1985, p. xii, although Harvey has assured me these are scare quotes and that it is not a quotation (personal correspondence, 10 January 2002).
146 Richard Peet, *Global Capitalism: Theories of Societal Development*, London and New York: Routledge, 1991, pp. 178–9.
147 On the circulation of capital, see Karl Marx, *Capital: A Critique of Political Economy* II, translated by David Fernbach, Harmondsworth: Penguin, 1978, *passim*, especially pp. 135, 225–9, 326–32; *Capital: A Critique of Political Economy* III, translated by David Fernbach, Harmondsworth: Penguin, 1981, p. 164; *Grundrisse: Foundations of the Critique of Political Economy (Rough Draft)*, translated by Martin Nicolaus, Harmondsworth: Penguin, 1973, pp. 521, 618–23. On spatial scarcity, see *Capital* I, pp. 442, 444, 596–8, 612; III, pp. 185–90; and 'The eighteenth Brumaire of Louis Bonaparte', in *Surveys from Exile: Political Writings Volume II*, translated by David Fernbach, Harmondsworth: Penguin, 1973. On the relation of town and country see *Capital* I, pp. 848–9, 877; III, pp. 789–90, 904–5; Karl Marx and Friedrich Engels, *The German Ideology*, edited by Chris Arthur, London: Lawrence & Wishart, 1970; and 'Manifesto of the Communist Party', in *The Revolutions of 1848: Political Writings Volume I*, translated by David Fernbach, Harmondsworth: Penguin, 1973. Concerning the army, the importance of the spatial analyses in Marx's work is suggested by Michel Foucault, 'Questions à Michel Foucault sur la géographie', in Daniel Defert and François Ewald (eds), *Dits et écrits 1954–1988*, Paris: Gallimard, 4 volumes, 1994, III, pp. 38–9. We can see this in practice in 'Articles from the *Neue Rheinische Zeitung*' in *The Revolutions of 1848*; 'The Class Struggles in France: 1848 to 1850'; 'Agitation against the Sunday Trading Bill'; 'The British rule in India'; and 'Articles on the North American Civil War', in *Surveys from Exile*.
148 Marx, *Grundrisse*, pp. 533–4.

149 *Une pensée devenue monde*, p. 149.
150 'Space: social product and use value', in J. W. Freiburg (ed.), *Critical Sociology: European Perspectives*, New York: Irvington Publishers, 1979, pp. 285–95; see *Espace et politique*, p. 127; *La production de l'espace*, pp. 119–21; *The Production of Space*, pp. 100–2.
151 *Espace et politique*, p. 147.
152 See Louis Althusser, Etienne Balibar, Roger Establet, Jacques Rancière, and Pierre Macherey, *Lire le Capital*, Paris: François Maspero, 2 volumes, 1965, especially I, pp. 28–31. For a discussion of Althusser and Foucault, see Neil Smith and Cindy Katz, 'Grounding metaphor: towards a spatialised politics', in Michael Keith and Steve Pile (eds), *Place and the Politics of Identity*, London: Routledge, 1993, pp. 67–83. Smith and Katz liken Foucault to Althusser, and criticize his use of metaphors without analysis. I have tried to show in my *Mapping the Present*, particularly Chapter 5, just how erroneous this judgement is.
153 *Au-delà du structuralisme*, p. 416.
154 Doreen Massey, 'Politics and space/time', *New Left Review* 196, November/December 1992, pp. 65–84, p. 66. See *La production de l'espace*, pp. 9–10; *The Production of Space*, pp. 3–4.
155 This makes Andrew Merrifield's 'Place and space: a Lefebvrian reconciliation', *Transactions of the Institute of British Geographers* 18, 1993, pp. 516–31, fundamentally misconceived: it reads a problematic into Lefebvre that he did not use in order to suggest he can resolve it. For a discussion of the notion of *l'espace* and its polyvalence, see Shields, *Lefebvre, Love and Struggle*, p. 154. Shields generally provides a useful discussion of *The Production of Space*.
156 *La production de l'espace*, pp. 7–8; *The Production of Space*, pp. 1–2; *Espace et politique*, p. 46.
157 *Le matérialisme dialectique*, Paris: PUF, 6th edition, 1971 (1939), pp. 119, 130; *Dialectical Materialism*, translated by John Sturrock, London: Jonathan Cape, 1968, pp. 122, 133.
158 *Descartes*, Paris: Éditions Hier et Aujourd'hui, 1947, p. 106.
159 For example, *Descartes*, pp. 187–243; see *Logique formelle, logique dialectique*, p. 28.
160 René Descartes, *The Geometry of René Descartes*, French-Latin-English edition, translated by David Eugene Smith and Marcia L. Latham, New York: Dover, 1954, pp. 2/3, 216/17.
161 *Logique formelle, logique dialectique*, p. 90. On this in more detail, see Stuart Elden, 'The place of geometry: Heidegger's mathematical excursus on Aristotle', *The Heythrop Journal* 42(3), July 2001, pp. 311–28.
162 *Descartes*, p. 144.
163 *Descartes*, pp. 145–6.
164 *Descartes*, pp. 146–7.
165 *La fin de l'histoire*, p. 190; *Key Writings*, p. 177.
166 Elden, 'The place of geometry'; *Mapping the Present*; see also Didier Franck, *Heidegger et le problème de l'espace*, Paris: Les Éditions de Minuit, 1986; Edward S. Casey, *The Fate of Place: A Philosophical History*, Berkeley: University Presses of California, 1997.
167 Heidegger, *Being and Time*.
168 *La production de l'espace*, p. 280; *The Production of Space*, p. 242.
169 Many references could be given here, but see for example, Heidegger, *Being and Time*, pp. 143–4, 412–13; *The Basic Problems of Phenomenology*, translated by Albert Hofstader, Bloomington: Indiana University Press, 1982, pp. 162–6.

170 Martin Heidegger, *Hölderlins Hymnen 'Germanien' und 'Der Rhein', Gesamtausgabe Band 39*, Frankfurt am Main: Vittorio Klostermann, 1980; *Hölderlin's Hymn 'The Ister'*, translated by William McNeill and Julia Davis, Bloomington: Indiana University Press, 1996.

171 Martin Heidegger, *Poetry, Language, Thought*, translated by Albert Hofstadter, New York: Harper & Row, 1971.

172 Friedrich Hölderlin, *Selected Verse*, translated by Michael Hamburger, Harmondsworth: Penguin, 1961, pp. 245–6.

173 See, for example, Heidegger, *Poetry, Language, Thought*, p. 213.

174 See Heidegger, *The Question Concerning Technology*. For a commentary, see Stuart Elden, 'Taking the measure of the *Beiträge*: Heidegger, National Socialism and the Calculation of the Political', *European Journal of Political Theory* 2(1), January 2003, pp. 35–56.

175 *La production de l'espace*, p. 273; *The Production of Space*, p. 236.

176 *Espace et politique*, p. 167.

177 *La survie du capitalisme*, p. 85; *The Survival of Capitalism*, p. 89.

178 *La révolution urbaine*, p. 203.

179 *La révolution urbaine*, pp. 240–1.

180 *La production de l'espace*, p. 407; *The Production of Space*, p. 352.

181 *La révolution urbaine*, p. 241; see *Espace et politique*, pp. 15–16; *Writings on Cities*, pp. 190–1.

182 *Espace et politique*, p. 16; *Writings on Cities*, p. 191.

183 *Espace et politique*, p. 149, see 147.

184 *Le matérialisme dialectique*, p. 165; *Dialectical Materialism*, p. 167; see Norbert Guterman and Henri Lefebvre, *La conscience mystifiée*, Paris: Éditions Syllepse, 3rd edition, 1999 (1936), p. 210.

185 *Critique de la vie quotidienne I: Introduction*. Paris: L'Arche, 2nd edition, 1958 (1947), p. 223; *Critique of Everyday Life Volume I: Introduction*, translated by John Moore, London: Verso, 1991, p. 209.

186 *La production de l'espace*, pp. 42–3, 48–9; *The Production of Space*, pp. 33, 38–9. The original French for the last of these is *les espaces de représentation*, and 'spaces of representation' seems a more felicitous translation than 'representational spaces' used by Nicholson-Smith. This has become standard practice. See Edward W. Soja's *Thirdspace: Journeys to Los Angeles and Other Real-and-Imagined Places*. Blackwell: Oxford, 1996, p. 61; Shields, *Lefebvre, Love and Struggle*, p. 161.

187 The reference to navigators and explorers is from *De l'État*, IV, p. 281.

188 See Soja, *Postmodern Geographies; Thirdspace*. The problem with this is that it turns an initial schema into an absolute, instead of realizing that it is then examined historically throughout the work. Shields, *Lefebvre, Love and Struggle*, is better on the historical dimension. See also *Espace et politique*, p. 25; see *Hegel, Marx, Nietzsche*, p. 90.

189 *La révolution urbaine*, p. 240; *La production de l'espace*, pp. 143–4; *The Production of Space*, pp. 121–2.

190 *Du rural à l'urbain*, Paris: Anthropos, 3rd edition, 2001 (1970), p. 160; *La révolution urbaine*, p. 111; *La production de l'espace*, p. 362; *The Production of Space*, p. 314.

191 *La production de l'espace*, pp. 143–4; *The Production of Space*, pp. 121–2; *La droit à la ville*, Paris: Anthropos, 1968, p. 41; *Writings on Cities*, p. 92. See Heidegger, 'Building dwelling thinking', in *Poetry, Language, Thought*; Gaston Bachelard, *The Poetics of Space*, translated by Maria Jolas, Boston: Beacon, 1969.

192 *La droit à la ville*, pp. 16, 18; *Writings on Cities*, pp. 76, 79; *La production de l'espace*, p. 362; *The Production of Space*, p. 314; *Critique de la vie quotidienne* III, p. 94.

193 *Du rural à l'urbain*, pp. 222, 241; *Vers le cybernanthrope*, Paris: Denoël/Gonthier, 1967, pp. 15–16.

194 *Du rural à l'urbain*, p. 161.

195 Monique Coornaert and Henri Lefebvre, 'Ville, urbanisme et urbanisation', *Perspectives de la sociologie contemporaine: Hommage à Georges Gurvitch*, sous la direction de Georges Balandier, Roger Bastide, Jacques Berque et Pierre George, Paris: PUF, 1968, pp. 85–105, p. 93.

196 *La vie quotidienne dans le monde moderne*, p. 215; *Everyday Life in the Modern World*, p. 113.

197 *La fin de l'histoire*, p. 113.

198 David Harvey, *Justice, Nature and the Geography of Difference*, Oxford: Blackwell, 1996, p. 267.

199 *La production de l'espace*, p. 362; *The Production of Space*, p. 314.

200 *Métaphilosophie*, Paris: Éditions Syllepse, 2nd edition, 2001 (1965), pp. 127–8.

201 *Métaphilosophie*, p. 288.

202 *Au-delà du structuralisme*, p. 161.

203 *La révolution urbaine*, pp. 111–12.

204 *La production de l'espace*, p. 250; *The Production of Space*, p. 217.

205 René Lourau, *L'analyseur Lip*, Paris: Union Générale d'Éditions, 1974, p. 141.

206 *De l'État*, Paris: UGE, 4 volumes, 1976–78, IV, p. 260.

207 Kirsch, 'The Incredible Shrinking World?' p. 548.

208 *La production de l'espace*, p. 144; *The Production of Space*, p. 122. This criticism is preceded by others, including the claims that space for Heidegger is 'nothing more and nothing other than "being-there"', than beings, than *Dasein*'; and that 'time counts for more than space; Being has a history, and history is only the History of Being' (*La production de l'espace*, p. 144; *The Production of Space*, p. 121). Both of these claims are contestable. See Elden, *Mapping the Present*.

209 On this, and other aspects of Lefebvre and space, see Mario Rui Martins, 'The theory of social space in the work of Henri Lefebvre', in R. Forrest, J. Henderson and P. Williams (eds), *Urban Political Economy and Social Theory: Critical Essays in Urban Studies*, Aldershot: Gower, 1982, pp. 160–85.

210 For example, Marx, *Capital* I, pp. 442, 444, 596–8, 612; III, pp. 185–90.

211 *La vie quotidienne dans le monde moderne*, p. 103; *Everyday Life in the Modern World*, p. 52; see *Espace et politique*, p. 58.

212 *La production de l'espace*, p. 381; *The Production of Space*, pp. 330–1.

213 *L'irruption de Nanterre au sommet*, pp. 86–7; *The Explosion*, p. 95.

214 *La production de l'espace*, p. 68; *The Production of Space*, p. 55.

215 *La production de l'espace*, p. 370; *The Production of Space*, p. 321.

216 See for the former, in Lefebvre's work, for example, *La pensée marxiste et la ville*, pp. 109–47; *Du rural à l'urbain*, pp. 80–7. Massimo Quani, *Geography and Marxism*, translated by Alan Braley, Oxford: Basil Blackwell, 1982; and David Harvey, *The Limits to Capital*, London: Verso, New Edition, 1999 (1982) offer some valuable pointers. There are some hints here which are developed in many of Harvey's other writings towards a politics of space. Lefebvre suggests that there is a danger in reducing the urban and spatial 'reality' to economic aspects in *De l'État* IV, p. 268.

217 *La production de l'espace*, pp. 167–8; *The Production of Space*, pp. 142–3.

218 Harvey, *Justice, Nature and the Geography of Difference*, p. 87.

219 *La production de l'espace*, p. 465; *The Production of Space*, p. 404.

220 *La production de l'espace*, p. 18; *The Production of Space*, p. 11.

221 *La production de l'espace*, p. 465; *The Production of Space*, p. 404. See *Le temps des méprises*, Paris: Stock, 1975, p. 247.

222 *La survie du capitalisme*, p. 12; *The Survival of Capitalism*, p. 18.

223 Caute, *Communism and the French Intellectuals*, p. 298.

224 I have in mind particularly Soja's *Thirdspace*, which I have critically reviewed in 'What about Huddersfield?', *Radical Philosophy* 84, July/August 1997, pp. 47–8. A different argument about the spatial turn in our 'postmodern' times is found in Jameson, *Postmodernism*.

225 Ross, *The Emergence of Social Space*, p. 9. Soja, *Postmodern Geographies*, pp. 69–70, 76ff.

226 Soja, *Postmodern Geographies*, p. 42.

227 Lynn Stewart, 'Bodies, visions and spatial politics: a review essay of Henri Lefebvre's The *Production of Space*', in *Environment and Planning D: Society and Space* 13(5), 1995, pp. 609–18, p. 617.

228 *La production de l'espace*, pp. 57, 130–1, 144; *The Production of Space*, pp. 46, 110, 122; see *De l'État* IV, pp. 264, 281, 409–11. On this criticism, see Tim Unwin, 'A waste of space? Towards a Critique of the Social Production of Space . . .', *Transactions of the Institute of British Geographers* 25, 2000, pp. 11–29, p. 21.

229 *La production de l'espace*, p. 465; *The Production of Space*, p. 405. See *De l'État* IV, p. 283.

230 *Le temps des méprises*, p. 238. See *La pensée marxiste et la ville*, p. 154, where he suggests the neglect of time.

231 *La production de l'espace*, p. 465; *The Production of Space*, p. 405; see *La production de l'espace*, pp. 236–8; *The Production of Space*, pp. 205–7; *Hegel, Marx, Nietzsche*, pp. 191–2, 195–6; *De l'État* IV, p. 280.

232 *Éléments de rythmanalyse*, p. 71; *Rhythmanalysis*, p. 51.

233 *Le temps des méprises*, p. 240; *De l'État* IV, p. 321; *Le langage et la société*, Paris: Gallimard, 1966, p. 66.

234 *Du rural à l'urbain*, p. 235; see pp. 224, 259.

235 See Elden, *Mapping the Present*.

236 *Contribution à l'esthétique*, p. 12.

237 Armand Ajzenberg, 'A partir d'Henri Lefebvre: Vers un mode de production écologique', *Traces de futures: Henri Lefebvre: Le possible et le quotidienne*, Paris: La Société Française, 1994, pp. 1–5, cited in Kofman and Lebas, 'Lost in transposition – time, space and the city', p. 7.

238 *Critique de la vie quotidienne* II, p. 233; *Critique of Everyday Life* II, p. 232.

239 *Critique de la vie quotidienne* III, p. 17. The most detailed discussion is in a section called 'Space and time', pp. 128–35.

240 Lefebvre and Régulier, 'Le projet rythmanalytique'; 'Essai de rythmanalyse des villes méditerranéennes', *Peuples méditerranéens* 37, October–December 1986, reprinted in *Éléments de rythmanalyse: Introduction à la connaissance de rythmes*. Paris: Éditions Syllepse, 1992, pp. 97–109.

241 *Éléments de rythmanalyse*, see Lourau's preface, 'Henrisques', pp. 5–10. Around the same time, see also *Le retour de la dialectique*, pp. 105–7.

242 'The Rhythmanalytical Project', *Key Writings*, pp. 190–8; 'Rhythmanalysis of Mediterranean cities', 'Seen from the window', *Writings on Cities*, pp. 228–40, 219–27.

243 *Éléments de rythmanalyse*, p. 18; *Rhythmanalysis*, p. 9. See *Critique de la vie quotidienne*

II, p. 233; *Critique of Everyday Life* II, pp. 232, 366 n. 17. See Gaston Bachelard, *The Psychoanalysis of Fire*, translated by Alan C. M. Ross, Boston: Beacon, 1964. For a detailed note on Bachelard, see *Critique de la vie quotidienne* II, pp. 334–5 n. 1; *Critique of Everyday Life* II, pp. 369–70 n. 9; for more general references, see *La somme et le reste*, pp. 142–3, 308 n. 1, 314; *L'existentialisme*, Paris: Anthropos, 2nd edition, 2001 (1946), pp. 67–8; *Le langage et la société*, p. 113. For a useful discussion, see Kofman and Lebas, 'Lost in transposition', pp. 28–9, 30–1. For a discussion which analyses Lefebvre's early pronouncements, but was written before the explicit formularization, see Meyer, *Henri Lefebvre*, pp. 126–8. More generally, see Derek Gregory, 'Lacan and geography: The production of space revisited', in Georges Benko and Ulf Strohmeyer (eds), *Space and Social Theory: Interpreting Modernity and Postmodernity*, Oxford: Blackwell, 1997, pp. 203–31. The influence of Lacan is also analysed in Virginia Blum and Heidi Nast, 'Where's the difference? The heterosexualization of alterity in Henri Lefebvre and Jacques Lacan', *Environment and Planning D: Society and Space* 14, 1996, pp. 559–80.

244 *Éléments de rythmanalyse*, p. 11; *Rhythmanalysis*, p. 3.

245 *Éléments de rythmanalyse*, p. 94; *Rhythmanalysis*, p. 69.

246 *Éléments de rythmanalyse*, p. 40; *Rhythmanalysis*, p. 26.

247 *Éléments de rythmanalyse*, pp. 13–14; *Rhythmanalysis*, p. 5.

248 *Éléments de rythmanalyse*, p. 24; *Rhythmanalysis*, p. 14.

249 *Éléments de rythmanalyse*, p. 25; *Rhythmanalysis*, p. 15.

250 Kostas Axelos, 'Entretien avec Henri Lefebvre', in *Entretiens*: 'Réels', *Imaginaires, et avec 'Soi-Même'*, Montpellier: Fata Morgana, 1973, pp. 69–84, p. 75.

251 *Éléments de rythmanalyse*, pp. 16–17; *Rhythmanalysis*, p. 8.

252 *Critique de la vie quotidienne* II, p. 54; *Critique of Everyday Life* II, p. 48. See *Du rural à l'urbain*, p. 137.

253 *Éléments de rythmanalyse*, p. 76; *Rhythmanalysis*, p. 55.

254 'Le projet rythmanalytique', p. 194; *Rhythmanalysis*, p. 77.

255 Amin and Thrift, *Cities*, p. 19.

256 *Critique de la vie quotidienne* II, p. 20; *Critique of Everyday Life* II, p. 14. See *La révolution urbaine*, p. 48.

257 *Critique de la vie quotidienne* II, pp. 52–3; *Critique of Everyday Life* II, p. 47. See *Diderot ou les affirmations fondamentales du matérialisme*, Paris: L'Arche, 2nd edition, 1983 (1949), p. 27.

258 *La présence et l'absence*, p. 151.

259 *Critique de la vie quotidienne* II, p. 53; *Critique of Everyday Life* II, p. 48.

260 *Éléments de rythmanalyse*, p. 100; *Rhythmanalysis*, p. 90; see *Le retour de la dialectique*, p. 12.

261 *Le retour de la dialectique*, p. 72.

262 *Critique de la vie quotidienne* II, p. 54; *Critique of Everyday Life* II, pp. 48–9.

263 'Le projet rythmanalytique', p. 192; *Rhythmanalysis*, p. 74.

264 *Le matérialisme dialectique*, p. 139; *Dialectical Materialism*, p. 142.

265 *Éléments de rythmanalyse*, p. 62; *Rhythmanalysis*, p. 43; 'Le projet rythmanalytique', p. 192; *Rhythmanalysis*, p. 74.

266 'Le projet rythmanalytique', p. 191; *Rhythmanalysis*, p. 73.

267 *Éléments de rythmanalyse*, pp. 55–63; *Rhythmanalysis*, pp. 38–45.

268 Axelos, 'Entretien avec Henri Lefebvre', pp. 76–7; see *Critique de la vie quotidienne* III, p. 17.

269 *Éléments de rythmanalyse*, p. 32; *Rhythmanalysis*, p. 19.

270 *Éléments de rythmanalyse*, p. 33; *Rhythmanalysis*, p. 21.
271 *Éléments de rythmanalyse*, p. 32; *Rhythmanalysis*, p. 20; 'Le projet rythmanalytique', pp. 196–7; *Rhythmanalysis*, p. 80.
272 *Éléments de rythmanalyse*, p. 57; *Rhythmanalysis*, pp. 39–40. See Michel Foucault, *Discipline and Punish: The Birth of the Prison*, translated by Alan Sheridan, Harmondsworth: Penguin, 1977.
273 *Critique de la vie quotidienne* II, p. 54; *Critique of Everyday Life* II, p. 49.
274 *Critique de la vie quotidienne* II, p. 54; *Critique of Everyday Life* II, p. 49.
275 *La droit à la ville*, p. 58; *Writings on Cities*, pp. 104–5. See *Du rural à l'urbain*, pp. 101, 137, 224.
276 *Éléments de rythmanalyse*, p. 35; *Rhythmanalysis*, p. 22.
277 *Éléments de rythmanalyse*, pp. 41–54, 97–109; *Rhythmanalysis*, pp. 27–37, 87–100.
278 *Éléments de rythmanalyse*, p. 97; *Rhythmanalysis*, p. 87.
279 For example, *Éléments de rythmanalyse*, pp. 71, 109; *Rhythmanalysis*, p. 51, 100. See also *Le temps des méprises*, p. 240.
280 *Éléments de rythmanalyse*, p. 14; *Rhythmanalysis*, p. 6.
281 *Éléments de rythmanalyse*, p. 91; *Rhythmanalysis*, p. 69.

6   Politics and the state

Even generally well-informed critics can give a very misleading impression of Lefebvre's work on politics. Talking of Sartre's transition from existentialism to a Marxist humanism, putting consciousness at centre stage in his *Critique of Dialectical Reason*, Merquior argues that

> as such, it was a steady reinforcement to the anti-positivist heretic Marxists gathered around *Arguments*, a journal founded in 1956. Its main figure, Henri Lefebvre (b. 1901), had discovered Marx through Hegel and Hegel on the advice of André Breton, the surrealists being very fond of dialectics at its most bacchic. Lefebvre devoted two decades to a 'critique of everyday life' hinging on the alleged ubiquity of alienation in modern capitalism. As with Sartre and German Western Marxism, his kind of Marxist approach had little in common with a critique of political economy.[1]

This is misleading for a number of reasons. As we have seen, Lefebvre was concerned with the notion of everyday life from as early as 1933 right up to his death. Equally, given the range of other concerns he had, it is hardly accurate to say that he 'devoted' any period of his career to just that concept. The *Arguments* journal was much more shaped by Edgar Morin and Kostas Axelos than Lefebvre, who only published two short pieces in it. But most seriously misleading is the suggestion that Lefebvre had little to say about political economy. This is simply wrong. As is clear from the preceding chapters of this study, Lefebvre was political in the broad sense of the term throughout his work. As he notes of his early work, 'the *Philosophies* group behaved *politically*'.[2] In 1975 he stated that he was a political writer – against fascism and Hitlerism; capitalism, bourgeois society and its organization; Stalinism and dogmatism in general; and on political themes of space, urban questions, architecture and spatial planning.[3]

It was in this year, just after the publication of *The Production of Space*, that Lefebvre began the production of yet another remarkable work. This final chapter draws together the contribution he made to social and political theory through an examination of the four volume *De l'État*. It is worth underlining that he was 75 when the first volume appeared. Over the more than 1,600 pages of this work Lefebvre both discusses theories of the state and analyses the state in the modern world, adding significantly to the literature on this topic. Although he had touched upon the state in some of his earlier writings – notably *La somme et le reste* and *The Sociology of Marx*[4] – he is critical of these discussions, suggesting that in the ensuing years, particularly since 1968, new problems and perspectives had arisen.[5] Some of these issues had been explored in his analysis of 1968, *The Explosion*, and the 1973 study, *The Survival of Capitalism*, which develops its insights (and in the French original, reprints much of the 1968 text).[6] Taken together with *De l'État* they demonstrate the enormous importance of Lefebvre's work on politics – work that includes, but cannot be reduced to, political economy.[7] As Lefebvre notes in relation to the analysis of 1968

> such an analysis cannot be limited to a 'point of view', whether economic, psychological or psychoanalytical, historical or sociological. It is essentially *political*.[8]

This stands as a useful motto for his work as a whole. Lefebvre argues that 'the theoretical structure elaborated by Marx remains solid', but it must be continued. This does not mean that it should be made more scientific or formally coherent, but that it needs to be related to contemporary problems such as the state; 'the relations between economic and political factors; the problems posed by growth and development, town and country, etc.'[9] We have seen how Lefebvre continually stresses that although Marx provides the approach, his work needs to be developed – understandable given that it was written over a hundred years ago. 'Marx's work is necessary but not sufficient to enable us to understand our time, grasp events, and, if possible, guide them.'[10] As Lefebvre stresses, the capitalist system has not lost its meaning since 1867 – the date the first volume of *Capital* was published – but 'it has become clearly and distinctly *political*'.[11]

As is well known, Marx had planned to write on the state, though as Ralph Miliband notes, he 'never attempted a systematic study'.[12] In two famous and much cited letters of 1858, Marx outlined his plans for future work. His work on the critique of economic categories would comprise six parts:

1. On Capital
2. On Landed Property
3. On Wage Labour
4. On The State
5. International Trade
6. World Market[13]

Of course, it was only the first of these six parts that Marx came anywhere close to completing (and that with considerable editorial work by Engels and Kautsky after his death).[14] Although there are discussions of all the above areas in the lengthy *Grundrisse* draft, even this says relatively little about the state.[15] Sometimes the suggestion is made that Marx abandoned the analysis of the role of the state as he turned toward political economy. This requires a very simplistic reading of certain claims in the Preface to *A Contribution to the Critique of Political Economy* (usually known as the '1859 Preface'). Marx famously claims here that:

> my inquiry led me to the conclusion that neither legal relations nor political forms could be comprehended whether by themselves or on the basis of a so-called general development of the human mind, but that on the contrary that they originate in the material conditions of life, the totality of which Hegel, following the example of English and French thinkers of the eighteenth century, embraces within the term 'civil [or bourgeois] society'; that the anatomy of this civil society, however, has to be sought in political economy ... In the social production of their existence, men inevitably enter into definite relations, which are independent of their will, namely relations of production appropriate to a given stage in the development of their material forces of production. The totality of these relations of production constitutes the economic structure of society, the real foundation, on which arises a legal and political superstructure and to which correspond definite forms of social consciousness. The mode of production of material life conditions the general process of social, political and intellectual life.[16]

Clearly this requires an analysis of political economy in order to shed light on the workings of civil society, which is the sum of the material conditions of life, and the realm of the social existence of humans. This enables us to comprehend political and legal forms, which cannot be understood in isolation, nor from a reductive idealism. However, as Neocleous convincingly argues, to suggest that this requires us to replace an analysis of the relation between state and civil society with one of base/superstructure leads to a 'crude economism'.[17] For one thing it neglects the *political* of 'political economy'. As Lefebvre insists, this is equally not a simplistic, mechanistic process – to think that is to use an 'elementary Marxism' that is undialectical.[18] What is important is the fundamental relation that unites '*historical materialism* and the revised and corrected *dialectical method*'.[19] Marx realized that we cannot conceive the state without analysing economic reality; but in distinction to many Marxists he did not think it could be reduced to just that.[20] *Capital* is not an 'economic' work, because it is a critique of *all* political economy – not just bourgeois political economy with an attempt to replace it with socialist political economy. Likewise the Marxist critique of the state is not just of the Hegelian or bourgeois state, but also of democracy and the democratic and socialist state.[21] As Neocleous continues, 'while a critique of political economy may be *necessary* for a materialist theory of the state it is not *sufficient*. The state-civil society model remains throughout Marx's work and needs to be maintained *alongside* base-superstructure.'[22] In Lefebvre's formulation, 'following the penetrating conception of Hegel, the political is at once *within* civil society – in the economic – and *above it*: at the same time within and without'.[23]

However, as Lefebvre notes, for those seeking a coherent and complete theory of the state in Marx's writings, 'we can say without further ado that it does not exist'. Lefebvre stresses insistently that this does not mean that Marx neglected the state. On the contrary, it was a constant preoccupation – there are plenty of propositions concerning the state and a well-defined orientation.[24] Lefebvre suggests that the topic of the state was for Marx the 'point of rupture' with Hegel, the point where their thought collided.[25] This is evident from Marx's early writings on Hegel's *Philosophy of Right*. Indeed, for Lefebvre,

> the theory of the state is the core, or if you will, the culmination of Marxian thought. Very naturally, from the outset it has led to particularly passionate controversies. No other aspect of Marxian thought has been so greatly blurred, distorted and obscured as this.[26]

That it does not receive the systematic elaboration Marx clearly planned means that Marxists have often turned to Lenin's *State and Revolution* to fill this perceived hole. From then until the 1960s the state received less analysis. For example, in 1969 Miliband suggested that since Lenin, 'the only major Marxist contribution to the theory of the state has been that of Antonio Gramsci'.[27] Two of the reasons why this is not the case today are Lefebvre's work and the famous Miliband-Poulantzas debate.

And yet *De l'État* is largely unknown as a work of state theory – both to Lefebvre scholars and to Marxists more generally. This is a significant loss: *De l'État* is a text that is central for understanding Lefebvre's work. Within continental thought his analyses are at least the equal in importance to those better known ones of Gramsci, Althusser and Foucault, though of course the lack of an English translation does not help. On the one hand its importance can be put down to political reasons. Earlier work on the urban, everyday life, and the production of space are cast within a more explicitly political context. Among other things, as Lefebvre notes, it 'sketches the history of the modern State'.[28] It also provides insight into the debates which were raging in the European Left in the mid-1970s, particularly around ideas of Eurocommunism and *autogestion*. On the other hand – although these are hands joined together – there are important philosophical reasons. There are recurrent themes about the mystification and the sacramentalism of power, a critique of Hegelian notions of the idea of the state, and of course the notion of alienation is returned to in relation to the state.[29] Its concerns are so wide-ranging as to make even a broad overview difficult. The first volume situates the state in the modern world, that is at the world scale; the second traces Marxist theories of the state from Hegel to Mao through Lenin, Stalin and Luxemburg; the third discusses the State Mode of Production; the fourth analyses the relation between the state and society. I will first give a summary of some of its most significant concerns – based on the introduction to the first volume – before focusing on some issues in more detail.[30]

De l'Etat – an overview

The first volume begins with issues of the definition of the state, and its impersonation – its taking on of moral or juridical personality; its reality, form, substance and the ensemble of relations. This leads Lefebvre to look at definitions of the political and politics. It moves to a discussion of the relation between the state and the nation both historically and conceptually, and looks at the recent planetary extension of the state. How has this Western invention colonized the world – both in terms of the imperial moment, but also in terms of importing the capitalist, statist system? This raises all sorts of questions about how capitalism functions at different levels and scales; and about how it can mask its contradictions at all of these points. Some of these are at the world scale – which raises the question of the world-system, if indeed such a thing exists. Some are at the internal level – the relation between state and civil society or the political and social body; the relation between state and government; questions of power, decision and causality; economic and political power; the state as a 'monopoly of violence' (Max Weber's phrase) through the police, the army and death. There is a great danger of what Lefebvre, following Jean-Clarence Lambert, calls *le Terricide*, the killing of the earth.[31] This includes the clash between the rational state and the irrational world system, the markets in arms, energy and technology, the violence inherent in the *system*, and the role of the military in the modern state, such as the USA.[32] Equally there are questions of the state's role in economic growth, the relation between economic dominance and political power, the state's role in the extraction of surplus-value, and issues of autonomy and technocracy. Finally in Volume I, the issues of occultation-fetishism-mystification, and how they play out in the state through alienation, ignorance and alterity are discussed. Various questions are raised about the state as an ideological power, the play of representations, various conflicts including securitization and risk, prohibition and transgression, institutionalized knowledge and critical responses.

The second volume looks at the Marxist theory of the state and the difficulties or aporias of Marxist thought. The opening pages of this volume are historical, looking at the sources of power in magic, sacred or religious contexts. Lefebvre is concerned with the birth of the Western *logos*, the religious powers of the feudal period, and the subsequent secularization of religious power.[33] The modern nation-state is born particularly in France and England, and is in part based on the implications of classical reason. For Lefebvre, classical reason manifests itself in three ways simultaneously, although with conflict:

1. *as philosophic and scientific reason* – mathematics, geometry, algebra, physics, in Descartes, Spinoza, and so forth;
2. *as critical and autonomous reason* – a kind of reason which admits no authority, such as that used by Montaigne or the Cartesians;
3. *as reason of state*, raison d'État.[34]

There is an analysis of the conflict between the French *Ancien Régime* and the new society under bourgeois hegemony, with the concomitant historical production of the people, the nation and the national. This leads to the state as measure and the institutor of the measure in the metric system. The metric system symbolizes and puts the finishing touches on the mastery, the measure of, the social by the state.[35] Napoleon installs the state order *par excellence*, a bureaucracy built upon military precision.[36] For Lefebvre, in its wake, a new trinity of nation-state-reason replaces the Christian trinity. The state replaces 'man' as the measure of things and the world, through the notion of number for time and space.[37] The state acts as a control over society through the combination of a triple norm: logical, juridical, ethical. 'It renders the heterogeneous – understood as a the heteroclite [the irregular or anomalous] – homogeneous.' It attempts to equalize the unequal, to make the non-equivalent equivalent.[38]

Lefebvre's analysis here is comparative between France, England and the USA, with some references to the rest of Europe and Japan. He suggests that this makes use of the analytic-regressive/genetic-progressive process discussed above in Chapter 1.

> The preceding considerations sketch the application of a specifically Marxist methodical process to the State; in two moments:
>
> a) the analytic-regressive moment, which goes back through time from the present [*actuel*], looking for the conditions (in the largest sense) which made possible this actuality;
> b) the genetic-progressive moment which attempts to follow the historic movement of the production of the present [*présent*] from these more or less distant conditions, through the sudden changes of fortune of events, the series of the determinisms (causes and reasons), chances (contingencies), and wills (choices and political decisions).[39]

There are a number of European models for the emergence of the state:

1. England – a state constructed on the parliamentary compromise between dominant classes;
2. France – à centralized state, very administrative, very bureaucratic;
3. Germany – a state that remained close to its feudal-military power structures, the importance of the Junker caste, but very decentralized.[40]

The remainder of the volume is largely a history of ideas, from Saint-Simon and Fourier[41] through Hegel, Marx, Lenin and Stalin. Lefebvre provides a useful summary of his approach to the history of ideas in this volume:

> Once more we are going to take up the 'grand texts'. To comment on them faithfully? In order to restore an authentic reading and institute a definitive one? Or, on the other hand, in order to deconstruct them and make the texts say what they did not say or mean? Neither one nor the other. In order to show that Hegel

and Marx, each in his own way, came to an impasse, and hit a limit against which subsequent thought was going to break.[42]

Lefebvre suggests that these texts, outside of a literary scientificism which is only within the 'textual' or the 'inter-textual', 'are nothing without context'.[43] But crucially, for Lefebvre, this is not that of the producer of the text, the writer, but the context of rereading, study, interpretation and the restitution of the text.[44]

The scope on Hegel alone is impressive, providing readings of him in opposition to Fichte and Schelling, as a theorist of the revolution and as a theorist of the state. The state is the central concept for Hegel, a system of systems, it transcends civil society and is the embodiment of the ethical idea. Hegel's state is 'god on earth', akin to the word made flesh.[45] The making concrete of this abstraction happens around the years 1789–1815 – in France the years between the revolution and Napoleon's Waterloo.[46] Napoleon made the state more than just a concept: Hegel was right to see the World Spirit in him. 'The State, a concrete abstraction, can not exist in itself and by itself, except in philosophy. It needs statesmen.'[47]

Right from his earliest writings, Marx was critical of Hegel, and Lefebvre provides a detailed compendium of his ideas of the state. For Marx, in distinction to Hegel, 'the state is just another institution dependent on historical conditions'.[48] Against Hegel, Marx contends that humans are not political animals, but social animals. 'Social relations, including contradictions that give rise to class struggles, explain the state, not the other way round, as it seemed to Hegel.'[49] One of the reasons why there is not *a* Marxist theory of the state in Marx or Engels is, Lefebvre suggests, because the modern state was being constituted under their eyes, under Bonapartism, under Bismarck. For that reason there are numerous theoretical sketches, which can be fairly divergent.[50] Lefebvre suggests that there are three key theories in Marx's writings:

1. 'The state as instrument of the dominant class – economically, then politically. The most well-known theoretical sketch, the most vulgarised';[51]
2. 'The state is autonomous in appearance, above classes', but is in reality parasitic upon social production of wealth;[52]
3. 'The State takes control of the whole society, in that it assumes administrative functions which have an economical efficiency, and though in appearance it continues to set itself up as above society, actually state power manages productive forces directly. In this analysis, the economic is not independent of the political, it is neither cause nor reason; it depends on it.'[53]

Of the three positions Lefebvre finds, the first would be that associated with Miliband's work, the second bears some relation to positions taken by Poulantzas, the third with Lefebvre, and the understanding of the State Mode of Production. For Miliband the class issues of the relation between

the economy and the state can be found in numerous inter-personal relationships; for Poulantzas social classes and the state are objective structures,
and it is the relationship between the structures that is important.[54] For
Lefebvre, as we shall see, the state intervenes in production, in the economy,
in a much more direct manner. In this respect we can suggest the possibility
of a Miliband-Poulantzas-Lefebvre debate, even though the first two did not
engage with the third.[55]

Here and elsewhere Lefebvre provides some brief discussion of contemporary writers on the state, also including Dahl. For example, he suggests that one of the errors of the thesis of the 'monopoly capitalism of the
state' is that it conceives of a single link between capitalism and the state,
when there are numerous forms of linkage. He suggests that in this, this
thesis accords with that of some of its critics, such as Poulantzas.[56] On the
other hand, some American ideologues of pluralism, such as Dahl have
coined the phrase 'polyarchy': 'this empiricist and behavioural formula
masks the pure and simple division of political labour and the unity in the
division of labour'.[57] Pluralist and liberal regimes allow the *historical compromise* – between the aristocracy and the bourgeoisie in England, followed by
one between the bourgeoisie and the working class (also in the USA). 'No
historical compromise, no peaceful coexistence without representative
democracy.'[58] In the only explicit mention of Miliband, Lefebvre notes that
Miliband critiques the pluralists, in that power *is* concentrated.[59]

Particularly important in terms of a solution, which refers back to the
discussion of the end of history in the previous chapter, is the suggestion
that in Marx's thought on the state there are three moments (each inherent
in those prior to it):

1. The return or reintegration of alienated elements to the social;
2. The dictatorship of the proletariat, with its corollary, the withering away
   of the state by democracy from the ground;
3. The series of ends – the end of the bourgeoisie, of capitalism, of the
   working class and classes, the end of scarcity in abundance, the end of
   religion, the family, the nation and the state, the end of work, history,
   philosophy, politics, and so forth. Political alienation and its end.[60]

The rest of the volume is concerned with the question of why this did not
easily come to pass, looking at the problems of Marx and Engels thought on
this subject: the difficulties, non-posed, badly posed, non-resolved and
uncertain questions and so on. Lefebvre suggests that Marx's work on the
state is largely limited to Europe and even to France, but that Engels makes
some moves toward a general theory, looking at the way society produces the
state.[61] Various questions about capitalism's flexibility and resilience are
raised, and about the legacy of Marxist thought sundered on this dual
problem (accumulation – state). Lefebvre suggests that an analysis of the
way the world process works requires the inverting of traditional analysis –
both Marxist and otherwise. Instead of the nation giving birth to the state,

the state makes the nation – a political and ideological effect; instead of the economic base generating political superstructures, the political 'head' generates the social body, the political or state superstructure modifies and sometimes gives rise to the economic base.[62] A number of central figures are brought into this analysis: Luxemburg, Kautsky, Lenin, Stalin, Trotsky, among others. Lefebvre closes this volume by analysing more recent Marxist thought, such as the Frankfurt School, Lukács, Gramsci; and the political actions of Tito and Mao in breaking with Soviet orthodoxy.

There is not the space here for a detailed discussion of Lefebvre's reading of all these thinkers, but I want to make a few points. As we have seen in previous chapters, Lenin is important to Lefebvre for a range of reasons, but here he is praised for introducing the concept of imperialism, which is developed by Leninists, including Rosa Luxemburg.[63] Luxemburg is complimented in a number of places, with Lefebvre suggesting that she is the nodal point in the history of Marxist thought.[64] Despite the flaws in her work – misunderstanding of monopolies, cartels and trusts, for example – Lefebvre claims Luxembourg has been badly mistreated by dogmatic and sectarianism.[65] Also important in terms of historical development is Ferdinand Lassalle, particularly because he is seen as central as the 'sketch and germ' of a socialism of the state. Lefebvre suggests that Lassalle 'accepts in advance that the state exists and envisages (as the first and against Marx) a state-socialism'.[66] In the world today there is no other kind of socialism, so for this reason alone, Lassalle is important, and needs, to a certain extent, rehabilitation.[67] In Lefebvre's stinging phrase, Lassalle was 'a Hegelian who thought he was a Marxist'.[68] Despite Marx's efforts in the *Critique of the Gotha Programme*, Lassallism, state socialism, has won out over Marxism.[69] As Lefebvre notes, it is an irony of history that the so-called socialist countries, attempting to institute Marxist philosophy have actually realized Hegel's programme.[70]

The linkage between socialism and the state is particularly played out in Stalin's thought and practice, and in many ways the whole of *De l'État* is an attempt to come to terms with the legacy of Stalin. As Lefebvre notes, 'Stalin? We can dispense with him in a few pages, since this entire work has as its objective and purpose the examination of "Stalinism", its conditions and consequences.'[71] Only understanding these issues can come to terms with the problem and possible alternatives, of which the neo-liberal programme is part of the former and not of the latter. Stalin is a problem for a number of reasons, including the question of dogmatism, as discussed in Chapter 1. Dogmatism is not just a theoretical problem. Stalinism is both 'a way of thinking and acting dogmatically'.[72] Getting rid of Stalinism and dogmatism has been the political objective of democracy, but what is at stake is nothing less than the perpetuity of the state.[73] Khrushchev is little better, with his proclamation of the monster of the 'state of the entire people'.[74] Lefebvre suggests that another issue is that of the mystification of political authority, the 'cult of personality'. 'This fiction, a veritable mixture of ideology and myth, has barred the way from an analysis of the Stalinist state – the apogee of state socialism and the model for the world scale – for more than twenty years.'[75]

Stalin plays a particularly central role in Volume III, which is devoted to the State Mode of Production (SMP). The SMP might be said to be the key theoretical innovation of this work.[76] For Lefebvre, 'Stalin produced the *state mode of production*, that is to say something new and unforeseen, incompatible with so-called Marxist-Leninist thought, but which has shown and continues to show its force.'[77] Lenin's grand project in 1917 was to destroy the existing state, and to construct a state that would wither. However, the result – due to Stalin – was the opposite, a strong state,[78] which is why Lefebvre describes him as 'the cancer of the revolution'.[79] As Lefebvre notes in 1959, Stalin was unable to see the difference between state socialism and the dictatorship of the proletariat.[80] The SMP should be distinguished from the totalitarian state,[81] although we should note that fascism closely follows Stalinism in its state-takeover (*étatisation*) of the economy.[82] Equally China works as a state-socialism on a Stalinist prototype.[83] We can find the exposé of SMP in Stalin's writings,[84] but also most evidently in his practice. 'The Stalinist State was and remains the prototype of the modern State', but behind state socialism comes state capitalism.[85] As he notes in a different context, Stalinist Russia is merely the exemplary case.[86] This does not change now that reason of State is concerned with worldwide space. Lefebvre suggests that on paper, the Stalinist state model functions perfectly. It is very close to Hegel's model, which Stalin disavows because he excels at clouding the issue.[87] 'Currently, "communism" does not exist in the political vocabulary. In pronouncing such a word, in admitting it, we admit that this analysis pierces, punctures, tears the surface. You have accepted, without knowing it, the State.'[88] The SMP will be discussed in a little more detail below.

Volume III begins with some clarifications on the Marxist concept or category of production,[89] and the role of economics and ideas in the establishment of the modern state. There are lengthy analyses of material exchange in different economic systems, looking particularly at the ways these are played out in space.[90] Capitalism is not looked at as a unified mode of production, but as having gone through various phases, particularly from a blind, quasi-autonomous process to one controlled by the state. The transition might be seen from competitive capitalism to capitalism of the state, and from there to the State Mode of Production; from merchandise to capital to the state, more and more homogeneous. This has been a move to political production.[91] Sports champions and records, for example, are political products.[92] There are huge number of disparate analyses in this volume, from economic analyses of accumulation, surplus-value and development to legal ones. There is an important discussion of the state as a concrete abstraction. This brings together previous analyses of alienation, mystification and reification, looking at how the state embodies abstractions in the economic and political realm (sovereignty, legitimacy, authority, legality). Sovereignty of course is both theoretical and practical – the two depend on each other. As discussed in previous chapters, some of Lefebvre's analysis bears relation to Heidegger, when he talks about the accumulation of resources and their turning into stock, and the move toward giganticism.[93]

There are plenty of other political analyses in this volume, of bureaucracy, parties, state-apparatuses, territory and state-leaders. The analysis of territory – which links back to *The Production of Space*, but also to the much more detailed reading in the fourth volume – looks at the way productive relations go beyond the state level to the planetary or semi-planetary. It opens up issues of global surplus-value, the transfer of surplus-value from one country to another.[94] Alongside political decolonization came the worldwide extension of the colonial phenomenon in the economic sphere.[95] One of the key claims is that state capitalism and state socialism are species of the same genre – that of the SMP, of a society dominated by the state.[96] The SMP, which is a development from previous relations of the state and capitalism, masters both markets and space. At this point Lefebvre makes a move from the more theoretical and historical analysis and discusses various state formations at the time he was writing. These analyses of the USSR, China, Japan, USA, European states, Chile, and so forth, are perhaps the least interesting for a contemporary reader, given that they are many years out of date, although they demonstrate the applicability of his ideas.

The final volume builds upon all of the preceding, summarizing some of the contradictions of the state in the modern world. Lefebvre talks of the dialectic and/of the state, the relationship between logic and the state, and how all of this plays out in the political themes of contradiction, conflict, resistance, identity and difference and homogeneity and heterogeneity. This is particularly important in terms of the state's role as the mediator between conflicts – social, spatial, intellectual, cultural or otherwise – and the play of forces between different parts and levels of society. Issues of centralization and decentralization become important leading to the central question: how can the centralized State subject millions and sometimes hundreds of millions of people to the management (*gestion*) and to the statist homogeneity (*homogénéité étatiques*) of their *private* business and their everyday life?[97] Does this lead to effective decentralization or repressive brutality, and how does the state integrate the normal and abnormal elements of society? This leads to questions of the state's role in organizing the homogeneity of the people, the production of entirely similar individuals (identical, identified, identifiable). Equally it raises the possibility of a revolt of the *lived* against abstractions, of the everyday against economicism, of the social and civil society against high growth and its requirements maintained by the state.

Recurrent themes include the relationship between knowledge and power, the role of information in the new economy and state dominance, and the growth of the world market and so called supra-national companies – themes that have come to pass in ways beyond what Lefebvre could have imagined. There are hints of the work on rhythm and the repetitive which would follow this, but here played out in a much more political context, in the disciplining of behaviour in work and everyday life through bureaucratic regulations and cultural stereotypes.[98] This trades on the understanding of measure, with a description of the clock as a 'coercive instrument'.[99] The control of production *and* consumption, reproduction of the human species, production of material goods and the reproduction of social relations, and the relation between exchange and use value are all crucial. The notion of everyday life is – as elsewhere in Lefebvre's work – central, with discussion of the state's role in its organization and regulation. There are also analyses of the notion of class and its relation to the state, with the suggestion that that state is not simply an effect of class struggle but also in part its cause and reason. There are discussions of the incorporation of the working class into the state, by the state, and the middle classes as supports to the state, and vice versa, and the possible response through the notion of *autogestion*.

The final volume also provides some extremely important analyses of the political production and use of space, and the politics of scale and the domination of the worldwide. It also includes a discussion of representation in the political realm. Lefebvre notes that this was not in the original plan, but that he became convinced of its importance whilst in Spain in late 1976 (following Franco's death), with the questions of elections and representative democracy.[100] The notion of representation is pursued in much more detail in *La présence et l'absence*, where it is discussed in scientific, philosophical and aesthetic as well as political contexts.[101]

From this profusion of ideas I will concentrate a little more detail on but a few: the State Mode of Production; the issues of the world scale; the politics of space, and the distinction between politics and the political. Following the first I will discuss his alternatives of *autogestion* and the right to difference; the question of politics and the political will provide the starting point for the book's conclusion.

The State Mode of Production

The major innovation of the text is the idea of the mode of statist production. For Lefebvre, Marx correctly discerned many of the crises that would beset capitalism, but did not foresee many of the ways in which it would respond to them. Capitalism has proved to be more resilient, flexible and adaptable than he believed it was.[102] It is important for Marxists to understand why this is so. For Lefebvre, the State Mode of Production is *the* significant event of the twentieth century, 'far more important than the landing of men on the moon'.[103] As I noted in the overview of this study, the concept of the SMP was explicitly intended to understand Stalinism and state socialism (the USSR and the PCF); but also fascism with its economic and political plans. State socialism and National Socialism, or perhaps – although Lefebvre does not use this term – state nationalism. As early as 1938 Lefebvre had shown an interest in this issue. Fascist economy is possibly the single biggest theme in his *Hitler au pouvoir*, suggesting that the 'national socialist state had worked for four years exclusively for the benefit of grand capital', and that its socialism and calls to the national community were ruses to get this to happen.[104] In this sense, chronologically, the SMP was announced by fascism and fully realized by Stalin.[105]

> First moment of this process: Stalinism, not as a local phenomenon (Russian, oriental, peasant, etc.) but as a prototype of the SMP. Second moment: through variable representations, through the dismissal of Stalinism, on the ideological plan, becoming worldly [*mondialisation*], the SMP. In the same way that the SMP accomplished the modern State, the Communist party leads the achievement of the concept and the reality of the political party.[106]

However, Lefebvre does not think that the mode of statist production is confined to totalitarian regimes or the aspirations of European communist parties, but also to movements in the centre of the political spectrum. Stalinism was a prototype of the SMP, but this was put into practice in a range of ways.[107] Americans are not rich Soviets, Soviets are not poor Americans,[108] but there are some underlying similarities.

For example, social liberalism, according to Lefebvre, does not fundamentally challenge the prevailing logic, but attempts to facilitate some redistribution without addressing the underlying issues. In other words what we have is the state appropriating the results of exploitation in order to partly redress the balance after the event. The American New Deal in the 1930s vastly increased the scope of the federal state, and Lefebvre suggests that along with fascism it was one of the first glimpses of this new model.[109] We could similarly look at the increase in social policy and the emergence of the welfare state in the UK, and similar programmes in other countries. It is worth noting, for example, that Keynes and Beveridge – the architects of the putative British post-war consensus in economic and social policy – were liberals. As Lefebvre argues, the problem facing the Left in the late 1960s – and we could add from much earlier, and there is surely no improvement since – is that it has made the same kinds of proposals as the Right, but 'to do it more and do it better – better rate of growth, better distribution of the national income, etc.' Instead of rethinking the state and its relation to society it has embraced state socialism, and 'like the state power, it has crushed democracy at the base and eliminated all mediations. Weak without a bureaucratic machine and strong with a bureaucratic machine, the Left is situated on the very terrain of those with whom it is engaged in combat.'[110]

A whole range of examples can be given for what is meant by the SMP. Essentially it means the mode of management and domination of the entire society by the state. It is perhaps most evident in the social production and the five-year plans of the total states, with their quest for the quantitative growth of productive forces. These programmes were partnered by gigantic publicity drives to show the world images of great works, canals, dams, and power stations, and the mechanization of Soviet agriculture. However, as is well known, the latter was only possible on the basis of the liquidization of the Kulak class, and was based upon faulty data and poor organization.[111] We could give similar examples with fascist regimes. Moreover, Lefebvre suggests that the nationalization of industries – a central part of the programme of post-war Labour government in Britain for example – was actually an *étatisation*, an untranslatable word that means the establishment of state control.[112] On the French state in the late 1960s, Lefebvre suggests that it

> stands above society but extends down to the base of this society. It is not at all confined to the superstructures but in a sense covers the whole of social life. It profoundly affects capitalist social relations, yet stands apart from these relations, guaranteeing and arbitrating them.[113]

As Kofman and Lebas note, in this period the French state was 'increasingly freed from its heavy investment in colonialism', and was able to attend to the restructuring of space and reorganization of capitalism.[114] In an important summary, written shortly after the fourth volume, Lefebvre describes the SMP in terms of three main dimensions in which the state works its way into everyday life:

1. managerial (*gestionnaire*) and administrative;
2. the power to protect, to make secure (*sécurisante*);
3. the power to kill (*mortelle*) – repression, the monopoly of violence, the army and military spending, the possibility of war.[115]

In the SMP – with neo-capitalism as much as neo-socialism – the global strategy sets prices – those of petrol, energy, armaments, investments and 'grey matter'.[116] Similarly, the State Mode of Production is related to ideological matters. Lefebvre claims that the mystifications of fascism and falsifications of Stalinism are part of the same issue – the elevation of the state's position.[117] Stalin and Stalinism can be simply understood as 'the fetishism of the state'.[118] We can therefore understand the purpose of Lefebvre's critique of Stalin. As he suggests as early as the mid-1960s, the liquidation of Stalinism is nothing other than the liquidation of a certain concept of the state.[119]

Lefebvre recognizes that the SMP works within a particular context, the nation-state. Taking the Marxist model of regressive-progressive steps in research it was necessary to analyse more deeply the genealogies of modern states in order to comprehend the contemporary situation.[120] It is for this reason that there is so much analysis of particular states and theorists of the state in the volumes. Instead of the standard story that 'the nation creates the state', Lefebvre argues that the reverse is closer to being true. The state produces the nation within a territory; political action produces a nationality as an ideology formed from various sources – ethnicity, myths and legends, religion and morals, linguistics and semantics.[121]

A quarter of a century later, Lefebvre's claims may look seriously outdated. Since he completed *De l'État* in the late 1970s we have seen the rise of the New Right and the advent of globalization. The nation-state obviously functions within a much wider context – that of the world system of states, the global or world system. We will look more at the way in which Lefebvre's work provides a basis for the examination of the world scale below. However, Lefebvre's analysis can be used to show how, for the New Right, it becomes more effective for capital to *seem* to remove the state from direction (Thatcher's 'roll back the frontiers of the state') whilst actually increasing state power in other areas. The increase in state power can be seen in the use of police in challenging organized labour; the providing of the institutional support for the free market; and the protection of property through the administration of justice and talk of 'law and order'. As Andrew Gamble describes this, this is the rhetoric of the free economy and the strong state – 'neo-classical' liberalism and political conservatism.[122] At the same time that the role of the state in redistribution is challenged with the removal of the highest bands of taxation and the move away from expenditure on the social services, the role of the state in promoting, financing and subsidizing capitalist growth increases. We can see this in the giving of subsidies to the privatized industries, the establishment of 'development' agencies, the lack of accountability in quangos, which demonstrates the increase in state apparatuses but without the accountability of government, and so forth.[123]

Part of the reason for these changes is that the state is no longer the target market. It is the supra- or multi-national corporations' global or world scope that removes – ostensibly – the role of the state in regulating. However, much contemporary debate is about precisely how the state can best compete in this globalized environment. Rather than the state being the container, the place where the market operates, the state is now one of the key players. 'On the planetary [*planétaire*] scale and on the worldwide market, the unit is no longer the enterprise or the business but the Nation-State.'[124] While Lefebvre is certainly inaccurate in suggesting that the enterprise or business is not a key player, he is correct in diagnosing the new role for the state. The state takes on a particular role in promoting growth, promoting the national economic interest on the world stage. 'A qualitative transformation occurs from the moment in which the state takes charge of growth, whether directly or indirectly. From this moment forward, economic failures are attributed to the State.'[125] Equally, and as a development of this, the state needs to ensure the reproduction of the relations of production, to allow the continuation of the relations of domination.[126] It is not a simple case of providing either the means of fair competition within the nation-state, or, alternatively, mobilizing the state to the best advantages of its citizens, but of improving the competitiveness of national firms on a global basis. Hence the uneasy tension between promoting free trade and protectionism, as shown recently in the steel tariffs' row.

The danger is therefore that the debate is of *how* to promote capitalist growth, rather than a challenge to what capitalism is and should be about – even for the Left. This is even more the case with the putative Third Way or *Neue Mitte* of more recent years – associated with the likes of Clinton, Blair and Schröder. Thatcher famously suggested that 'there is no alternative', and the worry is that much of the Left has accepted this as true.[127] In a sense then, the twentieth century can be read as a progressive move toward acceptance of the state and its role within a capitalist system. The various third ways, or middle ways that have been proposed have been a sequence of compromises – charting a movement from communism to socialism to social democracy to social liberalism to the Third Way. A 'ratchet effect', but to the Right and not to the Left, as Keith Joseph suggested.

Autogestion and the right to difference

In the *Communist Manifesto* Marx famously suggests that the executive of the state is but a committee for managing the common affairs of the bourgeoisie.[128] Clearly things are not nearly as straightforward today. The Miliband-Poulantzas debate was around the understanding of the state and its relation to organized capitalism. Was this an instrumental or structural relation? In other words, can the state be harnessed to progressive political goals? Lefebvre's answer is that only a radical rethink of the state, and essentially a wholesale removal of its power, is sufficient to achieve this. Although Lefebvre only rarely provides a positive alternative to the problems he identifies, there are two principal components to his rethinking – a programme of *autogestion* and a reformulated understanding of citizenship, which would include a rethinking of rights. Taken together, they provide the basis for a reorientation of the state – albeit in a radically transfigured form – for progressive goals. In the *Critique of the Gotha Programme* Marx talks of the state being converted 'from an organ superimposed on society into one thoroughly subordinate to it'.[129] This passage, which is also cited by Miliband,[130] in some ways provides the framework for understanding Lefebvre's work. The theme of *autogestion* is widespread in Lefebvre's work and emerges from his engagement with the journal *Autogestion*;[131] the emphasis on rights and citizenship appears in fewer places – notably his work *Le manifeste différentialiste* and his introduction to a collection of essays written by the *Groupe de Navarrenx*, entitled 'From the Social Pact to the Contract of Citizenship'.[132]

The term *autogestion* is best left untranslated. Literally it means 'self-management', or 'self-government', but with a sense of it being workers' or citizens' control.[133] The term, much used in the 1970s around Eurocommunism and other leftist groups, has connotations of radical democracy, of greater direct democracy, of a moving beyond mere 'representation', of returning power to local communities and so on.[134] As Marković suggests, 'self-government is the dialectical negation of state socialism with its inherent tendencies towards bureaucratisation'.[135] One of the most famous examples of it in practice was the Lip watch factory which was taken over by its workers when threatened with closure.[136] As Brenner notes, the French Socialist Party embraced the term in the early 1970s, and the PCF 'tentatively adopted a politics of *autogestion* in conjunction with its experiments with Eurocommunist ideology, particularly between 1975 and 1978'.[137] In one of his last works, Lefebvre proves a useful overview definition:

Autogestion is defined as knowledge of and control (at the limit) by a group – a company, a locality, an area or a region – over the conditions governing its existence and its survival through change. Through *autogestion*, these social groups are able to influence their own reality. The right to *autogestion*, like the right to representation, can be proclaimed as a citizen's right, with the ways in which it is applied being spelled out later. Action and initiative by the rank-and-file are always desirable. But have we to wait until the practice is working before espousing the principle? The growth of democracy goes like this: either democracy declines – or the right to *autogestion* is brought into the definition of citizenship . . . The right to *autogestion* involves the right to democratic control of the economy, and therefore of companies, including national or nationalised companies, i.e. those up to now under some degree of state control.[138]

It is remarkable just how similar this exposition is to the work he was writing decades before. As Lefebvre notes, *autogestion* is not something established but is itself the 'site and stake of struggle'.[139] *Autogestion* has to be applied both at the level of the unit of production – the firm or enterprise – and the territorial level of government – local communities, towns or regions. We cannot simply wait for this to happen, it is not going to happen from nowhere, although spontaneity, as he would stress, is crucial. It needs to be prepared for theoretically, by being posed as an axiom and its implications worked through.[140] In fact, Lefebvre argues that the issue of *autogestion* is becoming increasingly concerned with issues over the organization of space – urban campaigns and so on – than of enterprises.[141] *Autogestion* would require much more active participation in the political process, and would dissolve the relations between the rulers and the ruled, the active and passive, subjects and objects. New technology can be used, but only on the condition that this promotes the withering of the state and bureaucracy.[142] Indeed, it is this withering away of the state that is central to the notion:

The state cannot coexist peacefully with radicalised and generalised *autogestion*, as it must be put under the democratic control 'of the base'. The state of *autogestion*, that is to say a State in which an internalised *autogestion* gains power, could only be a State that is withering away. The party of *autogestion* could therefore only be that the party which leads politics towards its conclusion and the end of politics, beyond political democracy.[143]

Although Marx's work does not presuppose the idea of *autogestion*, it does have this notion of democracy from the ground up.[144] Lefebvre argues that in this regard, Marx's work is situated between the anarchists (inspired by Bakunin) and the reformists like Lassalle. However, Lefebvre suggests that his work is also rather different from certain types of revolutionaries. For both Marx and Lenin there was a threefold aim of widening and deepening democracy; the withering away of the state; and the dictatorship of the proletariat.[145] As Engels notes in *Anti-Dühring* there must be a period of transition.[146] The anarchist aim of the end of the state and with it the abolition of private property is laudable, but this cannot be achieved overnight. For Marx, the three elements above cannot be disassociated. Reformists may put the emphasis on the democracy but leave the dictatorship and the withering away of the state on one side; the revolutionaries emphasize the dictatorship and neglect the other two. While these latter two groups disagree violently, both neglect the central aim of the gradual abolition of the state.[147] 'The so-called revolutionary tendency, and the so-called reformist one are, in fact, none other than variants on state socialism, that is to say, Lassallism.'[148] Lefebvre notes that there is a tension in Lenin's work on this point of the withering away of the state, and that it is most glaring in *State and Revolution*. Though Lenin abandoned the idea of a rapid or immediate withering away of the state, Lefebvre believes that he never would have embraced the idea of the strengthening of, the consolidation of the state, which was so central to Stalin. This is the tension in *State and Revolution*.[149]

Lefebvre contends that 'Louis Althusser and his followers have sealed [*obturé*] the political break [*coupure*] which separates Marx from Hegel: the critic of the state from its apologist.'[150] In Marx's work this break was apparent as early as 1842–3.[151] This is another aspect of the dangers posed by structuralism. They miss the crucial differences, because instead of recognizing breaks as political, they are described as epistemological or philosophical.[152] For Lefebvre, there are similarly political breaks between Marx and Lenin, and Lenin and Stalin. These are crucial to a proper understanding of Marxist state theory.[153] For example, the notion of the dictatorship of the proletariat is viewed through the distorting lens of Stalinism, and is therefore seen as 'bloody and brutal'. For Lefebvre though, the dictatorship of the proletariat proposed by Marx and Lenin would not be the dictatorship of Stalin.[154] The risk of abandoning this idea is that we return to Hegel, with the idea that the state is unconditional, even eternal. This is yet another flaw with Stalinism. The crimes are important, but the essential problem was the idea that the revolution required the unlimited reinforcement of the state. The PCF has embraced this.[155] As Lefebvre notes:

> When in our writing we affirm the truth of the proposition, 'between the state and the market there is nothing', we pose a false dilemma, because between the two there is already the bureaucracy; tomorrow there may be *autogestion*.[156]

Lefebvre's conception of *autogestion* is linked to his work on everyday life, which it should be remembered is in a state of crisis because of the control exerted over it by the capitalist system. One of the things he thinks striking about the events of May 1968 is how much everyday life – the provision of services such as the post, banking and petrol – was disrupted by the protests. For Lefebvre, 'everyday existence is a solid terrain which supports the structure because the structure was built on this terrain and made it hospitable to itself. The process – contestation, strike, the whole movement – shook up this terrain.' Of course, it was very quickly restored to how it was before.[157] Although Lefebvre thinks it encouraging that the French socialist party and various trade unions adopted the concept of *autogestion* in the early 1970s, he fears little has come of it.[158] *Autogestion* is an opening toward the possible, it coincides with the notion of freedom, made practical and political.[159] For Lefebvre, '*autogestion* indicates the road toward the transformation of every-day existence'. It was this that was behind the call of the 1968 protestors to 'changer la vie', to change life,[160] a phrase originating in Rimbaud.[161] As this slogan was often partnered by 'changer la ville', change the city, Lefebvre's thought was at the heart of the protests.

Lefebvre believes that spontaneity – one of the central things found in both the events of 1871 and 1968 – is essential to a revitalized Marxist theory. The form that spontaneous revolution takes today, he suggests, is not anarcho-syndicalism, but *autogestion*.[162] As we saw in Chapter 4, Lefebvre believed that the events in Paris in 1968 were a challenge to state capitalism; those in Prague the same year a challenge to state socialism. Lefebvre reads these struggles, and the Commune almost a hundred years before, as dir-ected against the state, its bureaucracy, military, and other institutions.[163] The desire to achieve *autogestion* enables the taking control of the things that effect their life, the conquest of power by the working classes, and therefore a fundamental change in how that power operates. Social relations will become stronger and more complex. Instead of the state being above soci-ety, to echo Marx, the state will become dependent upon it. This is the dictatorship of the proletariat, the widening and deepening of democracy. It will lead to the withering away of the state.

Despite Lefebvre's interest in contemporary movements that made use of some of the ideas of *autogestion* he is critical. As he notes in *The Survival of Capitalism*, there were so many different senses of the term that it was 'a great outburst of confusion'.[164] *Autogestion* is neither a magic formula that will solve all problems nor a recipe that can be applied immediately.[165] One of the most striking examples of an inspiration is the alternative route to Communism taken in Yugoslavia, a place he calls the 'laboratory of *autoges-tion*'.[166] However, by the end of the 1970s Lefebvre is somewhat more sceptical. As was suggested above, he did not view *autogestion* as an achieve-ment but as a process, a process of continual struggle. He argues that every time workers contest decisions, to take control of the conditions of their exist-ence, then *autogestion* is occurring.[167] The problem with Yugoslavia was that

> certain Yugoslavs committed the error of seeing in *autogestion* a system, and therefore a model, that could be established juridically and that could function without clashes and contradictions, in a sort of social and political harmony. Instead, *autogestion* reveals contradictions in the State, because it is the very trigger of those contradictions . . . *Autogestion* must continually be enacted. The same is true of democracy, which is never a 'condition' but a fight.[168]

Lefebvre believes that we need simultaneously to rethink the notion of rights. To rights to work, to education, leisure, health, housing and so on, we need to add the right to the city – as discussed in Chapter 4 – and the right to be different.[169] The right to be different is the right 'not be classified forcibly into categories which have been determined by the necessarily homogenising powers'.[170] If there are calls for women's and children's rights this is because they are different from an abstract notion of 'man' in general.[171] Declarations of the rights of men – in the French Revolution, or the US declaration of independence – need to be partnered by declarations of the rights of women – the work of Mary Wollstonecraft or the Seneca Falls declaration. For Marxists it is not a question of rejecting such declarations, but of rendering them more concrete, of completing them. Abstract rights of the 'man' and 'citizen' are made applicable in concrete situations by the introduction of rights of workers, of women and children, of youth and old age. Equally there are differences within women and children as groups, and within different peoples and ethnic groups within modern societies and world society.[172] This is what Lefebvre means by the right to difference.

In the twenty-first century, such a call may not seem particularly radical. But it is worth underscoring that Lefebvre was writing this at the very beginning of the 1970s. Lefebvre contends that classical philosophy 'eludes difference'.[173] His discussion of the confrontation between 'homogenising powers and differential capacities'[174] has substantial overlap with the work of feminism, race and queer theory, but is substantially earlier than much of that work. More important than chronology is that Lefebvre believes this is possible within a Marxist analysis, whereas much recent debate has been about the superposed inability of Marxists – tied to class analysis, so the story goes – to come to terms with 'other' differences. Struggle is today not (simply) between classes, but between peoples, nations, tribes, ethnicities, religions.[175] Just as the notion of alienation needed to be developed from within Marxist thought, and that of 'everydayness' added to it, so too does the concept of *difference*.[176] The transformation of everyday life requires this rethinking.[177] It is, yet again, an example of Lefebvre's pluralist approach to Marxism.[178]

Very late in life, and in the last book that appeared in his own lifetime, Lefebvre returned to these themes. This was a collaborative project with a group of researchers who used to visit Lefebvre in the Pyrenees. Known as the *Groupe de Navarrenx*, they produced a volume of essays entitled *Du contrat de citoyenneté*.[179] Old forms of contract between the state and the people were no longer workable for a range of reasons. Citizenship had to take into account the new world scale, difference and heterogeneity, migration and immigration. Lefebvre argues that there is a fundamental difference between human rights and citizen rights. While the first grabs the headlines and leads to struggles and conferences; the second is misunderstood and forgotten. By citizen rights he means those concerned with the relationship between the ruled and the ruler. Early forms of citizen rights included the right to move freely within one's own state's boundaries; freedom of thought; and the right to the vote. The advent of Europe as a form of government and the movements of population are two reasons why we need to rethink these carefully. Previously established forms of identity, of belonging, are changing. Identity is no longer a straightforward matter – we can have numerous nested or overlapping identities because, as Lefebvre suggests 'we all "belong" to our family, to a village or a town, a region, a trade or occupation, a country (homeland, nation and nationality), a State, a continent (in our case, Europe), and to one or more cultures, etc.'[180]

The situation is difficult, and we need to rethink the relationship between the members of a society and the state. For Lefebvre this requires a contract, between state and citizen, which will diminish, and eventually remove, 'the distance between the State, the government, established power, on the one hand, and the citizens – civil society – on the other'.[181] It will eventually remove the distance, he believes, because it will curtail the autonomy of the state. Citizenship is a fundamental source of obligations such as a liability to taxation, to obey laws, do military service, and so forth, but Lefebvre argues that, other than the right to vote, it has given little in return. He suggests that it should be broadened to include such things as the right to information; the right to free expression; the right to culture (to enjoy art and explore the world); the right to identity and equality within an understanding of difference; the right to the city; the right to public services and the right to *autogestion*.[182]

Many of these have been at the forefront of political debate in recent years, and have important implications particularly, as Lefebvre suggests, in the light of immigration. Recent debates in Germany about the citizenship of *Gastarbeiter* and discussions in Britain about the status of asylum seekers; as well as more general questions about the erosion of civil liberties in the wake of 11 September highlight these issues. For Lefebvre, this new call for citizenship and rights is an important political movement. It 'would complete, democratically, the abandoned project of the dictatorship of the proletariat'. The stress on the democratic means is important: Lefebvre would have written these lines around the time of the 1989 revolutions and the fall of the Berlin Wall. Peacefully, 'avoiding brutality, it would cause the political State to wither away'.[183]

> The new rights of the citizen, tied in to the demands of everyday life in the modern world, should have been the subject of a detailed declaration at the time of the bicentenary of the French Revolution, which would then not have been reduced to pomp and circumstance, but would have served as the basis for a new beginning.[184]

The world scale

The problem of scale is central to Lefebvre's concerns, from the politics of the local through to the national and to the world. For Lefebvre, 'the question of scale and level implies the multiplicity of scales and levels',[185] it is the point of departure, the foundation of textual analysis and interpretation of events.[186] The issue of levels – global, mixed or urban, and private habitation – was discussed in Chapter 4 in the context of Lefebvre's historical sociology of the transition from the rural to the urban. While there is naturally an overlap between levels and scales, they are not quite the same. As Brenner notes, scale can be 'the body, the local, the urban, the regional, the national, the supernational, the worldwide [*mondial*] and the planetary'. He continues to suggest that the work on the urban – such as *La révolution urbaine* – looks more at the question of scale as level, while *The Production of Space* and *De l'État* look more at the issue of scale as territory.[187]

The shift from the nation-state to a world scale is seen as particularly important and is a process Lefebvre calls *mondialisation*. This is not quite the same as the current vogue word globalization, but Lefebvre certainly prefigures many of the substantial points of the analysis.[188] What is important in *mondialisation* – as Derrida has insisted – is the distinction between the globe and *le monde*, the world.[189] It is for this reason that I would caution against neglecting the difference between the level of the global and the world scale in Lefebvre's work. Lefebvre is quite careful in distinguishing between *le global* and *le mondial*. *Mondialisation* – the making worldly of phenomena – was, for Lefebvre, first announced in a prophetic and quasi-metaphysical way by Heidegger, and then more concretely by Kostas Axelos.[190] Today it can be seen in practice, from everyday life to the spaces of strategy.[191] The concept of *mondialisation* is designed to replace those of philosophical provenance – totality and globality, and the equation of universality-rationality-totality. It is a matter of the Terrestrial, of the Planetary, but not of the Cosmos (which we can also name as 'world').[192] The notion of the 'worldwide' (*le mondial*) can be useful, but is not a panacea: 'Sometimes it obscures, sometimes it illuminates: global by definition, it does not just deal with the economic, nor the sociological in isolation . . . it implies the criticism of separations.' It looks at the state, its interrelation with the worldwide market, worldwide technicity, but goes beyond these determinations.[193] The worldwide now acts as a third term in relation to the country and the city.[194] It is an ongoing process rather than an accomplishment.[195] In distinction, 'the total, the global, is the totality of knowledge and the world as a totality'.[196]

A number of things are implied by *mondialisation*. For one it requires the homogenization of space and time,[197] a direct consequence of Cartesian determinations and the calculative casting of being.[198] By conceiving of matter, the material world as something that can be calculated, measured, *res extensa*, Descartes provides modern science with a particular way of grasping and comprehending the world. It is this that Heidegger would describe as the world-picture, the world made picture.[199] We can see the Heideggerian tone of much of Lefebvre's discussion when he talks about the role of technology, the conflict between temporality and spatiality, the treating of the earth as a resource, as stock:[200]

> At the world scale, the system of states introduces the worldwide [*mondialité*] against historicity; it delineates the contours of planetary space, which does not result from the historical past but from new factors (energy, techniques, strategies, productive forces.[201]

The state tries to achieve two goals – the annihilation of history and the thoughtless utilization of everything in the past as resources.[202] For Lefebvre then, who says '*mondiality*' says *spatiality* and not *temporality*.[203] For an investigation it is crucial to look at the interrelation of these three terms, what Lefebvre calls the trilogy of 'historicity – worldliness – spatiality'. The conflict between historicity and worldliness, *mondiality*, is resolved 'in and by the production of worldwide space, the work of a historical time in which it is realised'.[204] Lefebvre suggests that 'when philosophy has explored worldliness, it has established significant propositions'. Lefebvre finds Heidegger's suggestion that 'Welt *ist* nie, sondern *welten*' – 'world never *is*, but *worlds*' important.[205] Although it is close to a tautology, it implies that 'the worldwide conceives itself in and by itself and not by another thing (history, spirit, work, science, etc.). The world becomes world, becoming what virtually it was. It transforms itself by becoming world-wide.'[206]

We already know how the state is becoming world-wide [*se mondialise*] and at the same time opposes the worldwide. The nation-states, attached to a territory, managers of this space, arbitrate and act as dominant power from and by this space. They manage it as *eminent* owners [*propriétaires éminents*], almost in the way this word meant under the *ancien régime*, whereby the written rights and powers of the nobles and the king were superimposed upon the common rights of the peasants, 'commoners', holders of perpetual usufruct. An analogous superimposition governs the modern State and its relationship to its space (territory). Methods (sometimes compelling and sometimes violent) and multiple procedures, the best known of which is 'expropriation', give concrete expression to this eminent right which we know extends itself to under the ground and to air space, forests and water sources, rivers and coasts, maritime territories and to recently extended territorial waters. Productive forces tend to the worldwide. Unfortunately, this tendency of productive forces – the latest worldwide experiences and of primary importance – has engendered 'supra' or 'multi' firms and companies which, as we know, tend to outclass States, and to use them to dominate and manage a territory to their profit.[207]

Equally, *mondialisation* demonstrates how the transfer, extraction, of surplus value is today not just from one class, but from one country to another. The developing world has become the global proletariat, or the proletariat for the first world. As political de-colonization began, economic colonization moved into a new phase. Colonization, and with its end the problems of neo-colonization, have similar characteristics as well as the more overt distinctions. As Lefebvre notes, this is principally for the benefit of some nations: 'A neo-imperialism constitutes and establishes the world scale, based admittedly in some States (USA, Japan, Germany, etc.) but overflowing them little by little in order to produce a planetary system.'[208]

The scale question is therefore more complicated that the micro/macro model of economics – but also more complicated than that of the geographical reduction of nested hierarchies. The micro level of the local needs to be supplemented with the macro level of the national or the worldwide, but the modern state cannot be understood without an examination of relations of dependence. In other words we need to look at the interrelation of spatial scales rather than distinct elements within hierarchies. Just as we should not look at the relation between the state and civil society as one level over another, and not look at base/superstructure as having merely one-way relations, we should look at the dialectical relations between the different scales of local, regional, national and the worldwide.[209] The state becomes worldly just as it fragments.[210] 'No space disappears in the process of growth and development: the *worldwide does not abolish the local*.'[211]

Recognizing the way in which these scales interrelate is useful in terms of challenging some of the more recent understandings of globalization as deterritorialization.[212] For Lefebvre,

> The world market is not detached from space; there is no 'deterritorialised' abstraction, even if some extra-territorial forces (the heads of some so-called supra-national businesses) operate there.[213]

Even 'multinationals' – 'the most abstract form of capital' – cannot be wholly deterritorial.[214] Territory, historically, has been associated with the state. This is misleading, and we would be better advised if we recognized that the modern state is, in part, dependent on a particular conception of space, which, when related to the state, is understood as territory. Modern concepts of territory, in terms of the state, rest upon an understanding of space as bounded, quantifiable, and exclusive; space which can be mapped, demarcated and controlled. Such a conception of space was not always held, and, for example, in the Middle Ages land was poorly mapped, non-contiguous and there were many cases of overlapping sovereignty. The intellectual development whereby space became understood scientifically can be traced through scholastic readings of Aristotle, but the central figure is Descartes.

The suggestion that modern conceptions of territory are founded upon a particular ontological determination of space requires us to rethink globalization. Because, I believe, we find that globalization – ontologically – rests upon exactly the same idea of homogeneous, calculable space, an abstract space imposed on an already existing landscape, but in this case extended to the globe as a whole rather than within the confines of a single state. Politically then, globalization may be a break (although that too is debatable), but ontologically it is the same, a continuation of Cartesianism by other means. In other words, what we currently discuss as globalization is in some sense dependent on what Lefebvre calls *mondialisation*, the grasping or conceiving of the world as a whole. Of this *mondialisation* Lefebvre suggests that we must look for its conditions of possibility, but this cannot be reduced to linear causality or mechanistic determinism.[215]

The making worldly of the state goes with the extension and the strengthening of the world market. When competitive capitalism was first installed, it consisted of a relatively limited number of companies together with a

larger number which were dependent on them, either for or
finance.[216] However, today there has of course been an enormous gro...
the number and scope of capitalist firms. This is particularly notable with
the commodification of information – to sit alongside products, labour
power and energy.[217] Similarly, as we have seen, this extension of the world
market is at the same time as the growth of multi-national firms.[218] Lefebvre
suggests, that we can see three periods in the history of the world market:

1. Pre-industrial capitalism, that is commercial capitalism. This is related to
   imperialism and the use of the oceans – particularly by the British – to
   establish trade routes.
2. Industrial capitalism and the spread of world trade.
3. After two world wars and the defeat of the socialist market, the opening
   up of this market more generally.[219]

Marx's analysis, naturally, is of the transition between stages 1 and 2. For
Lefebvre, 'he started the elaboration of the concept without finishing it. He
distinguishes periods of the worldwide market: before capitalism and after
capitalism.'[220] Following him, Lefebvre suggests that England, France and
Germany, sometime in the eighteenth and nineteenth centuries, inaugurated the worldwide beyond the nationality that they were striving for.[221] The
relationship between the national and the worldwide, and the link between
the transnational and international that it must pass through is central.[222]
Going beyond Marx, Lefebvre thinks it is crucially important that the world
market remained a single market, despite the advent of communism in the
USSR. Indeed, he suggests that if we were to draw up a balance sheet on
Stalinism then the debit side would obviously have all the oppression, but
most significantly 'its incapacity, in spite of all its efforts and abuses of
power, to constitute a world market other than the capitalist one'.[223] It is not
noted what might fall on the positive side of this balance.

We should also note here that Lefebvre expresses some scepticism about
the idea of an *Imperialist State of the Multinationals* (*Stato imperialisto delle multina-
zionale*), which was discussed by the Red Brigade in Italy. The nation-state
has indeed operated in the interests of multinationals, but equally the
reverse has happened.[224] As a summation of his position Lefebvre suggests
that there is a central tension between the state and the notion of the
worldwide. The state's becoming worldly is at the same time its end, its
withering away. This links into the discussion of metaphilosophy and the
role of philosophy becoming worldly that Lefebvre and Axelos were so
interested in, as was discussed in Chapter 2. For Lefebvre, the 'last image of
historical time is also the first of world-wide space [*l'espace mondial-figure*] – an
image which will fade and already is becoming blurred before other con-
figurations'.[225] Our understanding of the world as a whole, as planetary, is
an example of what might be meant by the production of space. It is one
of the central ways in which capitalism has been able to supersede its
limitations, through the production of the world, of the world as market.[226]

The state organization of space

It was noted above that Lefebvre suggested that Marx believed that the contradictions of capitalism would lead to its demise, and that we need to come to terms with why this has not turned out as he expected. Hints for this can be found in Marx's own work, with the idea of the re-production of the relations of production, outlined above all, in the *Grundrisse*.[227] Lefebvre argues that social space is

> the place of the reproduction of the *relations* of production (super-imposed on the reproduction of the means of production); at the same time, it is the occasion for and the instrument of a form of planning (land development), of a logic of growth.[228]

Capitalism has found a way to 'attenuate (if not resolve) its internal contradictions' for a century since the writing of *Capital*. We cannot calculate the price of this 'growth', but 'we do know the means: *by occupying space, by producing a space*'.[229] (It is worth noting that the French title of this work – *La survie du capitalisme* – is more ambiguous than the English, because *survie* means 'afterlife' as well as 'survival'). The reproduction of the relations of production happens on the world scale,[230] a scale that has been produced or constituted by and for capitalism,[231] and capitalism's survival has also constituted new sectors of production and therefore of exploitation and domination (leisure, everyday life, knowledge (*connaissance*), art and urbanization).[232] As we have seen in Chapter 5, Lefebvre's work on space needs to be understood in relation to his work on history, but also in terms of its relation to production. I argued that both of these were occluded in much of the work that has drawn upon his ideas. Here, further emphasizing the latter, I want to make some more general comments about the intersection between politics and space. The most extensive analysis is found in the final volume of *De l'État*, which provides some extremely important analysis of the political production and use of space, which complements and develops the work of *The Production of Space*, but also in *The Survival of Capitalism*. There are discussions of the circulation of goods and people, patterns of migration, the creation of short-lived towns and enterprises, de-location and de-territorialization, the notion of flux or flow, ghettos and urbanization. For Lefebvre the control of space is central to the SMP with social and spatial relations closely intertwined, the networks and layout (*les maillages et quadrillages*) of space, centre-periphery relations, dominant and dominated space. Some of these analyses are at the abstract level, and some at the more concrete level of readings of France, Japan and the USA.[233]

Curiously, Lefebvre notes, the notion of space is rarely examined politically. Or rather, politics is rarely examined spatially – political thought is examined without reference to the ground it is based on, or even national territory. The nation is examined as idea; space is left to geographers in the academic division of labour.[234] And yet, 'each state *has* its space . . .

moreover, each state *is* a social space'.[235] The concentration on the state, yet without its spatial elements, has led to a neglect of questions of peripheries, margins, regions, towns, communities. Classical liberalism operates without reference to territory; even the notion of right, of sovereignty has a poor grasp of territorial concerns: sovereignty is exercised over people rather than things. 'The state is conceived in itself and by itself, as a real abstraction, without a spatial body, without concrete support other than "subjects" or "people".' For Lefebvre, in distinction, '*relations have social space* (spaces) *as support*'. Political thought should be *spatialized* – we should examine places and regions, the differences and multiple associations, some conflictual, attached to the soil, to habitation, to circulation of people and goods. The economy should likewise be reconsidered in terms of its spatial elements – flows and stores; mobility and stability; and the production and reproduction of space.[236] Democracy is linked to space both in terms of the space, that is the extent of the region being governed and the type of space – urban or rural.[237]

Lefebvre provides some important hints concerning the transition between the Greek *polis*, and the Roman notions of *civitas* and *res publica* and the related notions of *Imperium* and *Dominium*. In the Middle Ages the term *Regnum* was used for monarchies and *Civitas* for city-states, in opposition to the *Respublica christiana*. The territorial link was considerably weaker at this time, with sovereignty plural and overlapping. In Machiavelli's work, in the context of Renaissance city-states, we find the notion of *principauté*, and Bodin reintroduces that of *res publica*. Following Bodin's work, sovereignty characterizes the state, and distinguishes it from all other associations, contractual or natural, such as families or corporations, because it is exercised over a territory. This territory, and the subjects that make it up, is the focus of sovereign power. This is perhaps most fully developed with Hobbes's work on the *commonwealth*. It would become known as the national, but it is the territorial aspect which seems important, but which is often neglected.[238] Through various processes such as wars and the consolidation of powerful interior markets, cities are joined together, urban relations are integrated to much larger wholes (*ensembles*), which are territorially defined by so-called natural borders, and these wholes are called 'nations'.[239] This process is not without conflict – indeed it is a class conflict between the urban bourgeoisie and the feudal lords in the villages and their landed strongholds (*fiefs territoriaux*).[240] It is the incorporation of town and countryside together into the national – that is the entire territory – that is a crucial development within capitalism.[241]

As well as the large-scale question of territory, the relation between state and space works on a number of other levels. State control leads to the development of regions such as the Pyrenees, and changes to metropolitan space because state capitalism needs the town as a centre, a 'centre of decision making, wealth, information, of the organisation of space'.[242] The needs of capitalism are paramount. Communication and transport networks – rivers, maritime and terrestrial – enable the circuits of exchange.

Circuits and spatial connections develop into spatial networks for the distribution of industrial products.[243] The growth of the state and the economy is therefore linked to the transformation of space in the nineteenth century by the grand industrial countries through railways and stations. Old towns either became part of the new network or are allowed to waste away. The building of airports and motorways, the location or relocation of heavy industry in strategic places or near convenient transport hubs, are all part of the reorganization of space, the state organization of space; the political production of space, controlled by the central state power.[244]

We therefore need to think about both the abstract space of business and information networks, but also the concrete space of capital flows, trade routes, production lines, cities, buildings, and tourist destinations.[245] The domination of the space of the ocean and thereby the world market was by England, but things have developed far beyond this.[246]

> Capitalism seizes the whole space. Without appropriating it to its use, it dominates it and modifies it for exchange; it produces its space, that of domination, around centres of decision, of wealth, of knowledge and information.[247]

Lefebvre suggests that state is involved in three types of planning – material and financial accounting, and spatial planning. The last of these includes the unity of codes, ordinances and institutions for construction and architecture, urbanism, and the development of territory – which together institute a space. Drawing on French organizations, Lefebvre notes the way in which homogeneous, logistic, optico-geometric, quantitative space is created and organized. But this is not simply a passive process, because space developed in this way takes on an organizing function in the economy and planning.[248] Space is not therefore something passive, there to be shaped by material forces, but a condition of the very operation of those forces. Territory is the support for these developments, and the territory of the national is distinct from both planetary space and the space of nature.[249] There are a range of levels of the spatial from the immediate neighbourhood of the local, to the mediations of exchanges, flux, networks, and circuits, to the larger scale of the region or the country. Each of these has a particular form of *autogestion* pertaining to it; equally direct democracy or *autogestion* requires a knowledge of the social conditions and spatial scale it is being applied to.[250]

It is therefore essential to understand the power relations at play between state and space.

> Reproduction (of the relations of production, not just the means of production) is located not simply in *society as a whole* but in *space as a whole*. Space, occupied by neo-capitalism, sectioned, reduced to homogeneity yet fragmented . . . becomes the seat of power.[251]

Lefebvre further suggests that though power is in everyday discourse as well as police batons, it is like a Shakespearian tragedy, because 'the more it consolidates, the more afraid it is'.[252] We can see this taken to its extreme in particular places, because those 'where power makes itself accessible and visible – police stations, barracks, administrative buildings – ooze with anxiety'.[253] The architecture of these buildings can be seen in this light – 'it attempts to conceal the meaning but only succeeds in proclaiming it: these are the places of official Power, the places where Power is concentrated, where it reflects itself, looks down from above – and is transparent. The Phallic unites with the political; verticality symbolizes Power. Transparent, metal and glass, constructed space tells of the ruses of the will to power.'[254] However, it would be misleading to think that these are the only sites of power.

> Power, the power to maintain the relations of dependence and exploitation, does it keep to a defined 'front' at the strategic level? No. The 'front' of power is not like a frontier on the map or a line of trenches on the ground. Power is everywhere; it is omnipresent, assigned to being. It is everywhere *in space* . . . Social relations remain entangled in the constraints, and except in the case of revolt, confrontation or revolution, social space remains that of Power.[255]

This looks very similar to Foucault's analyses, made at a similar time, of the power of buildings and spaces. However, *De l'État* contains an interesting and powerful criticism of Foucault's work, precisely because of the question of the state. It is useful both in terms of illuminating Lefebvre's purpose and because it shows some points of comparison and contrast between these two thinkers. Lefebvre suggests that 'revived by the Marxist and Nietzschean critique, current philosophy attempts to renew history itself, by transforming positive historicity into critical history. The most prominent works in this approach carry the signature of Michel Foucault.'[256] Foucault's thesis, in *Histoire de la folie à l'âge classique* and *Discipline and Punish*, is about the importance of confinement in France. Lefebvre's focus is on the former book, known in an edited version in English as *Madness and Civilisation*.[257] For Lefebvre, Foucault uses historical material to support a philosophical project, an attack on the Western *logos*, and its historical consequences in classicism and humanism. It is, Lefebvre suggests, a 'powerful book'.[258]

Foucault is successful in showing how difficult people, abnormals or those who appear abnormal, are got rid of. He shows how classical reason distinguishes between the normal and norms on the one hand, and abnormals and anomaly on the other.[259] As Lefebvre recognizes, 'this thesis gained rapid success', because philosophy has regained some ground as speculative activity, and 'because the society where we live, composed of ghettos, has generalised confinement'.[260]

> However, this thesis does not get to the heart of the analysis. It mentions some phenomena but does not discover what is concealed in them . . . Michel Foucault has retrospectively illuminated a fragment of the historical past from present experience and state repression. A worthwhile step provided that we do not stop there. What characterizes the formation of capitalism in the West is not confinement, but *putting people to work*.[261]

For Lefebvre it is the production of workers that is the most significant thing to analyse. This is because Foucault neglects the analysis of the state, the way the state operates at the side of reason, how reason becomes *raison d'Etat*.[262] To study the state in this way would incorporate an analysis of confinement, but although this is significant it is a minor element within the wider picture. It is the state that makes decisions about who is normal and abnormal, replaces communal life with its own laws, and puts certain people outside the law. The flaw of Foucault's work is that there is some kind of *deus ex machina*, a hidden god, but that he does not recognize the role of the state.[263] As Lefebvre notes elsewhere, it is a philosopher's illusion that it is reason, and not the state. Although he admires the book, it therefore suffers from an error of perspective and appreciation – not a falsification but an illusion.[264]

More generally, Lefebvre broadens this critique to suggest that contemporary concentration on marginal/peripheral groups 'neglects the centres and centrality; in a word the global'. These are pin-prick operations, suggesting that we should 'enjoy yourselves! Don't work! We are all delinquents, sexually obsessed, schizophrenics.'[265] By this it is clear he has Deleuze and Guattari and the Situationists in his sights as much as Foucault.[266] Instead of just examining the isolated and the isolation, we need to look at the centre and the incorporation within contemporary society. This is shown by Lefebvre's insistence that the 'the expulsion of whole groups towards the spatial, mental and social peripheries' should be partnered with an analysis of integration.[267]

> Having become political, social space is on the one hand centralised and fixed in a political centrality, and on the other hand specialised and parcelled out. The state determines and congeals the decision-making centres. At the same time, space is distributed into peripheries which are hierarchised in relation to the centres; it is atomised. Colonisation, which like industrial production and consumption was formerly localised, is made general. Around the centres there are nothing but subjected, exploited and dependent spaces: neo-colonial spaces.[268]

We can see the questions of centre-periphery and the notion of neo-colonization particularly in Lefebvre's reading of the situation in the Pyrenees, with the building of the new towns and the exploitation of resources, as was discussed in Chapter 4.

> Of the contradictions of space, the problems and concepts which have recently arisen concerning 'the environment', the depletion of resources, the destruction of nature, etc., only tell half the story. They are only fragmentary manifestations; they mask the global problem, of space as a whole, its production and management.
> The 'centre-periphery' relation, in spite of its importance, is neither the sole nor the essential conflictive relation. It is subordinate to a deeper conflictive relation: the relation between, on the one hand, the *fragmentation* of space (first *practical*, since space has become a commodity that is bought and sold, chopped

up into lots and parcels; but also *theoretical*, since it is carved up by scientific
specialisation), and, on the other hand, the global capacity of the productive
forces and of scientific knowledge to produce spaces on a planetary and even
interplanetary scale.

*This dialectised, conflictive space is where the reproduction of the relations of production is
achieved. It is this space that produces reproduction, by introducing into it its multiple contradictions, whether or not these latter have sprung from historical time.*[269]

In this remarkable passage Lefebvre brings several strands of his work
together. The well-known notion of the production of space is balanced by
a historical and temporal analysis, shot through with themes of politics and
political economy, dialectically analysed both in its theoretical and practical
instances, and related to issues of the world scale. As such it is a powerful
example of how the work on capitalism and the state is related to recurrent
themes throughout Lefebvre's work, and how at the end of this book, the
practical analyses send us back to the theoretical suggestions, with the
continual aim of reworking, rebalancing and rethinking them.

Politics, the political and the possible

An importance distinction is now often drawn between 'politics' (*la politique,
die Politik*) – concrete policy-making, decisions and actions – and the 'political' (*le politique, das Politische*) – the frame of reference within which 'politics'
occurs.[270] When Lefebvre makes the distinction between *le (la) politique* it
partners ones he would make between the logical and logic – *le (la) logique* –
and the dialectical and the dialectic – *la (le) dialectique*.[271] For Lefebvre the
distinction between *le politique* and *la politique* enables a distinction between
the thinking of the political and political action. This is a distinction and not
a disassociation; a distinction and not a separation. The political thinker and
thought on the one side; the political human and action on the other.[272]
With his favoured thinkers it enables him to turn their thought to political
purposes other than those they favoured, initiated or influenced (the Prus-
sian state for Hegel, Stalinism for Marx, Hitler and Nazism for Nietzsche
and Heidegger).[273] At one point Lefebvre notes that Marx's work differs as
much from the Gulag as Christ's teachings do from Torquemada.[274] Equally
it is worth noting Eduard Baumgarten's recollection that at one point
'Heidegger was working through a pile of Marxist writings so that he would
be in a position to reign as *der deutsche Philosoph* no matter who prevailed in
the ensuing political struggle'.[275] This is a distinction between their thought
and their action, not a disassociation. What it allows is a means of appropriating their thought against their action, or against the actions of those
putatively informed by their thought. As demonstrations, witness the critique of Stalin in *Dialectical Materialism*, which continues in *De l'État*; and for
early critiques of Nazism, see *La conscience mystifiée, Le nationalisme contre les
nations* and *Hitler au pouvoir*.[276]

Lefebvre notes that the distinction between politics and the political tends
to disappear because the political becomes absorbed in politics in the eyes of

most people and in public opinion. 'To rehabilitate the *political* is one *moment* in a vast project. Difficult to accomplish.'[277] The lack of a theory of *the political* means that the actions and choices made by politicians are contingent and short-term. There will be a lack of strategy. Strategy is what gives generalized context to action, to individual tactics; it provides theory, although this may be unexpressed. Whilst this may not be of concern to statesman, in the long term it can only cause problems.[278]

Lefebvre's formative political and philosophical years were the 1920s and 30s. He is dismissive of his own work of the 1920s, and realizes that it was only somewhat later that he reached a mature view. Two central texts appeared in this period – Heidegger's *Being and Time*, and Marx's *1844 Manuscripts*. Lefebvre explicitly notes the way in which the publication of the latter was both in competition and confrontation with Heidegger's work.[279] This is of central importance to understanding the formation of Lefebvre's political and philosophical views. His work may have tended more toward Marxism, was indebted to other thinkers, and was certainly shot through with a profound originality, but the role of Heidegger should not be forgotten. If Lefebvre's politics were Marxist, his view of the political was close to both Marx and Heidegger. As I have suggested, this is not dissimilar to Marx's own appropriation and critique of Hegel. Because of his abstraction and mystification, Heidegger needs to be constantly stood on his feet, grounded, rooted in material reality. A related argument can be made for Lefebvre's interest in Nietzsche.

This book has shown how Nietzsche and Heidegger are important to Lefebvre alongside Hegel and Marx. It has attempted to demonstrate how Lefebvre's broad range of concerns have to be understood in the context of his Marxism and his active engagement with philosophy more generally. Lefebvre was well-read in classical and contemporary theory, and his writings similarly need to be situated in a range of political and social contexts. In addition to the attempt to use these as a starting point for analysis, this book has shown how notions of festivity and revolution are crucial to his work on everyday life; how his writings on cities develop from a concern with rural communities; and how the idea of the production of space emerges from this work on the rural and the urban, an interest in aesthetic representation and discussion of time and history. In this final chapter many of these themes are returned to in an explicitly political way. In doing this the book demonstrates the way in which Lefebvre's various interests interlink and disrupts both chronological and simplistic disciplinary divisions of his work.

Lefebvre's work is potentially open to use beyond a Marxist framework but it seems essential that this and his other contexts are understood before an attempt is made at this kind of utilization. Much of the recent appropriation of Lefebvre has seemingly neglected this straightforward proposition. Lefebvre was able to use Hegel, Nietzsche and Heidegger in new and progressive ways precisely because he understood the way in which politics and thought intertwined in their work. The danger in the uncritical appropriation of thinkers is that their philosophical complexity is denied and their political edge blunted – or perhaps more dangerous, that the political issues of their work are ignored altogether. This book has not solved all the problems with Lefebvre and not sought to render him entirely consistent. It has taken both a wide angle on his work, but also focused in on selective specifics. It has attempted to highlight crucial parts of his work that have been neglected in much of the available secondary literature, and perhaps given less attention to well-known areas of his work than might be expected.

Lefebvre argues insistently that progressive thought is an opening up, a making possible of opportunities. Just as he describes Marx, Lefebvre is a thinker of the possible.[280] We find this in a number of places in his work – his call for a new romanticism is revolutionary for precisely this reason; similarly the notion of *autogestion* offers future promise, new potentials. Above all we find it in his use of Marx's approach, the dialectic at work, which he summarizes as the regressive-progressive mode of analysis. The successive regressive-progressive steps, Lefebvre claims, allow us to explore the possible,[281] that is both a regressive, historical analysis of the conditions of possibility of the present, using the present to understand the past, and the past to understand the present; and a revolutionary, progressive analysis that opens us to the future, to the possible.

In the investigation of the conditions of possibility he is engaged in an ostensibly Kantian project, but rendered historical, as it is in both Heidegger and Marx's work.[282] In relation to capitalism, asking how it has been able to survive and overcome its contradictions, Lefebvre notes that its conditions of possibility are not static.[283] Lefebvre similarly asks how fascism is possible, how the city emerged from the countryside, how the state functions on the world scale, how everyday life has been colonized, and numerous other investigations. From these investigations come the potential overcomings. The contradictions within capitalism make possible its transition to a worldwide level, but they also lead to moments of profound 'crisis', making possible social transformation and revolution.[284] As Lefebvre notes, in addition to the rich Hegelian-Marxist tradition that this derives from, it was from Nietzsche in particular that he derived the revolutionary theory of the possible-impossible.[285] What is there embedded in the past becomes present through a 'realisation of the possibilities objectively implied in this past'.[286] Rather than merely seeking to transform the world, we need to ask how revolutionary thought is rendered *possible*.[287] As Lefebvre notes, 'utopia today is the possible of tomorrow'.[288]

The purpose of this book is usefully summed up in Lefebvre's outline of one of the many books he wrote on Marx: 'One has to – obviously – read Marx himself! This small book does not aim to give a complete understanding of Marxism and to replace the reading of the works.'[289] This book is for its readers not as a directive but as a tool. If it helps demonstrate the wide range of Lefebvre's concerns and their potentially rich applicability outside of the context in which he wrote them then it will have served its purpose. It is not designed to close off or complete discussion, but as an introduction in the best sense of the word – a leading into a topic, a problematic, an understanding of a thinker's work, an opening to the possible.

Notes

1 J. G. Merquior, *Western Marxism*, London: Paladin, 1986, p. 145.
2 *La somme et le reste*, Paris: Méridiens Klincksieck, 3rd edition, 1989 (1959), p. 394.
3 *Le temps des méprises*, Paris: Stock, 1975, p. 10.
4 *La somme et le reste*, pp. 183–202; *Sociologie de Marx*, Paris: PUF, 1966, pp. 104–62; *The Sociology of Marx*, translated by Norbert Guterman, Harmondsworth: Penguin, 1968, pp. 123–85; see *Le marxisme*, Paris: PUF, 1948, p. 100; 'Les rapports de la philosophie et de la politique dans les premières oeuvres de Marx (1842–1843)', *Revue de métaphysique et de morale* 63(2–3), April–September 1958, pp. 299–324; *Problèmes actuels du marxisme*, Paris: PUF, 2nd edition, 1960 (1958), pp. 30–5, 77–83.
5 *De l'État*, Paris: UGE, 4 volumes, 1976–8, II, p. 255 n. 1.
6 On this, see Rémi Hess, 'La place d'Henri Lefebvre dans le collège invisible, d'une critique des superstructures à l'analyse institutionnelle', in *La survie du capitalisme: La re-production des rapports de production*, Paris: Anthropos, 3rd edition, 2002 (1973), p. 199.
7 For an early study, see 'La crise du capitalisme français: Essai de définition du problème', *La pensée* 17, March–April 1948, pp. 39–50. This, according the editorial note on p. 50, is the introduction and résumé of a forthcoming study entitled *L'avenir du capitalisme*, which never appeared.
8 *L'irruption de Nanterre au sommet*, Paris: Éditions Syllepse, 2nd edition, 1998 (1968), p. 4; *The Explosion: Marxism and the French Upheaval*, translated by Alfred Ehrenfeld, New York: Modern Reader, 1969, p. 8.
9 *L'irruption de Nanterre au sommet*, p. 11; *The Explosion*, p. 15. Lefebvre argues that a conference at UNESCO tried to 'drown Marxist thought once and for all in academicism'. Marcuse was a key speaker. *L'irruption de Nanterre au sommet*, p. 19; *The Explosion*, p. 24.
10 *L'irruption de Nanterre au sommet*, p. 17; *The Explosion*, p. 23.
11 *L'irruption de Nanterre au sommet*, p. 10; *The Explosion*, p. 15.
12 Ralph Miliband, *The State in Capitalist Society*, London: Quartet, 1969, p. 7.
13 Letter from Marx to Ferdinand Lassalle, 22 February 1858; letter from Marx to Engels, 2 April 1858, in Karl Marx and Frederick Engels, *Collected Works* 40, London: Lawrence & Wishart, 1983, pp. 270, 298. Lefebvre cites these letters in *De l'État* II, pp. 212–13. See also Karl Marx, 'Preface (to *A Contribution to the Critique of Political Economy*)', in *Early Writings*, translated by Rodney Livingstone and Gregor Benton, Harmondsworth: Penguin, 1975, p. 424.
14 Karl Marx, *Capital: A Critique of Political Economy* I, translated by Ben Fowkes, Harmondsworth: Penguin, 1976; *Capital: A Critique of Political Economy* II, translated by David Fernbach, Harmondsworth: Penguin, 1978; *Capital: A Critique of Political Economy* III, translated by David Fernbach, Harmondsworth: Penguin, 1981; *Theories of Surplus Value*, London: Lawrence & Wishart, 3 volumes, 1967–72. For a note on the changes, see Ernest Mandel, 'Introduction', in Marx, *Capital* I, pp. 11–86.
15 Karl Marx, *Grundrisse: Foundations of the Critique of Political Economy (Rough Draft)*, translated by Martin Nicolaus, Harmondsworth: Penguin, 1973. For a

discussion, see Roman Rosdolsky, *The Making of Marx's 'Capital'*, translated by Peter Burgess, London: Pluto, 1977.

16 Marx, 'Preface', p. 425.

17 Mark Neocleous, *Administering Civil Society: Toward a Theory of State Power*, London: Macmillan, 1996, p. 16.

18 *De l'État* III, p. 255.

19 *Pour connaître la pensée de Karl Marx*, Paris: Bordas, 1947, p. 187.

20 *De l'État* IV, p. 17.

21 *La pensée marxiste et la ville*, Paris: Casterman, 1972, p. 70.

22 Neocleous, *Administering Civil Society*, p. 17.

23 *De l'État* III, p. 134.

24 *De l'État* II, p. 212; *Hegel, Marx, Nietzsche ou le royaume des ombres*, Paris: Casterman, 1975, p. 105. At this time, Lefebvre claims that his work seeks to restore the unity of Marx's work around two guiding threads – alienation and the state. See *Le temps des méprises*, p. 192.

25 *Sociologie de Marx*, p. 20; *The Sociology of Marx*, p. 26.

26 *Sociologie de Marx*, p. 104; *The Sociology of Marx*, p. 123.

27 Miliband, *The State in Capitalist Society*, p. 8. The same point is made in Nicos Poulantzas' review of Miliband's book, 'The problem of the capitalist state', *New Left Review* 58, November–December 1969, pp. 67–78, p. 67. In his later *Marxism and Politics*, Oxford: Oxford University Press, 1977, p. 3, Miliband questions why 'more by way of a Marxist political theorization of some of the most important experiences of our times, and of a Marxist political theory in general, should not have been constructed in, say, the last fifty years, on the foundations provided by classical Marxism'. At least part of the answer, he suggests, is down to Stalin.

28 *De l'État* IV, p. 325.

29 See also *Le temps des méprises*, p. 213.

30 The following few pages are closely based on the outline in the introduction (*De l'État* I, pp. x–xlix), which was also published separately the previous year as 'L'Etat dans le monde moderne', *L'homme et la société* 37–8, 1975, pp. 3–23.

31 See *De l'État* I, p. 39. Lefebvre's reference is to J.-C. Lambert, *Opus International* 50.

32 This is a neglected part of the analysis – for various discussions see *De l'État* II, pp. 8, 139–40, 155; III, p. 58.

33 For a much more detailed – but broadly complimentary – analysis see Perry Anderson, *Passages from Antiquity to Feudalism*, London: NLB, 1974; and *Lineages of the Absolutist State*, London: NLB, 1974.

34 *De l'État* II, p. 29.

35 *De l'État* II, pp. 230–1.

36 *De l'État* II, p. 62, and see II, p. 222.

37 *De l'État* III, p. 62.

38 *De l'État* III, p. 184.

39 *De l'État* II, p. 28. On the use of this method in the work on the state, see Patrick Dieuaide and Ramine Motamed-Nejad, 'Méthodologie et hétérodoxie en économie: retours sur Henri Lefebvre', *Espaces et sociétés* 76, 1994, pp. 69–98.

40 *De l'État* II, p. 74. On the former, see *Une pensée devenue monde: Faut-il abandonner Marx?* Paris: Fayard, 1980, pp. 186–7.

41 On Fourier see also the introduction to *Actualité de Fourier: Colloque d'Arcs-et-Senans sous la direction de Henri Lefebvre*, Paris: Anthropos, 1975.

42 *De l'État* II, p. 118.

43 For a related criticism of 'deconstruction' as modern ideological-scientific jargon, see *De l'État* II, p. 341.
44 *De l'État* II, p. 118.
45 *De l'État* II, p. 157.
46 *De l'État* II, p. 162.
47 *De l'État* II, p. 62. For an early discussion of the forerunners of the Marxist theory of the state – notably including Hegel – see 'Les sources de la théorie Marxiste-Leniniste de l'État', *Les cahiers du centre d'études socialistes* 42–3, 1964, pp. 31–48.
48 *Sociologie de Marx*, p. 21; *The Sociology of Marx*, p. 26.
49 *Sociologie de Marx*, p. 104; *The Sociology of Marx*, p. 123.
50 *De l'État* II, p. 177.
51 *De l'État* II, p. 216.
52 *De l'État* II, pp. 218, 226.
53 *De l'État* II, p. 226.
54 Poulantzas, 'The problem of the capitalist state', p. 70. In his reply, 'The capitalist state: reply to Nicos Poulantzas', *New Left Review* 59, January–February 1970, pp. 53–60, p. 57, Miliband describes Poulantzas' view as 'structural determinism or structural super-determinism'.
55 To my knowledge Miliband never acknowledges Lefebvre's work, and Nicos Poulantzas does only rarely. There are some criticisms – both explicit and implicit – in *Political Power and Social Classes*, edited by Timothy O'Hagan, London: NLB, 1973 (see, for example, pp. 135 n. 13, 310 n. 4); and some more complimentary references in a few places in *State, Power, Socialism*, translated by Patrick Camiller, London: NLB, 1978, pp. 50, 190, 193. The most substantive reference is p. 50: 'Here I will simply mention Henri Lefebvre's very recent work on the state, which is closer than others to my positions.' In a note on that page he talks of the 'value' of Lefebvre's work, which 'contains some remarkable analyses'. For some pointers toward the debate that never happened – though no direct discussion – see Ivan Szelenyi, 'The relative autonomy of the state or State Mode of Production', in Michael Dear and Allen J. Scott (eds), *Urbanization and Urban Planning in Capitalist Society*, London: Methuen, 1981, pp. 565–91.
56 *De l'État* II, p. 163. The reference is to Nicos Poulantzas, *Les Classes sociales dans le capitalisme aujourd'hui*, Paris: Éditions de Seuil, 1974, pp. 169ff; *Classes in Contemporary Capitalism*, translated by David Fernbach, London: NLB, 1975, pp. 177ff. Other, brief, references to Poulantzas are found in *De l'État* III, pp. 14, 247 and IV, p. 334.
57 *De l'État* III, p. 229.
58 *De l'État* IV, p. 127.
59 *De l'État* IV, p. 120.
60 *De l'État* I, p. xxi; and see II, pp. 431; IV, p. 124.
61 *De l'État* II, p. 218.
62 *De l'État* II, pp. 65–6.
63 *De l'État* I, p. 82.
64 *De l'État* II, p. 422; see also II, p. 176; III, p. 120.
65 *De l'État* II, pp. 326–7.
66 *De l'État* II, pp. 258–9.
67 *De l'État* II, p. 270.
68 *Sociologie de Marx*, p. 159; *The Sociology of Marx*, p. 181; see *Au-delà du structuralisme*, Paris: Anthropos, 1971, p. 329.

69 *De l'État* II, p. 277; see 'Problèmes théoriques de l'*autogestion*', *Autogestion* 1, 1966, pp. 59–70, p. 61.
70 *La fin de l'histoire*, Paris: Les Éditions de Minuit, 1970, p. 116. see *Problèmes actuels du marxisme*, p. 116.
71 *De l'État* II, p. 393.
72 *De l'État* I, p. 179. See *La somme et le reste*, p. 497, on anti-Stalinism, which may be as much of a problem.
73 *De l'État* II, p. 432.
74 *De l'État* III, p. 240. Lefebvre recalls that Nietzsche describes the state as 'the coldest of all cold monsters' in *La fin de l'histoire*, p. 89. In fact, the full quote is even more relevant. See Friedrich Nietzsche, *Thus Spoke Zarathustra*, in *The Portable Nietzsche*, edited and translated by Walter Kaufmann, Harmondsworth: Penguin, 1954, p. 160 – 'state is the name of the coldest of all cold monsters. Coldly it tells lies, too; and this lie crawls out of its mouth: "I, the state, am the people".'
75 *De l'État* I, p. 172.
76 See *La survie du capitalisme*, p. 62; *The Survival of Capitalism*, p. 66; *De l'État* IV, pp. 304–6 for a discussion of the capitalist mode of production (CMP), which precedes it. See Marx, *Capital* I, p. 274: 'Capital, therefore, announces from the outset a new epoch in the process of social production.' The CMP is also discussed under this acronym in Poulantzas, *Political Power and Social Classes*.
77 *De l'État* II, p. 396; III, p. 283.
78 *De l'État* II, p. 349. On Lenin and politics, see also Chapter V of *Pour connaître la pensée de Lénine*, Paris: Bordas, 1957. This is obviously not entirely accurate. Lenin's initial reforms were designed to consolidate the Bolshevik grasp on power rather than dismantle the state. He wanted to pursue a state capitalism, a command economy. As Conquest notes, his famous phrase that 'Communism is nothing but Soviet rule plus the electrification of the entire country' lacks Marxist content. See Robert Conquest, *Lenin*, London: Fontana, 1972, p. 97. See *Métaphilosophie*, Paris: Éditions Syllepse, 2nd edition, 2001 (1965), p. 282.
79 *Qu'est-ce que penser?* Paris: Publisad, 1985, p. 129.
80 *La somme et le reste*, p. 133.
81 See *De l'État* III, p. 292.
82 *De l'État* III, p. 235; see Henri Lefebvre and Catherine Régulier, *La révolution n'est plus ce qu'elle était*, Hallier: Éditions Libres, 1978, p. 199.
83 *De l'État* II, p. 416.
84 *De l'État* II, p. 397; III, p. 283.
85 *De l'État* II, p. 396.
86 *De l'État* III, p. 88.
87 *De l'État* II, p. 396.
88 *De l'État* IV, p. 150.
89 Much of this has informed the discussion of this notion in Chapter 1 above.
90 In a sense these are an extension and updating of Marx's analyses on the circulation of capital in *Capital* II.
91 *De l'État* III, p. 157.
92 *De l'État* III, p. 221.
93 For a discussion of Heidegger in this respect, see Stuart Elden, 'Taking the Measure of the *Beiträge*: Heidegger, National Socialism and the Calculation of the Political', *European Journal of Political Theory* 2(1), January 2003, pp. 35–56.
94 *De l'État* III, p. 122; II, p. 325.
95 *De l'État* IV, p. 178.

96 See *De l'État* I, p. 71.

97 *De l'État* I, p. xxxvi.

98 *De l'État* I, p. 388. See also *Critique de la vie quotidienne* III, pp. 135–8.

99 *De l'État* III, p. 62. See *La présence et l'absence: Contribution à la théorie des representations*, Paris: Casterman, 1980, p. 29.

100 *De l'État* IV, p. 170.

101 *La présence et l'absence*, most explicitly p. 7, where he links this work back to that on the state.

102 *L'irruption de Nanterre au sommet*, pp. 13–14; *The Explosion*, p. 19.

103 *De l'État* III, p. 300. At the time, Lefebvre described it as 'the sacrifice of a considerable part of the earth's resources in order to gain possession of one of the ghastliest of all the piles of pebbles rattling around in space'. *La fin de l'histoire*, p. 212; *Key Writings*, edited by Stuart Elden, Elizabeth Lebas and Eleonore Kofman, London: Continuum, 2003, p. 182.

104 *Hitler au pouvoir: Les enseignements de cinq années de fascisme en Allemagne*, Paris: Bureau d'Éditions, 1938, p. 72.

105 *De l'État* IV, p. 22.

106 *De l'État* III, p. 300.

107 *De l'État* III, p. 300.

108 *La fin de l'histoire*, p. 174.

109 *De l'État* IV, p. 22. As David Harvey, *Social Justice and the City*, Oxford: Basil Blackwell, 1973, p. 15, perceptively notes, John Rawls, *A Theory of Justice*, Oxford: Clarendon, 1971, makes no reference to production, treating redistribution as something subsequent and therefore separate. On this critique see also Harvey, *Social Justice and the City*, pp. 108–9; Marx, 'Critique of the Gotha programme', in *The First International and After*, pp. 344–8.

110 *L'irruption de Nanterre au sommet*, pp. 117–18; *The Explosion*, pp. 128–9.

111 *De l'État* III, p. 280.

112 *De l'État* IV, p. 21.

113 *L'irruption de Nanterre au sommet*, pp. 40–1; *The Explosion*, pp. 44–5.

114 Eleonore Kofman and Elizabeth Lebas, 'Lost in transposition – time, space and the city', in Henri Lefebvre, *Writings on Cities*, translated and edited by Eleonore Kofman and Elizabeth Lebas, Oxford: Blackwell, pp. 3–60, p. 14.

115 'A propos d'un nouveau modèle étatique', *Dialectiques* 27, 1979, pp. 47–55, pp. 50–1; 'Comments on a new state form', translated by Neil Brenner and Victoria Johnson, *Antipode* 33(5), November 2001, pp. 769–82, p. 774; *Le retour de la dialectique: 12 mots clefs*, Paris: Messidor/Éditions Sociales, 1986, p. 27.

116 *De l'État* III, p. 233.

117 *De l'État* I, p. 210.

118 *De l'État* I, p. 281.

119 'L'État et la société', *Les cahiers du centre d'études socialistes* 42–3, 1964, pp. 17–29, p. 17.

120 *De l'État* III, p. 253.

121 *De l'État* IV, p. 202. See the analysis of nationalism discussed in Chapter 2.

122 Andrew Gamble, *The Free Economy and the Strong State*, London: Macmillan, 1988.

123 For a discussion see Neil Brenner, 'State theory in the political conjuncture: Henri Lefebvre's "Comments on a new state form" ', *Antipode* 33(5), November 2001, pp. 783–808, pp. 798–9.

124 *De l'État* III, p. 260; see *La survie du capitalisme*, p. 103; *The Survival of Capitalism*, p. 106.

125 'A propos d'un nouveau modèle étatique', p. 50; 'Comments on a new state form', p. 773. For the phases of transition, see *De l'État* IV, pp. 407–9.

126 *De l'État* IV, p. 409.

127 See Brenner, 'State theory in the political conjuncture', p. 802.

128 Karl Marx and Friedrich Engels, 'Manifesto of the Communist Party', in *The Revolutions of 1848: Political Writings Volume I*, translated by David Fernbach, Harmondsworth: Penguin, 1973, p. 69.

129 Karl Marx, 'Critique of the Gotha Programme', in *The First International and After: Political Writings Volume III*, translated by David Fernbach, Harmondsworth: Penguin, 1974, p. 354.

130 Miliband, *The State in Capitalist Society*, p. 247.

131 This journal became *Autogestion et socialisme*, and then later *Autogestions*. See René Lourau, 'Lefebvre, "parrain" de la Maffia "Analyse institutionnelle" ', in *La somme et le reste*, pp. ii–iii.

132 *Le manifeste différentialiste*, Paris: Gallimard, 1970; 'Du pacte social au contrat de citoyenneté', in Henri Lefebvre et le Groupe de Navarrenx, *Du contrat de citoyenneté*, Paris: Éditions Syllepse, pp. 15–37; *Key Writings*, pp. 238–54.

133 In leaving *autogestion* untranslated I am following Brenner's suggestion in his note to Lefebvre's 'Comments on a new state form', p. 781 n. 5. His commentary on this piece, 'State theory in the political conjuncture', is an invaluable discussion of *autogestion* and indeed, Lefebvre's state theory more generally. The literature on *autogestion* is vast, but for a sampling see also Félix Damette and Jacques Scheibling, *Pour une stratégie autogestionnaire*, Paris: Éditions Sociales, 1979; and Bernard E. Brown, *Socialism of a Different Kind: Reshaping the Left in France*, Westport: Greenwood Press, 1982. The links to the Italian variant are usefully explored in Steve Wright, *Storming Heaven: Class Composition and Struggle in Italian Autonomist Marxism*, London: Pluto, 2002.

134 On the problems of representation in the political sphere see *La présence et l'absence*, especially p. 67.

135 Mihailo Marković, *Democratic Socialism: Theory and Practice*, Sussex: Harvester Press, 1982, p. 32.

136 On this event see René Lourau, *L'analyseur Lip*, Paris: Union Générale d'Éditions, 1974; and Brown, *Socialism of a Different Kind*, pp. 104–17. See also the brief comments in Jacques Guignou, 'Préface à la troisième édition', in *La survie du capitalisme*. Lourau was a colleague at Nanterre, and his book *L'analyse institutionnelle*, Paris: Éditions de Minuit, 1970, was important for Lefebvre in the gestation of *De l'État*, and is cited both there (for example, IV, p. 260) and in *La survie du capitalisme*, p. 52 n. 1; *The Survival of Capitalism*, p. 56, although these are sometimes critical references. There is also an overlap of themes with *De l'État* in René Lourau, *L'État-inconscient*, Paris: Éditions de Minuit, 1978. For a discussion of the relation, see Hess, 'La place d'Henri Lefebvre dans le collège invisible', pp. 201–12.

137 Brenner, 'State theory in the political conjuncture', p. 789. For a discussion of the contemporary events, see Lefebvre and Régulier, *La révolution n'est plus ce qu'elle était*, pp. 188–9.

138 'Du pacte social au contrat de citoyenneté', p. 35; *Key Writings*, pp. 252–3.

139 'A propos d'un nouveau modèle étatique', p. 54; 'Comments on a new state form', p. 779.

250 UNDERSTANDING HENRI LEFEBVRE

140 *La survie du capitalisme*, pp. 34–5; *The Survival of Capitalism*, p. 40.
141 'Interview – Débat sur le marxisme: Léninisme-stalinisme ou autogestion?' *Autogestion et socialisme* 33/34, 1976, pp. 115–26, pp. 123, 125; On *territorial autogestion*, see *De l'État* IV, pp. 323–4; *Critique de la vie quotidienne* III, p. 114.
142 *L'irruption de Nanterre au sommet*, p. 79; *The Explosion*, pp. 86–7.
143 'Problèmes théoriques de l'autogestion', p. 69.
144 'Interview – Débat sur le marxisme', p. 123.
145 'Problèmes théoriques de l'autogestion', p. 60; 'Interview – Débat sur le marxisme', p. 119; *Introduction à la modernité: Préludes*, Paris: Les Éditions de Minuit, 1962, p. 199 n. 2; *Introduction to Modernity: Twelve Preludes*, translated by John Moore, London: Verso, p. 394 n. 14. Marx suggests that '*the political state disappears [untergehe]* in a true democracy', in 'Critique of Hegel's doctrine of the state', in *Early Writings*, p. 88. Engels is responsible for the phrase 'withers away' in *Socialism: Utopian and Scientific*, Peking: Foreign Languages Press, 1975, p. 94. For a note on the phrase, see *Key Writings*, p. 264 n. 3. On the dictatorship of the proletariat, see Karl Marx to Joseph Weydemeyer, 5 March 1852, *Collected Works* 39, London: Lawrence & Wishart, 1983, pp. 62–5, which is discussed in *Pour connaître la pensée de Lénine*, p. 17.
146 Engels, *Socialism: Utopian and Scientific*, p. 94.
147 'Problèmes théoriques de l'autogestion', p. 60.
148 'Problèmes théoriques de l'autogestion', p. 61.
149 'Interview – Débat sur le marxisme', pp. 118–19. For Lenin's discussion see *The State and Revolution: The Marxist Theory of the State and the Tasks of the Proletariat in the Revolution*, Moscow: Progress Publishers, 1965; and see *Pour connaître la pensée de Lénine*, especially pp. 321ff.
150 *L'idéologie structuraliste*, Paris: Anthropos, 1975, p. 11; see *De l'État* III, pp. 61–2; 'Interview – Débat sur le marxisme', p. 118.
151 *Logique formelle, logique dialectique*, Paris: Anthropos, 2nd edition, 1969, p. xxxii.
152 See *Au-delà du structuralisme*, pp. 373–5, 413.
153 'Interview – Débat sur le marxisme', p. 118.
154 'Interview – Débat sur le marxisme', p. 119.
155 'Interview – Débat sur le marxisme', pp. 121–2; see 'A propos d'un nouveau modèle étatique', p. 48; 'Comments on a new state form', p. 770.
156 'Du pacte social au contrat de citoyenneté', p. 24; *Key Writings*, p. 243.
157 *L'irruption de Nanterre au sommet*, pp. 80–1; *The Explosion*, pp. 88–9.
158 *La survie du capitalisme*, p. 35; *The Survival of Capitalism*, p. 40.
159 'Problèmes théoriques de l'autogestion', p. 68. See more generally *Marx 1818–1883*, Genève-Paris: Trois Collines, 1947, which examines the understanding of freedom in Marx's writings.
160 *L'irruption de Nanterre au sommet*, pp. 81–2; *The Explosion*, pp. 89–90.
161 See Kurt Meyer, *Henri Lefebvre: Ein Romantischer Revolutionär*, Wien: Europaverlag, 1973, p. 77.
162 'Problèmes théoriques de l'autogestion', p. 62.
163 See also *Le temps des méprises*, pp. 107, 123.
164 *La survie du capitalisme*, p. 35; *The Survival of Capitalism*, p. 40.
165 'A propos d'un nouveau modèle étatique', p. 54; 'Comments on a new state form', p. 779.
166 *Le retour de la dialectique*, p. 34; 'Interview – Débat sur le marxisme', p. 125. On the Yugoslavian model, see the essays in Mihailo Marković and Gajo Petrović, *Praxis: Yugoslav Essays in the Philosophy and Methodology of the Social Sciences*, trans-

lated by Joan Coddington, David Rougé and others, Dordrecht: D. Reidel, 1979; Gerson S. Sher (ed.), *Marxist Humanism and Praxis*, Buffalo: Prometheus Books, 1978; and Mihailo Marković, *From Affluence to Praxis: Philosophy and Social Criticism*, Ann Arbor: University of Michigan Press, 1974; Marković, *Democratic Socialism*.

167 'A propos d'un nouveau modèle étatique', p. 54; 'Comments on a new state form', p. 779.

168 'A propos d'un nouveau modèle étatique', pp. 54–5; 'Comments on a new state form', p. 780.

169 *Le manifeste différentialiste*, Paris: Gallimard, 1970, p. 44.

170 *La survie du capitalisme*, p. 30; *The Survival of Capitalism*, p. 35.

171 *Le manifeste différentialiste*, p. 45; *Espace et politique: Le droit à la ville II*, Paris: Anthropos, 2nd edition, 2000 (1972), p. 145.

172 *Le manifeste différentialiste*, pp. 44–5; *Espace et politique*, p. 145.

173 *Le manifeste différentialiste*, p. 73.

174 *Le manifeste différentialiste*, p. 49.

175 *Le manifeste différentialiste*, pp. 49, 168.

176 *Le manifeste différentialiste*, p. 140; 'Le marxisme éclaté', *L'homme et la société* 41/42, July–December 1976, pp. 3–12, p. 6.

177 *Critique de la vie quotidienne* III, p. 108.

178 On the link to Deleuze, see Rémi Hess, 'Henri Lefebvre et le projet avorté du *Traité de matérialisme dialectique*', in *Méthodologie des sciences: Inédit*, Paris: Anthropos, 2002, pp. v–xxvi, p. xiii; and *Logique formelle, logique dialectique*, p. xvii.

179 On the foundation and work of the group see Armand Ajzenberg, 'Henri Lefebvre: La société au point critique ou de l'individu écartelé', *Regards* 38, September 1998, www.regards.fr/archives/1998/199809/199809ide01.html. This piece includes a plan of an unpublished work on society by the group. Lefebvre highlights how the original plan of the journal *M, mensuel, marxisme, mouvement* was to pursue this research in 'Chers amis, lecteurs, abonnés, collaborateurs de M', *M, mensuel, marxisme, mouvement* 14, October 1987, pp. 6–7.

180 'Du pacte social au contrat de citoyenneté', pp. 31–2; *Key Writings*, pp. 249–50.

181 'Du pacte social au contrat de citoyenneté', p. 32; *Key Writings*, p. 250.

182 'Du pacte social au contrat de citoyenneté', pp. 33–6; *Key Writings*, pp. 250–3. See Engin F. Isin and Patricia K. Wood, *Citizenship and Identity*, London: Sage, 1999, p. 104, where, drawing upon Lefebvre, they argue that 'urban citizenship becomes part of rethinking a multilayered conception of citizenship'.

183 'Du pacte social au contrat de citoyenneté', p. 37; *Key Writings*, pp. 253–4.

184 'Du pacte social au contrat de citoyenneté', p. 33; *Key Writings*, p. 250.

185 *De l'État* II, p. 67.

186 *De l'État* II, p. 68.

187 Neil Brenner, 'The urban question as a scale question: reflections on Henri Lefebvre, urban theory and the politics of scale,' *International Journal of Urban and Regional Research* 24(2), June 2000, pp. 360–77, p. 367 n. 12. On scale generally, developing ideas from Lefebvre, see his 'State territorial restructuring and the production of spatial scale: urban and regional planning in the Federal Republic of Germany, 1960–1990', *Political Geography* 16(4), 1997, pp. 273–306; 'Between fixity and motion: accumulation, territorial organization and the historical geography of spatial scales', *Environment and Planning D: Society and Space* 16(5), 1998, pp. 459–81; and 'The limits to scale? Methodological

reflections on scalar structuration', *Progress in Human Geography* 25(4), 2001, pp. 591–614.

188 On this see Neil Brenner, 'Global, fragmented, hierarchical: Henri Lefebvre's geographies of globalization', *Public Culture* 10(1), Fall 1997, pp. 135–67.

189 See, for example, Jacques Derrida, *Without Alibi*, edited and translated by Peggy Kamuf, Stanford: Stanford University Press, 2002, p. 203.

190 See particularly, Kostas Axelos, *Le jeu du monde*, Paris: Les Éditions de Minuit, 1969 and *Vers la pensée planétaire: le devenir-pensée du monde et le devenir-monde de la pensée*, Paris: Éditions de Minuit, 1964. Lefebvre's review of the last book shows the impact Axelos had on this notion in his work. See 'Kostas Axelos: *Vers la pensée planétaire*', *Esprit* 338, May 1965, pp. 1114–17. See also 'Interview – Débat sur le marxisme', pp. 124–5; *Une pensée devenue monde*, p. 258.

191 *De l'État* III, p. 133.

192 *Le retour de la dialectique*, p. 135.

193 *De l'État* III, p. 133. For some caution, see also 'Le marxisme éclaté', p. 10.

194 *Qu'est-ce que penser?* p. 110.

195 *De l'État* II, p. 67.

196 *Une pensée devenue monde*, p. 69.

197 *De l'État* III, p. 133.

198 Lefebvre hints at this in *De l'État* II, p. 72.

199 Martin Heidegger, 'The age of the world picture', in *The Question Concerning Technology and Other Essays*, translated by William Lovitt, New York: Harper & Row, 1977; and see Elden, 'Taking the Measure of the *Beiträge*'.

200 See also 'Le mondial et le planétaire', *Espace et sociétés* 8, February 1973, pp. 15–22, p. 15.

201 *De l'État* IV, p. 95.

202 *De l'État* IV, p. 94.

203 *De l'État* IV, p. 326.

204 *De l'État* IV, p. 435; *Key Writings*, p. 203.

205 Martin Heidegger, 'Vom Wesen des Grundes', in *Wegmarken*, Frankfurt am Main: Vittorio Klostermann, 1967, p. 60; 'On the essence of ground', translated by William McNeill, in *Pathmarks*, Cambridge: Cambridge University Press, p. 126.

206 *De l'État* IV, p. 416; *Key Writings*, p. 200.

207 *De l'État* IV, pp. 415–16; *Key Writings*, p. 200.

208 *De l'État* IV, p. 195.

209 See *De l'État* II, pp. 67–70; III, p. 164; IV, pp. 165–6; *La production de l'espace*, p. 106; *The Production of Space*, p. 88.

210 *Une pensée devenue monde*, pp. 172–3.

211 *La production de l'espace*, p. 103; *The Production of Space*, p. 86.

212 See, for example, Jan Aart Scholte, *Globalization: A Critical Introduction*, Basingstoke: Macmillan, 2000. A more complicated and nuanced analysis of this issue is found in Ash Amin, 'Spatialities of globalisation', *Environment and Planning A* 34(3), 2002, pp. 385–99.

213 *De l'État* IV, p. 29.

214 *De l'État* III, p. 134.

215 *De l'État* IV, p. 23.

216 *La survie du capitalisme*, p. 77; *The Survival of Capitalism*, pp. 81–2.

217 *De l'État* IV, p. 25.

218 *De l'État* IV, p. 26.

219 *De l'État* IV, pp. 27–8. In *Une pensée devenue monde*, p. 8, Lefebvre describes the third stage as post-industrial, noting the importance of new technologies of computers and information.

220 *De l'État* IV, p. 419; *Key Writings*, p. 201.

221 *Le retour de la dialectique*, p. 136.

222 *Le retour de la dialectique*, p. 139.

223 *La survie du capitalisme*, p. 106; *The Survival of Capitalism*, pp. 108–9

224 'A propos d'un nouveau modèle étatique', p. 53; 'Comments on a new state form', pp. 777–8.

225 *De l'État* IV, p. 421; *Key Writings*, p. 202.

226 See also *Au-delà du structuralisme*, p. 414.

227 *La pensée marxiste et la ville*, p. 145.

228 *La survie du capitalisme*, p. 11; *The Survival of Capitalism*, p. 17.

229 *La survie du capitalisme*, p. 15; *The Survival of Capitalism*, p. 21. For a similar enquiry, see Scott Lash and John Urry, *The End of Organized Capitalism*, Cambridge: Polity Press, 1987.

230 *Hegel, Marx, Nietzsche*, p. 142.

231 *Une pensée devenue monde*, p. 39.

232 *La pensée marxiste et la ville*, p. 152. See also *De l'État* II, pp. 322–3; IV, pp. 403–5.

233 The most extensive discussion is in *De l'État* IV, pp. 259–324. A slightly edited translation of this chapter has recently appeared as 'Space and the state', in *State/Space: A Reader*, edited by Neil Brenner, Bob Jessop, Martin Jones and Gordon MacLeod, Oxford: Blackwell, 2003, pp. 84–100. See also *Une pensée devenue monde*, pp. 156–61.

234 *De l'État* IV, p. 164.

235 *De l'État* IV, p. 261.

236 *De l'État* IV, pp. 164–5.

237 *De l'État* IV, pp. 166–7. For useful discussions of Lefebvre's work on the state/space relation, see Brenner, 'Global, fragmented, hierarchical'; and 'State territorial restructuring and the production of spatial scale', pp. 276–80.

238 *De l'État* III, pp. 40, 44–5; see IV, p. 259.

239 *De l'État* III, p. 89.

240 *De l'État* III, p. 98.

241 *De l'État* III, pp. 98–9.

242 *La survie du capitalisme*, p. 12; *The Survival of Capitalism*, p. 17.

243 *De l'État* III, p. 134; IV, p. 259.

244 *De l'État* I, p. 55; IV, pp. 301–2.

245 On leisure spaces on the Mediterranean see *La survie du capitalisme*, p. 80; *The Survival of Capitalism*, p. 84. More generally, see *La production de l'espace*, p. 357; *The Production of Space*, p. 310; *De l'État* IV, pp. 276–8; *Une pensée devenue monde*, pp. 150–1.

246 *De l'État* III, p. 89. For a discussion of this, in part inspired by Lefebvre, see Philip E. Steinberg, *The Social Construction of the Ocean*, Cambridge: Cambridge University Press, 2001.

247 *De l'État* III, p. 120.

248 *De l'État* III, pp. 222–3; *De l'État* IV, pp. 299, 306–7, 308.

249 *De l'État* III, p. 134.

250 *De l'État* IV, pp. 168–9.

251 *La survie du capitalisme*, pp. 79–80; *The Survival of Capitalism*, p. 83.

252 *La survie du capitalisme*, p. 82; *The Survival of Capitalism*, p. 86.

253 *La survie du capitalisme*, p. 83; *The Survival of Capitalism*, pp. 86–7.

254 *La survie du capitalisme*, p. 84; *The Survival of Capitalism*, p. 88.

255 *La survie du capitalisme*, pp. 82–5; *The Survival of Capitalism*, pp. 86–8.

256 *De l'État* II, p. 42.

257 *Histoire de la folie à l'âge classique*, Paris: Gallimard, 1976 (1961); translated by Richard Howard as *Madness and Civilisation*, London: Routledge, 1967.

258 *De l'État* II, p. 161; see IV, p. 408.

259 *De l'État* I, p. 161.

260 *De l'État* II, p. 42.

261 *De l'État* II, pp. 42–3.

262 *De l'État* I, p. 162.

263 *De l'État* I, pp. 162–3. See *Qu'est-ce que penser?* pp. 162–3. The hidden god (*dieu caché*) may be a reference to Lucien Goldmann's book of that title.

264 *Le temps des méprises*, p. 87.

265 *La survie du capitalisme*, p. 114; *The Survival of Capitalism*, p. 116. See Derek Gregory, *Geographical Imaginations*, Oxford: Blackwell, 1994, p. 365. A similar critique is made in *La présence et l'absence*, pp. 38, 159.

266 For critiques of *Anti-Oedipus* and Debord, see also *Le temps des méprises*, pp. 160–1, 172.

267 *La survie du capitalisme*, p. 18; *The Survival of Capitalism*, p. 23.

268 *La survie du capitalisme*, pp. 80–1; *The Survival of Capitalism*, pp. 84–5.

269 *La survie du capitalisme*, pp. 13–14; *The Survival of Capitalism*, pp. 18–19.

270 For a slightly longer discussion and some references, see Elden, *Mapping the Present*, pp. 74–5. A rather different distinction is made by Poulantzas, *Political Power and Social Classes*, p. 37, where the political is the 'juridico-political super-structure of the state' and politics 'political class practices (political class struggle)'.

271 *Le retour de la dialectique*, pp. 59, 70, 88.

272 *Le retour de la dialectique*, p. 89.

273 *Hegel, Marx, Nietzsche*, pp. 46–9.

274 'Toward a leftist cultural politics: remarks occasioned by the centenary of Marx's death', in Cary Nelson and Lawrence Grossberg (eds), *Marxism and the Interpretation of Culture*, London: Macmillan, 1988, pp. 75–88, p. 84. See also 'Lettre', in *Marx . . . ou pas? Réflexions sur un centenaire*, Paris: Études et Documentation Internationales, 1986, pp. 21–5, p. 24.

275 David Luban, 'A conversation about Heidegger with Eduard Baumgarten', in Berel Lang, *Heidegger's Silence*, Ithaca: Cornell University Press, 1996, pp. 101–11, p. 109. This comes in the context of a fairly general assault on Heidegger's character. Luban suggests that 'Baumgarten's portrait is different [from one of a man of "substantial Nazi conviction"]: it shows a man who was driven not so much by political or ideological passion as by personal pettiness, more than usual vanity, and a desire for philosophical glory', and, 'a measure of – at least – social anti-Semitism'.

276 *Le matérialisme dialectique*, Paris: PUF, 6th edition, 1970 (1939); *Dialectical Material-ism*, translated by John Sturrock, London: Jonathan Cape, 1968; *De l'État*; Norbert Guterman and Henri Lefebvre, *La conscience mystifiée*, Paris: Éditions Syllepse, 3rd edition, 1999 (1936); *Le Nationalisme contre les nations*, Paris: Méridiens Klincksieck, 2nd edition, 1988 (1937); *Hitler au pouvoir*.

277 *Le retour de la dialectique*, p. 88.

278 *Le retour de la dialectique*, pp. 17–18; *Key Writings*, p. 61.

279 *Le retour de la dialectique*, p. 143.
280 *Une pensée devenue monde*, p. 215.
281 *Le retour de la dialectique*, p. 47.
282 For this as a reading of Marx, see *Une pensée devenue monde*, pp. 219–23, more generally, pp. 240–1. For a discussion of this question see my 'Reading genealogy as historical ontology', in Alan Rosenberg and Alan Milchman (eds), *Foucault/Heidegger: Critical Encounters*, Minneapolis: University of Minnesota Press, 2003, pp. 187–205.
283 *Une pensée devenue monde*, p. 221.
284 *Une pensée devenue monde*, p. 222.
285 *Le temps des méprises*, pp. 201–2.
286 *Au-delà du structuralisme*, p. 86; 'What is the historical past?' *New Left Review* 90, 1975, pp. 27–34, p. 34.
287 *Une pensée devenue monde*, p. 180.
288 Lefebvre and Régulier, *La révolution n'est plus ce qu'elle était*, p. 200 See also 'Lettre', p. 21.
289 *Pour connaître la pensée de Karl Marx*, p. 43.

Bibliography

Books by, or edited by, Henri Lefebvre

(1934) *Morceaux choisis de Karl Marx*, Paris: Gallimard. With Norbert Guterman.
(1936) *La conscience mystifiée*, Paris: Éditions Syllepse, 3rd edition, 1999. With Norbert Guterman.
(1937) *Le nationalisme contre les nations*, Paris: Méridiens Klincksieck, 2nd edition, 1988.
(1938) *Hitler au pouvoir, les enseignements de cinq années de fascisme en Allemagne*, Paris: Bureau d'Éditions.
(1938) *G. W. F. Hegel, Morceaux choisis*, Paris: Gallimard. With Norbert Guterman.
(1938) *Cahiers de Lénine sur la dialectique de Hegel*, Paris: Gallimard. With Norbert Guterman.
(1939) *Nietzsche*, Paris: Éditions Sociales Internationales.
(1939) *Le matérialisme dialectique*, Paris: PUF, 6th edition, 1971. Translated by John Sturrock as *Dialectical Materialism*, London: Jonathan Cape, 1968.
(1946) *L'existentialisme*, Paris: Anthropos, 2nd edition, 2001.
(1947) *Logique formelle, logique dialectique*, Paris: Anthropos, 2nd edition, 1969.
(1947) *Descartes*, Paris: Éditions Hier et Aujourd'hui.
(1947) *Marx 1818–1883*, Genève-Paris: Trois Collines.
(1947) *Pour connaître la pensée de Karl Marx*, Paris: Bordas.
(1947) *Critique de la vie quotidienne* I: *Introduction*, Paris: L'Arche, 2nd edition, 1958. Translated by John Moore as *Critique of Everyday Life Volume I: Introduction*, London: Verso, 1991.
(1948) *Le marxisme*, Paris: PUF.
(1949) *Diderot ou les affirmations fondamentales du matérialisme*, Paris: L'Arche, 2nd edition, 1983.
(1949) *Pascal: Tome Premier*, Paris: Nagel.
(1953) *Contribution à l'esthétique*, Paris: Anthropos, 2nd edition, 2001.
(1954) *Pascal: Tome Deux*, Paris: Nagel.
(1955) *Musset*, Paris: L'Arche, 2nd edition, 1970.
(1955) *Rabelais*, Paris: Anthropos, 2nd edition, 2001.
(1956) *Pignon*, Paris: Édition Falaise.
(1957) *Pour connaître la pensée de Lénine*, Paris: Bordas.
(1958) *Problèmes actuels du marxisme*, Paris: PUF, 2nd edition, 1960.
(1959) *La somme et le reste*, Paris: Méridiens Klincksieck, 3rd edition, 1989.
(1961) *Critique de la vie quotidienne* II: *Fondements d'une sociologie de la quotidienneté*, Paris:

L'Arche. Translated by John Moore as *Critique of Everyday Life Volume II: Foundations for a Sociology of the Everyday*, London: Verso.

(1962) *Introduction à la modernité: Préludes*, Paris: Les Éditions de Minuit. Translated by John Moore as *Introduction to Modernity: Twelve Preludes*, London: Verso, 1995.

(1963) *La vallée de Campan: Étude de sociologie rurale*, Paris: PUF.

(1963) *Karl Marx, Oeuvres choisis*, Tome I, Paris: Gallimard. With Norbert Guterman.

(1964) *Marx*, Paris: Gallimard.

(1964) *Allemagne*, Paris: Braun & Cie. Photos et notices par Martin Hurlimann.

(1965) *La proclamation de la commune*, Paris: Gallimard.

(1965) *Pyrénées*, Pau: Cairn, 2nd edition, 2000.

(1965) *Métaphilosophie*, Paris: Éditions Syllepse, 2nd edition, 2001.

(1966) *Le langage et la société*, Paris: Gallimard.

(1966) *Sociologie de Marx*, Paris: PUF. Translated by Norbert Guterman as *The Sociology of Marx*, Harmondsworth: Penguin, 1968.

(1966) *Karl Marx, Oeuvres choisis*, Tome II, Paris: Gallimard, with Norbert Guterman.

(1967) *Position: Contre les technocrates en finir avec l'humanité-fiction*, Paris: Gonthier.

(1968) *La vie quotidienne dans le monde moderne*, Paris: Gallimard. Translated by Sacha Rabinovitch as *Everyday Life in the Modern World*, Harmondsworth: Allen Lane, 1971.

(1968) *La droit à la ville*, Paris: Anthropos. Translated and edited by Eleonore Kofman and Elizabeth Lebas as 'The right to the city', in *Writings on Cities*, Oxford: Blackwell, 1996, pp. 63–181.

(1968) *L'irruption de Nanterre au sommet*, Paris: Éditions Syllepse, 2nd edition, 1998. Translated by Alfred Ehrenfeld as *The Explosion: Marxism and the French Upheaval*, New York: Modern Reader, 1969.

(1970) *Du rural à l'urbain*, Paris: Anthropos.

(1970) *La révolution urbaine*, Paris: Gallimard. Translated by Robert Bononno as *The Urban Revolution*, Minneapolis: University of Minnesota Press, 2003.

(1970) *La fin de l'histoire*, Paris: Les Éditions de Minuit.

(1970) *Le manifeste différentialiste*, Paris: Gallimard.

(1971) *Au-delà du structuralisme*, Paris: Anthropos.

(1971) *Vers le cybernanthrope*, Paris: Denoël/Gonthier.

(1972) *La pensée marxiste et la ville*, Paris: Casterman.

(1972) *Espace et politique: Le droit à la ville II*, Paris: Anthropos, 2nd edition, 2000.

(1972) *Trois textes pour le théâtre*, Paris: Anthropos.

(1973) *La survie du capitalisme: La re-production des rapports de production*, Paris: Anthropos, 3rd edition, 2002. Abridged version translated by Frank Bryant as *The Survival of Capitalism*, London: Allison & Busby, 1976.

(1973) *Le jeu de Kostas Axelos*, Paris: Fata Morgana, with Pierre Fougeyrollas.

(1974) *La production de l'espace*, Paris: Anthropos. Translated by Donald Nicholson-Smith as *The Production of Space*, Oxford: Blackwell, 1991.

(1975) *Le temps des méprises*, Paris: Stock.

(1975) *Hegel, Marx, Nietzsche ou le royaume des ombres*, Paris: Castermann.

(1975) *L'idéologie structuraliste*, Paris: Anthropos.

(1975) *Actualité de Fourier: Colloque d'Arcs-et-Senans sous la direction de Henri Lefebvre*, Paris: Anthropos.

(1976–8) *De l'État*, Paris: UGE, 4 volumes.

(1978) *La révolution n'est plus ce qu'elle était*, Hallier: Éditions Libres. With Catherine Régulier.

(1980) *Une pensée devenue monde: Faut-il abandonner Marx?* Paris: Fayard.

(1980) *La présence et l'absence: Contribution à la théorie des representations*, Paris: Casterman.

(1981) *Critique de la vie quotidienne III: De la modernité au modernisme (Pour une métaphilosophie du quotidienne)*, Paris: L'Arche.

(1985) *Qu'est-ce que penser?* Paris: Publisad.

(1986) *Le retour de la dialectique: 12 mots clefs*, Paris: Messidor/Éditions Sociales.

(1986) *Lukács 1955*, with Patrick Tort, *Être marxiste aujourd'hui*, Paris: Aubier.

(1990) *Du contrat de citoyenneté*, Paris: Éditions Syllepse. With le Groupe de Navarrenx.

(1991) *Conversation avec Henri Lefebvre*, Paris: Messidor. With Patricia Latour and Francis Combes.

(1992) *Éléments de rythmanalyse: Introduction à la connaissance de rythmes*, Paris: Éditions Syllepse. Translated by Stuart Elden and Gerald Moore as 'Elements of rhythmanalysis: introduction to the understanding of rhythms', in *Rhythmanalysis: Space, Time and Everyday Life*, London: Continuum, 2004, pp. 1–69.

(1996) *Writings on Cities*, translated and edited by Eleonore Kofman and Elizabeth Lebas, Oxford: Blackwell.

(2002) *Méthodologie des Sciences: Un inédit*, Paris: Anthropos.

(2003) *Key Writings*, edited by Stuart Elden, Elizabeth Lebas and Eleonore Kofman, London: Continuum.

Shorter works by Henri Lefebvre

(1924) 'Une tentative métaphysique: "La dialectique du monde sensible" de Louis Lavelle', *Philosophies* 3, pp. 241–8.

(1924) 'Critique de la qualité et de l'être: Fragments de la philosophie de la conscience', *Philosophies* 4, pp. 414–21.

(1925) 'Positions d'attaque et de defence du nouveau mysticisme', *Philosophies* 5/6, pp. 471–506.

(1925) 'La revolution d'abord et toujours', *La revolution surréaliste* 5, pp. 31–2, cosignatory with several others.

(1926) 'La pensée et l'esprit', *L'esprit* 1, pp. 21–69.

(1926) 'Description de ce temps: Misère de M. Jacques Maritain', *L'esprit* 1, pp. 258–71.

(1926) 'Introduction: Le même et l'autre', in Friedrich Schelling, *Recherches philosophiques sur l'essence de la liberté humaine et sur les problèmes qui s'y rattachent*, translated by Georges Politzer, Paris: F. Rieder, pp. 7–64.

(1927) 'Reconnaissance de l'unique', *L'esprit* 2, pp. 5–37.

(1927) 'Notes pour le process de la chrétienté', *L'esprit* 2, pp. 121–47.

(1929) '*Verdun, par le maréchal Pétain*', *La revue marxiste* 6, pp. 719–20.

(1932) 'Du culte de "l'esprit" au matérialisme dialectique', *La nouvelle revue française* 39(231), pp. 802–5.

(1933) 'Individu et classe', *Avant-Poste* 1, pp. 1–9. With Norbert Guterman.

(1933) 'Le fascisme en France', *Avant-Poste* 1, pp. 68–71.

(1933) 'André Breton, *Les vases communicants*', *Avant-Poste* 1, pp. 75–7.

(1933) 'La mystification: pour une critique de la vie quotidienne', *Avant Poste* 2, pp. 91–107, with Norbert Guterman.

(1933) 'Autocritique', *Avant-Poste* 2, pp. 142–3.

(1933) 'Le Karl Marx de M. Otto Ruhle', *Avant-Poste* 3, pp. 199–201.

(1933) 'Mussolini: le fascisme', *Avant-Poste* 3, pp. 201–2.

(1934) '*Madame 60 Bis*, par Henriette Valet (Grasset)', *La nouvelle revue française* 43(255), pp. 921–3.

(1935) 'Qu'est-ce que la dialectique?', *La nouvelle revue française* 45(264) pp. 351–64 and 45(265), pp. 527–39.

(1944) 'Georges Politzer', *La pensée* 1, pp. 7–10.

(1945) 'Existentialisme et Marxism', *Action* 40, pp. 5–8.

(1945) 'La pensée militaire et la vie nationale', *La pensée* 3, pp. 49–56.

(1948) 'Marxisme et sociologie', *Cahiers internationaux de sociologie* IV, pp. 48–74.

(1948) 'Le Don Juan du Nord: Pièce en 3 actes', *Europe: Revue mensuelle* 28, pp. 73–104.

(1948) 'La crise du capitalisme français: Essai de définition du problème', *La pensée* 17, pp. 39–50.

(1949) 'Autocritique: Contribution à l'effort d'éclaircissement idéologique', *La nouvelle critique* 4, pp. 41–57.

(1949) 'L'homme des revolutions politiques et sociales', *Pour un nouvel humanisme*, textes des conférences et des entretiens organisés par les Rencontres Internationales de Genève, Neuchâtel: Éditions de la Baconnière, pp. 115–35.

(1950) 'Connaissance et critique sociale', in Marvin Farber (ed.), *L'activité philosophique contemporaine en France et aux États-Unis – Tome Second: La philosophie Française*, Paris: PUF, pp. 298–319.

(1950) 'Knowledge and social criticism', in Marvin Farber (ed.), *Philosophic Thought in France and the United States: Essays Representing Major Trends in Contemporary French and American Philosophy*, New York: University of Buffalo Publications in Philosophy, pp. 281–300.

(1951) 'Lettre sur Hegel', *La nouvelle critique* 22, p. 99–104.

(1953) 'Structures Familiales Comparées', in Georges Friedmann (ed.), *Villes et campagnes: Civilisation urbaine et civilisation rurale en France*, Paris: Armand Colin, pp. 327–62.

(1955) 'La notion de totalité dans les sciences sociales', *Cahiers internationaux de sociologie* XIII, pp. 55–77.

(1955) 'Une discussion philosophique en URSS. Logique formelle et logique dialectique', *La pensée* 59, pp. 5–20.

(1956) 'De l'explication en économie politique et en sociologie', *Cahiers internationaux de sociologie* XXI, pp. 19–36.

(1956) 'Une philosophie de l'ambiguïté', in Roger Garaudy *et al.*, *Mésaventures de l'antimarxisme: Les malheurs de M. Merleau-Ponty*, Paris: Éditions Sociales, pp. 99–106.

(1956) 'Divertissement pascalien et alienation humaine', in *Blaise Pascal: L'homme et l'oeuvre*, Paris: Les Éditions de Minuit, pp. 196–224.

(1956) 'La communauté villageoisie', *La pensée* 66, pp. 29–36.

(1956–57) 'M. Merleau-Ponty et la philosophie de l'ambiguité', *La pensée* 68, pp. 44–58 and 73, pp. 37–52.

(1957) 'Le marxisme et la pensée française', *Les temps modernes* 137–38, pp. 104–37.

(1957) 'Vers un romantisme révolutionnaire', *Nouvelle revue française* 58, pp. 644–72.

(1958) 'L'exclu s'inclut', *Les temps modernes* 149, pp. 226–37.

(1958) 'Réponse à camarade Besse', *Les temps modernes* 149, pp. 238–49.

(1958) 'Les entretiens philosophiques de Varsovie', *Comprendre: Revue de politique de la culture* 19, pp. 237–45.

(1958) 'Les rapports de la philosophie et de la politique dans les premières oeuvres de Marx (1842–1843)', *Revue de métaphysique et de morale* 63(2–3), pp. 299–324.

(1958) 'Retour à Marx', *Cahiers internationaux de sociologie* XXV, pp. 20–37.

(1958) 'Avant-propos de la 2ᵉ édition', in *Critique de la vie quotidienne* I: *Introduction*, Paris: L'Arche, 2nd edition, pp. 9–111. Translated by John Moore as 'Foreword to the second edition', in *Critique of Everyday Life Volume I: Introduction*, London: Verso, 1991, pp. 3–99.

(1958) *Le romantisme révolutionnaire, Cercle Ouvert: Confrontations*, Paris: La Nef de Paris, with Colette Audry, Jacques Nantet and Claude Roy.

(1959) 'Justice et vérité', *Arguments* 15, pp. 13–19.

(1959) 'Les cadres sociaux de la sociologie marxiste', *Cahiers internationaux de sociologie* XXVI, pp. 81–102.

(1959) 'Le soleil crucifié', *Les temps modernes* 155, pp. 1016–29.

(1959) 'Karl Marx et Heidegger', in Kostas Axelos, *Argument d'une recherche*, Paris: Éditions de Minuit, 1969, pp. 93–105, with Kostas Axelos, Jean Beaufret, François Châtelet. Originally published in *France Observateur* 473, 28 May 1959.

(1960) 'Psychologie des classes sociales', in Georges Gurvitch (ed.), *Traité de sociologie*, Paris: PUF, 2 volumes, 1958–60, II, pp. 364–86.

(1960) 'Avant-propos à la deuxième édition', in *Problèmes actuels du marxisme*, Paris: PUF, 2nd edition, 1960, pp. vii–viii.

(1961) 'Avant-propos', in *Le matérialisme dialectique*, Paris: PUF, 6th edition, pp. 5–12. Translated by John Sturrock as 'Foreword to the fifth edition', in *Dialectical Materialism*, London: Jonathan Cape, 1968, pp. 13–19.

(1961) 'Critique de la critique non-critique', *Nouvelle revue marxiste* 1, pp. 57–79

(1961) 'Les dilemmes de la dialectique', *Médiations* 2, pp. 79–105.

(1962) 'Le concept de structure chez Marx', in Roger Bastide (ed.), *Sens et usages du terme structure dans les sciences humaines et sociales*, The Hague: Mouton, 2nd edition, 1972, pp. 100–6.

(1962) 'Marxisme et technique', *Esprit* 307, pp. 1023–8.

(1962) 'La signification de la commune', *Arguments* 27–28, pp. 11–19.

(1962) 'Les myths dans la vie quotidienne', *Cahiers internationaux de Sociologie* XXXIII, pp. 67–74.

(1964) 'L'État et la société', *Les cahiers du centre d'études socialistes* 42–3, pp. 17–29.

(1964) 'Les sources de la théorie Marxiste-Leniniste de l'État', *Les cahiers du centre d'études socialistes* 42–3, pp. 31–48.

(1965) 'Kostas Axelos: *Vers la pensée planétaire: le devenir-pensée du monde et le devenir-homme* [sic] *de la pensée* (Ed. de Minuit)', *Esprit* 338, pp. 1114–17.

(1966) 'Problèmes théoriques de l'*autogestion*', *Autogestion* 1, pp. 59–70.

(1967) 'Sur une interpretation du marxisme', *L'homme et la société* 4, pp. 3–22.

(1967) '1925', *La nouvelle revue française* 172, pp. 707–19.

(1967) 'Le droit à la ville', *L'homme et la société* 6, pp. 29–35.

(1968) 'Ville, urbanisme et urbanisation', *Perspectives de la sociologie contemporaine: Hommage à Georges Gurvitch*, edited by Georges Balandier, Roger Bastide, Jacques Berque and Pierre George, Paris: PUF, pp. 85–105. With Monique Coornaert.

(1968) 'Bilan d'un siècle et de deux demi siècles (1867–1917–1967)', in Victor Fay (ed.), *En partant du 'capital'*, Paris: Anthropos, pp. 115–42.

(1969) 'Pascal et l'ordre des *Pensées*', in A. Lanavère (ed.), *Pascal*, Paris: Firmin-Didot Étude/Librairie Marcel Didier, 1969, pp. 154–73. With Lucien Goldman.

(1970) 'Réflexions sur la politique de l'espace', *Espaces et Société* 1, pp. 3–12. Translated as 'Reflections on the politics of space', *Antipode* 8(2), 1976, pp. 30–7.

(1971) 'Musique et sémiologie', *Musique en jeu* 4, pp. 52–62.

(1973) 'Le mondial et le planétaire', *Espace et société* 8, pp. 15–22.

(1974) 'La production de l'espace', *L'homme et la société* 31–32, pp. 15–32.
(1974) 'Evolution or Revolution', in Fons Elders (ed.), *Reflexive Water: The Basic Concerns of Mankind*, London: Souvenir Press, pp. 201–67. With Leszek Kolakowski.
(1975) 'What is the Historical Past?' *New Left Review* 90, pp. 27–34.
(1975) 'Les autres Paris', *Espaces et sociétés* 13–14, pp. 185–92.
(1976) 'Interview – Débat sur le marxisme: Léninisme-stalinisme ou autogestion?', *Autogestion et socialisme* 33/34, pp. 115–26.
(1976) 'Le marxisme éclaté', *L'homme et la société* 41/42, pp. 3–12.
(1979) 'A propos d'un nouveau modèle étatique', *Dialectiques* 27, pp. 47–55. Translated by Neil Brenner and Victoria Johnson as 'Comments on a new state form', *Antipode* 33(5), 2001, pp. 769–82.
(1979) 'Space: Social Product and Use Value', in J. W. Freiburg (ed.), *Critical Sociology: European Perspectives*, New York: Irvington Publishers, pp. 285–95.
(1982) 'Préface à la troisième édition: Douze thèses sur logique et dialectique', in *Logique formelle, logique dialectique*, Paris: Terrains/Éditions Sociales, 3rd edition, pp. 3–8.
(1985) 'Le projet rythmanalytique', *Communications* 41, pp. 191–9. With Catherine Régulier.
(1985) 'Préface: La production de l'espace', in *La production de l'espace*, Paris: Anthropos, 4th edition, 2000, pp. xvii–xxviii.
(1986) 'Lettre', in *Marx . . . ou pas? Réflexions sur un centenaire*, Paris: Études et Documentation Internationales, pp. 21–5.
(1986) '1956', *M, mensuel, marxisme, mouvement* 1, pp. 31–5.
(1986) 'Le renouveau philosophique avorté des annés trente: Entretien avec Henri Lefebvre', *Europe: Revue littéraire mensuelle* 683, pp. 29–41, with Michel Trebitsch.
(1987) 'An Interview with Henri Lefebvre', translated by Eleonore Kofman. *Environment and Planning D: Society and Space* 5(1), pp. 27–38.
(1987) 'The Everyday and Everydayness', in *Everyday Life: Yale French Studies* 73, pp. 7–11.
(1987) 'Quelques questions sur le questionnement', *M, mensuel, marxisme, mouvement* 7, pp. 52–4.
(1987) 'Le quotidien (mise au point)', *M, mensuel, marxisme, mouvement* 11, p. 9.
(1987) 'Chers amis, lecteurs, abonnés, collaborateurs de M', *M, mensuel, marxisme, mouvement* 14, pp. 6–7.
(1988) 'Toward a leftist cultural politics: remarks occasioned by the centenary of Marx's death', in Cary Nelson and Lawrence Grossberg (eds), *Marxism and the Interpretation of Culture*, London: Macmillan, pp. 75–88.
(1995) 'A group of young philosophers: a conversation with Henri Lefebvre', in Bernard-Henri Lévy, *Adventures on the Freedom Road: The French Intellectuals in the Twentieth Century*, translated by Richard Veasy, London: Harvill, pp. 131–8.
(1997) 'Lefebvre on the Situationists', conducted and translated by Kristin Ross, *October* 79, pp. 69–83.
(2003) 'Space and the State', in *State/Space: A Reader*, edited by Neil Brenner, Bob Jessop, Martin Jones and Gordon MacLeod, Oxford: Blackwell, 2003, pp. 84–100.

This is not a complete list of Lefebvre's shorter writings. Several of these are collected in his books, and several others are reviews or other pieces not used in this book. For fuller – yet still incomplete – listings, see Rémi Hess, *Henri Lefebvre et l'aventure du siècle*, Paris: A. M. Métailié, 1988, pp. 334–45, or Rob Shields, *Lefebvre, Love and Struggle: Spatial Dialectics*, London: Routledge, 1999, pp. 190–204.

Index of Names

There are no references for Hegel, Marx or Lefebvre himself. Discussion of them is found on almost every page.